IMPEACH THE PRESIDENT

IMPEACH THE PRESIDENT
THE CASE AGAINST BUSH AND CHENEY

EDITED BY DENNIS LOO & PETER PHILLIPS
Introduction by Howard Zinn

SEVEN STORIES PRESS
New York | Toronto | London | Melbourne

Seven Stories Press
140 Watts Street
New York, NY 10013
http://www.sevenstories.com

In Canada: Publishers Group Canada, 250A Carlton Street, Toronto, ON M5A-2L1

In the UK: Turnaround Publisher Services Ltd., Unit 3, Olympia Trading Estate, Coburg Road,
Wood Green, London N22 6TZ

In Australia: Palgrave Macmillan, 627 Chapel Street, South Yarra VIC 3141

Library of Congress Cataloging-in-Publication Data
Impeach the president : the case against Bush and Cheney / [edited by] Dennis Loo and Peter
Phillips. — Seven Stories Press 1st ed.
p. cm.
ISBN-13: 978-1-58322-743-5 (pbk. : alk. paper)
ISBN-10: 1-58322-743-1 (pbk. : alk. paper)
1. Bush, George W. (George Walker), 1946—Impeachment. 2. Cheney, Richard B.—Impeach-
ment. 3. Political corruption—United States. 4. Political crimes and offenses—United States. 5.
United States—Politics and government—2001–
6. United States—Foreign relations—2001– I. Loo, Dennis. II. Phillips, Peter, 1947–

E903.3.I46 2006
973.931092'2—dc22
2006017826

College professors may order examination copies of Seven Stories Press titles for a free
six-month trial period. To order, visit www.sevenstories.com/textbook
or fax on school letterhead to (212) 226-1411.

Book design by Phoebe Hwang
Printed in the USA
9 8 7 6 5 4 3 2 1

We dedicate this book to free speech, due process, human rights, personal privacy, and the right of the people to challenge empire and end tyranny.

CONTENTS

12 REASONS WHY GEORGE W. BUSH AND RICHARD CHENEY MUST BE IMPEACHED

1. Stealing the White House in 2000 and 2004 through outright voter fraud.

2. Lying to the American people and deliberately misleading Congress in order to launch an unprovoked war of aggression upon Iraq.

3. Authorizing and directing the torture of thousands of captives, leading to death, extreme pain, disfigurements, and psychological trauma. Hiding prisoners from the International Committee of the Red Cross by deliberately failing to record them as detainees and conducting the rendition of hundreds of prisoners to "black sites" known for their routine torture of prisoners. Indefinitely detaining people and suspending habeas corpus rights.

4. Ordering free fire zones and authorizing the use of antipersonnel weapons in dense urban settings in Iraq, leading to the deaths of tens of thousands of civilians—war crimes under international law.

5. Usurping the American people's right to know the truth about governmental actions through the systematic use of propaganda and disinformation.

6. Building an imperial presidency by issuing signing statements to laws passed by Congress that negate congressional intent. Hiding government decisions from public and congressional view through subverting

the Freedom of Information Act. Illegally spying on millions of Americans without court authorization and lying about it for years.

7. Undermining New Orleans' capacity to withstand a hurricane, allowing New Orleans' destruction by Katrina, and failing to come to victims' aid in a timely fashion, leading to thousands of Americans dead or missing.

8. Denying global warming, disregarding Peak Oil, and placing oil-industry profits over the long-term survival of the human race and the viability of the planet.

9. Violating the constitutional principle of separation of church and state through the interlinking of theocratic ideologies in the decision-making process of the U.S. government.

10. Failing to attempt to prevent the 9/11 attacks, despite a wealth of very specific evidence of a pending terrorist attack upon New York, and the World Trade Center in particular. Using this *failure* as a rationale for preemptive attacks on other countries and for the suspension of Americans' fundamental civil liberties and our right to privacy.

11. Promotion of U.S. global dominance of the world and the building and use of illegal weapons of mass destruction.

12. Overthrowing Haiti's democratically elected president, Jean-Bertrand Aristide, and installing a highly repressive regime.

PREFACE

Dennis Loo and Peter Phillips

> The people can always be brought to the bidding of the leaders.
> ... All you have to do is tell them they are being attacked, and
> denounce the pacifists for lack of patriotism and exposing the
> country to danger.
>   —Hermann Goering, Luftwaffe Commander and Nazi Leader[1]

The Bush-Cheney administration and the radical right-wing forces that it represents constitute an extraordinary threat to the world. As events unfold, this becomes ever more painfully evident: the appalling debacle of Katrina; the disastrous and immoral occupation of Iraq with no end in sight; the murder of prisoners by American personnel in Iraq, Afghanistan, and Guantánamo, and the covert rendition of prisoners to nations known for torture; Bush's admission that he secretly and illegally authorized spying on all Americans, and his brazen declaration upon being caught that he will continue to do so, and on and on. Their corruption, incompetence, criminal activity, and disregard for human rights and the law seem endless. The White House has become increasingly embattled as a result of these events, but it will take unprecedented popular action to end this regime. Governments do not fall of their own weight; they must be driven out.

In 1960 social psychologist Stanley Milgram conducted a now famous experiment. He planned to test his pilot study on Americans, and then take it to Germany. His object? To explore what it was about Germans that made them so willing to obey Hitler and the Nazis in the 1930s and 1940s. His hypothesis?

Fascism came to power because Germans were somehow more obedient and compliant than others. His experiment consisted of asking subjects to administer what they thought were progressively more and more severe electrical shocks to someone in another room when that person gave incorrect answers to a test. The shock scale went from 15 volts up to 450 volts. Several stops prior to the 450 volts the scale was labeled "Danger: Severe Shock." The person answering the questions—a study collaborator not actually hooked up for electrical shocks—began to scream in agony as the test proceeded, declaring that he had a heart condition, and then, eventually, as the shocks continued, he stopped making any sounds, with only ominous silence coming from the room he was in.

Milgram expected that only a small number of subjects would carry out the shocks to the very end of the scale. He was astonished to discover that his American subjects, primarily Yale University students, were all too willing to go all the way. Milgram never did take his experiment to Germany because the answer was right here at home: obtaining obedience to authority was as easy among Americans as it had been among Germans.

The United States today under George W. Bush and Dick Cheney is the Milgram Experiment writ large. The experimental subjects this time are each and every one of us. Unlike the Germans under Hitler, however, who claimed that they didn't know that Jews, Communists, trade unionists, homosexuals, and other political opponents of the Third Reich were being incinerated in concentration camps, none of us can claim that we do not know that torture is going on in our name. The news coverage, partial and abbreviated as it has been, makes this clear.

More shocking, however, than finding our government now *openly* endorsing and practicing torture is how easily they have accomplished this—and so many other egregious things—and how paltry and ineffectual the opposition has been to these crimes by our political institutions and media.

The National Security Agency (NSA) spying scandal illustrates this graphically. In an April 20, 2004, speech in Buffalo, New York, Bush reassured Americans that "a wiretap requires a court order." He said this knowing that since at least 2002 he had secretly ordered the government to spy on Americans *without* a court order. Because of a whistle-blowing NSA official, this warrantless spying came to light in 2005. Now no longer able to pretend that he wasn't violating the 1978 Federal Intelligence Security Act that Congress had passed to prevent exactly this scenario, Bush fired back that the real criminal was the person who blew the whistle and that his administration was going to continue to spy.

What did Congress do about this singular declaration of a felon declaring, in essence, that he was above the law—that is, that he was a dictator? A few cried foul, but within a short time, with the exception of a handful of congresspeople who tried their best to object, Congress decided to set up a seven-member panel to "oversee" the spy program. In other words, an administration declared that it was doing something far worse than what had forced Richard Nixon out of office, declared that it was not subject to any laws passed by Congress, and Congress *looked the other way.*

It does not end there—nothing about this administration "ends there." In trying to cover their tracks when the spying scandal first broke, the White House claimed that they had been spying without court orders only on *suspected terrorists* making *international* calls. Americans' civil liberties and privacy were being safeguarded, they loudly proclaimed.[2] Then in May 2006 came another bombshell: whistleblowers revealed that the White House has in fact been spying on *ALL* Americans' calls, foreign *and* domestic. And Congress . . . *looked the other way.*[3]

We face a situation today in which political institutions, public officials, the two major parties, and the mainstream and right-wing media are all more out of touch and *at odds* with the public than at any other time in this country's history. Pulitzer Prize–winning journalist Seymour Hersh, in his recent book *Chain of Command*, put it this way: "How did eight or nine neoconservatives . . . redirect the government and rearrange long-standing American priorities and policies with so much ease? How did they overcome the bureaucracy, intimidate the press, mislead the Congress, and dominate the military? Is our democracy that fragile?"[4]

How indeed? The central problem here is that truth and facts have been barricaded off from reaching most of the American people. If Americans *truly* knew exactly what was going on in their names, they would mass outside 1600 Pennsylvania Avenue, scale the gates, haul these perpetrators out of the White House by their shirt collars, and put them on trial immediately for crimes against humanity. Such an event has yet to happen because the right wing has been resoundingly successful in the plans it laid beginning in the early 1970s to dramatically alter the political landscape. Through the very deep pockets of such people as Rupert Murdoch, Adolph Coors, and the

"Four Sisters,"[5] they have invested tens of billions of dollars in establishing their own media empire, such as Fox News and Clear Channel, their own think tanks, their own publishing houses, their heavy subsidy and cultivation of right-wing scholars and writers, and so on. From these pulpits they have bullied, lied and twisted. Their media empire's impact cannot be overestimated. They have cowed the Democratic Party and the mainstream media. Like the shadow cast by the immense alien ship in the movie *Independence Day*, Bush-Cheney and the radical right have generated a black cloud over this country. We wrote this book to help to dispel this state of affairs.

These times call for nothing less than that the people take extraordinary measures to repudiate these "leaders." An unprecedented mass popular upheaval is what must occur.

The "high" in "high crimes and misdemeanors" refers to the high office of the one being impeached. As ex-president Gerald Ford once put it, impeachable offenses are whatever Congress decides they are. The chapters in this book make a painstakingly meticulous case for the plethora of reasons present for impeachment. But the ultimate issue is one of political will. We hope to encourage a movement that shakes this country to the core. A movement so potent that Congress is compelled to act, no matter who is in Congress at the time or what their party affiliation. Nixon, it should be recalled, did not want to pull out of Vietnam. The Vietnamese people's resistance and the antiwar movement forced him to do so.

Many of the acts discussed in these chapters constitute grounds not only for impeachment but also for criminal prosecution. Every single day that this regime is allowed to continue in office means that numerous crimes against humanity will continue. As you read these words, numerous people in places like Abu Ghraib, Guantánamo, or Uzbekistan are being beaten until they cannot walk, waterboarded until they drown, electroshocked in their genitals, and suffocated with sleeping bags wrapped around their heads "like yo-yos."

Chapter 1: "Impeachment: The People's Nuclear Option," by constitutional attorney Judith Volkart surveys the history of past impeachments and describes why impeachment is the Constitution's safeguard of last resort for holding federal officials accountable for misconduct that subverts our constitutional government.

Chapter 2: "Never Elected, Not Once: The Immaculate Deception and the Road Ahead," by Dennis Loo. After the 2004 presidential election, millions were stunned by Bush's win and suspected that something was deeply awry. Drawing upon overwhelming evidence, Loo shows how the theft of the 2000 and 2004 elections was accomplished. He analyzes the ways the GOP has fabricated the impression of majority popular support for its policies. Loo further accounts for why the Democratic Party and mainstream media have cooperated with this deception and what this cooperation means for the future.

Chapter 3: Dahr Jamail in "The 'Free Fire Zone' of Iraq" recounts first hand (and with photographs) his experience as an unembedded reporter in Iraq witnessing U.S. troops' systematic commission of war crimes under White House military and political strategists' direction. He documents collective punishment, illegal weapons (for example, cluster bombs used against civilian populations), disrupted medical care, press censorship, and the torturing of Iraqis, all express violations of international law. He looks especially at the siege of Fallujah, declared a "free fire zone" by the U.S. military. Jamail witnessed grave breaches of the Geneva Conventions of 1949, for which those convicted can be subject to the death penalty.

Chapter 4: "War Crimes Are High Crimes" by Jeremy Brecher, Jill Cutler, and Brendan Smith. The tyranny that sparked the American Revolution characterizes the Bush administration like no other in U.S. history. Bush-Cheney have asserted that they have the authority to attack other countries that have not attacked the U.S., to operate death squads engaged in killings not sanctioned by law, to engage in cruel abuse of prisoners without legal oversight, and to unilaterally annul the Geneva Conventions and other treaties authorized by Congress.

Chapter 5: Dennis Loo's "Defending the Indefensible: Torture and the American Empire" links Bush-Cheney's antirational worldview to the neocons' wild ambitions of unrivaled world dominance to explain their open embrace of torture—an extremely ominous development. He further shows that the administration's and its apologists' justification for torture doesn't wash on either ethical or practical grounds. Indeed, he points out the startling similarities between Bush-Cheney and al-Qaeda.

Chapter 6: "Iraq: Phase Two in an Unbounded War on the World" by Larry Everest exposes the underlying rationale for the war on both Iraq and the entire Arab world. The U.S. government openly debated, and actually attempted, the overthrow of Hussein's regime a decade before 9/11, and not because Iraq posed a military threat or was linked to al-Qaeda. Instead, the U.S. administration felt that Saddam Hussein's regime was undermining its control of the Middle East and impeding its global ambitions. The decision to invade Iraq was made by November 2001, nearly a year before the U.S. attempted to secure the United Nation's approval of the invasion in the fall of 2002.

Chapter 7: "The Downing Street Memos, Manipulation of Prewar Intelligence, and Knowingly Withholding Vital Information from a Grand Jury Investigation" by Greg Palast features the first U.S. publication of the full text of Matthew Rycroft's July 23, 2002, Downing Street Memo that proved that Bush's WMD rationale was bogus. "Here it is. The smoking gun. The memo that has IMPEACH HIM written all over it." Palast, considered by many the top investigative journalist in the U.S. and a former racketeering investigator, recounts how the smoking gun was dismissed both by Congress and mainstream U.S. journalism as not worth a second look.

Chapter 8: "Propaganda, Lies, and Patriotic Journalism" by Nancy Snow. Snow knows propaganda when she sees it. She was a Presidential Management Fellow for the U.S. Information Agency. Snow describes the ways 9/11 was a potent gift to any propagandist, especially to this administration, which purposely and cynically manipulated public opinion to anchor misperceptions about Iraq, 9/11, and al-Qaeda's role, and was generously helped along in this process by the patriotic, unquestioning mainstream media.

Chapter 9: Barbara J. Bowley's "The Campaign for Unfettered Power: Executive Supremacy, Secrecy, and Surveillance" shows how Bush has become the "first dictator of the Information Age" through presidential fiat and massive, illegal surveillance. Given the complex and covert nature of the methods by which Bush-Cheney have accomplished much of their aims, Bowley compiles and chronicles this process in a highly readable and immediately understandable way.

Chapter 10: "Bush-Cheney's War on the Enlightenment" by Mark Crispin Miller is a wide-ranging piece that explains why the Bush-Cheney regime's most dangerous aspect is their imperial crusade for total power. Miller shows that the war on terror is not only unending, unlike all prior wars in human history, but an unprecedented national crusade to wipe out all the world's evil. The Bush enterprise is conjointly headed by apocalyptic Christianists, eager for worldwide theocracy, and an influential network of Straussian neoconservatives, who have made an unholy alliance with the Christian right in an effort to create a docile populace.

Chapter 11: "Denying Disaster: Hurricane Katrina, Global Warming, and the Politics of Refusal" by Kevin Wehr shows graphically and convincingly how global climate change represents a clear, present, and dire danger that Bush-Cheney have continued to remain oblivious to, imperiling the planet. Wehr links these environmental changes to the Katrina disaster, showing that Katrina was a social, not a natural, disaster and was preventable, not inevitable. He recounts Bush-Cheney's incredible malfeasance prior to, during, and after the hurricane. Wehr shows why Bush-Cheney's continued misleadership on these urgent life-and-death issues can be tolerated no longer.

Chapter 12: "Ignoring Peak Oil: Beyond Incompetence" by Richard Heinberg outlines how world oil production's peaking presents the U.S. and the world with an unprecedented problem in risk management, and how the Bush-Cheney administration's inaction constitutes dereliction of duty on a global scale.

Chapter 13: "The Other Regime Change: Overthrowing Haiti's President Jean-Bertrand Aristide" by Lyn Duff and Dennis Bernstein documents the Bush administration's illegal overthrow of the democratically elected Haitian president Jean-Bertrand Aristide. Duff and Bernstein's report covers the journey of portions of 20,000 M-16 semiautomatic assault rifles with 20-round magazines, shipped by the U.S. to the Dominican Republic, to end up in the hands of Haitian rebels. They uncover the ways the U.S. funded the Haitian political opposition, blocked military assistance to the government, kidnapped Aristide, and established a highly repressive regime.

Chapter 14: "The Global Dominance Group: A Sociological Case for Impeachment of George W. Bush and Richard Cheney" by Peter Phillips, Bridget Thornton, Lew Brown, and Andrew Sloan documents the oligarchical nature of U.S. politics, showing the incestuous relationships that exist between the neocons, corporate media, and the military-industrial complex. The chapter lists 240 advocates of global dominance who have been the primary promoters and beneficiaries of the war on terrorism before and after 9/11, and demonstrates how these advocates dominate the U.S. government today.

Chapter 15: "Beyond Impeachment: Rebuilding a Political Culture" by Cynthia Boaz and Michael Nagler argues that impeachment isn't enough. The advertising culture's promotion of private comforts and feel-good narcissism, the authors point out, provides fertile ground for the neocons' finessing accountability to truth and to justice. Challenges to that culture of private comforts therefore need to occur to set things right.

Chapter 16: "What Can Be Done?" by the editors recommends steps that can be taken to carry forward the fight for impeachment.

We stand at a crossroads. Will we obey and be "good Germans"? In the years preceding Hitler's naming to the German chancellorship many German Jews and others kept telling themselves that it can't possibly get any worse and it can't possibly go any further. Except that it did. The 1933 Reichstag Fire, set by Herman Goering and the Nazis but blamed on the Communists,[6] was the Nazis' excuse to suspend civil liberties and freedom of the press entirely. It was the German equivalent of our 9/11.

Impeachment advocates are widely mobilizing in the U.S. By March 2006 over a thousand letters to the editors of major newspapers had been printed in the preceding six months calling for impeachment. George Matus, writing to the *Pittsburgh Post-Gazette*, stated, "I am still enraged over unasked questions about exit polls, touch-screen voting, Iraq, the cost of the new Medicare . . . who formulated our energy policy, Jack Abramoff, the Downing Street Memos, and impeachment." David Anderson in McMinnville, Oregon, wrote to the *Oregonian*, "Where are the members of our congressional delegation now in demanding the current president's actions be investigated to see if impeachment or censure are appropriate actions?" William Dwyer's letter in the *Charleston Gazette* read, "Congress will never have the courage to start the impeachment process without a groundswell of outrage from the people."

City councils, boards of supervisors, and local and state Democratic central committees have voted for impeachment. Arcata, California, voted for impeachment on January 6, 2006. The City and County of San Francisco voted Yes on February 28, 2006. The Sonoma County, California, Democratic Central Committee voted for impeachment on March 16, 2006. The townships of Newfane, Brookfield, Dummerston, Marlboro, and Putney in Vermont, all voted for impeachment the first week of March 2006. The New Mexico State Democratic Party convention rallied on March 18, 2006, for the "impeachment of George Bush and his lawful removal from office." Texas Democrats called for impeachment on April 9, 2006, joining other proimpeachment Democrats from Nevada, North Carolina, and Wisconsin. The national Green Party called for impeachment on January 3, 2006. Op-ed writers at the *St. Petersburg Times, Newsday, Yale Daily News, Barrons, Detroit Free Press*, and the

Boston Globe have called for impeachment. It was as if the call for impeachment was emerging from a national collective consciousness when the *San Francisco Bay Guardian* (January 25, 2006), *The Nation* (January 30, 2006), and *Harper's* magazine (March 2006) each published cover articles calling for impeachment within weeks of each other.

Stephen T. Jones threw one of the first punches in his article in the *San Francisco Bay Guardian* on January 25, 2006, "The Case for Impeachment: It's Not Just for Radicals Anymore." Jones describes the events of a town hall meeting Nancy Pelosi held in San Francisco in mid-January 2006, where she was confronted by "a new political reality." Jones described the meeting and how "the real eruption came when a questioner listed several war-related Bush misdeeds and asked, are these not high crimes and misdemeanors?" The room went "nuts," Jones wrote, with sustained applause and chants of "Impeach, impeach."

The irascible long-time editor of *Harper's*, Lewis Lapham, wrote, "The Case for Impeachment: Why We Can No Longer Afford George W. Bush" for the periodical's March 2006 issue. In the article Lapham applauds Rep. John Conyers (D-Michigan) for introducing on December 18, 2005, into the House of Representatives a bill to investigate grounds for impeachment. Lapham wrote:

> We have before us in the White House a thief who steals the country's good name and reputation for his private interest and personal use, a liar who seeks to instill in the American people a state of fear, a televangelist who engages the United States in a never-ending crusade against all the world's evil, a wastrel who squanders a vast sum of the nation's wealth on what turns out to be a recruiting drive certain to multiply the host of our enemies. In a word, a criminal—known to be armed and shown to be dangerous.

The Nation contributor and former member of Congress, Elizabeth Holtzman—a Representative during Nixon's presidency—started her article by noting that "people have begun to speak of impeaching President George W. Bush—not in hushed whispers but openly, in newspapers, on the Internet, in ordinary conversations and even in Congress." Holtzman advocates impeachment based on Bush's scorn for international treaties, lies about Iraq, and violations of the U.S. Foreign Intelligence Surveillance Act (*The Nation*, January 30, 2006).

As of March 16, 2006, thirty-two members of the U.S. House of Representatives had signed on as cosponsors to House Resolution 635, which would create a Select Committee to look into the grounds for recommending President Bush's impeachment.

The International Commission of Inquiry on the Crimes Against Humanity Committed by the Bush Administration met in October 2005 and January 2006 in New York City and heard wide-ranging and searing testimony documenting extensive and ongoing crimes against humanity.

Despite all this advocacy and sentiment for impeachment, corporate media has yet to cover this emerging mass movement as of this writing. *The Bangor Daily News* simply reported on March 17, 2006, that former U.S. Attorney General Ramsey Clark had set up the Web site Votetoimpeach.org and that other groups were using the Internet to push for impeachment. The *Wall Street Journal,* on March 16, editorialized to the effect that it was just "the loony left" seeking impeachment, but perhaps some Democrats in Congress would join in feeding on the "bile of the censure/impeachment brigades."

The corporate media are ignoring the broadening call for impeachment—wishing perhaps that it might just go away. Nothing on the television news programs has yet given the impression that millions of Americans are calling for Bush and his cohorts' impeachment. Despite the corporate media's inability to hear the demands for impeachment, the groundswell of outrage continues to expand. Will it be enough? Will it grow to the size of the elephant in the room that no one can afford to ignore?

Had we a system that could protect itself against the predations and subversions of threats such as Bush-Cheney, there would be no reason for this book. Bush and his cohorts would have been driven from office and put on trial for their crimes long ago. Indeed, they would never have been allowed to seize the White House in the first place. It is up to the rest of us to rouse ourselves and rouse others, to bring forth from the grassroots new social movement leaders to constitute an alternative and powerful counterforce that fundamentally alters the overall political atmosphere, providing a competing legitimate authority to the bankrupt and illegitimate authority now leading this country. The existing establishment has left us no other choice.

Times of great peril are also times of great opportunity. What we do or fail to do at this critical juncture over the course of the next months and years will have profound ramifications for both this generation and future generations, for the people of this country and of the entire world.

In an episode of the television show *The Simpsons*, Homer finds himself in an alien spaceship orbiting Earth. The aliens have managed to kidnap the Republican and Democratic Party nominees for president and have them imprisoned in capsules on their ship. Hitting buttons randomly on the ship's control, Homer inadvertently jettisons the two candidates into deep space. Doh! After this, Homer somehow manages to steer the spaceship back to Earth, and upon landing in Washington, DC, he finds the two aliens, disguised as the two presidential candidates, giving campaign speeches together on the Capitol steps. Homer unmasks the aliens, revealing them to be two very large, very grotesque, octopus-looking creatures. The crowd gasps. The aliens hesitate for a moment. Then one of them says to the crowd: "It's a two-party system; you have to vote for one of us." There is a pause and then someone from the crowd says, "He's right!"[7]

Is he?

Notes:

1. A conversation Gustave Gilbert held with Goering in his cell on the evening of April 18, 1946, recorded in Gilbert's book, *Nuremberg Diary* (New York: Signet, 1961), pp. 255–256.
2. Cheney, for example, stated in a January 19, 2006, speech: "[Y]ou frequently hear this called a 'domestic surveillance program.' It is not. We are talking about international communications, one end of which we have reason to believe is related to al Qaeda or to terrorist networks affiliated with al Qaeda . . . a wartime measure, limited in scope to surveillance associated with terrorists, and conducted in a way that safeguards the civil liberties of our people." (Press release, "Vice President's Remarks on Iraq and the War on Terror at the Manhattan Institute for Policy Research.") The White House was clearly expecting, when making these false claims in early 2006, that no other whistleblowers would step forward to reveal their new cover stories to be further lies.
3. See Chapter 9 in this book for further details.
4. Seymour Hersh, *Chain of Command: The Road From 9/11 to Abu Ghraib* (New York: HarperCollins, 2004), p. 362.
5. The John M. Olin, Bradley, Smith Richardson, and Scaife foundations.
6. "[T]here is enough evidence to establish beyond a reasonable doubt that it was the Nazis who planned the arson and carried it out for their own political ends. . . . General Franz Halder, Chief of the German General Staff during the early part of World War II, recalled at Nuremberg how on one occasion Goering had boasted of his deed. 'At a luncheon on the birthday of the Fuehrer in 1942 the conversation turned to the topic of the Reichstag building and its artistic value. I heard with my own ears when Goering interrupted the conversation and

shouted: "The only one who really knows about the Reichstag is I, because I set it on fire!" With that he slapped his thigh with the flat of his hand.'" (William L. Shirer, *The Rise and Fall of The Third Reich*, Simon and Schuster: New York, 1960, pp. 192–193).

7. "Treehouse of Horror VII," Episode #801 4F02, *The Simpsons*, original airdate October 27, 1996.

ACKNOWLEDGMENTS

Dennis Loo

Thanks to Howard Zinn, Stacey McGoldrick for her valuable feedback, Jennifer Wong, Marcos Ibarra, Katherine Lawson, and Morgan Love for their research assistance. My gratitude to coeditor Peter Phillips for being my collaborator on this project. His extensive experience, sound judgment, and invaluable contacts have made this book project possible. Finally, I want to thank Barbara for her loving support, forbearance, and encouragement throughout this major enterprise.

Peter Phillips

Thank you, Dennis Loo, for approaching me in the fall of 2005 on doing the book together. I have been glad ever since. You are great to work with and a dedicated scholar and true radical democrat. Howard Zinn is a long-time associate with us at Project Censored and a wonderful introducer to this work. I want to personally thank those close friends and intimates who have counseled and supported me through the past six months. Most important, my wife Mary Lia, who as my lover, friend, and partner provides daily hearing and consultative support on my many issues. It is her centeredness and thoughtful analysis that helps keep me on track. The men in the Green Oaks breakfast group—Noel Byrne, Bob Butler, Bob Klose, Derrick West, Colin Godwin, and Bill Simon—are personal advisors and confidants who help with difficult decisions. Kate Sims, Andy Roth, and Trish Boreta are supportive professionals working closely with me at Sonoma State University. Thanks very much also to Lew Brown, Bridget Thornton, and Andrew Sloan, Sonoma State University student research assistants and cowriters.

We both extend big thanks to the people at Seven Stories Press. They are not just a publishing house, but rather progressive friends who helped edit our book in record time and served as advisors in its development. Publisher Dan Simon is a visionary who deserves full credit for assembling an excellent support crew including Jon Gilbert, Lars Reilly, Ria Julien, Phoebe Hwang, Anna Lui, Crystal Yakacki, Theresa Noll, Ruth Weiner, Tara Parmiter, and George Mürer, along with interns Lauren Hougen, Sinan Schwarting, Anastassia Fisyak, and Jason Spears. Thanks also to designer Stewart Cauley for an excellent cover.

Special thanks to the sales staff at Consortium Books, who will see to it that every independent bookstore, chain store, and wholesaler in the U.S. is aware of *Impeach the President*. Thanks to Publishers Group Canada, our distributor in Canada, as well as Turnaround Publishers Services Ltd. in Great Britain and Palgrave Macmillan in Australia.

And thank you to our twenty coauthors who, often on short notice, worked diligently to build this collection on the importance of impeaching the Bush-Cheney regime. The book is a summary of many minds presenting the impeachment forest filled with many trees.

We thank also the many, many activists who have ordered this book and are using it to spread the word for a national populist impeachment movement in the U.S.

Thank you all!

INTRODUCTION

Howard Zinn

The essays in this volume are part of a growing demand in the United States for the impeachment of George W. Bush and anyone else in his administration committed to his policies. This campaign for impeachment, it should be understood, is not just a condemnation of the Bush administration but also a recognition of the flawed nature of the American political system.

There is a kind of conventional "wisdom" slightly to the left of center that analyzes the United States this way: we have political democracy but not economic democracy. It points to the "democratic" institutions: the three branches of government and the "checks and balances" that are presumed to prevent a monopoly of power by any one branch; the voting process for the president and Congress (especially now that women and black people have the right to vote); the Bill of Rights.

What this viewpoint ignores is the economic basis of politics, the fact that if the economy is dominated by corporate wealth, wealth will inevitably corrupt the political process, irrespective of the fact that on paper the institutions appear to be democratic.

The nation's history shows as much from the start. The much praised "democracy" created by the Constitution after the Revolutionary War was a showpiece created by the Founding Fathers in response to popular participation in the Revolution and to rebellions in the various states afterward. In fact the new nation was dominated by slaveholders, bondholders, merchants, and land speculators, all of whom established a central government strong enough to put down popular protest and to serve the interests of the wealthy.

What was established at that early point in the nation's history continued to be true for the next two centuries and more. Any honest look at national policy would conclude that, except for certain moments when massive social movements have forced reforms (the 1930s, the 1960s), the government has legislated as the Founding Fathers did, in the interests of the wealthy classes.

Furthermore, whatever pretense there has been for "checks and balances" among the three branches of government evaporates when it comes to foreign policy. The expansion of the empire, first across the continent and then across the world, has come as a result of military interventions, commanded by the president, with Congress abjectly going along, and the Supreme Court silent in the face of clear violations of the Constitution.

The administration of George W. Bush has taken this historic path further, and with more ruthless disregard of public opinion, than any other presidency. After losing the popular vote in 2000 to Al Gore by several hundred thousand, and then being installed as president by five Republican-appointed justices of the Supreme Court, Bush launched two wars in less than two years.

The huge increases in expenditures for war and tax cuts for the superrich have created an enormous national debt and have been accompanied by severe cuts in social programs for the poor. The unashamed subservience to corporate profit has created an environmental crisis of which the human effects have only just begun to be felt, such as the devastation of New Orleans by the hurricane Katrina.

In a political system that does not make the president subject to recall before his four-year term is up, impeachment by the House of Representatives (and then removal by the Senate) is the only recourse the Constitution provides. Because of the general submissiveness of Congress to presidential power, the impeachment process has only rarely been used.

After the Civil War, President Andrew Johnson, incurring the wrath of congressmen who opposed his pro-Southern policy, was impeached, but he managed to avoid removal by one vote in the Senate. Richard Nixon faced impeachment in 1974 but resigned before it could come to a vote. Bill Clinton was impeached for lying about his sexual activities but won the vote in the Senate.

Although Nixon had illegally invaded Cambodia and Laos and secretly bombed Cambodia, the bill of impeachment did not deal with Nixon's foreign policy. It emphasized, rather, his financial shenanigans and other matters peculiar to him, rather than dealing with larger issues fundamental to the American system. Similarly, Clinton was impeached, not for raising a false issue of "weapons of mass destruction" as an excuse for bombing Iraq, but for personal misbehavior.

In other words, on the rare occasions when impeachment proceedings have been initiated, the indictment has carefully avoided calling into question policies that would expose the long-term nature of the system.

However, the actions of the Bush administration clearly match the level of "high crimes and misdemeanors," which the constitutional provision on impeachment requires. Its policies have resulted in the deaths of over two thousand American soldiers and a hundred thousand Iraqi civilians, as well as the devastation of a country already ruined by two wars and ten years of economic sanctions. To pay for all this, the administration has been looting our country's national wealth.

Therefore the present campaign for the impeachment of George W. Bush has the possibility of going beyond the previous experiences, by calling into question the fundamental thrust of American foreign policy, the class nature of national politics, and the corporate domination of the culture. A public campaign for the removal of the Bush administration from office has the potential for a far-reaching critique of the very idea of the American empire and its consequences for the well-being of the people of this country.

We cannot expect either Republicans or Democrats in Congress to initiate any challenge to the existing order of things. In the history of the nation, serious injustices—slavery, racial segregation, the rights of working people, the condition of women, the war in Vietnam—have only been remedied by powerful social movements that have forced the government to change its policies.

Now we have another such time. This important volume, contributing powerfully to the campaign for impeachment, must be welcomed by anyone concerned for peace, justice, and a truly democratic nation.

Chapter 1

IMPEACHMENT
The People's Nuclear Option

Judith Volkart, Esq.

I do solemnly swear that I will faithfully execute the Office of President of the United States, and will, to the best of my ability, preserve, protect and defend the Constitution of the United States.
—Inaugural Oath in 2000 and 2004 of George Walker Bush[1]

Ask any American to name the most recently impeached president, and chances are they will answer, "Richard Nixon." Of Watergate notoriety, Nixon commandeered the break-in to Democratic national headquarters during the 1972 presidential campaign, an event that resulted in many of his key people's being indicted, convicted, and sent to prison.[2] Rather than face certain impeachment, Nixon resigned after negotiating a full pardon from his successor, President Gerald Ford.

The correct answer is "Bill Clinton," a fact that escapes memory, most probably because, although impeached, Clinton was neither convicted nor removed from office. What was this president's high crime or misdemeanor? Did he admit to illegally tapping the phone calls and e-mail messages of Americans? Did he lie to Congress and the public in order to garner support for a preemptive war? Did he condone, outsource, and advocate legalizing torture? Dismantle our Bill of Rights? Perhaps he seized unprecedented executive power while cloaking his administration from congressional and judicial oversight. Or did he merely ignore the predictions and victims of our country's worst national disaster? No, Bill Clinton lied under oath about having sex with Monica Lewinsky.

Less than an administration later, talk of impeachment is back. This time the issue is not coming to public discourse top down, as it did with Clinton. No special prosecutor with a Ken Starr take-no-prisoners mentality is advocating impeachment. Nor is Congress waving the banner. Today's call to remove from office Bush—and Cheney, too—is building steadily from the bottom up.[3] "Impeach Bush-Cheney" is a people's movement galvanized in large part by the countless executive abuses that have turned our country into a Homeland.[4]

The constitutional crisis facing us today is Nixonian—on steroids. Like Nixon, this president and his senior officials have broken the law.[5] Not unlike King Richard, who on television pled to the American public, "I am not a crook," President George Walker Bush on radio unapologetically admits to the nation that for more than four years under his command the National Security Agency[6] has violated the Foreign Intelligence Surveillance Act (FISA).[7] And, so this president says, to save us from terrorism, the NSA will continue to tap America's e-mails and phone calls indefinitely, regardless of what the law prescribes.[8] John Dean, former Nixon legal counsel, has thoughtfully observed, "Bush is the first president to admit to an impeachable offense."[9] Those of us who love peace and justice, and honor the rule of law simply cannot let this president have his way with our Constitution.

The Unimpeachable Power of the People

As the Constitution's preamble reminds us, in the U.S. ultimate power resides with the people.[10] So it is with removing President Bush and Vice President Cheney from office. More about process than result, impeachment is the Constitution's own safeguard. It is the last resort for holding federal officials accountable for misconduct that subverts our constitutional government.[11] Since the Constitution cannot protect itself, it places definitive power in the hands of the people's elected representatives in Congress, dividing responsibility for the process between the House and the Senate. The House impeaches,[12] the Senate convicts and removes.[13]

The initial call for impeachment must be raised in the House, and that can happen in several ways. A member may introduce a resolution asking the House to create a committee to investigate alleged misconduct to determine whether it rises to the level of an impeachable offense, as John Conyers

(D-Mich) has done in Bush's case. Such a request to open an impeachment inquiry or the referral of formal articles of impeachment may be made by any member, a special prosecutor, an independent counsel (as in Clinton's case), an investigative committee (as in Nixon's case), a grand jury, or even a state legislature.[14] (Illinois[15] and California[16] are in the early stages of invoking this final method.) Once the issue of impeachment is raised, the process moves forward in the House only with majority approval.[17]

The House has a few options. It can take action on the impeachment referral, or in some cases it may decide simply not to act. If the House chooses to do nothing, power reverts to those with the political will to compel the House to act. If the House decides to move forward, it may send the matter to a select committee for a preliminary inquiry or to its Judiciary Committee for a full impeachment hearing.

Select committees are set up as needed for a specifically defined purpose. With impeachment, the House may authorize a select committee simply to decide whether the impeachment referral is sufficient to allow the House to exercise its constitutional power to impeach, but the House can ask it to do more.[18] Before the select committee can act, it must be staffed and funded, and that is the job of the Rules Committee.[19] When the select committee completes its assignment, it delivers a report with recommendations to the full House. If the House votes to move forward with impeachment, it will refer the matter to its Judiciary Committee—a standing committee, one that is already staffed, funded, and active.[20] In any event, the House Judiciary Committee plays the central role in presidential impeachments.

The House Judiciary Committee conducts the investigatory hearings that are at the heart of the impeachment process. The committee's duty is to adopt formal impeachment charges called *articles of impeachment*. The articles list the alleged impeachable offenses and for each sets out the most important supporting evidence. Acting much like a grand jury, the committee has the subpoena power necessary to call witnesses and to require the production of documents. In its hearings the Judiciary Committee listens to testimony, questions witnesses, and reviews documents—all in an effort to determine whether sufficient evidence exists to support a conclusion that an impeachable offense has been committed. At the end of the investigatory hearings, which in Clinton's case lasted only a few months, the Judiciary Committee by majority vote adopts the articles of impeachment, then delivers them to the full House. If a simple majority—51 percent—of the House approves the articles, the president is impeached.

Only the Senate can remove an impeached president from office, and it can do so only after a jury reaches a guilty verdict. The trial takes place in the Senate. All one hundred Senators are sworn in as jurors by the Chief Justice of the Supreme Court—now John Glover Roberts, Jr.—who serves as trial judge.[21] The House selects a trial management team, headed most likely by the House Judiciary Committee chair, to prosecute the case by presenting to the jury the articles of impeachment, the evidence gathered by the House Judiciary Committee, and at its discretion, witness testimony. The senator-jurors listen to the evidence, deliberate to determine whether the president has committed an impeachable offense, and deliver a verdict of innocence or guilt. Conviction requires agreement by two-thirds of the Senators present (sixty-seven, if all one hundred participate) to vote guilty to at least one of the charges in the articles of impeachment. The only punishment the Senate can impose on a convicted president or vice president is disqualification from holding a federal fiduciary position and—of far more consequence—removal from office.[22]

Under the rules of presidential succession, the consequence of impeaching, convicting, and removing Bush from office is that Vice President Cheney will assume the presidency.[23] If the vice president leaves office while the president remains, then Bush is free, subject to congressional consent, to select a successor, as Richard Nixon did when he chose Gerald Ford to replace outgoing Vice President Spiro Agnew.[24] (The importance of this executive appointment power cannot be underestimated considering the fact that less than a year later, when Nixon resigned, Ford became president.) If both the president and vice president are removed, succession falls to the Speaker of the House,[25] then to the President Pro Tem of the Senate.[26] Since the basis of an impeachment conviction is political misconduct, the impeachment itself does not exonerate a convicted official from being sued in civil court or being indicted criminally.[27]

Resolution to Impeach Bush—H.R. 635

Representative John Conyers (D-Mich), the House Judiciary Committee's ranking member, has taken the first institutional step in the impeachment process for Bush-Cheney by introducing H.R. 635 on the House floor.[28] This resolution calls on the House to authorize a select committee (1) to investigate alleged misconduct by Bush's administration and determine whether it constitutes a possible impeachable offense, and (2) to report to the Judiciary Committee any offenses that appear to rise to the level of impeachment. House Resolution 635 expressly directs the select committee to investigate Bush's intent to go to war before obtaining congressional authorization, his manipulation of prewar intelligence, his encouragement and countenance of torture, and his retaliation against critics.[29]

The executive misconduct alleged in the Conyers resolution is supported by a 250-page report (the Conyers Report), a year in the making, entitled *The Constitution in Crisis*.[30] Conyers directed the preparation of this report out of frustration with the Bush administration's refusal to answer the question of whether the Downing Street Minutes' assertions were accurate.[31] The report concludes that enough evidence exists to show that Bush, Cheney, and other members of their administration violated a long list of federal laws and treaties.[32] Crimes include fraud against the United States; making false statements to Congress; misuse of government funds; violating treaties prohibiting torture and cruel, inhuman, and degrading treatment; retaliation against witnesses; and misuse of intelligence and other laws prohibiting leaking.[33] It recommends that Conyers and others consider referring the matter to the Department of Justice for criminal investigation. The report includes recommendations for needed legislation, such as laws to limit government secrecy and to enhance oversight of the executive branch.

Within a few months thirty-six House members signed on as cosponsors of H.R. 635, representing over 8 percent of all representatives and about 17 percent of all House Democrats. Representatives from California, New York, Massachusetts, Minnesota, and Illinois comprise well over half of the cosponsors.[34] According to Conyers, as of April 2006, over 42,000 people had added their names to his Web site's citizen cosponsorship page.[35]

The House has taken no action on the Conyers Resolution other than to refer it immediately to the Rules Committee, directing that committee to create, fund and staff a select committee. Since Republicans on the Rules Committee outnumber Democrats about two to one and none of the Democrats on the Rules Committee have cosponsored H.R. 635, quick action is not expected. In fact, the media predict that H.R. 635 will die in committee. However, if support for impeachment in the House increases, Conyers could bypass the select committee and on the floor of the House directly introduce articles of impeachment. If the Democrats win a majority in the House in the 2006 fall elections, Conyers, by virtue of his position as ranking member, will become chair of the Judiciary Committee.[36] This event would dramatically change the impeachment dynamic.

Censure Is Not Impeachment[37]

Censure is a process of congressional reprimand—a purely political slap on the wrist.[38] In December 2005 Conyers introduced two censure resolutions—one directed at Bush, H.R. 636,[39] and the other at Cheney, H.R. 637,[40] asking the House to reprimand the administration for failing to respond to congressional requests for information, giving misleading statements to Congress and the public regarding the decision to go to war, manipulating intelligence to justify the war, and countenancing torture and cruel and inhumane treatment of Iraqi prisoners. The more conservative Senate is also considering censuring Bush for authorizing the illegal NSA program of warrantless domestic surveillance under S.R. 398,[41] introduced in March of 2006 by Senator Russell Feingold (D-Wis), one of nine Democrats serving on the Senate's twenty-member Judiciary Committee. Commenting in a television interview on his censure action, Feingold acknowledged that Bush's violations of FISA are "right in the strike zone of the concept of high crimes and misdemeanors."[42]

The good news is that talk of censure in both the upper and lower houses introduces executive accountability into public discussion, signaling as it does that some members of Congress recognize the need to reprove Bush's administration. The bad news is that congressional support even among Democrats is nearly absent[43] and—even with support—censure of a president or vice president has no effect other than making a record of congressional disapproval.[44] Neither the Constitution nor the House and Senate rules authorize censure of a president or vice president. Unlike impeachment, censure requires no investigation, no hearing, no opportunity for public accountability, no sanctions. Censure will not stop this administration from stonewalling, steamrolling, and intimidating Congress to avoid oversight. It will not stop illegal domestic spying.[45] Nor will it stop the war or the torture.[46] Moreover, there is no guarantee of once-censured, always-censured. Andrew Jackson, who holds a place of honor on the front of our twenty-dollar bills, is the only president ever censured. By the end of his term a sympathetic Congress expunged the censure from the Congressional Record.[47] With impeachment, there is no pardon.[48]

High Crimes and Misdemeanors

President Bush and Vice President Cheney will be removed from office only if they are convicted of at least one impeachable offense of treason, bribery, or other high crime or misdemeanor.[49] The Constitution is very specific that treason and bribery are grounds for impeachment. Less clear is what constitutes "high crimes and misdemeanors," because no court has definitively interpreted or defined the phrase. Its origins trace to England, where it was used for centuries in impeachment proceedings in Parliament. Already familiar with the phrase, the framers of our Constitution with little debate selected it to augment the more defined impeachable offenses of treason and bribery.

In the two hundred years since the ratification of our Constitution, the House has begun impeachment proceedings sixty times with about one in four instances concluding in a majority vote to impeach. Of those impeached, the Senate has convicted and removed from office only seven (less than half)—all federal judges. With little precedent on impeachment, legal scholars differ on the issue of what level of misconduct constitutes an impeachable offense. Or, more directly, how bad does it have to get to be a high crime or misdemeanor?

Most legal scholars agree with four general conclusions about what constitutes high crimes and misdemeanors. One, impeachable offenses are not limited to criminal offenses but may include such noncrimes as abuse of official power, neglect of constitutional duties, encroachment on the power of another branch of government, undermining the integrity of the office, and betrayal of trust. Two, criminal conduct can be an impeachable offense, but not all crimes merit conviction and removal from office. Three, the term *misdemeanor* bears no relationship to the minor criminal offenses we today usually associate with the word. And four, though an impeachable offense need not be criminal, it must be misconduct that in the context of the office is serious and substantial, such as in the case of a president, conduct that subverts the integrity of government.

Articles of impeachment charging Bush, Cheney, and even Secretary of Defense Donald Rumsfeld with proposed high crimes and misdemeanors are widely available, mostly on the Internet.[50] Among the more compelling are those drafted by the Center for Constitutional Rights (CCR), a highly regarded nonprofit legal and educational organization.[51] In making the legal case for impeachment, CCR details four separate articles of impeachment. For each impeachable offense, CCR provides abundant evidence.

As outlined by Michael Ratner, president of CCR,[52] the first article is based on warrantless electronic surveillance in violation of FISA and the Constitution. FISA prohibits wiretaps without a warrant. Bush admits to authorizing a program of wiretapping e-mails and phone calls with no warrant. This is a criminal offense that carries a five-year sentence for each count. Additionally, warrantless wiretaps violate the Fourth Amendment of the Constitution, which prohibits unreasonable searches and seizures. More fundamentally, the president is usurping congressional power by claiming that executive privilege and national security interests give him authority to disregard the law. This charge is very similar to Article II in Nixon's impeachment proceedings, in which the House Judiciary Committee voted to impeach Nixon, in part, for violating the law by engaging in warrantless wiretapping of Vietnam War protesters.

The second article stems from the lies used to justify the Iraq war; this misdemeanor is the focus of the Conyers Report. This issue arises from Bush's statements that Iraq has a relationship to 9/11, al-Qaeda, and Osama bin Laden and that Iraq had weapons of mass destruction. In the year and a half leading up to the war, the time during which Bush was making these statements, he knew that they were false. Lying to Congress and the American people to prompt war contains two serious impeachable issues. First, the Iraq war is an aggressive, preemptive war, contrary to the United Nations Charter and contrary to law that does not allow war unless it is in self-defense. Second, providing false intelligence is illegal and undermines the authority of Congress and the American people to decide when war is necessary. By lying, Bush convinced and defrauded Congress, thereby undercutting Congress' constitutional authority.

The third impeachable offense deals with the President's action in regard to torture, arbitrary long-term detentions, disappearances, and special trials. Our law is very clear: we cannot torture, we cannot commit war crimes, we cannot send people to countries where they will be tortured, and we cannot set up special courts for trial. The Geneva Conventions are a part of our law, as is the International Covenant on Civil and Political Rights. In authorizing these actions, Bush has breached his constitutional obligation to faithfully execute the law. Congress tried to rein in the Bush administration by enacting the McCain amendment, which prohibits cruel, inhumane, and degrading treatment. But Bush, in a signing statement, essentially proclaimed that he reserved the right to ignore what Congress has resolved. What Bush did is not just a violation of the law; the President is destroying the checks and balances of our Constitution.

Last is a general article combining all three impeachable offenses. As a whole, the President's misconduct is essentially subverting our republic, our democracy, and our Constitution. These violations of law are a breach of Bush's oath of office and a violation of his constitutional duty to faithfully execute the law. This is as bad as it has to get to be a high crime and misdemeanor. Bush needs to be impeached.

No American president has ever been convicted of an impeachable offense. Only two presidents have been impeached—Andrew Johnson and Bill Clinton. A third, Richard Nixon, would have been impeached had he not removed himself from office. Congress has never considered the impeachment of a vice president, although it may have had the opportunity to do so had Spiro Agnew, who served under Nixon, not resigned in October 1973, less than a year before Nixon himself stepped down. Agnew, a rabid critic of anyone opposing Nixon's policies, especially the press (those "nattering nabobs of negativism"), was charged by the Justice Department with taking kickbacks from contractors when he was a county executive.[53] Although vehemently denying the charges, Agnew pled no contest to tax fraud and was sentenced to a fine and probation. Portending the lesser fate of many in the Nixon administration, including Nixon himself, Agnew left office a criminal. He has the distinction of being the only vice president to have done so.

Saved By a Single Vote—Andrew Johnson

Congress has never come closer to removing a president from office than it did in 1868, when the House impeached Andrew Johnson and the Senate failed by only one vote to convict him. Never elected president, Johnson took office just days after the Civil War ended, when Abraham Lincoln was assassinated. Suddenly a Southern Democratic president was vetoing major Reconstruction laws passed by a Congress controlled by Northern Republicans. Earlier the House Judiciary Committee had investigated Johnson as a preliminary to impeachment, but Johnson survived this first attempt to remove him. However, when Johnson intentionally defied Congress and fired the secretary of war for administering the very Reconstruction laws Congress had passed by overriding Johnson's vetoes, the House successfully renewed its impeachment effort.

In a strict party vote the House adopted eleven articles of impeachment against Johnson, most of them relating to his deliberate violation of the Tenure of Office Act.[54] This law prohibited the president from dismissing any official without the Senate's approval. As principal support, the first article of impeachment charged Johnson not just with violating the Act, but by violating the Act, being "unmindful" of his official duties, of his oath of office, and of the Constitutional requirement that he take care that the laws be faithfully executed. In the Senate impeachment trial, Johnson defended his action, arguing that the Act was unconstitutional because it interfered with the execution of executive power.[55]

Other articles of impeachment focused not on violations of law but on what the House called "high misdemeanors," based on the disdain Johnson publicly exhibited for members of Congress who opposed his own Reconstructionist view. Specifically Johnson was charged with bringing the office of the presidency into "contempt, ridicule and disgrace, to the great scandal of all good citizens" through a series of "loud threats and bitter menaces" and otherwise contemptuous reproaches against the legislative branch and the laws it enacted—perhaps the historical equivalent of Dick Cheney's mal mot.[56] Ultimately Johnson was saved from conviction by one vote, and he continued to hold the office of the president until his term ended in 1869.

No doubt Johnson's impeachment came at a time when the nation and its elected officials were bitterly divided by the consequences of the Civil War. At the heart of the Johnson impeachment ordeal was the issue of separation of power between the executive and legislative branches. Johnson's presidency, not unlike Clinton's, was plagued by political intrigue and acrimony between the two branches. Legal scholars agree that the Senate got it right—Johnson's misconduct did not merit conviction because the charges did not constitute a high crime or misdemeanor. Most scholars believe that Johnson's impeachment was in reality a partisan effort to remove a political enemy from office.

While some of the many grounds supporting a Bush impeachment resemble those of Johnson in that both presidents deliberately violated a law passed by Congress, we should not be discouraged by Johnson's acquittal. The two cases are easily distinguished by the highly serious nature of the charges against President Bush, which show a pattern, practice, and degree of impeachable misconduct that far surpasses Johnson's sole act of illegally firing the secretary of war. Impeaching Bush is not a mere political ploy. It is an effort to remove from office a president who has violated a myriad of federal laws and flagrantly subverted the Constitution.

He Cheated, He Lied—Bill Clinton

The voyeuristic impeachment of William Jefferson Clinton was back in the news with the resignation of former House Majority Leader Tom "The Hammer" DeLay. Among his most notable achievements, DeLay is credited with coercing the House to adopt articles of impeachment against President Clinton.[57] If it were not for DeLay's twisting the arms of moderate members of his own party with threats of obstructing the interests of their financial backers and of funding right-wing candidates to run against them, President Clinton's impeachment would have failed in favor of censure, which, in the absence of DeLay's crude yet effective bullying, had bipartisan support.[58]

The attempt to remove Clinton from office is as much a model of congressional expediency as it is a testimony to the price of democracy. Five months is all it took Congress to impeach and acquit—proving that with sufficient motivation our elected officials can move quickly on matters of impeachment. The independent counsel Kenneth Starr's investigation of Clinton, which laid the foundation for the House impeachment, lasted four years and focused on acts of personal indiscretion, beginning with the Whitewater scandal and ending with Lewinsky. The price tag: an estimated $40 million. The House impeachment process was rancorous and emotionally charged, but at the conclusion of the Senate trial, the Constitution prevailed.

Clinton's acquittal after a five-week trial in the Senate prosecuted by the

House Judiciary Committee Chair Henry Hyde (R-Ill) was a victory for the Constitution. The Senate needed sixty-seven votes to convict, but neither the charges of grand-jury perjury[59] nor of obstruction of justice[60] came close. Clinton's defense rested on three principal arguments: (1) Clinton did not lie to the grand jury; (2) a jury would be unlikely to convict Clinton for dancing around questions that demanded admission of marital infidelity; and (3) even if he did lie, his conduct, though morally reprehensible, did not rise to the level of an impeachable offense.

Perjury and obstruction of justice can without doubt be impeachable offenses, but the level of Clinton's impropriety was not substantially serious enough to support conviction and removal from office. Republicans who broke from their party to vote against conviction conceded that the charges against Clinton did not constitute the kind of high crimes the nation's Founding Fathers had contemplated when they wrote the impeachment clause of the Constitution. Many people believe that the impeachment of Clinton was political retribution for the televised investigation of Nixon that eventually drove him from office and assured a Democratic victory in the following election. In a candid interview in April 2006, retiring Rep. Hyde, who served as prosecutor in Clinton's trial in the Senate, was asked whether the impeachment of Clinton was payback for Nixon. Hyde answered, "I can't say it wasn't."[61]

Regardless of motivation, the fact is that though he was not convicted, Clinton was impeached. If a president can be impeached for lying about an extramarital affair that in no way invokes issues of executive power, then President Bush's lying to and misleading Congress and the public about the reasons for the Iraq war and numerous other known and unknown matters also must be an impeachable offense. The impeachment of Clinton underscores the fact that the serious charges of misconduct levied against Bush most certainly satisfy a standard of high crimes and misdemeanors substantial enough for impeachment and—more likely than in Clinton's case—conviction.

Many of the representatives who voted for impeachment and senators who voted for conviction of Clinton are still in office. Partisanship aside, those same members who voted to impeach Clinton should be leading the pack in the effort to impeach President Bush. Given Senate Judiciary Chair James Sensenbrenner's impassioned support for the rule of law and fear of a return to an imperial presidency when the target was Clinton, he too should be a vocal proponent for a full-scale investigation of Bush's conduct. The charges against Clinton do not even come close to the abuse of official power and betrayal of trust that underlie the impeachable offenses of President Bush.

The One Who Went Away—Richard Nixon

Just over thirty years ago John Dean, President Richard Nixon's White House counsel, put loyalty to the Constitution and the rule of law above his own interests and those of the president who appointed him. Dean's testimony before the Senate Watergate Committee was the defining moment that sealed the fate of the Nixon presidency. "What did the president know, and when did he know it?" It was the question of the day, asked by the committee's vice chair, Howard Baker (R-Tenn), who, like other Republicans on the committee, began the impeachment investigations as one of Nixon's defenders.

The Watergate affair began in the June run-up to the 1972 presidential election, when five men were caught at 2:30 a.m. inside Washington, DC's Watergate building trying to bug the Democratic national headquarters by using electronic surveillance equipment. The burglars all wore rubber gloves and suits and had crisp $100 bills in their pockets and White House phone numbers in their address books. One of the men, an ex-CIA agent formerly associated with the Committee to Re-Elect the President (CREEP), implicated the Nixon administration. Within two months investigators revealed that a $25,000 cashier's check intended for the Nixon reelection campaign had been deposited in one of the burglars' accounts. An audit of Nixon's campaign finances was immediately ordered, and a grand jury was convened.

Two *Washington Post* reporters, Bob Woodward and Carl Bernstein, doggedly investigated and reported on the Watergate scandal often relying on leads provided by their anonymous source, Deep Throat.[62] Within four months of the bugging attempt the *Post* in its page-one story, "FBI Finds Nixon Aides Sabotaged Democrats," published the fact that the Watergate break-in stemmed from a massive campaign of political spying and sabotage conducted on behalf of the Nixon reelection effort.[63] Other media had not picked up the Watergate story except in an attempt to discredit the *Post's* reporting. By the end of October, with the support of CBS News, the *Post*, under enormous pressure from the American public with its need to know, got a break—Walter Cronkite devoted two consecutive broadcasts to Watergate.[64] By the time other press, radio, and television outlets got on board, however, Richard Nixon was reelected in one of American history's largest landslides.

Heavily influenced by public opinion spurred by Woodward and Bernstein's reporting,[65] in October 1973 the Senate took the first step leading to Nixon's impeachment with a unanimous and bipartisan vote of those present (77–0) to create a select committee with subpoena power to investigate the allegations of illegal political campaign activities. To minimize partisanship, the committee was required to have seven members, four from the Democratic majority, three from the Republican minority, and none with presidential aspirations. Senator Sam Ervin (D-NC) chaired, and the decision was made to televise the hearings.

At the committee hearings John Dean testified that there indeed was a cover-up and that the president knew of it. Other witnesses revealed the existence of the infamous Nixon tapes, with their eighteen-minute gap (erased by Nixon, according to Dean's speculation). Claiming executive privilege, Nixon fought release of the tapes but lost when the Supreme Court ordered their production just one month before the House Judiciary Committee adopted articles of impeachment. Those secret tapes captured in Nixon's own voice proof that not only did he know about the cover-up, but also that he directed it. Nixon was also heard to instruct his chief of staff to tell the CIA leadership to dissuade the FBI from pursuing crucial Watergate leads by making up a phony reason of national security. (The tapes also allowed us to eavesdrop on the private Nixon, showing him to be vindictive, profane, and racist, despite his Quaker upbringing.)

The Watergate break-in and Nixon's cover-up proved to be just the tip of the iceberg that John Mitchell, Nixon's attorney general, dubbed the White House Horrors. The testimony of the president's men under oath revealed a shocking pattern of criminal and unconstitutional executive conduct unimagined before the hearings. Secret slush funds used by Nixon's administration financed widespread intelligence gathering operations against political enemies. Lawbreaking was enthusiastically played out as dirty tricks, such as forging racist letters and distributing them under Democratic candidates' names. Nixon corrupted government agencies to "screw" political enemies by means of tax audits and manipulation of federal contracts, grants, and lawsuits. When Daniel Ellsberg leaked The Pentagon Papers, Nixon created the "plumbers," whose first job was breaking into Ellsberg's psychiatrist's office hoping to find some way to besmirch him.

After the *New York Times* revealed the secret bombing of Cambodia, Nixon ordered the FBI to conduct illegal wiretaps of suspected leakers—journalists and members of his own administration.[66] Other horrors include proposed firebombing of the Brookings Institution as a diversion for theft of documents, willingness to use thugs to brutalize antiwar protestors, and deliberate falsification of government documents to enhance Nixon's own agenda. And if the plumbers didn't know who to go after, Nixon maintained an "Enemies" list that included Democratic fund-raisers, a union official, a newspaper editor and columnist, actor Paul Newman, and Rep. John Conyers.[67] This proclivity for secret criminal and unconstitutional misconduct led to the Watergate break-in and Nixon's downfall.

In early February 1974 the House voted 410–4 to empower its Judiciary Committee to begin an impeachment investigation of Nixon, which concluded at the end of July.[68] The House Judiciary Committee approved three articles, all premised on abuse of presidential power.[69] Article I charged Nixon with obstructing justice during the investigation of the Watergate burglary, a charge that also carried criminal charges.[70] Another article (III) indicted Nixon for defiance of Congress based on his refusals to comply with the Judiciary Committee's subpoenas.[71] The committee rejected proposed charges relating to Nixon's secret bombing in Cambodia, believing that the action was within his powers as Commander-in-Chief.[72] Also rejected were personal income-tax irregularities, on the grounds they were too personal to warrant impeachment.[73]

Article II, referenced earlier, charged Nixon with abuse of his presidential power based on illegal surveillance and on the warrantless wiretapping of journalists and government staffers as well as political opponents.[74] Nixon defended his actions by claiming that because the country was at war, he needed to prevent leaks of classified information harmful to national security. However, Nixon's tricksters could not resist using some of the information collected for political purposes. The House Judiciary Committee concluded that the illegal wiretapping, compounded by the misuse of the information, was an impeachable offense.[75] Nixon's when-the-president-does-it-it's-not-illegal mindset made the exercise of unlimited executive power under the auspices of national security commonplace.[76]

Nixon's misuse of the FBI to conduct illegal domestic wiretapping led the Senate during the Ford administration to create a select committee headed by Senator Frank Church (D-Idaho) to investigate the use and misuse of electronic surveillance. The Church Committee Report provided the groundwork for Congress to enact the Foreign Intelligence Surveillance Act (FISA) that is at the heart of the illegal NSA domestic surveillance matter facing the Bush administration.[77]

Vice President Cheney held a number of positions in the Nixon administration, and when Nixon left office Cheney was offered a post in President Ford's administration. There, as Ford's chief of staff, Cheney witnessed the checks Congress placed on the executive branch. Many people have speculated that Cheney's current mission is to restore to the presidency the power he believes to have been lost when Congress, controlled by a Democratic majority, passed FISA, the Church Guidelines, and other laws to curb Nixon's excesses. John Dean goes even further to suggest that in the context of the current NSA illegal spying scandal, the reason Cheney and company did not ask Congress for the additional power was because he wanted to make the point that he thought it was within a president's power to ignore congressional laws relating to executive power.[78]

Nearly half of the Republicans on the House Judiciary Committee voted in favor of impeachment on the grounds of defiance of Congress and abuse of presidential power, sending a strong bipartisan message to President Nixon. On July 30, 1974, the Judiciary Committee referred the three articles to the full House for the impeachment vote. Before a vote could be cast, the Republican congressional leadership, led by Senator Barry Goldwater, arrived at the White House to give Nixon an ultimatum—either he step down or the Senate would convict and remove him from office. On August 9, 1974, Nixon resigned.

Over the twenty-six months from the Watergate break-in to the day Nixon was forced from office, many of those closest to the President resigned, only to face indictment, conviction, and prison terms.[79] Most notable are his attorney general, John Mitchell;[80] his chief of staff (Nixon's fierce gatekeeper, who once called himself "the president's-son-of-a-bitch"), H. R. Haldeman;[81] Nixon's assistant for domestic affairs who directed the White House "plumbers" unit, John Ehrlichman;[82] and his White House legal counsel, John Dean.[83] In total, twenty-five of the many indicted in Nixon's administration were convicted and sentenced to prison terms. Nixon was pardoned.

Absolute Conviction—Conclusion

Representative John Conyers, the current House Judiciary Committee's rank-ing member, is the only committee member to have served on two impeach-ment panels—Bill Clinton's in 1998 and Richard Nixon's in 1974.[84] On reflection, Conyers, who introduced H.R. 635 and was on Nixon's enemies list, compares the executive office abuses of Nixon and Bush, commenting, "I see parallels with the Watergate incident with Nixon, even though that really quite frankly pales in comparison to the issues here [in the Bush administra-tion] that have yet to be examined."[85]

Carl Bernstein, the Pulitzer Prize–winning *Washington Post* reporter who helped unravel Watergate, would agree that the abuses of Bush win out. In his April 2006 article in *Vanity Fair* Bernstein points to the dangerous simi-larities of Bush to Nixon that demand immediate Senate investigation: their contempt for legitimate oversight, their passion for secrecy, their exploitation of national security and executive privilege as its justification, their maniacal zeal to ferret out leakers and eliminate enemies, their unwillingness to deal truthfully with the public, and their shameful disregard for the Constitution and the law. Advocating an immediate Senate investigatory hearing, Bern-stein observes, "Raising the worse-than-Watergate question and demanding unequivocally that Congress seek to answer it is, in fact, overdue and more than justified by ample evidence stacked up from Baghdad back to New Orleans and, of increasing relevance, inside a special prosecutor's office in downtown Washington."[86]

In March of 2006 John Dean made a second appearance before the Senate, this time not to answer questions but to implore the Senate not to sit idly by while executive abuses more serious than Watergate unfold before it. Dean testified, in part:

> It has been the announced policy of the Bush/Cheney presidency
> from its outset to expand presidential power for its own sake, and
> it continually searched for avenues to do just that, while constantly
> testing to see how far it can push the limits. I must add that never
> before have I felt the slightest reason to fear our government. Nor
> do I frighten easily. I do fear the Bush/Cheney government and the
> precedents they are creating because this administration is caught

up in the rectitude of its own self-righteousness, and for all practical purposes this presidency has remained largely unchecked by its constitutional coequals.[87]

A Nixon insider, a Watergate reporter, and a House Judiciary Committee member, each representing a different interest group in the Nixon impeachment proceedings—the presidency, the media, and the legislature—have independently reached the same conclusion: We do not know what the Bush administration has done under its cloak of secrecy. Congress doesn't know either. And it's about time we all find out.

Impeachment is the tool the Constitution has given the American people to use when all else fails. With absolute conviction those of us who have the political will to restore peace, justice and the rule of law must invoke this nuclear option to end the lunacy of the Bush-Cheney regime.

Notes:

1. The words of the oath of office are mandated by the U.S. Constitution in Article II, section 1, clause 8.

2. A total of forty of the Nixon administration officials were indicted as a result of Watergate. See http://www.washingtonpost.com/wp-srv/national/longterm/watergate/front.htm. Twenty-five were convicted.

3. In April 2006 Bush's approval rating was at 32 percent at the same time 33 percent of Americans supported impeaching and removing Bush from office, which is about the same percentage that supported impeaching Nixon at the beginning of the Watergate investigation. The number increases to 50 percent of Americans supporting impeachment if Bush lied about the reasons for going to war. This means that many more favor impeaching Bush if he lied than supported impeaching Clinton over the Lewinsky matter. See http://www.truthout.org/docs_2006/042406B.shtml and http://www.latimes.com/media/acrobat/2006-04/229 15725.pdf. For polling results see http://democrats.com/bush-impeachment-polls; http://impeachpac.org/taxonomy/term/4; http://www.pollingreport.com/BushJob.htm.

4. See http://www.dhs.gov/dhspublic/.

5. In January 2006 the Center for Constitutional Rights filed a lawsuit against Bush, the NSA, and other security agencies challenging the NSA warrantless surveillance within the U.S. You can find a case synopsis, legal filings and relevant reports at http://www.ccr-ny.org/v2/legal/govt_misconduct/govtArticle.asp?ObjID=RovrtPD8Bc&Content=694.

6. The NSA is so secret it is nicknamed "No Such Agency." *Newsweek*, "Full Speed Ahead," January 9, 2006.

7. Congress passed FISA in response to the Nixon administration's abuses of power. It was drafted to distinguish between domestic criminal investigations and foreign intelligence investigations, the former subject to Fourth Amendment protection against unreasonable searches and the latter enjoying an expedited process for searches that eliminate Fourth

Amendment protections. Court orders allowing wiretapping under FISA are issued through a closed FISA court, referred to by the press as the "secret court," administered by judges appointed to temporary terms by the Chief Justice of the Supreme Court. All reports indicate that the FISA court rubber-stamps the government's requests. FISA allows the government to request a wiretap order retroactively—no wait, no oversight. You can find a detailed yet clear explanation of FISA and the implications of its violation in Articles of Impeachment Against George W. Bush, pp. 15–16, by the Center for Constitutional Rights; it can be ordered through the Center's Web site at http://www.ccr.org.

8. You can find the full text of Bush's Saturday, December 17, 2005, radio address at http://www.whitehouse.gov/news/releases/2005/12/20051217.html.

9. See http://www.dailykos.com/story/2005/12/18/21310/392.

10. The preamble reads, "We the People of the United States, in Order to form a more perfect Union, establish Justice, insure domestic Tranquility, provide for the common defense, promote the general Welfare, and secure the Blessings of Liberty to ourselves and our Posterity, do ordain and establish this Constitution for the United States of America."

11. Article II, section 4 of the Constitution reads, "The President, Vice President and all civil Officers of the United States, shall be removed from Office on Impeachment for, and Conviction of, Treason, Bribery, or other high Crimes and Misdemeanors." Subsequent case law holds that members of Congress are not considered civil officers for purposes of impeachment.

12. Article I, section 2, clause 5 of the Constitution declares, "The House of Representatives . . . shall have the sole Power of Impeachment." Each House has its own rules for impeachment proceedings, which it can amend.

13. Article I, section 3, clause 6 of the Constitution states, "The Senate shall have the sole Power to try all Impeachments." Two sets of rules control Senate impeachment proceedings. One is the Rules of Procedure and Practice in the Senate When Sitting on Impeachment Trials, which can be found at http://jurist.law.pitt.edu/rules.htm. The other is A Manual of Parliamentary Practice: for the Use of the Senate of the United States by Thomas Jefferson at http://www.constitution.org/tj/tj-mpp.htm.

14. A complete list of ways impeachment charges can be raised before the House can be found in Section 603 of the House Rules and Manual entering the terms "603 impeachment" at http://www.gpoaccess.gov/hrm/index.html.

15. Illinois HJR 00125 urges the Assembly to submit charges to the House to impeach Bush based on illegal spying, torture, detentions without charge or trial, manipulation of prewar intelligence, and the leaking of classified information. The full bill can be found and its progress tracked at http://www.ilga.gov/legislation/billstatus.asp?DocNum=0125&GAID=8&GA=94&DocTypeID=HJR&LegID=25794&SessionID=50. A full story can be found at http://www.truthout.org/docs_2006/042406B.shtml.

16. California AJR 39 charges Bush and Cheney with intentionally misleading Congress and the American people regarding the threat from Iraq in order to justify an unnecessary war that has cost billions of dollars and thousands of lives and casualties; exceeding constitutional authority to wage war by invading Iraq; exceeding constitutional authority by federalizing the National Guard; conspiring to torture prisoners in violation of the "Federal Torture Act" and indicating intent to continue such actions; spying on American citizens in violation of the 1978 Foreign Intelligence Surveillance Act; leaking and covering up the leak of the identity of Valerie Plame Wilson; and holding American citizens without charge or trial. A full story is found at http://www.afterdowningstreet.org/node/9249.

17. In April 2006 the House consisted of a total membership of 438, of which 232 are Republicans, 205 are Democrats, and 1 is an Independent. Updates can be found at http://www.capwiz.com/thenation/directory/demographics.tt?catid=party&chamber=house.

18. It was a Senate select committee headed by Senator Sam Ervin (D-NC) (known as the Watergate or Ervin Committee) that conducted the in-depth hearings investigating President Nixon.
19. In April 2006 the Rules Committee consisted of 9 Republicans and 4 Democrats, plus the Ranking Member Louise Slaughter (D-NY) and Chair David Drier (R-Cal). Updates are found at http://www.capwiz.com/thenation/directory/committees.tt?commid=hrule.
20. In April 2006 the House Judiciary Committee consisted of 22 Republicans and 18 Democrats, plus Ranking Member John Conyers (D-Mich) and Chair James Sensenbrenner (R-Wisc). Updates are found at http://judiciary.house.gov/CommitteeMembership.aspx.
21. In Article 1, section 3, clause 6 the Constitution regulates, "When sitting for that purpose, [the Senate jurors] shall be on Oath or Affirmation. When the President of the United States is tried, the Chief Justice shall preside: And no Person shall be convicted without the Concurrence of two thirds of the Members present."
22. Article I, section 3, clause 7 of the Constitution declares, "Judgment in Cases of Impeachment shall not extend further than to removal from Office, and disqualification to hold and enjoy any Office of honor, Trust, or Profit under the United States."
23. See the U.S. Constitution, Amendment XXV, section 1.
24. See the U.S. Constitution, Amendment XXV, 1, section 2.
25. As of April 2006, the Speaker of the House is J. Dennis Hastert (R-Ill). Updates are found at http://speaker.house.gov/.
26. As of April 2006, the President Pro Tempore of the Senate is Ted Stevens (R-Ark). Updates can be found at http://www.capwiz.com/thenation/directory/congdir.tt.
27. Article I, section 3, clause 7 of the Constitution notes, "the Party convicted shall nevertheless be liable and subject to Indictment, Trial, Judgment, and Punishment according to Law."
28. A full story is found at http://www.thenation.com/blogs/thebeat?bid=1&pid=43981.
29. For the full text of H.Res. 635, see http://thomas.loc.gov/cgi-bin/query/z?c109:H.RES.635:.
30. The text of *The Constitution in Crisis* is at http://www.afterdowningstreet.org/.
31. As revealed the *Sunday Times*, in "The 2002 Downing Street Memo," Richard Dearlove, then head of MI6, wrote in reference to preemptive war with Iraq, "the intelligence and facts were being fixed around the policy" of removing Saddam Hussein.
32. The Conyers Report does not specifically address the NSA spying issues because Congress learned about this matter just as the report was being finalized. The issue is referenced only in the report's executive summary.
33. You can find an excellent discussion of the issues in the Conyers Report in an excerpt of a *Harper's* magazine article, "The Case for Impeachment, Why We Can No Longer Afford George W. Bush," by Lewis Lapham at http://www.harpers.org/TheCaseForImpeachment.html or in the full article in the March 2006 issue.
34. You can find out if your representative is a cosponsor in two ways. One, go to http://www.capwiz.com/thenation/dbq/officials/. Identify your elected representative by using your zip code, then click "info" under the picture. There you will find cosponsorship status, as well as the representative's voting record on key legislation, the committees they serve on, and how to contact them. Two, go to http://www.capwiz.com/thenation/issues/bills/. Click on H.R. 635 to link to "About This Legislation," then click on "detail" for an up-to-date status and a complete list of cosponsors.
35. A current count of citizen cosponsors is found at http://johnconyers.com.
36. Conyers is the only Judiciary Committee member to serve on the committee during two impeachments—Richard Nixon and Bill Clinton's.
37. Inspiration for this chapter heading is provided by U.S. Secretary of State Condoleezza Rice's recent statement, "Iran is not Iraq." See http://www.sfgate.com/cgi-bin/article.cgi?f=/n/a/2006/04/02/international/i044927D35.DTL.

38. General information about censure is found at http://www.senate.gov/reference/reference_index_subjects/Censure_vrd.htm.

39. A copy of H.R. 636 calling for the censuring of President Bush is found at http://thomas.loc.gov/cgi-bin/query/z?c109:H.RES.636:.

40. A copy of H.R. 637 calling for the censuring of Vice President Cheney is found at http://thomas.loc.gov/cgi-bin/query/z?c109:H.RES.637:.

41. A copy of S.R. 398 is found at http://thomas.loc.gov by entering the terms "S.R. 398" under "Bill Search." As of April 2006, the resolution had two cosponsors: Sen. Barbara Boxer (D-Cal) and Sen. Tom Harkin (D-Iowa).

42. See http://thinkprogress.org/2006/03/12/feingold-censure/.

43. An intriguing look at the lack of support for censure and its impact on Sen. Feingold can be found in "Russ Never Sleeps" at http://www.observer.com/20060327/20060327_Chris_Lehmann_pageone_coverstory1-3.asp.

44. Some people believe that censure delivers a serious psychological effect, but a recent analysis of the Bush personality indicates that it would only push him to become more strident. "If the Past is Prologue, George Bush is Becoming an Increasingly Dangerous President" by John Dean can be found at http://writ.news.findlaw.com/dean/20060421.html.

45. "The Bush-Cheney administration's position is crystal clear. It claims there is no place for congressional or judicial oversight of any of its activities in any way related to national security in the post-9/11 world. Through stonewalling, steamrolling and intimidation, this Administration is running roughshod over the Constitution and hiding behind inflammatory rhetoric demanding Americans blindly trust every one of its decisions." Such is the conclusion of Senator Patrick Leahy (D-Vt), the Ranking Member of the Senate Judiciary Committee, which is currently conducting hearings on the president's wartime executive power and the surveillance authority of the NSA. Senator Leahy's full comments are found at http://leahy.senate.gov/press/200602/022806.html.

46. An excellent critique of the Bush Administration's position on presidential war power by Georgetown law professor David Cole is found at http://www.nybooks.com/articles/18431?email.

47. See http://www.senate.gov/reference/reference_index_subjects/Censure_vrd.htm.

48. Article I, section 2, clause 1 of the Constitution affirms that the president "shall have Power to Grant Reprieves and Pardons for Offenses against the United States, except in Cases of Impeachment." President Ford pardoned Nixon before the full House could vote to impeach.

49. Article II, section 4 of the Constitution reads, "The President, Vice President and all civil Officers of the United States, shall be removed from Office on Impeachment for, and Conviction of, Treason, Bribery, or other high Crimes and Misdemeanors."

50. See, for example, http://www.impeachpac.org/?q=articles.

51. The Center for Constitution Rights is an excellent source of clear, well-reasoned analysis of executive-branch abuses. Its Articles of Impeachment Against George W. Bush was a guiding reference for this chapter. A copy can be ordered at http://www.mhpbooks.com/aoi.html, where interview and commentary about impeachment can also be found. CCR's Web site is www.ccr-ny.org.

52. The full interview is at http://www.mhpbooks.com/aoiClips/alternet.html.

53. Referring to the press, Agnew charged in a 1970 speech, "In the United States today, we have more than our share of the nattering nabobs of negativism. They have formed their own 4-H Club—the hopeless, hysterical hypochondriacs of history." Though spoken by Agnew, these alliterative phrases were coined by New York Times columnist William Safire, who at the time was a Nixon and Agnew speechwriter.

54. The articles of impeachment for Andrew Johnson can be found at http://www.law.umkc.

edu/faculty/projects/ftrials/impeach/articles.html.

55. Twenty years later Congress repealed the Tenure of Office Act. Then in 1926, in *Myers v. U.S.*, the Supreme Court effectively ruled the Act unconstitutional when it decided that Congress did not have the authority to limit the removal power of the president with regard to purely executive officials. Thus based on *Myers v. U.S.*, Johnson's defense that the Act interfered with his executive powers had constitutional merit.

56. Cheney admits to telling Senator Patrick Leahy, who is critical of Halliburton's war profiteering in Iraq, on the floor of the Senate to "go fuck yourself." Cheney said that he felt much better afterwards. See http://www.harpers.org/DickCheney.html.

57. DeLay is quoted as announcing his mission to drive Bill Clinton from office by telling his aides, "This is going to be the most important thing I do in my political career and I want all of you to dedicate yourselves to it or leave." http://www.law.umkc.edu/faculty/projects/trials/clinton/clintontrialaccount.html. A detailed yet amusing account of Clinton's Senate impeachment trial is found at this Web site.

58. An analysis of DeLay's impact on the balance of power by Sydney Blumenthal, former senior advisor to Clinton and one of three witnesses deposed in Clinton's impeachment trial, can be found at http://commentisfree.guardian.co.uk/sidney_blumenthal/2006/04/i_delay.html. See also http://www.pbs.org/newshour/bb/congress/jan-june06/delay_4-4.html.

59. On the grand-jury perjury charge of which Clinton was acquitted, the Senate vote of 55–45 by party was: Republicans 45 guilty, 10 not guilty; Democrats 45 not guilty. A list of how each Senator voted is found at http://www.washingtonpost.com/wp-srv/politics/special/clinton/stories/rollcall1_021299.htm.

60. On the obstruction-of-justice charge of which Clinton was acquitted, the Senate vote of 50–50 by party was: Republicans 50 guilty, 5 not guilty; Democrats 45 not guilty. A list of how each Senator voted is found at http://www.washingtonpost.com/wp-srv/politics/special/clinton/stories/rollcall2_021299.htm.

61. A report of the Hyde interview is at http://www.freerepublic.com/focus/f-news/1388597/posts. See also a report that ABC pulled the Hyde story from its Web site, http://rawstory.com/exclusives/byrne/clinton_impeachment_hyde_abc_yanks_422.htm.

62. According to Ben Bradlee, the *Washington Post's* executive editor, the paper filed over three hundred stories on Watergate from the time of the break-in until Nixon resigned. A chronology of major events, complete with links to the *Washington Post's* coverage is found at http://www.washingtonpost.com/wp-srv/onpolitics/watergate/chronology.htm.

63. The full story is at http://www.washingtonpost.com/wp-dyn/content/article/2002/06/03/AR2005111001232.html.

64. The *Post's* former executive editor, Ben Bradlee's 1992 retrospective of Watergate can be found at http://www.washingtonpost.com/wp-dyn/content/article/2002/06/03/AR2005111001251.html.

65. Both Bob Woodward and Carl Bernstein were awarded the Pulitzer Prize for their Watergate reporting. Their notes from source interviews, drafts of stories and memos are at http://www.hrc.utexas.edu/exhibitions/online/woodstein/.

66. See http://writ.news.findlaw.com/dean/20051230.html.

67. A copy of the original twenty names on Nixon's enemy list are found at http://en.wikipedia.org/wiki/Nixon's_Enemies_List.

68. House Resolution 803, authorizing an impeachment investigation, simply noted that the House Judiciary Committee "is authorized and directed to investigate fully and completely whether sufficient grounds exist for the House of Representatives to exercise its constitutional power to impeach Richard Nixon, president of the United States of America."

69. The articles of impeachment and a full list of the thirty-eight House Judiciary Committee members and how they each voted on each article are found at http://watergate.info/

impeachment/impeachment-articles-analysis.shtml.

70. On adopting Article I, the vote of 26–11 by party was: Democrats 21 yes; Republicans 5 yes, 11 no.

71. On adopting Article III, the vote of 19–15 by party was: Democrats 19 yes, 2 no; Republicans 2 yes, 15 no.

72. See U.S. Constitution, Article II, section 2.

73. A full list of the thirty-eight House Judiciary Committee members and how they each voted on each article of impeachment can be found at http://watergate.info/impeachment/impeachment-articles-analysis.shtml.

74. On adopting Article II, the vote of 21–11 by party was: Democrats 21 yes; Republicans 6 yes, 11 no.

75. See http://writ.news.findlaw.com/dean/20051230.html.

76. Nixon made such a statement to David Frost. See http://www.landmarkcases.org/nixon/nixonview.html.

77. In response to grave civil-liberties abuses during the Nixon administration, the committee also developed guidelines, known as the Church Guidelines, limiting government infiltration of religious or political organizations. The Bush Justice Department has taken the position that the guidelines no longer apply, given the powers under the USA PATRIOT Act and its successors. A copy of the Church Committee Report is at http://www.icdc.com/~paulwolf/cointel pro/churchfinalreportIIIe.htm.

78. John Dean's December 30, 2005 article, "George W. Bush as the New Richard M. Nixon: Both Wiretapped Illegally and Impeachably," can be found at http://writ.news.findlaw.com/dean/20051230.html.

79. The specific crimes and sentences for each person in the Nixon administration who was prosecuted for misconduct in connection with Watergate or the other illegal activities of the White House "plumbers," as well as an update about what they are doing today can be found at http://www.washingtonpost.com/wp-srv/onpolitics/watergate/keyplayers.html.

80. John Mitchell was convicted of conspiracy, perjury, and obstruction of justice. He served nineteen months in a minimum-security prison before being paroled for medical reasons.

81. HR Haldeman was convicted of conspiracy and obstruction of justice. He served eighteen months in prison.

82. John Ehrlichman was convicted of obstruction of justice and perjury in the Watergate case and of conspiracy in the Pentagon Papers case. He served eighteen months in prison.

83. John Dean was convicted of obstruction of justice and spent four months in prison.

84. Elizabeth Holtzman also served on the House Judiciary Committee with Conyers during the Nixon impeachment proceedings. Her excellent article, "The Impeachment of George W. Bush," originally published in *The Nation* is at http://www.thenation.com/doc/20060130/holtzman.

85. The full story is at http://www.detnews.com/apps/pbcs.dll/article?AID=/20060405/POLITICS/604050415/1022/rss10.

86. The full text of the *Vanity Fair* article, "Senate Hearings on Bush, Now," by Carl Bernstein can be found at http://www.vanityfair.com/features/general/articles/060417fege08.

87. The full text of John Dean's Senate Judiciary Committee testimony is found at http://www.rawstory.com/news/2006/Testimony_of_John_Dean_on_censure_0331.html.

Chapter 2

NEVER ELECTED, NOT ONCE
The Immaculate Deception and the Road Ahead

Dennis Loo

> Alice laughed: "There's no use trying," she said; "one can't believe impossible things." "I daresay you haven't had much practice," said the Queen. "When I was younger, I always did it for half an hour a day. Why, sometimes I've believed as many as six impossible things before breakfast."
>
> —Lewis Carroll, *Alice Through the Looking Glass*

In order to believe that George W. Bush won the November 2, 2004, presidential election, you must also believe each and every one of the following extremely improbable or outright impossible things.[1]

1. New voter registrations in the lead-up to the election hit record levels, with Democrats swamping Republicans in voter registrations (outstripping them by a factor of 5:1 in Florida and by 6:1 and better in Ohio), but despite this increase Bush still somehow won.[2]

2. Pre–Election Day momentum carried through on Election Day with a record turnout and a highly energized and motivated electorate, but for the first time in history a large turnout favored the GOP instead of the Democrats.[3]

3. CNN reported at 9 p.m. EST on election evening that Kerry was leading by 3 points in the national exit polls based on well over 13,000 respondents. Several hours later, at 1:36 a.m., CNN reported that the exit polls, now based on a few hundred interviewees more—13,531 respondents—were showing Bush leading by 2 points, *a 5-point swing.*

In other words, a swing of 5 percentage points from a tiny increase in the number of respondents somehow occurred, despite it being mathematically impossible.[4]

4. Early-day voters picked up by initial exit polls (showing Kerry rolling to a 5-million-vote landslide win) apparently reflected the fact that GOP supporters waited to vote until very late in the day, even though there was a complete lack of evidence of any late GOP surge to observers on the ground. This was, moreover, contrary to the historic patterns of GOP supporters voting early.[5]

5. Bush loses big to Kerry nationally among the only groups from which Bush could legitimately fashion a win: first-time voters, lapsed voters (those who didn't vote in 2000), and undecideds. In addition, Bush loses people who voted for him in the cliffhanger 2000 election. Like Athena springing full-grown from Zeus' brow, however, Bush is nonetheless credited ex nihilo with a 3.4 million-vote surplus in the official tally.[6]

6. Bush far exceeded the 85 percent of registered Florida Republicans' votes he got in 2000, receiving in 2004 more than 100 percent of the registered Republican votes in 24 out of the 67 Florida counties, more than 200 percent of registered Republicans in 10 counties, over 300 percent of registered Republicans in 4 counties, more than 400 percent in 2 counties, and over 700 percent in 1 county. Bush's share of crossover votes by registered Democrats in Florida, however, *did not actually increase* over 2000 and he *lost ground* among registered Independents, dropping 15 points.[7] Floridians were just so enthusiastic about Bush and Cheney that they somehow managed to overrule basic math.

7. Bush got *more votes than there are registered voters*, and by stark contrast participation rates in many Democratic strongholds in Ohio fell to as low as less than 8 percent. Tens of thousands of voters waited in long lines for hours and hours in heavily Democratic precincts in Ohio, apparently only to then go into the booth and *pretend* to vote.[8]

8. Bush won reelection despite approval ratings of 48 percent, below the 50 percent tipping point—the first time in history such a disproportion has happened. Harry Truman has been cited as also having achieved the same, but Truman's polling numbers were trailing so much behind challenger Thomas Dewey that pollsters stopped surveying two weeks before the 1948 elections,[9] thus missing the late surge of support for

Truman. Unlike Truman, Bush's support was clearly eroding severely on election eve.[10]

9. The "challenger rule"—an incumbent's final results won't be better than his final polling—was wrong for the first time in polling history.[11]

10. Even though Harris' and Zogby's last-minute polling in 2000 were exactly on the mark, their last-minute polls projecting a Kerry victory in 2004 were wrong.[12]

11. There was no fraud in Warren County, Ohio, where officials admitted counting the votes in secret before bringing them out in public to count, citing an unidentified FBI agent's warning of a terrorist incident as the rationale—a report that the FBI denies ever making.[13]

12. Bush "won" Ohio by 51–48%, even though the hand count of the 147,400 absentee and provisional ballots had Kerry receiving 54.46 percent of the vote,[14] and exit polls showed Kerry winning Ohio by a four-point margin.[15]

13. A Florida computer programmer, Clinton Curtis (a lifelong registered Republican), must be lying when he stated in a sworn affidavit that his employers at Yang Enterprises, Inc. (YEI) and Tom Feeney (general counsel and lobbyist for YEI, GOP state legislator, and Jeb Bush's 1994 running mate for Florida Lieutenant Governor) asked him in 2000 to create a computer program to undetectably alter vote totals. Curtis, under the initial impression that he was creating this software in order to forestall possible fraud, handed over the program to his employer, Mrs. Li Woan Yang, and was told: **"You don't understand, in order to get the contract we have to hide the manipulation in the source code. This program is needed to control the vote in south Florida"** (boldface in original).[16]

14. Diebold CEO Walden O'Dell's declaration in a August 14, 2003, letter to GOP fundraisers that he was "committed to helping Ohio to deliver its electoral votes to the president next year," and the fact that Diebold is one of the three major suppliers of the electronic voting machines in Ohio and nationally, did not result in any fraud by Diebold.[17]

15. The nonpartisan Government Accounting Office Report on the 2004 vote in Ohio, released in September 2005, found that "(1) some electronic voting systems did not encrypt cast ballots or system audit logs and it was possible to alter both without being detected; (2) it was possible to alter the files that define how a ballot looks and works so that

the votes for one candidate could be recorded for a different candidate; and (3) vendors installed uncertified versions of voting system software at the local level . . . *resulting in the loss or miscount of votes*" (p. 7, italics added).[18] The GAO, known for its independence, thoroughness and objectivity, must have somehow gotten it wrong this time.

16. Exit polls in the November 2004 Ukrainian presidential elections, paid for in part by the Bush administration, were correct in showing election fraud, but exit polls in the U.S., where exit polling was invented, were very wrong.[19]

17. The National Election Pool's exit polls[20] were so far off that since their inception twenty years ago, they have never been this wrong, more wrong than statistical probability indicates as a possibility.

18. In *every* single instance where exit polls were wrong, the discrepancy favored Bush, even though statistical probability tells us that any survey errors should show up in both directions. Half a century of polling and centuries of mathematics must be wrong.[21]

19. In 2004 the U.S. Computer Emergency Readiness Team warned that "[a] vulnerability exists due to an undocumented backdoor account, which could [allow] a local or remote authenticated malicious user [to] modify votes" on Diebold GEMS Central Tabulator 1.17.7, 1.18 voting equipment (a central tabulator collects all the votes from the different precincts). They further noted that "[n]o workaround or patch [is] available at time of publishing."[22] This alert was posted on the Department of Homeland Security's Web site in late August 2004, but despite this warning, nothing was done to prevent tampering from occurring. Altering the votes in a state using Diebold equipment could therefore have been carried out by just one person over an ordinary phone line from a remote location. However, this admission that Diebold machines could be readily hacked raises no red flags about the election's outcome.

In short, people who want to claim that Bush won the 2004 election legitimately must argue that despite pre-election registration trends dramatically in Kerry's favor; despite election-eve polls showing momentum turning sharply against Bush; despite a record turnout; despite exit polls—the gold standard of vote-count validity internationally—showing Bush losing decisively; despite the fact that precedents of all prior elections were violated; despite massive evidence of vote tampering and disenfranchisement—despite all these indicators, millions of people suddenly and unaccountably are supposed to have done an about-face on Election Day, and the hand of God intervened to suspend the laws of math and statistics to permit another Bush presidency.

No wonder the White House considers itself part of the "faith-based community" rather than of the "reality-based community."[23]

The Emperor (and the Electoral Process) Have No Clothes

The list of nineteen improbables/impossibles recounts only some of the evidence of fraud in the 2004 election, since it ignores the scores of instances of voter disenfranchisement that assumed many different forms—for example, in Florida, banning black voters who had either previously been convicted of a felony or who were "inadvertently" placed on the felons list, while not banning convicted Latino felons;[24] in Ohio, providing extraordinarily few voting machines in predominately Democratic precincts (fewer than in 2000 in the full knowledge that 2004 would see a huge increase in turnout); for the first time disallowing Ohio voters from voting in any other precinct when they were unable to find their assigned precincts; and so on. A plethora of reasons clearly exists to conclude that widespread and historic levels of fraud were committed in this election. Meanwhile there are *no* reasons to think that these official results are in the least believable.[25]

Indeed, some items in the preceding list of improbables and impossibles separately point *definitively* to fraud. In whole—or in part—then, the evidence of a stolen election is overwhelming. The jarring strangeness of the results and the prevalence of complaints from voters (for example, those who voted for Kerry and then saw to their shock on the electronic voting machine screen that their vote had just been recorded for Bush), require some kind of explanation, or the legitimacy of elections and of the presidency would be imperiled.

Explanations from public officials and major media came in three forms. First, exit polls, not the official tallies, were labeled spectacularly wrong. Second, the so-called "moral-values" voters—expressed in the now ubiquitous "red state/blue state" formula—were offered as the underlying reason for Bush's triumph. And third, people who brought forth any of the evidence of fraud were dismissed as "spreadsheet-wielding conspiracy theorists," while mainstream media censored the vast majority of the evidence of fraud so that most Americans to this day have never heard a fraction of what was amiss. I will discuss each of these three responses, followed by a discussion of the role of electronic voting machines in the 2002 elections that presaged the 2004 election fraud, and then wrap up with a discussion of these events' significance taken as a whole and the question of what can be done.

Killing the Messenger: The Exit Polls

Exit polls are the gold standard of vote-count validity internationally. Since exit polls ask people as they emerge from the polling station whom they just voted for, they are not projections as are polls taken in the months, weeks, or days before an election. They are not subject to faulty memory, voter capriciousness (voters voting differently than they indicated to a pollster previously), or erroneous projections about who will actually turn up to vote. Pollsters know who turned up to vote because the voters are standing there in front of the exit pollsters. Because of these characteristics, exit polls are exceptionally accurate. They are so accurate that in Germany, for example, the winners are announced based on the exit polls, with paper ballots being counted as a backup check against the exit polls.[26] Exit polls are used worldwide, for this reason, as markers of fraud.[27]

Significant, inexplicable discrepancies between exit polls and official tallies started showing up in the U.S. in 2000, and *only in Florida* (Florida, of course, decided the outcome of the 2000 election). The discrepancy was not the fault of the exit polls, however, but in the official tallies themselves. Although the mainstream media fell on their swords about their election evening projections that called Florida for Gore in 2000, their projections were right. In analyses conducted by the National Opinion Research Center in Florida after the U.S. Supreme Court aborted the vote recount, Gore emerged the winner over Bush, no matter what criteria for counting votes were applied.[28] The fact that this is not widely known makes it a major untold story.

The pollster Dick Morris further affirms the validity of exit polling. Immediately after the 2004 election he wrote:

Exit polls are almost never wrong. They eliminate the two major potential fallacies in survey research by correctly separating actual voters from those who pretend they will cast ballots but never do and by substituting actual observation for guesswork in judging the relative turnout of different parts of the state. . . .

To screw up one exit poll is unheard of. To miss six of them is incredible. It boggles the imagination how pollsters could be that incompetent and invites speculation that more than honest error was at play here.[29]

Confounded by and suspicious of the results, Morris resorted to advancing the bizarre theory that there must have been a conspiracy among the networks to suppress the Bush vote in the West by issuing exit-poll results that were far off the final tallies.

A number of different statisticians have examined the 2004 election results. Most notably, a University of Pennsylvania statistician, Steve Freeman, Ph.D., analyzed the exit polls of the swing states of Pennsylvania, Ohio, and Florida and concluded that the odds of the exit polls being as far off as they were are 250 million to 1.[30] Exit polls in Florida had Kerry leading by 1.7 points and in Ohio by 2.4 points. These exit-poll figures were altered at 1:36 a.m. on November 3, 2004, on CNN to conform to the "official" tally. In the end Kerry lost Florida by 5 percent and Ohio by 2.5 percent. This is a net shift of 6.7 points in Florida and 4.9 points in Ohio in Bush's favor, beyond the margin of error. By exit poll standards, this net shift is unbelievable.

A team at the University of California at Berkeley, headed by sociology professor Michael Hout, found a highly suspicious pattern, in which Bush received 260,000 more votes in those Florida precincts that used electronic voting machines than past voting patterns would indicate, compared to those precincts that used optical scan-read votes, where past voting patterns held.[31]

The Edison-Mitofsky polling group that conducted the National Exit Poll issued a 77-page report on January 19, 2005, to account for the unexpected discrepancy of their exit polls.[32] Edison-Mitofsky ruled out sampling error as the problem and indicated that systemic bias was responsible. They concluded that their exit polls were wrong because Kerry voters must have been more willing to talk to their poll workers than Bush voters and because their poll workers were too young and inexperienced. Edison-Mitofsky offers no evidence to indicate that its conclusion about more talkative Kerry voters is based on actual occurrences, merely that such a scenario would explain the discrepancy. In fact, as nine statisticians[33] who conducted an evaluation of the Edison-Mitofsky data and analysis point out, Bush voters appeared to be slightly *more* willing to talk to exit pollsters than were Kerry voters. This fact would make the exit polls' discrepancy with the official tallies even more pronounced. In addition, the Edison-Mitofsky explanation fails to explain why exit polls were only exceptionally wrong in the swing states.

Red State, Red Herring: The "Moral Values" Voters

A plausible explanation still needs to be offered for the startling 2004 election outcome: how did Bush, caught in a lie about the reasons we went to war with Iraq, racked by prison abuse and torture scandals at Abu Ghraib and Guantánamo, bogged down in Iraq, failing to catch Osama bin Laden, badly embarrassed during the debates,[34] caught sleeping prior to 9/11, and so on, manage to win a resounding victory? Enter here the "moral values" rationale. As Katharine Q. Seelye of the *New York Times* wrote in a November 4, 2004, article entitled "Moral Values Cited as a Defining Issue of the Election":

> Even in a time of war and economic hardship, Americans said they were motivated to vote for President Bush on Tuesday by moral values as much as anything else, according to a survey of voters as they left their polling places. In the survey, a striking portrait of one influential group emerged—that of a traditional, church-going electorate that leans conservative on social issues and strongly backed Mr. Bush.

In the same issue, another article by Todd S. Purdum, entitled "Electoral Affirmation of Shared Values Provides Bush a Majority," cited one-fifth (more precisely, 22 percent) of the voters as mentioning "moral values" as their chief concern. This finding was echoed throughout the major media.[35] The only person in the mainstream media to challenge this theory was *New York Times* columnist Frank Rich, on November 28, 2004, in an opinion piece entitled "The Great Indecency Hoax":

The mainstream press, itself in love with the "moral values" story line and traumatized by the visual exaggerations of the red-blue map, is too cowed to challenge the likes of the American Family Association. So are politicians of both parties. It took a British publication, *The Economist*, to point out that the percentage of American voters citing moral and ethical values as their prime concern is actually down from 2000 (35 percent) and 1996 (40 percent).[36]

As Rich correctly points out, no American media outlet repeated this statistic. Instead, the widely mentioned and oft-repeated "moral values" vote took on the status of an urban—or in this instance, suburban/rural—legend.

Shocked by the election results, many people took out their anger at the perceived stupidity of Bush voters, especially those in the so-called red states. This fury, while understandable given Bush's record, badly misses the point. Voters did not heist this election. As others have pointed out eloquently, many of the people who *really did* vote for Bush did so primarily because they were misled through systematic disinformation campaigns.[37]

"Spreadsheet-Wielding Conspiracy Theorists"

In November 2004 major U.S. media gave headline treatment to the Ukrainian presidential election fraud, *explicitly citing the exit polls as definitive evidence of fraud*. At the very same time major U.S. media dismissed anyone who pointed out this same evidence of likely fraud in the U.S. elections as conspiracy-theory crazies. A November 11, 2004, *Washington Post* article, for example, described people who raised the question of fraud as "mortally wounded party loyalists and . . . spreadsheet-wielding conspiracy theorists."[38] Tom Zeller, Jr., handled it similarly, writing in the November 12, 2004, issue of the *New York Times* ("Vote Fraud Theories, Spread by Blogs, Are Quickly Buried"); "[T]he email messages and Web postings had all the twitchy cloak-and-dagger thrust of a Hollywood blockbuster. 'Evidence mounts that the vote may have been hacked,' trumpeted a headline on the Web site CommonDreams.org. 'Fraud took place in the 2004 election through electronic voting machines,' declared BlackBoxVoting.org."[39]

Neither of these articles bothered to address even a fraction of the evidence of fraud. The *Washington Post* passed off the exit polls discrepancy as "not being based on statistics," since the exit polls "are not publicly distributed." Both of these statements are untrue. The *New York Times* article for its part *failed to even mention exit polls*. Both articles explained away the glaring and unbelievable totals for Bush in hugely Democratic districts in Florida as due to the "Dixiecrat" vote. This explanation would be plausible except for two things: first, Bush did not win over any more crossover votes in 2004 than he did in 2000; and second, these votes, far in excess of Republican registered voters, occurred primarily in nonrural areas. In just one example, in Baker County, Florida, out of 12,887 registered voters, of whom 69.3 percent were Democrats and 24.3 percent Republicans, Bush received 7,738 votes, while Kerry only received 2,180.[40] As Robert Parry of Consortiumnews.com points out,

> Rather than a rural surge of support, Bush actually earned more than 7 out of 10 new votes in the 20 largest counties in Florida. Many of these counties are either Democratic strongholds—such as Miami-Dade, Broward, and Palm Beach—or they are swing counties, such as Orange, Hillsborough, and Duval.
>
> Many of these large counties saw substantially more newly registered Democrats than Republicans. For example, in Orange County, a swing county home to Orlando, Democrats registered twice as many new voters than Republicans in the years since 2000. In Palm Beach and Broward combined, Democrats registered 111,000 new voters, compared with fewer than 20,000 new Republicans.[41]

The only person in the major media to treat these complaints seriously and at any length was Keith Olbermann at MSNBC who ran two stories on it, citing Cuyahoga County's surplus 93,000 votes over the registered voter count and the peculiar victories for Bush in Florida counties that were overwhelmingly Democratic scattered across the state.[42] For his trouble, media conservatives attacked him for being a "voice of paranoia" and spreading "idiotic conspiracy theories."[43]

The Oh-So Loyal Opposition: The Democratic Party

An obvious question here is: Why haven't the Democrats been more vigorous in their objections to this fraud? The fact that they haven't objected more (with a few notable individual exceptions) has been taken by some as definitive evidence that no fraud happened, because the Democrats would have the most to gain from objecting. In part the answer to this puzzle is that the Democrats don't fully understand what has hit them. The Kerry campaign's reaction to the Swift Boat Veterans' attack ads that damaged them so much is a good illustration of this failure. The right-wing media hammered away at Kerry through their by now very heavy presence on talk radio, the Internet, Fox News, and other outlets. The mainstream media, such as ABC, CBS, NBC, CNN, and major newspapers and magazines, still adhering to the standards of "objective" journalism, which the right-wing media consider "quaint,"[44] legitimated these false allegations about Kerry by presenting "the two sides" as if one side made up entirely of lies and half-truths could be considered a legitimate "side." The Kerry campaign concluded that these ads were all lies and wouldn't have any effect, and thus they took too long to respond to them. By the time they did, the damage had been done. In a CBS/*New York Times* poll taken in the period of September 12–16, 2004, 33 percent said they thought that the Swift Boast Veterans' charges against Kerry were "mostly true."[45] A remarkable feat, given that Kerry volunteered and was decorated several times for heroism, while Bush used his father's connections to dodge real service.

The Democrats' meek acceptance of the extremely peculiar outcomes of other races prior to the 2004 elections illustrates this point further. As a result of the 2000 Florida debacle, Congress passed the "Help America Vote" Act in October 2002. While this act introduced a number of reasonable reforms, it also resulted in the widespread introduction of paperless electronic voting machines. This change meant that there was no way to determine if the votes recorded by these computers were accurate and free from tampering. The GOP majority has blocked subsequent efforts by a few Democratic congresspeople, led by Michigan Rep. John Conyers, to rectify this situation and ensure a paper ballot.

The following is a partial list of 2002 discrepancies that can be understood as dress rehearsals for the stolen presidential election of 2004:

On November 3, 2002, the *Atlanta Journal-Constitution* poll showed Democratic Senator Max Cleland with a 49-to-44-point lead over Republican Rep. Saxby Chambliss. The next day, Chambliss, despite trailing by 5 points, ended up winning by a margin of 53 to 46 percent. This was, in other words, an unbelievable 12-point turnaround over the course of one day!

In the Georgia governor's race, Republican Sonny Perdue upset incumbent Democratic Governor Roy Barnes by a margin of 52 to 45 percent. This outcome was especially strange given that the October 16–17, 2002, Mason Dixon Poll (Mason Dixon Polling and Research, Inc. of Washington, DC) had shown Democratic Governor Barnes ahead by 48 to 39 percent, with a margin of error of ± 4 points. The final tally was, in other words, a jaw dropping 16-point turnaround! What the Cleland "defeat" by Saxby and the Barnes "defeat" by Perdue have in common is that nearly all the Georgia votes were recorded on computerized voting machines, which produce no paper trail.

In Minnesota, after Democratic Senator Paul Wellstone's death in a plane crash,[46] former Vice President Walter Mondale took Wellstone's place and was leading the Republican Norm Coleman in the days before the election by 47 to 39 percent. Despite the fact that he was trailing just days before the race by 8 points, Coleman beat Mondale by 50 to 47 percent. This was an 11-point turnaround! The Minnesota race was conducted with paper ballots, read by optical scan readers, but Mondale never bothered to ask for a recount.[47]

The delicious irony for the GOP is that the Help America Vote Act, precipitated by the theft of the Florida 2000 presidential vote, made GOP theft of elections as in the preceding examples easy and unverifiable except through recourse to indirect analysis such as pre-election polls and exit polls. (Republican National Committee Chair Ed Gillespie, in remarks to the National Press Club on November 4, 2004, took the next logical step, calling for the elimination of exit polls on the grounds that the 2000, 2002, and 2004 exit polls showed the Republican candidates losing).[48] This is the political equivalent of having your cake and eating it, too. Or, more precisely: stealing elections, running the country, and aggressively, arrogantly, and falsely claiming that "the people" support it.

Welcome to a world where statistical probability and normal arithmetic no longer apply! The Democrats, rather than vigorously pursuing these patently obvious signs of election fraud in 2004, have nearly all decided that being gracious losers is better than being winners,[49] probably because—and this may be the most important reason for the Democrats' relative silence—a full-scale uncovering of the fraud runs the risk of mobilizing and unleashing popular forces that the Democrats find just as threatening as the GOP does.

Our Hope: The Popular Forces

What are these popular forces? There are two groups here, the lower strata and the middle classes. The lower strata include the working class and people such as those left to fend for themselves, to drown and die in New Orleans by the Bush administration, who had no way out of the city and who couldn't afford even bus fare, who were called "looters" by the media and the government when they broke into stores and restaurants in order to feed and give water to everyone who hadn't had any in days. These people recognize from their everyday experiences in this society that those who rule, those who run this country, aren't compassionate and aren't legitimate. The lower strata only go along with the status quo because they know that if they don't they will get cracked on the head by a policeman's club or worse.

Belief in the system's legitimacy plays an absolutely crucial role among the middle classes in the U.S., but not among the disenfranchised lower strata. While illusions and hopeless dreams—such as hoping you'll win the lottery—definitely help to hold the more oppressed in line, intimidation and the ubiquitous use of force are the *main* way they are kept down. Police in communities of color and among the poor are the most obvious symbols and first-line practitioners of this. Social workers and other "professionals of the poor" also play an important role "managing" the lower strata. One need only note what happens when a citywide blackout occurs, for example, to see what the oppressed will do when the normal forces of order are unable to perform their usual functions.

The cynicism the oppressed feel about the legitimacy of those who rule them and over the whole of society comes from the lessons of their *everyday* existence. The dispossessed do not rise up in ordinary times, not *mainly* because they are under illusions about the system's nature, but *mainly* because they know that if they rose up, they would be immediately crushed by the forces of the state. Only during times of general upheaval in the society, where those who rule them every day are preoccupied with internecine battles or handicapped or wounded because of some other crisis or crises, do rebellions and insurrections stand a chance.

The middle classes, by contrast, go along because they have a strong belief in this system's legitimacy and the electoral process in particular. They believe that the candidate with the greatest number of votes takes office. They believe that their votes matter and that public opinion overall guides public policy. They believe that the United States is a democracy. Should enough of the middle class conclude that the process is rigged, illegitimate, and corrupt, that those who lead us are dangerously incompetent and that they are endangering our lives and this planet, elements of the middle class will, together with the lower strata, begin to act outside the normal channels of electoral politics and shake this system to its core.

Any serious attempts to change a society must involve the lower strata together with the middle strata. The Democrats find the prospect of the genie being released from the bottle in the form of the masses springing into political life just as threatening as the GOP does, because they agree with the GOP that this system of globalized capitalism, this new American empire, is the proper order of things. Recall that John Kerry and John Edwards promised to continue the war in Iraq. Their platform, in fact, was Bush-lite. Their platform was essentially that of W.'s dad when he was president. This tells you something crucial about what is afoot in a larger sense.

Globalization and the Rise of the Neoliberal/Security State

We have been witnesses to momentous public policy changes over the last thirty years: the systematic dismantling of the New Deal/welfare state and its replacement by the security, or neoliberal, state. The neoliberal state (which takes its name from "liberal" in the sense of laissez-faire capitalism à la Adam Smith, the eighteenth century economist) features deregulation, deindustrialization, reengineering, privatization, downsizing, globalization, and in our case, an American imperialist empire. It means that social safety-net programs are being slashed right and left while the state's coercive apparatus—the military, the criminal-justice system, and security and surveillance activities and agencies—are being vastly expanded. When the GOP speaks of curbing government (or, as tax activist Grover Norquist has famously stated, shrinking the government so much that it can be drowned in a bathtub) they mean curbing the social safety net. They do not mean shrinking military or police or spy functions.

The key figures in this new economic and political order are transnational corporations that dwarf most of the world's national economies. As of 2000, of the 100 largest economic entities in the world, 51 were transnational *corporations*. Wal-Mart was larger, in economic terms, than 182 countries. The combined sales of the 200 largest corporations were larger than all of the world's countries' economies less the top 10 countries in economic size![50] Moreover, this concentration of wealth and power is *accelerating*. The dominance of these giant conglomerates and their allies in government means that we can expect ever rising levels of job and social insecurity, since such is the fundamental logic driving globalization. The Democrats are not going to stand up to these transnationals; they have not done so, nor are they capable of doing so. Hoping and praying that electing Democrats in 2006 will somehow turn this trend around is a losing strategy. The main problem isn't that the Democrats are spineless or that they can't get their act together. The main problem is that both major parties are the political representatives of big capital and of globalization.

It's important to further recognize that this isn't just because the Democrats are beholden to big campaign contributors, a situation that is resolvable through campaign reform legislation, although that is obviously part of the picture. The essence of the problem is that this situation is precisely what we should expect. When you're talking about economies on a world scale, in which the major players are monstrously large and the stakes involved are gigantic, there is no reason to expect that the people who run in these kind of circles, whether they are CEOs or public officials, are going to truly subject their fantastic power and wealth to the whims of an electorate in which everyone, rich and poor alike, has one vote. Would you, if you had their level of power and wealth and their ideology? If you had more power than 182 countries and you were one corporation, would you let the electorate decide that they were going to, for example, nationalize you? Would you put the fate of your extremely concentrated power and wealth in the hands of "the people"?

Both major parties in this country are in agreement that this new economic order of globalization, this security state, is the right thing. They differ somewhat over some particular policies, with some sectors, for example, more based in science and more concerned about the environment (for example, Al

Gore), but they don't differ on the fundamentals. The media are themselves fully embedded within this new economic order; they are themselves major corporations. The Democrats aren't the leading political representatives of this new order because, in their highest and best expression, the Democrats are FDR New Dealers, and the material basis for that stance has been getting wiped out systematically over the last thirty years. That is why the Democrats appear to be so hapless and so feeble against the GOP's cutthroat viciousness, for the GOP represents the most aggressive, the most in-your-face cutting edge of the ascendant neoliberal state.

The Faux, err, Fourth Estate

This brings us to the matter of the corporate media, who have completely failed to raise any questions about the obvious theft of the last two presidential elections. Worse, they have actively suppressed and ridiculed those who have pointed out the fraud, painting them as malcontents and conspiracy theorists. We have a situation today in which, as a concentrated example, a leading reporter for the most prestigious news organization in the country, Judith Miller of the *New York Times*, cannot distinguish between being a government mouthpiece and a part of the fourth estate and who, instead of scrutinizing the government's self-serving lies that got us into the war on Iraq, went to jail to protect her two sources, Lewis Libby and Karl Rove, claiming that she doesn't remember who told her that the CIA undercover agent Valerie Plame was Joe Wilson's wife. Essentially the same can be said of the *Washington Post* reporter Bob Woodward, who exchanged his proper journalistic skepticism for insider access to the Bush-Cheney administration.[51]

Two factors have combined to produce the media picture we have today. First, corporate consolidation has led both to highly concentrated, oligopolistic media ownership and to news organizations as merely one arm of corporations that are engaged in many other, non-news activities. News divisions, which formerly were not required to be profitable in their own right, have been forced to become profit-making centers. As a result, news gathering and news analysis have been cut back sharply. Media are, in general, much more dependent upon news feeds from the government and corporate business interests and right-wing think tanks. They are also much more likely, for business reasons, to devote space and time to infotainment, sex, sensationalism, and fluff, depriving the public, who rely heavily on TV for their news, of sound information.[52]

These mega media conglomerates are part of the same concentrated corporate power that is evident in the non-media world of petrochemical companies, and so on. Acting as the watchdogs for the public interest has become, *at the very best*, a rare occurrence, because it goes against corporate interests. Several years ago the film *The Insider* depicted the real-life struggle that went on at *60 Minutes* over whether to broadcast an explosive interview with a former tobacco insider, Jeffrey Wigand (played by Russell Crowe). The film is heartening in the sense that the producer, Lowell Bergman (played by Al Pacino), goes to the mat and puts his job on the line to get the interview on the air. But what is striking about this story is the fact that such bravery is so rare, that it took an extraordinary and selfless effort of going against the grain to get this *one* story on the air. Consider all the stories that get buried, never to be heard or seen by the public, in the ordinary course of events, either because it gets pulled by management or, much more frequently, because reporters engage in self-censorship and never write the stories in the first place.[53]

Consider two recent examples of what journalists fear. In February 2005 CNN's *chief* news executive, Eason Jordan, was forced to resign after his comments at the World Economic Forum in Switzerland were roundly attacked by right-wing bloggers and by liberals. Jordan apparently remarked (accurately) that journalists were not being killed accidentally but were being aimed at by American troops in Iraq. Dan Rather, in a more famous case, was forced into early retirement by a story about Bush's National Guard service. The secretary of Bush's commander, while saying that the memos were apparently recreated, stated that the content of the memos was accurate. No matter, Rather and two or three others went down. By contrast, Ann Coulter, for example, can say the most extreme, untrue, and outrageous things, Bill O'Reilly and Rush Limbaugh can say anything they want, frequently simply making things up, and they see no repercussions whatsoever from this. Indeed, in the current atmosphere, such behavior enhances their careers.

Secondly, the right-wing plans that were put together in the 1970s for their own media—TV, radio, magazines, think tanks, publishing houses, and so on—into which they have sunk tens of billions of dollars, has been a spectacular success.[54] Today, Bush can screw up—which, of course, he does constantly—

and the right-wing media have his back. On top of this, the mainstream media now *largely take their political cues from the right* and frequently ape the right-wing media, trying to position themselves in a number of instances to the right of the right.[55] This, more than anything, testifies to how successful the radical right has been in its media strategy.

Some people might ask, "If the evidence is so unmistakable that the elections were stolen, then how could the media ignore it?" "Why haven't we heard more about this?" "Wouldn't this be a huge story for them?" Yes, *too huge.* A combination of denial and collusion are at work here. For most people in the mainstream media, the very idea of American vote fraud on this scale is simply out of the question. Elections are stolen in other countries, *not here in the United States.* For the mainstream media to even accept the idea that the electoral process has been rigged would further mean that they would have to blow the lid on a scandal that would make Watergate look like a small hiccup by comparison. Major media corporations fear a popular upheaval for fundamentally the same reasons that the GOP and Democrats do. When it comes down to it, they choose national stability over truth nearly every time. These media conglomerates are also loath, especially in these times, to stick their necks out very far. They know that the GOP now wields major institutional power, and media also do not generally seek to rock a boat in which they themselves are heavy occupants.[56]

Flavor Flav of the rap group Public Enemy used to wear a big clock around his neck in order to remind us all that we'd better understand what time it is. Or, as Bob Dylan once said, "Let us not speak falsely now, the hour's getting late." To all of those who said before the 2004 elections that this was the most important election in our lifetimes, to all of those who plunged into that election hoping and believing that we could throw the villains out via the electoral booth, to all of those who thought that "being realistic" and backing Kerry-Edwards was the only responsible choice, to all of those who held their noses and voted for Democrats thinking that at least they were slightly better than the theocratic fascists running this country now, this must be said: *voting doesn't make public policy.* If we weren't convinced of that truth before the 2004 elections, then now is the time to wake up to that fact. Even beyond the fraudulent elections of 2000 and 2004, public policies are not now, nor have they ever been, settled through elections.

The Role of Mass Movements and Alternative Media

What can be done? The Eugene McCarthy campaign of 1968 and the George McGovern campaign in 1972 didn't end the war in Vietnam; the Vietnamese people and the antiwar movement ended the war. Civil rights weren't secured because JFK and LBJ suddenly woke up to racial discrimination; the civil rights movement and black-power movement galvanized public opinion and rocked this country to its foundations. Men didn't suddenly wake up and realize that they were male chauvinist pigs; women formed the women's movement, organized, marched, rallied, and demanded nothing less than equality, shaking this country to the core. The Bush administration is bogged down and sinking deeper in Iraq, not mainly because the top figures of the Bush administration consist of liars, blind (and incompetent) ideologues, international outlaws, and propagators of torture as an official policy, but because the Iraqi people have risen up against imperialist invasion. Prior to the war the international movement against the Iraq war brought millions of people out into the streets, the largest demonstrations in history, denying the U.S. imperialists the United Nations' sanction and leading to Turkey's denying U.S. requests to use their land as a staging area. These are major, world-historic feats.

The 2000, 2002, and 2004 election frauds underscores the critical importance of building a mass movement, a movement of resistance that doesn't tie itself to the electoral road and electoral parties. In addition, as Robert Parry has eloquently argued, a counterforce to the right-wing media empire must be built by the left and by progressive-minded people. As it stands today, the right can get away with nearly anything because it has talking heads on TV, radio, the Internet, and other outlets who set the tone and parameters of the political agenda, with mainstream media largely playing me-too.[57]

Like a bridge broken by an earthquake, the electoral road can only lead to plunging us into the sea—which is precisely what happened in the 2004 election.

The Immaculate Deception

When you examine the explanations offered for Bush's "election" closely, you find that they collapse the way vampires exposed to sunlight disintegrate into flame and ashes. Fundamentally the impression that the right has a mandate is a fraud. Major political figures and media have been carrying out a campaign to create the impression that the sweeping and dramatic public policy changes we've been seeing over the last thirty or so years are a product of a popular mandate and that popular sentiment is driving these momentous changes in our society. In a sense this impression management isn't brand new at all, but it has reached a qualitatively higher level for reasons I've indicated in this chapter.

There's a phenomenon that sociologist Noelle Neumann calls "The Spiral of Silence."[58] This occurs when people silence their true feelings because they believe that their opinion is in the distinct minority; they're outnumbered, and there's no hope of their opinion carrying the day. They may actually be in the majority, but if they *think* they're outnumbered, they'll censor themselves.

The right wing media (led by Fox News and Rush Limbaugh), the mainstream corporate media, and most public officials in this country have been assiduously conveying the impression that the right is riding high and is in power because it reflects the sentiments of most of the public. The sharp rightward trend in politics and public policy has been and is presented as the consequence of a rightward drift in public opinion. According to this dominant view, public opinion has been leading the way. Specifically around the so-called election of Bush, this line is expressed in the "moral values" voter. The evangelicals and social conservatives are in the driver's seat they've been claiming, and you can't resist them. As Robert Novak stated after the 2004 elections, "Let's face it, this is a conservative country."

This falsehood has bamboozled a lot of people. For instance, the left-wing magazine *The Nation*[59] ran an article shortly after the 2004 elections to the effect that the results showed that we just had to try harder next time and do more of what was done in 2004 in 2006 and 2008. This reminds me of that saying that insanity is continuing to do something that doesn't work, expecting it to work. For some reason they're blind to the fact that the election process has been rigged via paperless, easily hacked, electronic voting machines.

The Nation magazine's authors' faith in the electoral process and American-style democracy is so powerful that they can't seriously imagine that some people would brazenly steal elections. It is evidently much easier for them to conclude that millions of Americans are dupes than to believe that a small number of people are thieves. Why? Probably because stealing elections so undermines their belief in fair play and in democracy that it would mean that they and others must operate *outside* the bounds of the traditional politics of electioneering and voting, and *that* they aren't ready to accept.

Fundamentally, this impression that the right has a mandate is a fraud. It's a fraud specifically around the "moral-values vote" and the famous red state-blue state formula, and it's a fraud in general from well before the 2000 elections around a whole host of public-policy issues. It's a myth promoted in order to sell this entire neoliberalist program of deregulation, privatization, downsizing, globalization, and American imperialist empire under the pretense that the *people* support it.

To say that these are myths isn't the same as saying that the right doesn't have influence and doesn't have power. It has both influence and power. Tremendous influence. But it is not in the majority. We are. And we have truth on our side, which it has none of because its continued rule requires systematic lying and deception.

Injecting truth and facts into the public arena can and will alter the political landscape dramatically. The right has over the last three decades invested tens of billions of dollars in media because it understands so deeply the power of public opinion, the difference it makes in what information people get exposed to, and the interpretive frame they are presented with. We who want an entirely different world than it does must likewise recognize this.

The people who feel so outnumbered and/or disempowered now when armed with the truth and with information will feel unburdened, mad, passionate, and anxious to do what they can to change things. What a difference it makes to actually get truth and facts into the public arena.[60] How impoverished the public arena has become. Imagine for an instant how long this war on Iraq would last if Americans actually saw pictures of the civilian casualties caused by our military's use of cluster bombs. Imagine how many people would have supported this war if the media had actually brought up the issue of international law and what the United Nations charter specifies about attacking another country that has not attacked you.[61] Imagine what people would say if they knew exactly how precise exit polls are. People would be shocked and awed, and not in the way that Rumsfeld wants them to be.

The only hope we have is in building a movement that exposes this fraud, these schemes, these ugly reactionary policies, and drives the Bush team from

office. The Democrats won't do this. Simply voting won't do this. Only we—
you and I and many, many others—can do this. And we must.

Notes:

1   Several of the items in this list feature Ohio and Florida because, going into the election, it
was universally understood that the outcome hinged on these swing states.
     "TruthIsAll" (a pseudonym) on DemocraticUnderground.com offered a list that is similar
in format to my highly improbables and utterly impossibles list of the 2004 election results.
(http://www.democraticunderground.com/discuss/duboard.php?az=view_all&address
=203x22581), retrieved June 4, 2005.

2.   "The analysis by the *New York Times* of county-by-county data shows that *in Democratic areas
of Ohio*—primarily low-income and minority neighborhoods—*new registrations since January
have risen 250 percent* over the same period in 2000. In comparison, *new registrations have
increased just 25 percent in Republican areas.* A similar pattern is apparent *in Florida: in the
strongest Democratic areas, the pace of new registration is 60 percent higher than in 2000, while it
has risen just 12 percent in the heaviest Republican areas.* . . .
     "In rock-ribbed [Ohio] Republican areas—103 ZIP codes, many of them rural and subur-
ban areas, that voted by two to one or better for George W. Bush in 2000—35,000 new voters
have registered, a substantial increase over the 28,000 that registered in those areas in the
first seven months of 2000. . . .
     "But *in heavily Democratic areas*—60 ZIP codes mostly in the core of big cities *like Cleve-
land, Dayton, Columbus and Youngstown* that voted two to one or better against Mr. Bush—*new
registrations have more than tripled over 2000, to 63,000 from 17,000.*" (Italics added.) From
Ford Fessenden, "A Big Increase of New Voters in Swing States," *New York Times,* September 26, 2004; found at http://www.truthout.org/docs_04/printer_092704K.shtml, retrieved
March 13, 2006.
     "On Monday, the final day of voter registration in Ohio, the Board of Elections in Cleve-
land had a line out the door. 'I've never seen anything like this in my life,' said John Ryan,
head of the Cleveland AFL-CIO. 'We did a voter registration drive four years ago. We turned
in 14,399 new registration forms, and we were pleased with that. This time, there are about
100,000 newly registered voters.'" From Lisa Chamberlain, "GOP Dirty Tricks in Ohio?"
Salon.com, October 9, 2004; found at http://www.truthout.org/docs_04/101204X.shtml,
retrieved March 13, 2006.
     "A record surge of potential new voters has swamped boards of election from Pennsylva-
nia to Oregon, as the biggest of the crucial swing states reach registration deadlines today.
Elections officials have had to add staff and equipment, push well beyond budgets and work
around the clock to process the registrations. . . .
     "Officials across the country report similar patterns.
     "'Everything we're seeing is that there has been a tremendous increase in voter registra-
tion,' said Kay Maxwell, president of the League of Women Voters. 'In the past, we've been
enthused about what appeared to be a large number of new voters, but this does seem to be
at an entirely different level.'" Kate Zernike and Ford Fessenden, "As Deadlines Hit, Rolls of
Voters Show Big Surge," *New York Times,* October 4, 2004; found at http://www.truthout.
org/docs_04/100504W.shtml, retrieved March 13, 2006.

3.   Ordinarily, high turnout favors Democrats and more liberal-left candidates because the groups
who participate the least and most sporadically in voting are from lower socioeconomic groups,

who generally eschew more conservative candidates.

4. Michael Keefer, "Footprints of Electoral Fraud: The November 2 Exit Poll Scam," http://www. globalresearch.ca/articles/KEE411A.html, retrieved May 31, 2005. He recounts: "The same pattern is evident in the exit polls of two key swing states, Ohio and Florida. At 7:32 p.m. EST, CNN was reporting the following exit poll data for Ohio . . . Kerry was . . . leading Bush by a little more than 4 percent. But by 1:41 a.m. EST on November 3, when the exit poll was last updated, a dramatic shift had occurred . . . final exit polls showed Bush leading in Ohio by 2.5 percent.

    "At 7:32 p.m., there were 1,963 respondents; at 1:41 a.m. on November 3, there was a final total of 2,020 respondents. These fifty-seven additional respondents must all have voted very powerfully for Bush—for while representing only a 2.8 percent increase in the number of respondents, they managed to produce a swing from Kerry to Bush of fully 6.5 percent.

    "In Florida, the exit polls appear to have been tampered with in a similar manner. At 8:40 p.m. EST, CNN was reporting exit polls that showed Kerry and Bush in a near dead heat. . . . But the final update of the exit poll . . . at 1:01 a.m. EST on November 3, showed a different pattern: . . . Bush [with] a 4 percent lead over Kerry.

    "The number of exit poll respondents in Florida had risen only from 2,846 to 2,862. But once again, a powerful numerical magic was at work. A mere sixteen respondents—0.55 percent of the total number—produced a 4 percent swing to Bush."

5. "Election night, I'd been doing live election coverage for WDEV . . . and . . . during the 12:20 a.m. Associated Press Radio News feed, I was startled to hear the reporter detail how Karen Hughes had earlier sat George W. Bush down to inform him that he'd lost the election. The exit polls were clear: Kerry was winning in a landslide. 'Bush took the news stoically,' noted the AP report." Thom Hartmann, "Evidence Mounts That The Vote May Have Been Hacked," November 6, 2004, "Commondreams.org" at http://www.commondreams.org/ headlines04/1106-30.htm, retrieved March 21, 2006.

    Exit polls were altered by the NEP (National Election Pool) in the early morning hours of November 3, 2004, in order to make them conform to the official tallies that had started to change dramatically and unaccountably: "the final exit poll data used for analysis in 2004 was adjusted to match the actual vote returns." (Evaluation of the Edison/Mitofsky Election System 2004, prepared by Edison Media Research and Mitofsky International for the National Election Pool (NEP), January 19, 2005, p. 5, http://www.exit-poll.net/faq.html, retrieved April 2, 2005.) See Steven Freeman's discussion in "The Unexplained Exit Poll Discrepancy," November 10, 2004, election04.ssrc.org/research/ 11_10,unexplained_exit-poll.pdf.

    See also number 3 on my list of "improbables/impossibles." By altering the exit polls, the NEP obviated exit polls' most valuable purpose—detecting vote fraud.

6. 17 percent of the voters in 2004 did not vote in the 2000 election. Kerry defeated Bush among this group of first-time and lapsed voters by 9 points: 54 percent to 45 percent. (Katharine Q. Seelye, "Moral Values Cited as a Defining Issue of the Election," *New York Times*, November 4, 2004).

    Among undecideds, Kerry crushed Bush in the neighborhood of 4:1 or better. See number 5 in my list of "improbables/impossibles" and endnotes 11 and 12 herein.

    These data definitively contradict the widely held belief that Bush owes his victory to mobilizing conservative evangelicals and getting out the Republican base, as Alan Cooperman and Thomas B. Edsall note ("Evangelicals Say They Led the Charge for GOP," *Washington Post* November 8, 2004; p. A01; found at http://www.washingtonpost.com/wp-dyn/articles/ A32793-2004Nov7.html)

    Karl Rove believed he had to get the 4 million evangelicals who sat out 2000 in order to win.

As Sam Parry in "Bush's 'Incredible' Vote Tallies," *Consortium News*, November 9, 2004, http://www.consortiumnews.com/2004/110904.html, notes of this strategy, "even if one were to estimate that 100 percent of these Evangelical voters turned out for Bush in 2004 and that 100 percent of Bush's 2000 supporters turned out again for him, this still leaves about 5 million new Bush voters unaccounted for."

7.   For the breakdown of individual counties; see http://www.uscountvotes.org/index. php?option=com_content&task=view&id=78&Itemid=44, "ElectionArchive.org," the National Election Archive Project, retrieved March 13, 2006.

Liberty County was the most glaring case. 88.3 percent of the registered voters were Democrat and 7.9 percent GOP. Despite this ratio Bush received 4,075 votes to Kerry's 1,927. This translates to Bush receiving 712.3 percent of the registered GOP vote in Liberty.

Gore carried the 2000 Florida Independent vote by only 47 to 46 percent, whereas Kerry carried these voters by a 57 percent to 41 percent margin. In 2000 Bush received 13 percent of the registered Democratic voters votes and in 2004 he got the virtually statistically identical 14 percent of their votes. Sam Parry, "Bush's 'Incredible' Vote Tallies," *Consortiumnews.com*, November 9, 2004.

See also Colin Shea's analysis: "In one county, where 88 percent of voters are registered Democrats, Bush got nearly two-thirds of the vote—three times more than predicted by my model. In 21 counties, more than 50 percent of Democrats would have to have defected to Bush to account for the county result; in four counties at least 70 percent would have been required. These results are absurdly unlikely." http://www.freezerbox.com/archive/article. asp?id=321.

Crossover voting has been known to occur at times, but when it does, it occurs as part of a generalized trend evident across counties and across the country. In 2004 it occurred spectacularly in pockets only, violating logic. See Robert Parry, "Washington Post's Sloppy Analysis," consortiumnews.com, November 12, 2004 at http://www.consortiumnews. com/2004/111204.html, retrieved June 7, 2005.

8.   "[C]ertified reports from pro-Kerry Cleveland, in Cuyahoga County, [showed] . . . precincts with turnouts of as few as 22.31 percent (precinct 6B), 21.43 percent (13O), 20.07 percent (13F), 14.59 percent (13D), and 7.85 percent (6C) of the registered voters. Thousands of people in these precincts lined up for many hours in the rain in order, it would appear, not to vote.

"Meanwhile, in pro-Bush Perry County, the voting records certified by Secretary of State Blackwell included two precincts with reported turnouts of 124.4 and 124.0 percent of the registered voters, while in pro-Bush Miami County, there were precincts whose certified turnouts, if not physically impossible, were only slightly less improbable. These and other instances of implausibly high turnouts in precincts won by Bush, and implausibly low turnouts in precincts won by Kerry, are strongly suggestive of widespread tampering with the vote-tabulation processes." Michael Keefe, "The Strange Death of American Democracy: Endgame in Ohio," http://globalresearch.ca/articles/KEE501A.html; retrieved May 31, 2005.

9.   Roper stopped polling *two months* before the election, on September 9, 1948. Gallup's last poll was taken in the period of October 16–21, 1948. See "Classic Polling Surprises," http:// www.studyworksonline.com/cda/content/worksheet/0,,EXP545_NAV2-76_SWK543,00. shtml, retrieved March 22, 2006. See also the Roper Center at the University of Connecticut, Public Opinion Online.

10.   "Bush's job approval has slipped to 48% among national adults and is thus below the symbolically important 50% point." "Questions and Answers With the Editor in Chief," Frank Newport, Editor in Chief, *The Gallup Poll*, November 2, 2004, http://www.gallup.com/poll/ content/?ci=13948&pg=1, retrieved on May 27, 2005.

As Newport further notes, referring to the final Oct. 29–31, 2004 CNN/ USA Today/Gallup poll, "Among all national adults, 49% now choose Kerry as the candidate best able to handle Iraq, while 47% choose Bush. This marks a significant pickup on this measure for Kerry, who was down nine points to Bush last week. In fact, Kerry has lost out to Bush on this measure in every poll conducted since the Democratic convention.

"Bush's margin over Kerry as the candidate best able to handle terrorism is now seven points. 51% of Americans choose Bush and 44% choose Kerry. This again marks a significant change. Last week, Bush had an 18-point margin over Kerry, and the 7-point advantage is the lowest yet for Bush." In other words, momentum was on Kerry's side, with Bush losing 9 points of support on Iraq and 11 points on handling terrorism over the course of one week! These number were hardly a sign of someone about to win by 3.4 million votes.

11. Gallup explains: Challengers tend to get the votes of those saying that they are undecided on the eve of an election: "[B]ased on an analysis of previous presidential and other elections . . . there is a high probability that the challenger (in an incumbent race) will receive a higher percentage of the popular vote than he did in the last pre-election poll, while there is a high probability that the incumbent will maintain his share of the vote without any increase. This has been dubbed the 'challenger rule.' There are various explanations for why this may occur, including the theory that any voter who maintains that he or she is undecided about voting for a well-known incumbent this late in the game is probably leaning toward voting for the challenger." "Questions and Answers With the Editor in Chief," Frank Newport, Editor in Chief, The Gallup Poll, November 2, 2004, http://www.gallup.com/poll/content/?ci=13948&pg=1, retrieved on May 27, 2005.

12. http://www.harrisinteractive.com/harris_poll/index.asp?PID=515, dated November 2, 2004, retrieved on June 1, 2005: " Both surveys suggest that Kerry has been making some gains over the course of the past few days (see Harris Polls #83 http://www.harrisinteractive.com/harris_poll/index.asp?PID=512, and #78 http://www.harrisinteractive.com/harris_poll/index.asp?PID=507). If this trend is real, then Kerry may actually do better than these numbers suggest. In the past, presidential challengers tend to do better against an incumbent President among the undecided voters during the last three days of the elections, and that appears to be the case here. The reason: undecided voters are more often voters who dislike the President but do not know the challenger well enough to make a decision. When they decide, they frequently split 2:1 to 4:1 for the challenger." For Harris' last minute poll results before the 2000 election, see http://www.harrisinteractive.com/harris_poll/index.asp?PID=130, dated November 6, 2000, in which they call the election between Bush and Gore too close to call and predict that the result will depend upon the turnout.

On October 28, 2004, John Zogby was a guest on *The Daily Show* with Jon Stewart and called the election, without hesitation, for Kerry. See http://movies.internetvetsfortruth.org/misc/dailyshow/2004/10/28/10-28-04-johnzogby.mov.

After the election, Zogby said that "it would have required 'wrong sampling in wrong areas throughout the country,' or the purposeful manipulation of data to obtain exit poll results so significantly different from the official totals." (Ritt Goldstein, "US Election: Democracy in Question," Inter Press Service, November 18, 2004.)

13. Letter from Rep. John Conyers to Ken Blackwell, December 2, 2004, http://www.truthout.org/mm_01/5.120404W.pdf, retrieved March 23, 2006.

14. Bob Fitrakis, Steve Rosenfeld, and Harvey Wasserman, "Ohio's Official Non-Recount Ends amidst New Evidence of Fraud, Theft and Judicial Contempt Mirrored in New Mexico," *Columbus Free Press*, December 31, 2004, at http://www.freepress.org/departments/display/19/2004/1057, retrieved June 6, 2005.

15. See Steven Freeman, *op cit.* See also Greg Palast, "Kerry Won," *Common Dreams*, November 4, 2004, at http://www.commondreams.org/views04/1104-36.htm.

16. Curtis states in his affidavit that in the fall of 2000 he met with the principals of Yang Enterprises, Inc.—Li Woan Yang, Mike Cohen, and Tom Feeney (chief counsel and lobbyist for

YEI). Feeney became Florida's House speaker a month after meeting with Curtis. Curtis explains that he initially thought he was being asked to make such a program in order to prevent voter fraud. Upon creating the program and presenting it to Yang, he discovered that the company was interested in committing fraud, not preventing it. Curtis goes on to state: "She stated that she would hand in what I had produced to Feeney and left the room with the software." As the police would say, what we have here is motive and opportunity—and an abundance of evidence of criminal fraud in the Florida vote, together with Feeney's intimate connection to Jeb Bush. Curtis, on the other hand, as a lifelong registered Republican—as of these events at least—has no discernible motive to come forward with these allegations, and only shows courage for the risk to himself by doing so. For his full affidavit, see http://www.buzzflash.com/alerts/04/12/images/CC_Affidavit_120604.pdf, retrieved June 1, 2005.

17. Melanie Warner, "Machine Politics in the Digital Age," *New York Times*, November 9, 2003. See also: "The senior executives of each of the top 3 voting machine companies (ES&S, Diebold and Sequoia, accounting for over 90% of voting machines in use) have strong Republican ties. Key managers or funders of all three are significant Republican fundraisers and donors. Managers and/or affiliates of each of these have criminal records including cases of computer fraud, embezzlement and bid rigging. Two senior managers went directly from running the voting machine company to win unheard of success in politics, by means of machines sold to states by their companies." http://en.wikipedia.org/wiki/2004_U.S._Election_controversies_and_irregularities#Voting_machines_and_vendor_issues.

18. U.S. Government Accounting Office, "Elections: Federal Efforts to Improve Security and Reliability of Electronic Voting Systems Are Underway, but Key Activities Need to Be Completed," September 2005; at http://www.gao.gov/new.items/d05956.pdf.

19. In Ukraine, as a result of the exit polls' variance from the official tally, a revote was held. In the U.S., despite the fact that exit polls varied widely from the official tally, we had—an inauguration!

20. The NEP was a consortium of news organizations that contracted Edison Media Research and Mitofsky International to conduct the national and state exit polls. Warren Mitofsky created exit polling.

21. Freeman, *op cit*, http://truthout.org/unexplainedexitpoll.pdf, retrieved March 22, 2006.

22. See US-CERT National Cyber Alert System, Cyber Security Bulletin SB04-252 at http://www.us-cert.gov/cas/bulletins/SB04-252.html#diebold/.

23. The Bush White House consciously rejects empirical reality and inconvenient facts, considering these to be the province of what it calls the "reality-based community." As *New York Times* journalist Ron Suskind chillingly recounts: "In the summer of 2002 . . . I had a meeting with a senior adviser to Bush. . . . The aide said that guys like me were 'in what we call the reality-based community,' which he defined as people who 'believe that solutions emerge from your judicious study of discernible reality.' I nodded and murmured something about enlightenment principles and empiricism. He cut me off. 'That's not the way the world really works anymore,' he continued. 'We're an empire now, and when we act, we create our own reality. And while you're studying that reality—judiciously, as you will—we'll act again, creating other new realities, which you can study too, and that's how things will sort out. We're history's actors . . . and you, all of you, will be left to just study what we do.'" (Ron Suskind, "Without a Doubt," the *New York Times Magazine*, October 17, 2004.)

24. While blacks went to Kerry by 90:10, Latino voters were much more likely to vote for Bush.

25. A significant body of literature exists by now chronicling this fraud. See, for example, Mark Crispin Miller, *Fooled Again: How the Right Stole the 2004 Election (And How They'll Do It Again If We Don't Stop Them)*, the Conyers Report, "Preserving Democracy: What Went Wrong in Ohio," Status Report of the House Judiciary Committee Democratic Staff, January 5, 2005, http://www.house.gov/judiciary_democrats/ohiostatusrept1505.pdf, and Steven F. Freeman

and Joel Bleifuss, *Was the 2004 Presidential Election Stolen?: Exit Polls, Election Fraud, and the Official Count* (New York: Seven Stories Press, 2006).

26. I owe this example to Steven Freeman, *op cit.*

27. "So reliable are the surveys that actually tap voters as they leave the polling places that they are used as guides to the relative honesty of elections in Third World countries. When I worked on Vicente Fox's campaign in Mexico, for example, I was so fearful that the governing PRI would steal the election that I had the campaign commission two U.S. firms to conduct exit polls to be released immediately after the polls closed to foreclose the possibility of finagling with the returns. When the [exit] polls announced a seven-point Fox victory, mobs thronged the streets in a joyous celebration within minutes that made fraud in the actual counting impossible." GOP consultant and pollster Dick Morris, "Those Exit Polls Were Sabotage," http://www.thehill.com/morris/110404.aspx, dated November 4, 2004, retrieved June 4, 2005.

28. "Gore Won Florida," http://archive.democrats.com/display.cfm?id=181, retrieved May 28, 2005.

29. Dick Morris, "Those Exit Polls Were Sabotage," http://www.thehill.com/morris/110404.aspx, dated November 4, 2004, retrieved June 4, 2005.

30. Steven Freeman, *op cit.*

31. Ian Hoffman, "Berkeley: President Comes Up Short," the *Tri-Valley Herald*, November 19, 2004. The Berkeley report itself is at http://www.yuricareport.com/ElectionAftermath04/, retrieved June 7, 2005.

32. Evaluation of the Edison/Mitofsky Election System 2004 prepared by Edison Media Research and Mitofsky International for the National Election Pool (NEP), January 19, 2005, http://www.exit-poll.net/faq.html, retrieved April 2, 2005.

    MSNBC publicized this report (inaccurately) under the headline "Exit Polls Prove That Bush Won." Steve Freeman and Josh Mitteldorf, "A Corrupted Election: Despite What You May Have Heard, The Exit Polls Were Right," February 15, 2005, *In These Times*, www.inthese times.com/site/main/article/1970/, retrieved April 4, 2005:

    "The overall margin of error should have been under 1 percent. But the official result deviated from the poll projections by more than 5 percent—a statistical impossibility. . . .

    "Mitofsky and Edison vindicate a key piece of their methodology—the representativeness of their samples. . . .

    "On average, across the country, the President did 6.5 percent better in the official vote count, relative to Kerry, than the exit polls projected. . . .

    "Notably . . . only in precincts that used old-fashioned, hand-counted paper ballots did the official count and the exit polls fall within the normal sampling margin of error. . . .

    "[T]he report acknowledges that the discrepancy between the exit polls and the official count was considerably greater in the critical swing states."

33. Josh Mitteldorf, Ph.D., Temple University Statistics Department; Kathy Dopp, MS in mathematics, USCountVotes President; Steven Freeman, Ph.D., University of Pennsylvania; Brian Joiner, Ph.D. Professor of Statistics and Director of Statistical Consulting (ret.), University of Pennsylvania; Frank Stenger, Ph.D., Professor of Numerical Analysis, University of Utah; Richard Sheehan, Ph.D. Professor of Finance, University of Notre Dame; Paul Velleman, Ph.D. Assoc. Professor, Dept. of Statistical Sciences, Cornell University; Victoria Lovegren, Ph.D., Lecturer, Dept. of Mathematics, Case Western University; Campbell B. Read, Ph.D., Professor Emeritus, Dept. of Statistical Science, Southern Methodist University. http://uscountvotes.org/ucvAnalysis/US/USCountVotes Re Mitofsky-Edison.pdf.

34. "Mr. Bush has lost some or all of the lead he had before their first debate in Florida on Sept. 30, a series of recent polls suggests.

    "'By any objective measure—if Republicans are going to be intellectually honest with ourselves—prior to the first debate, we were pretty comfortable,' said Tony Fabrizio, a Republican pollster. 'It was a chance for the president to lay him out and just lock it. In the past two weeks, that's been turned on its head.'

"Gary Bauer, a conservative who ran for the Republican nomination in 2000, said . . . 'I don't mean to be disloyal to my friends, but I think the Kerry people are feeling pretty good about things.'"

See Adam Nagourney, "Tightening Race Increases Stakes of Final Debate," *New York Times*, October 13, 2004, http://www.truthout.org/docs_04/printer_101404Y.shtml, retrieved March 13, 2006.

35. An alternative theory, which was advanced by a few, was that fears about terrorism and the ongoing war in Iraq made many reluctant to kick out a sitting president. This theory has the benefit, at least, of being supported by some evidence. However, while it explains why so many ignored the fact that WMD were never found in Iraq, the given rationale for launching war on a country that had not attacked us, and a host of other scandals, such as torture and murder at Abu Ghraib, and why Bush did manage to receive a lot of votes, it didn't explain why he won by a margin of 3.4 million.

36. *The Economist*, "The triumph of the religious right," November 11, 2004, http://www.economist. com/printedition/displayStory.cfm?Story_ID=3375543, retrieved April 5, 2005.

37. See, for example, ex-conservative David Brock's *The Republican Noise Machine: Right-Wing Media and How It Corrupts Democracy* and Robert F. Kennedy, Jr., "How Washington Poisoned the News," *Vanity Fair*, May 2005.

38. Manuel Roig-Franzia and Dan Keating, "Latest Conspiracy Theory—Kerry Won—Hits the Ether," *Washington Post*, November 11, 2004, A-02, reprinted at http://www.washingtonpost. com/wp-dyn/articles/A41106-2004Nov10.html, retrieved June 7, 2005.

39. Available in its entirety at http://www.yuricareport.com/ElectionAftermath04/VoteFraud TheoriesNixed.html, retrieved June 6, 2005.

40. Greg Guma, "Election 2004: Lingering Suspicions," United Press International, November 15, 2004, http://www.upi.com/view.cfm?StoryID=20041112-010916-6128r, retrieved June 7, 2005.

41. Robert Parry, "Washington Post's Sloppy Analysis," consortiumnews.com, November 12, 2004, at http://www.consortiumnews.com/2004/111204.html, retrieved June 7, 2005.

42. "Liberty County—Bristol, Florida and environs—where it's 88 percent Democrats, 8 percent Republicans) but produced landslides for President Bush. On Countdown, we cited the five biggest surprises (Liberty ended Bush: 1,927; Kerry: 1,070), but did not mention the other 24, " at http://www.truthout.org/docs_04/111004B.shtml#1, retrieved June 7, 2005. See also David Swanson, "Media Whites Out Vote Fraud," January 3, 2005, http://www.truthout.org/ docs_05/010405Y.shtml for a good summary of this media whiteout.

43. Media Matters for America, "Conservatives rail against MSNBC's Olbermann for reporting election irregularities," http://mediamatters.org/items/200411600006, retrieved June 7, 2005.

44. The Fairness Doctrine that governed broadcasters from 1949 to 1987 required broadcasters, as a condition for having their FCC license, to provide balanced views on controversial questions. The elimination of the Fairness Doctrine was successfully lobbied for by well-heeled conservative groups during the Reagan administration and paved the way for the creation of a right-wing media empire that operates free of any need to provide opposing viewpoints to their own.

45. LexisNexis Academic database, Accession No. 1605983, Question No. 276, number of respondents 1,287, national telephone poll of adults.

46. Wellstone voted against the authorization to go to war on Iraq requested by George W. Bush's first-term administration.

47. I owe this summary to "The Theft of Your Vote Is Just a Chip Away," Thom Hartmann, Alter-

Net, http://www.alternet.org/story/16474, posted July 30, 2003, retrieved February 8, 2005. Chuck Hagel's story is worth mentioning here as well. As former conservative radio talk show host and current Senator from Nebraska Chuck Hagel (who is seriously considering a run for the White House) demonstrated back in 1996, being the head of the company that supplies the voting machines used by about 80 percent of the voters in Nebraska does not hurt you when you want to be the first Republican in twenty-four years to win a Senate seat in Nebraska. The fact that Hagel pulled off the biggest upset in the country in the 1996 elections by defeating an incumbent Democratic governor, and that he did so through winning every demographic group, including mainly black areas that had never voted Republican before, might have nothing to do with the paperless trail generated by the electronic voting machines his company provides, installs, programs, and largely runs. But then again, maybe it does have something to do with his stunning and totally unexpected victories (Thom Hartmann, "If You Want to Win An Election, Just Control the Voting Machines," January 31, 2003, http://www.commondreams.org/views03/0131-01.htm, retrieved April 10, 2005).

48. See http://www.buzzflash.com/analysis/04/11/ana04027.html, retrieved June 11, 2005.

49. By contrast, the GOP has decided that being "sore winners," as John Powers so aptly put it in his book *Sore Winners (and the Rest of Us) in George Bush's America* (New York: Doubleday, 2004), beats the hell out of being gracious losers.

50. Sarah Anderson and John Cavanagh, "Top 200: The Rise of Corporate Global Power," http://www.ips-dc.org/reports/top200text.htm.

51. See Robert Parry, "Woodward & Washington's 'Tipping Point,'" November 19, 2005, at http://www.consortiumnews.com/2005/111805.html, retrieved March 26, 2006.

52. See David Croteau and William Hoynes, *The Business of Media*.

53. While a majority of working journalists are registered Democrats, the people who sign their checks and decide whether they *stay* working journalists are overwhelmingly conservative Republicans. Right-wing media's canard that mainstream media are "liberal" in their news coverage simply does not match up with empirical reality. See, for example, Eric Alterman's *What Liberal Media?*, FAIR (Fairness and Accuracy in Reporting) at http://www.fair.org/index.php, and Media Matters at http://mediamatters.org/.

54. David Brock traces the roots from the early 1970s of this conservative assault on the media and their strategy to take over the political arena in *The Republican Noise Machine: Right-Wing Media and How It Corrupts Democracy* (New York: Crown, 2004). His book makes indispensable reading for anyone who wants to understand what we're up against.

55. MSNBC, for example, has tried to outfox Fox in its hirings of such reactionaries such as Michael Savage, Joe Scarborough, and bowtie Tucker Carlson.

56. See Howard Friel and Richard Falk, *The Record of the Paper: How the New York Times Misreports U.S. Foreign Policy* (New York: Verso, 2004).

57. Robert Parry, "Solving the Media Puzzle," May 15, 2005, http://www.consortiumnews.com/2005/051305.html, retrieved June 7, 2005.

58. Noelle-Neumann, E. (1984), *The Spiral of Silence: Public Opinion—Our Social Skin* (Chicago: University of Chicago Press, 1993).

59. Robert L. Borosage and Katrina Vanden Heuvel, "Progressives: Get Ready to Fight," November 11, 2004, http://www.thenation.com/doc/20041129/borosagekvh, retrieved March 22, 2006.

60. An excellent example of this is the famous October 14, 2004, guest appearance of Jon Stewart on CNN's *CrossFire*. Stewart made cohost Tucker Carlson look like a complete fool. CNN cancelled *CrossFire* not long afterward. Whether this was because of Stewart's skillful pillorying of Carlson and the show's overall character of bickering without substance or not we are left to speculate. Of course, *CrossFire* had been a long-standing show before Stewart's guest appearance. For the video and transcript, see http://mediamatters.org/items/200410160003.

61. Friel and Falk, *op cit.*

Chapter 3

THE "FREE FIRE ZONE" OF IRAQ

Dahr Jamail

Our aim is to put you in hell so you will tell the truth. These are the orders we have from our superiors, to turn your lives into hell.

—U.S. soldier to detainee in Abu Ghraib

Muna weeps while telling the story. The *abaya* (tunic) she wears cannot hide the shaking of her body as waves of grief roll through her. "I cannot get the image out of my mind of her fetus being blown out of her body."

Muna Salim's sister, Artica, was seven months' pregnant when two rockets from United States warplanes struck her home in Fallujah on November 1, 2004. "My sister Selma and I only survived because we were staying at our neighbors' house that night," Muna continued, unable to reconcile her survival with the fact that eight members of her family perished during the pre-assault bombing of Fallujah. The pre-assault campaign had already dragged on for several weeks.

Khalid, one of their brothers also killed in the attack, left behind a wife and five young children.

"There were no fighters in our area, so I don't know why they bombed our home," said Muna.

Muna and over a quarter of a million other residents of the city of Fallujah, do not know why most of their city and their former lives were destroyed by two United States sieges that killed *thousands* of innocent civilians.

When the most powerful military on the globe is given orders by its commander-in-chief to kill anything that moves in an entire city, it is indeed difficult for civilians to understand this sort of "reasoning."

The NBC war correspondent Kevin Sites, embedded with the United States Marines in Fallujah during the siege that was soon to follow the strike on Muna Salim's home, wrote in his web-log on November 10, 2004: "The Marines are operating with liberal rules of engagement." Sites wrote that he'd heard Staff Sgt. Sam Mortimer radio that "everything to the west is weapons-free." Sites explained that *weapons-free* "means that the Marines can shoot whatever they see—it's all considered hostile." Shortly after writing this entry, on November 13, Sites videotaped a U.S. Marine killing an unarmed, wounded Iraqi man in a mosque within the embattled city.

Collective Punishment

If I hadn't witnessed similar atrocities myself during the earlier April 2004 siege of Fallujah when I was inside that city, these blatant violations of international law, let alone inhumanity and indecency, would be difficult to believe.

Yet it was while I was hunkered down in a small makeshift clinic near the middle of Fallujah in early April, less than a week after the city was sealed and U.S. military snipers began their "turkey shoot" (as I heard one soldier refer to it), that I saw the slaughter with my own eyes.

Women and young children, along with the occasional man, were being carried into the clinic to be worked on by Iraqi doctors; each of the victims were saying the same thing: that they'd been shot by United States snipers when they were just outside of their home. I remember especially clearly one old woman who was carried into the clinic, gasping for air as the blood flowed from her body, still clutching a blood-stained white surrender flag.

The indiscriminate killing of civilians that resulted when Fallujah was being declared a "free fire zone" by the U.S. military is a grave breach of the Geneva Conventions[1] of 1949. Since the U.S. War Crimes Act considers grave breaches of the Geneva Conventions to be war crimes, those convicted can be subject to the death penalty.

Besides the Geneva Conventions, there is the International Criminal Court (ICC), which was formed in 1998 in response to the death of 174 million people who were killed in mass murders and genocides around the world in the last century. Yet the Bush administration refuses to join the court, and in fact opposes it.

For example, on July 15, 2002, Bush's deputy national security advisor at the time, Stephen J. Hadley, wrote an article for USA Today entitled, "Tribunal [ICC] is Threat to USA."[2] In Hadley's piece, which was and is distributed by the Office of International Information Programs through the U.S. Department of State, Hadley wrote, "The U.S. has a number of serious objections to the International Criminal Court. Among them are the lack of adequate checks and balances on the powers of the ICC prosecutor and judges, and the lack of any effective mechanism to prevent the politicized prosecution of U.S. citizens. That's why the Clinton administration voted against the ICC in 1998 (Clinton later signed the treaty at the end of his second term, but George W. Bush unsigned the treaty on May 6, 2002)[3] and why the Bush administration has consistently opposed it." He also added, "No one should underestimate Bush's commitment on this issue."

The United States is, essentially, at odds with the world in its refusal to abide by both the ICC and the Geneva Conventions.

The ICC, according to its Web site,[4] is "the first ever permanent, treaty based, international criminal court established to promote the rule of law and ensure that the gravest international crimes do not go unpunished."

As for membership, "The ICC was established by the Rome Statute of the International Criminal Court on 17 July 1998, when 120 States participating in the 'United Nations Diplomatic Conference of Plenipotentiaries on the Establishment of an International Criminal Court' adopted the Statute."[5]

By refusing to join the ICC, the United States finds itself in the company of several other nonmember states with records of horrific human rights abuses such as Libya, Saudi Arabia, China, North Korea, Sudan, and Pakistan.

As many as 192 states are signatories of the Geneva Conventions, including the U.S.—although the U.S. is blatantly disregarding them with regards to Iraq. If we ignore the ICC for the moment and look solely at the U.S.'s conduct through the lens of the four Geneva Conventions of 1949 that apply to civilians, the evidence is telling.

Article 48 from the 1949 Geneva Conventions states that the "basic rule" of the Geneva Conventions is to protect the civilian population: "In order to ensure respect for and protection of the civilian population and civilian objects, the Parties to the conflict shall at all times distinguish between the civilian population and combatants and between civilian objects and military objectives and accordingly shall direct their operations only against military objectives."

Article 51 adds, "The civilian population as such, as well as individual civilians, shall not be the object of attack. Acts or threats of violence the primary purpose of which is to spread terror among the civilian population are prohibited."

The Geneva Conventions go on to specify, "*Indiscriminant attacks are prohibited.*"

The April siege of Fallujah was launched under the pretext of finding those responsible for the deaths of four Blackwater USA mercenaries who had been killed less than a week before that siege was launched. The November siege, initially titled Operation Phantom Fury by the Department of Defense, was later renamed Operation al-Fajr (Arabic for dawn) by the U.S.-backed Iraqi Defense Minister.

According to the U.S. military, the reason given for the assault on the city was to regain control of the city from Iraqi resistance fighters before the upcoming January elections. However, the real reason for the siege was reprisal for the U.S. military's failure to take control of the city during the previous siege. The entire city, which overwhelmingly supported the Iraqi resistance, since Fallujah residents had long since grown weary of home raids, detentions, and killings at the hands of occupation forces, was about to be collectively punished.

Thus the stage was set for a massive attack against the city. One week before the siege was launched on November 8, Fallujah residents were told to leave the city or be killed. Only days after this announcement residents were told that they were not allowed to use their vehicles. During the November 2004 U.S. siege, in which an estimated 10,000–15,000 U.S. troops attacked the city, discriminating between fighters and civilians was intentionally avoided.

Burhan Fasa'a, an Iraqi journalist who works for the popular Lebanese satellite TV station, LBC, stated that he witnessed U.S. crimes up close. Fasa'a, who was in Fallujah for nine days during the most intense combat, told me that Americans grew easily frustrated with Iraqis who could not speak English.

"Americans did not have interpreters with them," Fasa'a said, "so they entered houses and killed people because they didn't speak English. They entered the house where I was with twenty-six people, and [they] shot people because [the people] didn't obey [the soldiers'] orders, even just because the people couldn't understand a word of English."

Fasa'a continued, "Soldiers thought the people were rejecting their orders, so they shot them. But the people just couldn't understand them."

Many refugees told me stories of having witnessed U.S. troops killing people who were already injured, former fighters and noncombatants alike.

"I watched them roll over wounded people in the street with tanks," said Kassem Mohammed Ahmed, a resident of Fallujah. "This happened so many times."

Other refugees reported similar stories. "I saw so many civilians killed there, and I saw several tanks roll over the wounded in the streets," said Aziz Abdulla, twenty-seven years old, who fled the fighting in November while the siege was still in progress. Another resident, Abu Aziz, said he also witnessed American armored vehicles crushing people he believes were still alive.

Abdul Razaq Ismail, another resident who fled Fallujah, reported, "I saw dead bodies on the ground and nobody could bury them because of the American snipers. The Americans were dropping some of the bodies into the Euphrates near Fallujah."

A man called Abu Hammad stated that he also witnessed U.S. troops throwing Iraqi bodies into the Euphrates River. Other refugees nodded in agreement while I interviewed him. Abu Hammed and others also said that they saw Americans shooting unarmed Iraqis who were waving white flags.

Believing that American and Iraqi forces were bent on killing anyone who stayed in Fallujah, Hammad said that he had watched people attempt to swim across the Euphrates to escape the siege. "Even then the Americans shot them with rifles from the shore," he said. "Even if some of them were holding a white flag or white clothes over their heads to show they are not fighters, they were all shot."

An Associated Press photographer, Bilal Hussein, reported witnessing similar events. After running out of basic necessities and deciding to flee the city at the height of the U.S.-led assault, Hussein ran to the Euphrates. "I decided to swim," Hussein told colleagues at the AP, who wrote up the photographer's harrowing story, "but I changed my mind after seeing U.S. helicopters firing on and killing people who tried to cross the river."

Hussein said that he saw soldiers kill a family of five as they tried to traverse the Euphrates, before he buried a man by the riverbank with his bare hands. "I kept walking along the river for two hours and I could still see some U.S. snipers ready to shoot anyone who might swim," Hussein recounted.

A man named Khalil, who asked me not to use his last name for fear of reprisals, told me that he had witnessed the shooting of civilians who were waving white flags while they tried to escape the city. "They shot women and old men in the streets," he said. "Then they shot anyone who tried to get their bodies."

"There are bodies the Americans threw in the river," Khalil continued, noting that he personally witnessed U.S. troops using the Euphrates to dispose of Iraqi dead. "And anyone who stayed thought they would be killed by the Americans, so they tried to swim across the river. Even people who couldn't swim tried to cross the river. They drowned rather than staying to be killed by the Americans," said Khalil.

According to the Director of Monitoring Net of Human Rights in Iraq (MHRI), Muhamad T. Al-Deraji, who is also a resident of Fallujah, an estimated 4,000–6,000 civilians were killed by U.S. forces during Operation Phantom Fury. Several mass graves were dug on the outskirts of Fallujah as the result of the U.S. siege.[6]

Let us be very clear about this. According to Protocol I, Article 85, Section 3, of the Geneva Conventions, "An indiscriminate attack affecting the civilian population or civilian objects and resulting in excessive loss of life, injury to civilians or damage to civilian objects is a grave breach of the Geneva Conventions."

Another aspect of collective punishment that was carried out in Fallujah, as well as other cities where the U.S. military has conducted operations, is the denial of food, water, and medical care to the civilian population as a method of warfare.

Not just in Fallujah but other cities, such as Ramadi, Samarra, Al-Qa'im, Haditha, and Baquba, and even parts of the capital city have had their water and electricity cut off, curfews imposed, and movement limited by U.S. forces.

These occurrences have been so frequent that it can easily be argued that such actions have become a standard operating procedure for U.S. military operations in Iraq in areas where occupation forces come under frequent attack.

Military forces may not starve out civilians nor deny food, water, medicine, or relief actions. In fact, the original purpose of the Geneva Conventions was to address these very points. It isn't just the U.S. soldiers who carried out the slaughter of civilians who are to blame. While they, of course, should be tried for the war crimes they so obviously committed, those giving the orders are, arguably, even more guilty.

"Criminal liability for war crimes extends beyond the perpetrator," writes

Marjorie Cohn, a professor of law. "Under the doctrine of command responsibility, higher-ups can be just as liable if they knew or should have known their underlings were committing war crimes, but they failed to stop or prevent it. Commanders have a responsibility to make sure civilians are not indiscriminately hurt and that prisoners are not summarily executed."[7]

Cohn, from the Thomas Jefferson School of Law in San Diego, California, wrote an article entitled "Setting the Conditions for War Crimes" following Operation Phantom Fury in November 2004.[8] In it she makes clear, "The rules of engagement are set at the top. The Marines are being told they can fire at anything that moves. Before entering Fallujah, the Marines had been pumped up by tough talking superiors."

Cohn goes on to add that a senior Pentagon consultant had told reporter Seymour Hersh that George W. Bush, Donald Rumsfeld, and Steven Cambone, undersecretary of defense for intelligence, had "created the conditions that allowed transgressions to take place."[9] Cohn writes, "the consultant was referring to torture at Abu Ghraib prison in Iraq. He could just as well have been talking about Operation Phantom Fury."

The fact that 70 percent of Fallujah was destroyed by the U.S. military operation, which, not so coincidentally, began just days after the U.S. presidential election adds further weight to the fact that the orders to lay siege to the city came from the very top.

The 1949 Geneva Conventions specify what attacks are considered to be indiscriminate; these include, "an attack by bombardment by any methods or means which treats as a single military objective a number of clearly separated and distinct military objectives located in a city, town, village or other area containing a similar concentration of civilians or civilian objects and an attack which may be expected to cause incidental loss of civilian life, injury to civilians, damage to civilian objects, or a combination thereof, which would be excessive in relation to the concrete and direct military advantage anticipated."

Water, food, and medical aid were cut off from Fallujah both before and during the siege of that city. This form of collective punishment, which I've seen first-hand in Ramadi and Samarra, has even led the United Nations to declare in October 2005, "The United States-led coalition's alleged practice of cutting off food and water to force Iraqi civilians to flee before attacks on insurgent strongholds is a flagrant violation of international law."

Jean Ziegler, the United Nations special reporter on the right to food stated, "The action is inhumane and causes innocent people to suffer. The Geneva Conventions on warfare, which form the basis of international humanitarian law, not only forbid denying food to civilians, but actually make the occupying force responsible to provide it."

A U.S. military spokesman in Baghdad, Lt-Col. Steve Boylan, dismissed the criticism as inaccurate. "Any accusations of coalition forces refusing basic needs from the citizens of Iraq are completely false," he asserted.

Mr. Ziegler promised that he would present a report on October 27, 2005, at the UN General Assembly in New York expressing his personal "outrage" at the alleged practice and calling on countries to condemn it in a resolution. He cannot submit a United Nations resolution himself.

The United States' food expert presents an oral report each autumn at the United Nations General Assembly and a written report each spring at the fifty-three-nation UN Human Rights Commission. "I can understand the military rationale, facing such a horrible enemy, this insurgent, who does not respect any law of war," Mr. Ziegler told reporters.

He conceded that the practice helped to "save tens of thousands of lives" but made the point that many civilians were unable to leave. Those that remained behind in insurgent strongholds such as Fallujah, Tal Afar, and Samarra have suffered as a result of broken supply lines, he asserted. And some have even starved, he claimed.

Either in part or in full, similar policies have been utilized by United States forces in the cities of Ramadi,[10] Samarra,[11] Haditha,[12] Al-Qa'im,[13] Abu Hishma,[14] Siniyah,[15] Baghdad,[16] and Mosul,[17] to name just a few.

Thus it is not surprising in the least that the initial figure published in the esteemed British medical journal, *The Lancet*, found the number of Iraqi deaths to be at least 100,000.[18]

The authors of the report interpret the results of their findings in the report summary as: "Making conservative assumptions, we think that about 100,000 excess deaths or more have happened since the 2003 invasion of Iraq. Violence accounted for most of the excess deaths and air strikes from coalition forces accounted for most violent deaths."[19] The figure of 100,000 Iraqis killed is too low for three reasons.

First, the fact that the results of this report were released in November 2004 means that they are already out of date.

Second, as stated in the full text of the report, so as not to skew the survey, the researchers did not include areas of major combat operations, such as Fallujah and Najaf, which eliminate thousands of deaths from the survey.

Finally, and most importantly, the baseline of the survey was the 14.5 month period prior to the invasion. This means that the baseline of the study was Iraq under the harshest economic sanctions in modern history—sanctions that caused the deaths of 1.7 million Iraqis.[20]

Thus, while Mr. Bush makes such statements as, "I would say 30,000 more or less have died as a result of the initial incursion and the ongoing violence against Iraqis," as he did in December 2005, he is clearly deliberately attempting to mislead the public about the deep level of violence that the Iraqi people suffer from the occupation.[21]

Illegal Weapons

The use of weapons deemed illegal under international law has also been prevalent in occupied Iraq. Cluster bombs, uranium munitions, white phosphorous and fuel/air bombs have been and are being used.

Protocol 1, Section I, of the Geneva Conventions applies to the "Methods and Means of Warfare," and Article 35 states that "[i]n any armed conflict, the right of the Parties to the conflict to choose methods or means of warfare is not unlimited. It is prohibited to employ weapons, projectiles and material and methods of warfare of a nature to cause superfluous injury or unnecessary suffering."[22] All of the aforementioned weapons cause "superfluous injury" and "unnecessary suffering."

I personally interviewed refugees and doctors from Fallujah regarding the use of white phosphorous during Operation Phantom Fury. One refugee I interviewed in a camp on the grounds of Baghdad University told me he'd witnessed some of the heaviest fighting in the Jolan district of Fallujah just before he escaped the city. "They used these weird bombs that put up smoke like a mushroom cloud," he said. He had seen "pieces of these bombs explode into large fires that continued to burn on the skin even after people dumped water on the burns."

A doctor from Fallujah working in Saqlawiyah, a small city on the outskirts of Fallujah, described treating victims during the siege "who had their skin melted." He asked to be referred to simply as Dr. Ahmed because of fear of reprisals for speaking out. "The people and bodies I have seen were definitely hit by fire weapons and had no other shrapnel wounds," he said.

Burhan Fasa'a, the aforementioned cameraman, also witnessed the use of illegal weapons. "I saw cluster bombs everywhere and so many bodies that were burned, dead with no bullets in them," he said. "So they definitely used fire weapons, especially in the Jolan district."

This is exactly what several civilians and doctors told me when I was in Fallujah during the April siege as well.

Impeding Medical Care

The intentional impeding of medical care was also a United States military tactic in Fallujah, as well as in other combat areas around Iraq. Fallujah, however, is the most obvious example. On November 7, 2004, the day before Operation Phantom Fury began, United States-Iraqi forces stormed and occupied Fallujah General Hospital. According to the military, the hospital was targeted because it was a "center of propaganda" that spread rumors of civilian casualties during the April assault. Patients and doctors alike were rounded up and ordered to lie on the floor with their hands tied behind their backs.

Just two days later, the United States bombed Fallujah's Central Health Center, killing twenty nurses and doctors and an uncounted number of patients.

According to the First Geneva Convention, Article 19, "Fixed establishments and mobile medical units must be protected and respected by all sides in a conflict." The U.S. military refused to allow emergency aid to be brought into Fallujah, in addition to refusing to allow doctors to evacuate wounded people outside of the city.

According to The Fourth Convention, Article 55, "In an occupied territory, the occupying power has the responsibility of assuring adequate medical supplies for the population." In addition, particularly relevant in a situation such as Fallujah, Article 59 in the same Convention states, "If there is a lack of medical supplies, the occupying power must agree to and support relief efforts by states or humanitarian organizations."

Attacks on civilian hospitals are grave breaches (war crimes) under Article 147 of the Fourth Geneva Convention of 1949. (An attack on even a military hospital is a grave breach of the provisions in the First Geneva Convention).

Despite the fact that the Fourth Geneva Convention, Article 18, is most specific—"Civilian hospitals organized to give care to the wounded and sick, the infirm and maternity cases, may in no circumstances be the object of attack but shall at all times be respected and protected by the Parties to the conflict"—I interviewed doctors during and after both the April and November sieges of Fallujah who told me that their hospitals, clinics, and ambulances had been fired upon by U.S. forces on a regular basis.

Ambulance in Fallujah, shot repeatedly by United States forces on driver's side of windshield.

Protocol 1, Section 1, of the Geneva Conventions applies to the "Methods and Means of Warfare." Article 21 states: "Medical vehicles shall be respected and protected in the same way as mobile medical units under the Conventions and this Protocol," and Article 12 adds, "Medical units shall be respected and protected at all times and shall not be the object of attack."[23]

In Iraq the Bush administration has openly defied the Geneva Conventions and continues to do so, with no statements of remorse.

Press Censorship

In addition, independent journalists who have tried to cover Fallujah (and other areas of conflict) have been detained and shot at by U.S. forces, an action that is, of course, a war crime. Journalists are granted the full rights of civilians in conflict zones, according to the Geneva Conventions.

A U.S. order issued in March 2004 gave the U.S.-installed Iraqi government broad powers to control the media—another violation of international law. Prime Minister Iyad Allawi in November 2004 issued a statement at a press conference telling the news media in Iraq to "stick to the government line on the U.S.-led offensive in Fallujah or face legal action."

To date estimates of journalists killed in Iraq range between sixty-four to over a hundred; the vast majority of these were of Arab descent. The Committee to Protect Journalists states that sixty-four journalists have been killed in Iraq since hostilities began in March 2003; forty-five of them Iraqi, three from other Arab countries; fourteen were killed by U.S. fire.[24]

Sixty-four dead is two short of all the journalists killed in the entire Vietnam conflict, according to some sources.[25] To add more perspective, a total of sixty-eight journalists were killed in all of World War II.[26]

A prime example of United States military hostility toward a news agency that is critical of U.S. policy in Iraq is the U.S.'s actions towards Al-Jazeera.

During the invasion of Iraq, U.S. tanks shelled the Al-Jazeera journalists in the Basra hotel where the journalists were the hotel's only guests in April 2003. Shortly after the Basra attack, the Al-Jazeera office in Baghdad was hit by a missile from a U.S. warplane, killing Al-Jazeera correspondent Tareq Ayoub on April 8. This happened despite the fact that Al-Jazeera had gone out of its way to provide the exact coordinates of their office in Baghdad to the Pentagon so as not to be bombed by U.S. warplanes.[27]

In addition to having its reporters detained by U.S. forces and placed in prisons in Iraq and Guantánamo Bay, Cuba, Al-Jazeera has weathered verbal attacks from government officials in many countries in the Middle East, as well as from the U.S. Secretary of Defense. "I can definitely say that what Al-Jazeera is doing is vicious, inaccurate, and inexcusable," Defense Secretary Donald Rumsfeld told reporters on April 15, 2004, when he referenced the showing by Al-Jazeera of bodies of women and children killed by U.S. bombs in Fallujah.

In late November, "top secret" minutes were leaked to Britain's *Daily Mirror* that stated that on the day after the aforementioned remarks made by Rumsfeld, during an April 2004 meeting in the White House, George W. Bush attempted to convince British Prime Minister Tony Blair to bomb the headquarters of Al-Jazeera in Doha, Qatar.[28]

"The Americans Brought Electricity to My Ass Before They Brought It to My House."

Another aspect that implicates the Bush administration in war crimes in Iraq is torture. Not abuse. Not mistreatment. Not cruelty. Not humiliation. Not degrading treatment. Torture.

Torture has been ongoing in Iraq since nearly the occupation's very beginning.

Despite the vehement denials of such people as George W. Bush and Secretary of State Condoleezza Rice that U.S. forces and their surrogate Western contractors have been and are currently torturing Iraqis, the fact remains that as you read this, torture is ongoing.

"As a matter of U.S. policy, the United States obligations under the Convention Against Torture, which prohibits, of course, cruel and inhumane and degrading treatment, those obligations extend to U.S. personnel wherever they are," said the Secretary of State on December 8, 2005, "whether they are in the United States or outside of the United States." The problem with Rice's statement is that the facts on the ground in Iraq completely contradict her claim.

Early on in the U.S. occupation of Iraq, evidence of torturing of Iraqis by U.S. soldiers began to appear. For example, in a home raid that produced no weapons, American soldiers detained fifty-seven-year-old Sadiq Zoman at his residence in Kirkuk on July 21, 2003. More than a month later, on August 23, U.S. soldiers dropped Zoman off, comatose, at a hospital in Tikrit. Although he was unable to recount his story, his body bore telltale signs of torture: what appeared to be point burns on his skin, bludgeon marks on the back of his head, a badly broken thumb, and electrical burns on the soles of his feet. Additionally, family members found whip marks and bruises across his back and more electrical burns on his genitalia.

According to further U.S. military documentation, on August 11 Mr. Zoman was transferred to the 28th Combat Support Hospital, where he was treated by Lt. Colonel Michael C. Hodges, M.D. Lt. Col. Hodges' medical report listed the primary diagnoses of Zoman's condition as hypoxic brain injury (brain damage caused by lack of oxygen) "with persistent vegetative state," myocardial infarction (heart attack), and heat stroke. The same medical report did not mention any bruises, lash marks, head injury, burn marks or other signs Iraqi doctors reported that they had found on Zoman's body upon his arrival at the Tikrit hospital.

According to documentation, on August 23, after two weeks of care at the Combat Support Hospital, the Army transferred Zoman from the Combat Support Hospital to the civilian Salahadeen Hospital in Tikrit. The Zoman family found Sadiq there on September 4, 2003, only because the Red Crescent of Tikrit had posted photos of him on buses around Tikrit in hopes that someone would recognize him. Remarkably, a friend saw one of the pictures and contacted the family.

Zoman has nine daughters; the oldest is thirty-two and the youngest fifteen. Rheem Zoman, Sadiq's nineteen-year-old daughter, spoke frankly with me about her father and his condition. "I was horrified," she said of his bittersweet return to his worried family. "He had whip marks all across his back and electrical burn marks all over his body."

The Army has so far offered no explanation to the family as to why their home was raided or the reason for Zoman's capture.

Sadiq Zoman remains completely unresponsive. His family cares for him in a stark home nearly devoid of furnishings, situated in the Al-Dora neighborhood of Baghdad. Entire rooms in their new home are completely empty since they have sold nearly everything that remained in order to purchase food and medical supplies. The family of Sadiq Zoman says that they have received no compensation for their situation from the United States military or the now obsolete United States-run Coalition Provisional Authority.

Hashimi Zoman, Sadiq's wife, stood over her comatose husband with a paper fan to cool him while telling me, "We make his food with a blender because it must be liquid. But with no electricity there is no blender, so no food for him at times."

Daughter Rheem pleaded to me, "Why have they done this to him? Can you tell me?"

With tears in her eyes Hashima Zoman added, "Is it fair for any man's family to be made to suffer like this? Is it right that his daughters must see him like this? Our lives will never be the same again, no matter what happens."

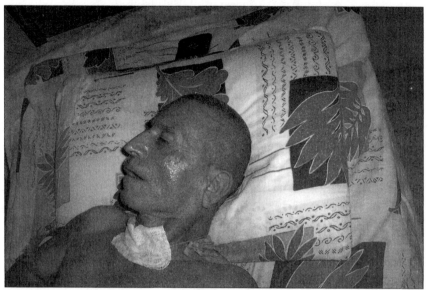

Sadiq Zoman, comatose as a result of beatings and electrical shocks sustained while in U.S. military custody.

With tens of thousands of Iraqis detained at military detention facilities across Iraq, the disappearing and torturing is a daily reality for Iraqis. That the U.S. caused prisoners to be tortured and subjected to cruel, unusual, and degrading punishment in violation of the Convention Against Torture (CAT), the International Covenant on Civil and Political Rights, The Human Rights Act of 1998, and the Criminal Justice Act of 1988 is no longer news.

Of course all of the cases, like Zoman's, are violations of the Geneva Conventions. These conventions apply to any person in a conflict—civilians (Fourth Geneva Convention) as well as military (Third Geneva Convention).

Article 13 of the Third Geneva Convention states clearly, "Prisoners of war must at all times be humanely treated. Likewise, prisoners of war must at all times be protected, particularly against acts of violence or intimidation and against insults and public curiosity."

Article 17 of the same convention adds, "No physical or mental torture, nor any other form of coercion, may be inflicted on prisoners of war to secure from them information of any kind whatever." During my eight months reporting from occupied Iraq I documented scores of instances of Iraqis being tortured while in U.S. custody. Another example is that of Ali Abbas.

In May 2004 I interviewed Abbas, who had just been released from Abu Ghraib. Like so many I interviewed from various U.S. military detention facilities who'd been tortured horrifically, he still managed to maintain his sense of humor. He began laughing when he told me how CIA agents made him beat other prisoners. He laughed, he said, because he had been beaten himself prior to this order and was so tired that all he could do to beat other detained Iraqis was lift his arm and let it drop on the other men. Later he laughed again as he said what else had been done to him, "The Americans brought electricity to my ass before they brought it to my house."

Ali Abbas lived in the Al-Amiriyah district of Baghdad and worked in civil administration. So many of his neighbors were detained that friends urged him to go to the nearby U.S. base to try and get answers for why so many innocent people were being detained. He went three times. On the fourth visit he was detained himself. Within two days he was transferred from the military base to Abu Ghraib, where he was held over three months without charges before being released.

"The minute I got there, the suffering began," said Abbas about his interrogator. "I asked him for water, and he said after the investigation I would get some. He accused me of so many things and asked me so many questions. Among them he said I hated Christians."

He was forced to strip naked shortly after arriving and remained that way for most of his stay in the prison. "They made us lie on top of each other naked, as if it was sex, and beat us with a broom," he said. In addition to being beaten on their genitals, detainees were also denied water and food for extended periods of time and then were forced to watch as their food was thrown in the trash.

Treatment also included having a loaded gun held to his head to prevent him from crying out in pain as his hand ties were tightened. "My hands were enlarged because there was no blood because they cuffed them so tight," he told me. "My head was covered with the sack, and they fastened my right hand to a pole with handcuffs. They made me stand on my toes to clip me to it."

Abbas said that soldiers doused him in cold water while holding him under a fan, and oftentimes "they put on a loudspeaker, put the speakers on my ears and said, 'Shut Up, Fuck! Fuck! Fuck!'" In this manner Abbas's interrogators routinely deprived him of sleep.

Abbas said that at one point, "two men came, one a foreigner and one a translator. He asked me who I was. I said I'm a human being. They told me, 'We are going to cut your head off and send you to hell. We will take you to Guantánamo.'"

A female soldier told him, "Our aim is to put you in hell so you will tell the truth. These are the orders we have from our superiors, to turn your lives into hell."

Abbas added, "They shit on us, used dogs against us, used electricity and starved us." He told me, "Saddam Hussein used to have people like those who tortured us. Why do they put Saddam into trial, but they do not put the Americans to trial?"

But unlike Saddam Hussein, the U.S. interrogators also desecrated Islam as part of their humiliation. Abbas was made to fast during the first day of Eid, the breaking of the fast of Ramadan, an action that is *haram* (forbidden).

Sometimes at night when he would read his Koran, Abbas had to hold it in the hallway for light. "Soldiers would walk by and kick the Holy Koran, and sometimes they would try to piss on it or wipe shit on it," he said.

Abbas did not feel that this treatment was the work of a few individual soldiers. "This was organized, it wasn't just individuals, and every one of the troops in Abu Ghraib was responsible for it."

Accounts by human rights groups support this charge. According to an April 2005 Human Rights Watch report, "Abu Ghraib was only the tip of the iceberg, it's now clear that abuse of detainees has happened all over—from Afghanistan to Guantánamo Bay to a lot of third-country dungeons where the United States has sent prisoners. And probably quite a few other places we don't even know about."[29]

The report adds, "Harsh and coercive interrogation techniques such as subjecting detainees to painful stress positions and extended sleep deprivation have been routinely used in detention centers throughout Iraq. An ICRC report concluded that in military intelligence sections of Abu Ghraib, 'methods of physical and psychological coercion used by the interrogators appeared to be part of the standard operating procedures by military intelligence personnel to obtain confessions and extract information.'"[30]

Amnesty International has released similar findings.[31]

Former Brigadier General Janis Karpinski who was in charge of Abu Ghraib, as well as sixteen other U.S. military detention facilities in Iraq, told reporters in June 2004 that she was being made a "convenient scapegoat" for abuse ordered by others.

In January 2006 Karpinski testified in a War Crimes Commission in New York City that I attended. During her testimony she revealed that Secretary of Defense Donald Rumsfeld had issued a memo while she was in charge of the military police unit that ran Abu Ghraib. The memo, signed by Rumsfeld, approved "harsher interrogation techniques" the Secretary of Defense wanted used in Abu Ghraib. Donald Rumsfeld even found it necessary, according to Karpinski, to handwrite in the left margin of the memo, "Make sure this happens!!"

When asked how high up the chain of command she thought this order could have originated, Karpinski said, "The Secretary of Defense would not have authorized without the approval of the Vice President. And so it filtered down."

Karpinski was asked if she believed that torture has stopped in Iraq. Her reply: "No. I don't have any reason; unfortunately, I have no reason to believe that it has. I believe that cameras are no longer allowed anywhere near a cellblock. But why should I believe it's stopped? We still have the captain from the 82nd airborne division that returned and had a diary, a log of when he was instructed, what he was instructed, where he was instructed, and who instructed him. To go out and treat the prisoners harshly, to set them up for effective interrogation. And that was recently as May of 2005."

War Criminals

Collective punishment, illegal weapons, impeding medical care, press censorship, and torturing Iraqis are but a few of the violations of international law committed by the U.S. military following orders from the commander-in-chief in Iraq.

In 1946 in Nuremberg, an American judge wrote: "To initiate a war of aggression, therefore, is not only an international crime; it is the supreme international crime differing only from other war crimes in that it contains within itself the accumulated evil of the whole."[32] The U.S.-led invasion of Iraq was judged by United Nations Secretary General Kofi Annan as "an illegal act that contravened the UN charter."[33]

Several members of the current and previous Bush administrations have demonstrated absolute contempt for international law regarding Iraq—from the illegal invasion of a sovereign country to virtually every aspect of the occupation. War crime after war crime continues to be committed on a daily basis.

Members of this administration and that which preceded it, such as George W. Bush, Richard Cheney, Donald Rumsfeld, Colin Powell, Condoleezza Rice, Richard Perle, and Paul Wolfowitz, to name just a few, are guilty of countless violations of international law and should be tried for war crimes.

These individuals are war criminals and should be treated as such: tried according to violations of the Geneva Conventions and brought to justice. Humanity should demand nothing less.

Notes:

1. The First Geneva Convention of 1864 dealt exclusively with the care of wounded soldiers; the law was later adapted to cover warfare at sea and prisoners of war. In 1949 the Conventions were revised and expanded. The First Geneva Convention deals with wounded soldiers on the battlefield. The Second Geneva Convention addresses those wounded and shipwrecked at sea. The Third Geneva Convention deals with prisoners of war, while the Fourth Geneva Convention addresses civilians under enemy control. In 1977 two Additional Protocols were added: The First Protocol deals with international conflicts, the Second Protocol addresses noninternational conflicts. More recently, in 2005, the Additional Protocol III was adopted; it deals with distinctive international emblems. The Geneva Conventions and their Additional Protocols are international treaties that contain the most important rules limiting the barbarity of war. They protect people who do not take part in the fighting (civilians, medics, aid workers) and those who can no longer fight (wounded, sick and shipwrecked troops, prisoners of war).
2. http://usinfo.state.gov/dhr/Archive_Index/tribunal_threat.html.
3. http://www.asil.org/insights/insigh87.htm.
4. http://www.icc-cpi.int/about.html.
5. http://www.icc-cpi.int/about/ataglance/history.html.
6. E-mail from Al-Deraji, 22 February 2006.
7. http://www.constitution.org/mil/ucmj19970615.htm.
8. http://www.truthout.org/docs_04/113004A.shtml.
9. Seymour Hersh, *Chain of Command: The Road From 9/11 to Abu Ghraib* (New York: Harper-Collins, 2004), pp. 71–72.
10. http://www.washingtonpost.com/wp-dyn/content/article/2005/10/17/AR2005101700808.html.
11. http://www.casi.org.uk/discuss/2003/msg05157.html.
12. http://www.irinnews.org/report.asp?ReportID=49396&SelectRegion=Middle_East&SelectCountry=IRAQ.
13. http://www.commondreams.org/headlines05/0519-07.htm.
14. http://www.truthout.org/docs_03/120803E.shtml.
15. http://www.dahrjamailiraq.com/hard_news/archives/hard_news/000351.php.

16. http://www.ipsnews.net/interna.asp?idnews=27077.
17. http://english.aljazeera.net/NR/exeres/3B46C2E3-26CB-4232-8C2E-1B9260D0BBFF.htm.
18. http://www.globalresearch.ca/articles/LAN410A.html.
19. Mortality before and after the 2003 invasion of Iraq: cluster sample survey, by Les Roberts, Riyadh Lafta, Richard Garfield, Jamal Khudhairi, and Gilbert Burnham. *The Lancet*, Volume 364, Number 9448, 20 November 2004.
20. http://www.mediamonitors.net/mosaddeq17.html, http://www.globalissues.org/Geopolitics/ MiddleEast/Iraq/Sanctions.asp, http://www.globalpolicy.org/security/sanction/iraqi/200105 10ina.htm.
21. http://www.cbsnews.com/stories/2005/12/12/politics/main1117045.shtml.
22. http://www.genevaconventions.org/.
23. *Ibid.*
24. http://www.cpj.org/Briefings/Iraq/Iraq_danger.html, as of 25 February 2006.
25. Freedom Forum lists sixty-six journalists killed covering the conflict in Vietnam from 1955 to 1975. The Foreign Correspondents Club of Japan, which surveyed the years 1962–1975, lists seventy-one journalists killed (http://www.cpj.org/Briefings/Iraq/Iraq_danger.html).
26. http://www.cpj.org/Briefings/Iraq/Iraq_danger.html.
27. "CPJ has seen a copy of Al-Jazeera's February letter to Pentagon spokeswoman Victoria Clarke outlining these coordinates" (http://www.cpj.org/protests/03ltrs/Iraq08apr03pl.html).
28. http://www.mirror.co.uk/news/tm_objectid=16397937&method=full&siteid=94762&headline =exclusive--bush-plot-to-bomb-his-arab-ally-name_page.html.
29. http://hrw.org/english/docs/2005/04/27/usint10545.htm.
30. http://www.globalsecurity.org/military/library/report/2004/icrc_report_iraq_feb2004.htm.
31. http://news.amnesty.org/index/ENGAMR510772004.
32. *Judgment of the International Military Tribunal for the Trial of German Major War Criminals—* Nuremberg, Germany 1946.
33. "Iraq war illegal, says Annan," BBC News Web site, Thursday, 16 September 2004.

Chapter 4

WAR CRIMES ARE HIGH CRIMES

Jeremy Brecher, Jill Cutler, and Brendan Smith

The founders of the American republic were deeply concerned that the executive branch might become a vehicle for tyranny. They worried that the government might come under control of what George Washington called "the frightful despotism of faction." They feared that the president's power to make war could become the vehicle for such a tyranny. So in their Constitution they included the famous "checks and balances" on presidential power. These included an independent Congress and judiciary; an executive branch subject to laws written by Congress and interpreted by the courts; an executive power to repel attacks but not to declare or finance war; election of top officials; and protection of the people from intimidation by state power through the Bill of Rights. Backing all the other checks and balances, as a last resort against their infringement, the founders established the power of Congress to impeach the president.

The drafters of the Constitution were well aware that the new republic would come into a world of other countries. They envisioned that world as regulated by international law and by treaties. In Article 1 the Constitution provided Congress with the power to define and punish "Offences against the Law of Nations." And they provided Congress with the power to ratify treaties that, under Article 6, would become the law of the land.

Over the centuries since, the U.S. has used national law, international law, and the treaty power to create an international order designed to provide security, limit war, and uphold human rights. Its principles are included in such international treaties as the United Nations Charter, the Geneva Conventions, and treaties against genocide, torture, and other abuses of human rights. These principles are also included in American law. The U.S. Constitution explicitly incorporates treaties into federal law. And laws passed by Congress also embody these principles; for example, the War Crimes Act makes grave violations of the Geneva Conventions a crime under American law. Whatever its flaws, the international order established under these principles has been superior to one based on the war of all against all.

The U.S. Constitution states that the president "shall take care that the laws be faithfully executed." But President George W. Bush, Vice President Dick Cheney, and officials appointed by them have systematically defied both national and international law. They have asserted the authority to attack other countries that have not attacked the U.S.; to operate death squads engaged in killings not sanctioned by law in countries around the world; to engage in cruel abuse of prisoners without legal oversight; and to unilaterally annul the Geneva Conventions and other treaties authorized by Congress. Not only have they claimed their right to take such illegal actions, but the evidence shows that they have repeatedly ordered and condoned them.

These actions are not just matters of policy or of competence. Rather, they are crimes that violate both international and national law. They are crimes that have come to be known as war crimes.

While the charge that Bush, Cheney, and their associates have committed war crimes may at first sound extreme, even voices inside the administration, as well as in the political mainstream, have concluded that they may have done so. When Colonel Larry Wilkerson, Colin Powell's top aide, was asked whether Cheney was guilty of a war crime, he said that the Vice President's actions were certainly a domestic crime and, he would suspect, "an international crime as well."[1] At a 2005 Pentagon meeting discussing interrogation policy the outgoing general counsel of the Navy, Alberto Mora, dramatically pulled out a copy of the U.S. War Crimes Act and read from it to a room full of high-level Pentagon and civilian officials. According to Mora he wanted to make the point that "it's a statute. It exists—and we're not free to disregard it. . . . It's been adopted by the Congress. . . . Other nations could have U.S. officials arrested."[2]

Days after the release of highly incriminating FBI torture e-mails the *Washington Post*, a newspaper that had enthusiastically supported the war in Iraq, published an editorial entitled "War Crimes" directly accusing the Bush administration of criminal behavior of the highest order. And according to NPR host and centrist Democrat Garrison Keillor, "The U.S. Constitution provides a simple, ultimate way to hold [the President] to account for war crimes and the failure to attend to the country's defense. Impeach him and let the Senate hear the evidence."[3] The Cato Institute's newly released report, *Power Surge: The Constitutional Record of George W. Bush*[4] concludes that we now have "a president who can launch wars at will, and who cannot be restrained from ordering the commission of war crimes, should he choose to do so."

Where evidence of its malfeasance has come to light, the Bush administration has tried to blame a few "bad apples" at the bottom for everything that has gone wrong, from false intelligence about Iraq to torture at Abu Ghraib prison. But American and international law put the responsibility squarely on those in a position to give orders—in this case, President Bush, Vice President Cheney, and their appointees and collaborators. They must be held accountable for the crimes they have ordered and condoned.

This issue is not fundamentally a partisan one. The plunge into criminality has seen complicity from both parties and from both the Congress and the judiciary. The restoration of law-abiding government is ultimately the American people's responsibility.

Impeachment represents one constitutional remedy. While it cannot correct the whole problem of an era and a country, a campaign for impeachment can be valuable. It can provide the frame for investigation into the illegality of Bush, Cheney, and their accomplices, who as the leaders of the U.S. government are legally accountable for acts conducted under their command. It can force political candidates who wish to represent the American people to take a stand. It may serve as a means to remove wrongdoers from power—and therefore deter their successors from similar acts. And it may begin to create the basis for a new relationship between the American people and the people of the rest of the world, one that pursues peace and mutual well-being through limits on leaders' abuse of national power.

In the impeachment proceedings against President Richard Nixon during the Watergate scandal, the investigating committee charged Nixon with burglary and other common criminal offenses—but decided not to charge the President with concealing from Congress the secret bombing of Cambodia.[5] The failure to charge him with his more significant crimes helped to clear the way for President Bush and Vice President Cheney's claims that they can initiate war, conduct occupations, and engage in torture, kidnapping, and murder with impunity. If impeachment is to serve as a deterrent to war crimes by leaders of the United States, such crimes must be among the "high crimes and misdemeanors" with which they are charged.

Defining War Crimes

National and international laws against war crimes have developed side by side. In 1863 President Abraham Lincoln promulgated the Lieber Code, which defined protections for civilians and prisoners of war. The following year a number of countries agreed to the Geneva Convention for the Amelioration of the Condition of the Wounded and Sick in Armies in the Field.[6] Diplomatic conferences in 1899 and 1907 produced the "Law of the Hague," which prohibited attacks on undefended towns, the use of arms designed to cause unnecessary suffering, poison weapons, collective penalties, and pillage.[7]

The Nuremberg Tribunal of Nazi war criminals following World War II established that "To initiate a war of aggression" is *the supreme international crime*, differing only from other war crimes in that it contains within itself the accumulated evil of the whole." The United Nations Charter provided that "all members shall refrain in their international relations from the threat or use of force against the territorial integrity or political independence of any state." Violations of this principle are crimes against peace. The devastation associated with World War II led to the recognition of a new category of international crimes, *crimes against humanity,* which involved acts of violence against a persecuted group in either war or peacetime.

Crimes against noncombatants, crimes against peace, and crimes against humanity have come to be summed up as *war crimes.*[8] War crimes were codified in the four Geneva Conventions of 1949 and have been further developed in subsequent protocols and agreements. By agreeing to the United Nations Charter, the Geneva Conventions, and other such treaties, nations agreed to bind themselves to limitations on their sovereign prerogatives.

Based on the understanding that the prosecution and enforcement of war crimes is not merely an international affair, Congress has embedded war-crimes law into national law. The United States War Crimes Act makes grave breaches of the Geneva Conventions by U.S. officials a federal crime; torture and conspiracy to commit torture are barred by the United States Anti-Torture Act; and Article VI of the Constitution turns Senate-ratified treaties into federal common law. Similarly, in 1950 the United States incorporated the Geneva Conventions into the Uniform Code of Military Justice and into the Army's field manuals.

Many laws, such as the laws against killing people, are suspended in times of war. But the law of war crimes applies even under conditions of emergency.[9] It is designed for conditions of war; absence of normal legality is no defense for war crimes. The Convention Against Torture, for example, provides that "no exceptional circumstances whatsoever, whether a state of war or a threat of war, internal political instability or any other public emergency, may be invoked as a justification of torture."[10]

The prohibition on war crimes is absolute, not relative. U.S. Justice Robert Jackson proclaimed at Nuremberg, "No grievances or policies will justify resort to aggressive war. It is utterly renounced and condemned as an instrument of policy."[11] The same applies to other war crimes as well. The war crimes of one's opponents are no justification for one's own.

Charges that opponents have committed war crimes have become common currency in international conflict. But *war criminal* is more than an epithet. Today there is a body of law that is clearly enough formulated and widely enough accepted to be interpreted by courts based on procedures similar to those used for judging other crimes. Those are the standards by which allegations of war crimes by Bush, Cheney, and their associates must be judged.

For the last sixty years, the U.S. Supreme Court, military judges, international lawyers, and American-sanctioned war-crimes tribunals have engaged in investigation and prosecution of war-crimes activity.[12] As early as 1946, the U.S. Supreme Court affirmed the criminal liability of a Japanese commander who failed to prevent atrocities by his troops.[13] U.S. military operations manuals regularly incorporate Geneva Conventions provisions, with, for example, clauses for mandatory POW tribunals set up in the battlefield.[14] And in the last decade alone, U.S. administrations have supported war-crimes tribunals in the former Yugoslavia, Rwanda, Sierra Leone, and East Timor. As U.S. troops readied their attack on Baghdad, President Bush proclaimed that if Iraqis "take innocent life, if they destroy infrastructure, they will be held accountable as war criminals. . . . War crimes will be prosecuted. War criminals will be punished."[15]

Criminal acts for which George Bush, Dick Cheney, and their collaborators should be investigated include such war crimes as initiating a war of aggression, abusing noncombatants, and engaging in torture and prisoner abuse.

A War of Aggression

Following the 2001 attacks on the World Trade Center, key members of the Bush administration began mobilizing support for the invasion of Iraq. Richard Clarke, the former counterterrorism czar for President Bush, recalls that Rumsfeld said that we needed to bomb Iraq because there aren't any good targets in Afghanistan.[16] This was despite clear evidence provided by the CIA and the U.S. State Department that Iraq played no role in the 9/11 attacks.

The Pentagon's war plans faced a serious hurdle, however: it is illegal to invade another country. Principle VI of the Nuremberg Charter, the first document to codify the ban on aggressive war, states that it is a crime to engage in the "planning, preparation, initiation or waging of a war of aggression or a war in violation of international treaties, agreements or assurances."[17] Of course nations still resort to war. But in the face of a general rule against the use of force, such violence must fall within one of two narrowly defined exceptions: either the attack has been authorized by the United Nations Security Council or it is justified under the doctrine of self-defense.

Well aware of this prohibition on the use of force, the Bush administration argued both exceptions simultaneously. First, asserting self-defense, it claimed Iraq to be a threat to the United States based on "evidence" of Iraq's stockpiling of weapons of mass destruction (WMD)—despite United Nations weapons inspectors' inability to find such evidence.[18] Second, unable to garner the United Nations Security Council's support, the administration argued an "implied" right to invade Iraq, drawn from former United Nations Security Council resolutions.

The response by the national and international legal community to these arguments was clear and resounding. A letter sent to the White House on behalf of over one thousand law professors and U.S. legal organizations stated, "We consider that any future use of force without a new U.N. Security Council Resolution would constitute a crime against peace or aggressive war in violation of the U.N. Charter." In a BBC interview more than a year after the invasion, United Nations Secretary-General Kofi Annan unequivocally stated that the U.S. war "was illegal." As subsequent documents, such as the Downing Street Memo, make clear, President Bush, Vice President Cheney, and their associates planned, prepared, and initiated a war of aggression.[19]

The invasion of Iraq is illegal for good reason. International law forbids aggressive war under any conditions, whether under the cloak of "military security," "democracy," or "fighting terrorism." It requires nations to present their claims and build consensus, and with a few but firm binding laws it works to promote peace by deterring raw, self-interested aggression.

Crimes of Occupation

On March 20, 2003, the United States began bombing Iraq. The strategy was to "shock and awe" the enemy, dropping nearly three thousand bombs in the first few days of the war.[20] As one Pentagon strategist boasted to CBS News, "There will not be a safe place in Baghdad." Immediately reports of civilian casualties began to pour in. The Los Angeles Times surveyed Baghdad hospitals and found records of 1,700 civilians killed and 8,000 injured in the battle for Baghdad alone.[21] The Associated Press deemed its hospital footage of babies cut in half and children with their limbs blown off too upsetting to air on television.[22]

The laws of war as codified in the Geneva Conventions prescribe rules for conducting battle as humanely as possible. They are guided by the principle that persons who do not take part in armed hostilities are entitled to special protection and humane treatment. In practice this principle means shielding civilians from battle, protecting the civilian infrastructure, and assuming responsibility for essential services as an occupying power. Both in conducting the war and as an occupying power the U.S. has failed to comply with these laws of war, and as a result unknown numbers of Iraqi civilians have been killed or maimed.

Despite the restrictions on journalists and the failure of the U.S. and Iraqi governments to investigate, the documented examples of such violations are myriad. Examples of illegal weapons include the use of cluster bombs in residential neighborhoods,[23] napalm, depleted uranium, and white phosphorus.[24] A senior British officer in Iraq stated, "The view of the British chain of command is that the Americans' use of violence is not proportionate. . . . American troops do shoot first and ask questions later."[25] According to UN human rights investigators, the U.S. is systematically using "hunger and deprivation of water as a weapon of war against the civilian population."[26] The systematic use of home demolitions has been documented by such groups as Human Rights Watch, which has pointed out that "destroying civilian property as a reprisal or as a deterrent amounts to collective punishment, a violation of the 1949 Geneva Conventions."[27]

It is not only bombs and bullets that kill or maim civilians in war zones. The Geneva Conventions require that when one nation invades another, the invading nation assumes responsibility for providing security for the civilian population. As a result, under occupation law, the U.S. is legally bound to provide services such as electricity, medical care, food, and education. But according to Columbia University professor Jeffrey Sachs, the U.S. occupation has allowed Iraqi children to "die in vast numbers from diarrhea, respiratory infections and other causes, owing to unsafe drinking water, lack of refrigerated foods, and acute shortages of blood and basic medicines in clinics and hospitals."

Although much attention has been paid to the buildup to war and the prisoner abuse scandal, the crimes associated with the war's conduct and occupation have gone largely unreported. These various crimes of occupation—whether targeting residential neighborhoods with cluster bombs or deliberately attacking hospitals—are not mere technical or minor breaches of international law. Rather, they violate the core principle of the Geneva Conventions—protection of civilians regardless of emergency.

Torture

Torture is illegal in all forms, in all places, and at all times.[28] In April 2004, Americans first learned of prisoner abuse from the television program 60 Minutes and from an article by Seymour Hersh in The New Yorker, which revealed shocking photographs from the Abu Ghraib prison in Iraq.

The Bush administration reacted to the Abu Ghraib scandal by arguing that a "few rotten apples" were to blame for the torture. But reporters at the Washington Post and Newsweek, followed by freedom-of-information lawsuits by the American Civil Liberties Union, soon uncovered a paper trail of legal memorandums, FBI e-mails, and other government documents indicating a common plan on the part of the administration to violate the laws of war.

These documents included White House Counsel Alberto Gonzales's memo to President Bush stating that a "new paradigm renders obsolete Geneva's strict limitations on questioning of enemy prisoners" and made other Geneva Convention provisions "quaint." This abandonment of international war crimes laws sanctioned, for example, the creation of six new "Enhanced Interrogation Techniques" authorized by top administration officials in March 2002. According to the CIA Inspector General, these techniques, including waterboarding, appeared "to constitute cruel, and degrading treatment under the [Geneva] convention."[29]

Meanwhile reports of torture, deaths, and "extraordinary rendition"—the CIA practice of spiriting people away to countries that may sanction torture—began to seep out of Guantánamo, Afghanistan, and Iraq. FBI agents at Guantánamo reported strangulation, routine beatings, lit cigarettes put out in detainees' ears, and mock executions. Sworn testimony from detainees documents instances of prisoners being burned with liquid chemical agents, sodomized with broom handles, forced to masturbate, and raped. Former Army interrogator Spc. Tony Lagouranis testified that the worst torture occurs in Iraqis' homes, where he witnessed U.S. soldiers smashing people's feet with the back of an axehead, and the regular breaking of bones to extract information.[30] *Nearly one hundred detainees have died* in U.S. custody in Iraq and Afghanistan since August 2002; *at least fifty-one detainees have died* in U.S. custody since Secretary of Defense Rumsfeld was informed of the abuses at Abu Ghraib on January 16, 2004.[31]

By 2005 the instances of publicly documented torture had become almost innumerable. These endless crimes have been followed by a constant flow of government reports, newspaper and human rights investigations, court documents, and victim statements. Yet those who ordered and/or created the conditions for torture have not even faced official investigation, let alone prosecution, trial, or punishment.

Accountability

Who bears the ultimate responsibility for an illegal invasion and occupation, dropping cluster bombs onto residential neighborhoods, attacking hospitals, and torturing prisoners?

The U.S. Supreme Court affirmatively answered this question in 1945 by upholding the conviction and death sentence of the Japanese commander Tomoyuki Yamashita for his failure to halt the crimes of his troops. According to the court's majority opinion, the law of war "presupposes that its violation is to be avoided through the control of the operation of war by its commanders."[32] Fifty years later this theory of *command responsibility* was the basis for The Hague Tribunal indictments of the Serbian civilian leader Radovan Karadzic and the commander of the army, Ratko Mladic. These courts understood that meaningful enforcement of the Geneva Conventions depends on holding those in power accountable for both the effects of their policy decisions and their troops' conduct.

Clearly the decisions about whether to invade Iraq and the conduct and character of the occupation are the responsibility of our national leadership. At minimum the doctrine of command responsibility implicates military and civilian leaders—including Paul Bremer, General Tommy Franks, Paul Wolfowitz, Condoleezza Rice, and others—for their policy-making roles in war crimes, such as the use of cluster bombs and napalm, denial of water to civilians, and waging an illegal war.[33]

In the Yamashita case, the U.S. Supreme Court took the doctrine of command responsibility even further to include the principle that "a person in a position of superior authority . . . should also be held responsible for failure to deter the unlawful behavior of subordinates."[34] Such standards, combined with the evidence of the crimes on the initiation and conduct of the Iraq war, fully establish President Bush and Vice President Cheney's culpability.

The culpability issues focus primarily on crimes for which the administration's responsibility is less self-evident, namely the war crimes of torture and prisoner abuse. With the criminal conviction of Corporal Charles Graner and other low-level individuals for prisoner abuse at Abu Ghraib, the Bush administration insists that justice has been served, as these "bad apples" acted alone, without orders. But as the *Washington Post* editorial "War Crimes" concluded, subsequent congressional hearings, internal investigations, and the release of thousands of pages of confidential documents under court order "establish beyond any doubt that every part of this cover story is false."

According to former Defense Secretary James Schlesinger, "The abuses were not just the failure of some individuals to follow known standards, and they are more than the failure of a few leaders to enforce proper discipline.

There is both institutional and personal responsibility at higher levels."[35] Eerily, Scott Horton, International Law Committee Chair of the Association of the Bar of the City of New York, in his article "A Nuremberg Lesson," details how U.S. prosecutors at Nuremberg rejected the "rotten apples" defense and held German Nazi officials accountable for the consequences of their policy decisions.[36]

How high up the chain of command does the evidence lead? All the evidence points to the top. FBI e-mails released under the Freedom of Information Act disclose torture techniques authorized by "Executive Order signed by President Bush" and "approved by the Sec. of Def."[37] Colin Powell's top aide, Colonel Larry Wilkerson, said in late 2005 that the U.S. has tortured, and "There's no question in my mind where the philosophical guidance and the flexibility in order to do so originated—in the vice president of the United States' office." According to Wilkerson, "His implementer in this case was Donald Rumsfeld and the Defense Department." Wilkerson explained, "The vice president had to cover this in order for it to happen and in order for Secretary Rumsfeld to feel as though he had freedom of action."[38] The former commander at Abu Ghraib prison, Brigadier General Janis Karpinski, confirms Wilkerson's charge: Abusive techniques at Abu Ghraib were "delivered with full authority and knowledge of the secretary of defense and probably Cheney."[39]

Administration officials are well aware that they risk being charged with war crimes. In his memo of January 25, 2002, then-White House counsel Alberto Gonzales warned President Bush that his circumvention of the Geneva Conventions exposed administration officials to war-crimes prosecution, since it "was difficult to predict with confidence" how prosecutors might apply the Conventions' limitations on "inhuman treatment" in the future.[40]

If equivalent evidence pointed to those responsible for a murder or burglary, our justice system would have opened a criminal investigation long ago. According to the United States Attorney General's office, investigations of crime may be initiated where facts or circumstance merely "reasonably indicate" that a crime has been committed.[41] As former Nixon Counsel John Dean concludes, there is "damning evidence suggesting a common plan on the part of the Administration to violate the laws of war," and "[s]trikingly, such a 'common plan,' or conspiracy, is itself a war crime."[42]

Cover-Up of War Crimes

The Bush administration is engaged in a large-scale cover-up of war crimes. According to the *New York Times,* it "drags its feet on public disclosure, stonewalls Congressional requests for documents, and suppresses the results of internal investigations."[43] Its suppression of information ranges from denying its use of illegal napalm on the battlefield and refusing to track the Iraqi civilian death toll to hiding "ghost detainees" from the International Committee of the Red Cross and withholding executive orders relating to the prisoner abuse at Abu Ghraib. These activities culminate in the systematic refusal of the administration to open full and proper investigations into allegations of war crimes. In the words of John Dean, the former whistle-blowing Nixon counsel, this is a cover-up "worse than Watergate."[44]

Despite more than a dozen investigations by the Department of Defense, not one addresses the central question of how the decisions of policy makers affected what soldiers and officers did to detainees.

This cover-up has obstructed the process of criminal investigation and prosecution of war crimes. As Scott Horton states in an affidavit supporting the "Criminal Complaint Against the United States Secretary of Defense Rumsfeld, et al.," brought before a court in Germany, "no such criminal investigation or prosecution would occur in the United States for the reason that the criminal investigation and prosecutorial functions are currently controlled by individuals who are involved in the conspiracy to commit war crimes." This failure to conduct a formal and proper investigation is itself a crime, meeting the requirements for misprision of a felony.

Subverting the Rule of Law

Under the principles of constitutional government, government officials are themselves required to obey the law. The authority of government officials was made conditional on their own obedience to law. Every schoolchild used to be taught that the United States Constitution provided "government under law"—that the United States was "a government of laws, not men."

The Constitution made the president the commander-in-chief of the armed forces but provided many legal constraints on the president's authority. Only

Congress had the authority to declare war, to conscript, to tax, or to appropriate funds. The President was subject to laws passed by Congress and interpreted by the courts.

The United Nations Charter, the Geneva Conventions, and other treaties ratified under the authority of the United States are the supreme law of the land under Article 6 of the U.S. Constitution. They are further reinforced by such U.S. laws as the War Crimes Act, which makes grave violations of the Geneva Conventions a crime punishable by imprisonment or even death.

The U.S. has a law-enforcement system responsible for investigating, apprehending, and sanctioning criminals. Unfortunately those who control the government have many opportunities to extend their authority beyond the limits provided in laws and constitutions—even to the point of committing crimes. Such "extended authority" has an old and ugly name: usurpation.

The modern United States has not been immune to such extended authority. In the 1960s Lyndon Johnson launched the Vietnam War without a congressional declaration of war; used a false account of an attack in the Gulf of Tonkin to panic Congress into granting him unlimited authority to make war; and ultimately sent half a million troops to Vietnam. Public antagonism eventually led Johnson to refuse to run for reelection.

In the 1970s Richard Nixon engaged in the massive abuse of presidential powers that came to be known as the Watergate scandals. On the heels of a landslide electoral victory the Nixon administration was subjected to investigation by a special prosecutor and by Congress; Nixon resigned rather than undergo impeachment.

Today the Bush administration has subverted constitutional government from within. It has paralyzed the constraints that would limit executive authority. A memo written by then-Assistant Attorney General Jay Bybee stated that prosecution under the U.S. law prohibiting torture could be barred "because enforcement of the statute would represent an unconstitutional infringement of the president's authority to conduct war." When asked at his Senate confirmation hearings whether he agreed that the President could simply refuse to obey a law he considered unconstitutional, President Bush's Attorney General nominee Alberto Gonzales assented. As Yale Law School Dean Harold Koh commented, "If the President has the sole constitutional authority to sanction torture, and Congress has no power to interfere, it is unclear why the President should not also have unfettered authority to license genocide."

The "new paradigm" the Bush administration has used to legitimate its war crimes is in truth not so new. It embodies practices well known to autocratic regimes throughout history. Seize on an emergency when people are panicked. Issue decrees that override established laws. Authorize your own henchmen to act outside the law. Restrict the courts. Appoint prejudiced judges. Threaten opponents. Conceal information. Construct phony plots and threats. Manufacture trumped-up law cases and phony evidence of wrongdoing. Criminalize the normal operations of dissent. The objective of such actions—to instill fear, confusion, acquiescence, submission, and withdrawal into private life—is often achieved, at least for a time.

The movement against autocracy and for democratic government is centuries old and worldwide. The effort to impeach President Bush and Vice President Cheney for war crimes is very much part of that struggle.

Web Resources:

After Downing Street: http://www.afterdowningstreet.org
American Civil Liberties Union: http://www.aclu.org
Amnesty International: http://www.ai.org
AntiWar.com: http://www.antiwar.com
Avalon Project at Yale Law School: http://www.yale.edu/lawweb/avalon/avalon.htm
Center for Constitutional Rights: www-ccr-ny.org
Center for Economic and Social Rights: http://www.cesr.org
Central Committee for Conscientious Objectors: http://www.objector.org/
Crimes of War Project: http://www.crimesofwar.org
Guantánamo Human Rights Organization: http://www.guantanamohrc.org
Human Rights Watch: http://www.hrw.org
Institute for Policy Studies: http://www.ips-dc.org
International Committee of the Red Cross: http://www.icrc.org
Lawyers Against the War: http://www.lawyersagainstthewar.org
Not In Our Name: http://www.notinourname.net
Occupation Watch: http://www.occupationwatch.org
Pro-Se Institute: http://www.internationallaw.pro-se-institute.org/index.htm
United Nations: http://www.un.org/law

United for Peace and Justice: http://www.unitedforpeace.org
War Crimes Watch: www.warcrimeswatch.org
World Tribunal on Iraq: http://www.worldtribunal.org

Notes:

1. Rupert Cornwell, "Cheney 'Created Climate' for U.S. War Crimes," *The Independent*, December 30, 2005.
2. Jane Mayer, "The Memo," *The New Yorker*, February 27, 2006.
3. Garrison Keillor, "What to Do When the Emperor Has No Clothes," *Chicago Tribune*, March 1, 2006.
4. Gene Healy and Timothy Lynch, *Power Surge: The Constitutional Record of George W. Bush*, Cato Institute, May 1, 2006, http://www.cato.org/pub_display.php?pub_id=6330.
5. Elizabeth Holtzman, "The Impeachment of George W. Bush," *The Nation*, January 13, 2006.
6. Frank Newman and David Weissbrodt, *International Human Rights*, 2nd ed. (Cincinnati: Anderson, 1969), p. 3.
7. Steven R. Ratner and Jason S. Abrams, *Accountability for Human Rights Atrocities in International Law*, 2nd ed. (Oxford: Oxford University Press, 2001), p. 81.
8. The law of war crimes has continued to evolve. The Geneva Conventions of 1949 built on the early conventions but provided far greater protections to civilians in armed conflicts. Two protocols in 1977 defined war crimes as "grave breaches" of the Geneva agreements.
9. "Humanitarian law applies specifically to emergency situations." Newman and Weissbrodt, *International Human Rights*, p. 17. For a discussion of the Bush administration's claims that law does not apply in an emergency, see Sanford Levinson, "Torture in Iraq and the Rule of Law in America," in *In the Name of Democracy*.
10. Convention Against Torture and Other Cruel, Inhuman or Degrading Treatment or Punishment, adopted and open for signature, ratification, and accession by General Assembly resolution 39/46 of December 10, 1984, article 16. Quoted in Human Rights Watch, "The Road to Abu Ghraib," reprinted in *In the Name of Democracy*.
11. Statement by Justice Jackson on War Trials Agreement, August 12, 1945.
12. While the modern origins of the laws of war trace back to President Lincoln's promulgation of the 1863 Lieber Code—primarily protecting prisoners of war—their twentieth-century incarnation resides in the Hague Conventions, Geneva Conventions, and Nuremberg Charter. Breaches of these laws include: initiating wars of aggression, murder or ill-treatment of civilians and prisoners of war, wanton destruction of cities not justified by military necessity, plunder of public and private property. See Roy Gutman and David Reiff, eds., *Crimes of War* (New York: Norton, 1999), pp. 374–375.
13. "The law of war imposes on any . . . commander a duty to take such appropriate measures as are within his power to control the troops under his command for the prevention of acts which are violations of the law of war . . . he may be charged with personal responsibility for his failure to take such measures when violations result." *In re Yamashita*, 327 U.S. 1 (1946) at 14. See also W. Hays Parks, "Command Responsibility for War Crimes," 62 *Mil. L. Rev.* 1 (1973).
14. See *United States Army Operations Law Handbook*, JA 422, at 272 (1997).
15. Barry Schweid, "War Planning Includes Targeting Saddam Hussein; Top Prospects Uncertain," Associated Press, February 26, 2003; Vivienne Walt, "U.S. Officials Expect to Find Evidence of War Crimes," *USA Today*, March 18, 2003.

16. Leslie Stahl, "Interviews with Richard Clarke," *Sixty Minutes*, March 21, 2004.

17. Charter of the Nuremberg Tribunals, principle VI. Full text published in *Report of the International Law Commission Covering Its Second Session, 5 June—29 July 1950*, document A/1316, pp. 11–14.

18. The strict limitations on self-defense as a justification for war were well established in international law long before the UN Charter. As Michael Byers, Associate Professor at Duke University Law School, explained, "customary law traditionally recognized a limited right of pre-emptive self-defense according to what are known as the '*Caroline criteria*.'" These date back to an incident in 1837, during a rebellion against British rule in Canada, when British troops attacked a ship (the *Caroline*) that was being used by private citizens in the United States to ferry supplies to the rebels. After a long diplomatic correspondence between the U.S. secretary of state, Daniel Webster, and the British foreign-office minister, Lord Ashburton, a form of words was agreed on to govern acts of anticipatory self-defense: there must be "a necessity of self-defense, instant, overwhelming, leaving no choice of means and no moment for deliberation" and the action taken must not be "unreasonable or excessive." "Iraq and the Bush Doctrine of Pre-Emptive Self-Defense," Crimes of War Project, http://www.crimesofwar.org/ experts/bush-intro.html.

19. This piece does not address the illegality of the U.S. invasion of Afghanistan. As Richard Falk states in *In the Name of Democracy*: "The Afghanistan war was undertaken without Security Council authorization, but at least there was a plausible case for American claims of self-defense, provided by the 9/11 attacks . . . [However,] even though the [Afghan war] had a legal basis, it was undertaken in a manner that makes it legally questionable, and possibly imprudent as well."

20. "Baghdad Wakes Up to Explosions," Fox News, March 22, 2003. Available at http://www.foxnews.com/story/0,2933,81791,00.html.

21. Laura King, "Baghdad's Death Toll Assessed," *Los Angeles Times*, May 18, 2003.

22. Amnesty International, *Iraq: Civilians Under Fire* (April 2002), p. 2. Available at http://www.web.amnesty.org/library/index/engmde140712003.

23. Ibid., p. 1.

24. George Monbiot, "Behind the Phosphorus Clouds are War Crimes Within War Crimes," *The Guardian*, November 22, 2005.

25. Sean Rayment, "U.S. Tactics Condemned by British Officers," *Telegraph*, April 11, 2004. Available at http://www.telegraph.co.uk/news/main.jhtml?xml=/news/2004/04/ 11/wtactii.xml.

26. http://news.bbc.co.uk/2/hi/middle_east/4344136.stm

27. Joe Stork and Fred Abrahams, "Sidelined: Human Rights in Post War Iraq," Human Rights Watch, January 1, 2004.

28. The definition of *torture* has been codified in the 1984 Convention for the Prevention of Torture and Inhuman or Degrading Treatment or Punishment. Available at http://www.yale.edu/lawweb/avalon/diana/undocs/33198-5.html. Article III of all four Geneva Conventions clarifies that "violence to life and person, in particular murder of all kinds, mutilation, cruel treatment and torture. . .outrages upon personal dignity, in particular humiliating and degrading treatment" are banned under all circumstances. See also Convention for the Prevention of Torture and Inhuman or Degrading Treatment or Punishment.

29. ABC News, "CIA's Harsh Interrogation Techniques Described," November 18, 2005.

30. Human Rights Watch, "Leadership Failure Firsthand Accounts of Torture of Iraqi Detainees by the U.S. Army's 82nd Airborne Division," December 2005; PBS Frontline, "Interview with Tony Lagouranis," September 25, 2005.

31. Human Rights First, "Command's Responsibility: Detainee Deaths in U.S. Custody In Iraq and Afghanistan," January 2006.

32. *The Matter of Yamashita*, 327 US I, 15 (1946).

33. The doctrine of command responsibility has been extended to civilian authorities exercising control over military forces. The International Criminal Tribunal for the Former Yugoslavia (ICTY) and the International Criminal Tribunal for Rwanda (ICTR) have held civilians criminally liable for the actions of militarized forces under their control. The term *command responsibility* is increasingly being replaced by *superior responsibility*.

34. *The Matter of Yamashita*, 327 US I, 15 (1946).

35. James Schlesinger, "Final Report of the Independent Panel to Review DoD Detention Operations," August 24, 2004, p. 5. Hereafter cited as Schlesinger Report.

36. Scott Horton, "A Nuremberg Lesson," in *In the Name of Democracy*.

37. ACLU, "FBI E-Mail Refers to Presidential Order Authorizing Inhumane Interrogation Techniques," December 20, 2004.

38. CNN, "Powell Aide: Torture 'Guidance' from VP," November 20, 2005.

39. Marjorie Cohn, "Abu Ghraib General Lambastes Bush Administration," http://www.truthout. org, August 24, 2005.

40. Alberto Gonzales, "Memorandum from Alberto R. Gonzales to the President," in *In the Name of Democracy*.

41. According to FBI guidelines, the "reasonable indication" threshold is substantially lower than probable cause. See "The Attorney General's Guidelines on General Crimes, Racketeering Enterprise and Terrorism Enterprise Investigation." Available at http://www.usdoj.gov/olp/ generalcrimes2.pdf.6. Scott Horton, "Expert Report by Scott Horton" (January 28, 2005, available at http:// www.ccr-ny.org/v2/legal/september_11th/docs/ScottHortonGermany013105. pdf.

42. John W. Dean, "The Torture Memo By Judge Jay S. Bybee That Haunted Alberto Gonzales's Confirmation Hearings," FindLaw.com, January 14, 2005.

43. "Time for Accounting," editorial, *New York Times*, February 19, 2005.

44. Dean, *op cit.*

Chapter 5

DEFENDING THE INDEFENSIBLE
Torture and the American Empire

Dennis Loo

We will not try to reform the existing institutions. We only intend
to weaken them, and eventually destroy them.
—A manifesto from Paul Weyrich's Free Congress Foundation.[1]

When fascism comes to America, it will be wrapped in the flag and
carrying a bible.

—Sinclair Lewis (1935)

Any reasonably aware student of history knows that torture and terror aren't
new to America—ask Native Americans slaughtered wholesale for Manifest
Destiny; ask the millions of Africans extirpated in blood and chains for the
slave trade; ask the people of Guatemala, Iran, the Dominican Republic, Chile,
Haiti, the Philippines, Dresden, Hiroshima and Nagasaki . . . the list goes on
and on.[2]

But what *is* new is how extensive and open torture has become under Bush-
Cheney and the fact that they are not just using proxies to carry out the torture
anymore. This is an extremely ominous development. Graphic pictures from
Abu Ghraib of torture and murder committed by American personnel were
leaked in 2003, and there are reports from Guantánamo and Afghanistan of
more of the same. Bad as these pictures are, there are even worse pictures that
the White House and Pentagon have so far successfully prevented from being
given general distribution, because they would "jeopardize national security
and the war in Iraq." In one of these Abu Ghraib photos, an attractive American woman interrogator (Spc. Sabrina Harmon) gives the thumbs up and

smiles beatifically, looking for all the world as if she were posing for the family album, as she leans over the ice-packed, duct-taped corpse of an Iraqi who was beaten to death during interrogation. I am reminded in looking at these pictures of the images of scores of Southern whites milling about and enjoying the picnic atmosphere, while in their midst, dangling from a tree, hangs a lynched black man. Do a Google search for "Abu Ghraib" and see for yourself what has been and is currently being done in your name.

Since this new campaign of "taking the gloves off" began, we have seen and heard Bush, Cheney, Alberto Gonzales, and Condi Rice denying that the U.S. uses torture. To the extent that the neocons have a social base among the populace outside of the plutocracy, these denials of torture on our part are aimed primarily at the misinformed and credulous—the approximately one-third of Americans who still support Bush (at this writing) and those who watch Fox News exclusively or nearly exclusively and/or listen to Rush Limbaugh. Limbaugh, doing his cheerleading part as usual, compared the torture at Abu Ghraib to Skull and Bones fraternity hijinks and "blowing some steam off."[3] Among the right-wing intelligentsia, who know too much to accept this cover story, the tact has been to argue that *some* torture is okay. As right-wing journal *National Review*'s Jonah Goldberg wrote in June 2004, for example:

> Today, we're getting shovelfuls of platitudes about how, if we become torturers, we will be no better than those we are fighting. . . . But at the same time, if we pulled out the fingernails of every single member of al-Qaeda, we wouldn't magically become a society where women have to wear burkas, homosexuals are crushed to death, and statues are blown up. In other words, the certainty we're now hearing from enlightened liberals that torture is manifestly wrong stems . . . from good old-fashioned dogmatism. A man who says torture is wrong in a "ticking time bomb" case isn't a man bereft of dogmatic certainty, but one weighed down by it.[4]

Michael Ignatieff, director of Harvard's Carr Center of Human Rights Policy, a liberal who endorsed the invasion of Iraq and who wrote in the *New York Times Magazine* an essay tellingly entitled, "The American Empire (Get Used to It),"[5] wrote on May 2, 2004, echoing Dick Cheney:

> To defeat evil, we may have to traffic in evils: indefinite detention
> of suspects, coercive interrogations, targeted assassinations, even
> pre-emptive war. These are evils because each strays from national
> and international law and because they kill people or deprive them
> of freedom without due process. They can be justified only because
> they prevent the greater evil.[6]

Ignatieff's "greater evil," he explains, is a second terrorist attack on the
U.S. According to his logic, then, the killing of more than a hundred thousand
Iraqis as a result of our invasion and occupation, in addition to the ongoing
"coercive interrogations" of Iraqis and others, is the "lesser evil." This logic
must mean that the greater evil was when Saddam tortured and killed Iraqis,
but when Americans torture and kill Iraqis it's the lesser evil. I'm glad we got
that straight.[7]

Rice and Gonzales were asked in 2005 by U.S. senators in their confirmation hearings if they would specifically rule out specific practices such as
waterboarding. Both Rice and Gonzales refused to rule out its use or countenance any restrictions whatsoever on their "war on terror." The rules of
war have changed because of terrorism, Rice stated, a war, it bears repeating,
Cheney has said will last for generations.

And Then There's Rendition

Rendition is the practice of secretly transporting prisoners to "black sites"
in places such as Uzbekistan, Egypt, Saudi Arabia, Pakistan, Romania, and
Poland for further "interrogation." The *Washington Post* broke the story about
rendition in November 2005. After this revelation Rice faced a firestorm of
criticism about this practice from Europeans during her tour there. According to a U.S. State Department February 2001 report, Uzbek police routinely
are guilty of "beating, often with blunt weapons, and asphyxiation with a gas
mask." Human rights groups reported that Uzbek jail torture included boiling of body parts, electroshock to genitals, and the use of pliers to pry off
fingernails and toenails. Two prisoners were boiled to death, these groups
reported. Despite the State Department's own report on torture, Rice and the
Bush administration have nonetheless been flying prisoners—some of whom

are "ghost" prisoners because their identity has been altogether hidden—to places like Uzbekistan. According to an April 4, 2006, Amnesty International investigation, the CIA has flown some thousand flights of this kind, with the number of rendition prisoners unknown—probably, according to Amnesty International, in the hundreds.

Rice's statements for the record on this practice were striking for their carefully worded character, as if she was trying to remain technically accurate and speaking for the sake of those who were looking only at the surface meaning, while leaving the door wide open to continue the torture that the European government leaders, military and intelligence officers *know full well* the U.S. is engaged in.[8] Rice stated that "as a matter of U.S. policy" U.S. adherence to the United Nations Convention Against Torture (which also bans cruel and inhumane treatment) applies to "U.S. personnel" in the U.S. and abroad. Conveniently left out of this statement were the possibility that practices were being engaged in that were at variance with U.S. policy, that U.S. security contractors might be carrying out torture for U.S. personnel, and any specifics about what the U.S. defines as cruel and inhumane treatment and torture.[9]

The McCain Amendment and Redefining Torture

Cheney fought openly, tooth and nail, in the fall of 2005 to prevent passage of Senator John McCain's amendment prohibiting torture. When the Senate passed it in October 2005 anyway, Bush made a big show of meeting with McCain and signing the legislation. Bush then immediately proclaimed, using a presidential "signing statement," that his intent in signing the law differed from the intent of Congress in passing the legislation, thus rendering the whole matter null and void.[10] Of critical importance here is what this incredible assertion of dictatorial powers elicited from Senator McCain, the rest of Congress, and the mainstream media. There were some protestations from editorial writers, but no calls for Bush's resignation and precious little talk of impeachment. Consider what this response means about how far things have come and where we are in this country: the President declares his intention to continue torturing, and the political leadership and opinion leaders *let this pass.*

The Bush administration can continue to argue with a straight face that we do not torture in part also because it has defined down what torture means. To Bush and Co., the official definition of torture is only when it causes organ failure, impairment of bodily function, or death; otherwise it's not torture.[11] This is a definition no one else in the world either believes or even dares to articulate. Not even Saddam Hussein was arrogant enough to attempt such a self-serving definition. Despite even this extraordinary redefinition of torture, the United States still condones causing organ failure and death with impunity, let alone humiliating detainees in cruel and unusual ways.

Marjorie Cohn, in an October 18, 2005, article entitled: "Continuing in His Defiance of the Law," wrote:

> Last month, an Army captain and two sergeants from the 82nd Airborne Division contacted Senator John McCain (R-Ariz) and Human Rights Watch with allegations that members of the unit routinely beat, tortured and abused detainees in 2003 and early 2004. Capt. Ian Fishback, a West Point graduate, said he was frustrated that his reports to superiors went unheeded.
>
> They reported seeing soldiers break prisoners' legs, and strike blows to the heads, chests, and stomachs of prisoners—on a daily basis. They described witnessing soldiers pour chemical substances on prisoners' skin and into their eyes. They said the mistreatment at a base near Fallujah was "just like" what happened at Abu Ghraib.
>
> Capt. Fishback told Human Rights Watch that he believes the abuses he witnessed in Iraq and Afghanistan were caused in part by Bush's 2002 decision not to apply the Geneva Conventions protections to detainees captured in Afghanistan.[12]

In another example, Chief Warrant Officer Lewis Welshofer, Jr., was put on trial in January 2006 for the death in custody of Maj. Gen. Abed Hamed Mowhoush. Mowhoush was subjected to waterboarding and beaten severely by Iraqis paid by the CIA, leaving him unable to walk before his final, fatal, torture session.

Welshofer admitted that during his final interrogation of the General he sat on Mowhoush's chest after covering Mowhoush's head with a sleeping blanket that was in turn bound to him with electrical wire wrapped like "a yo-yo," as

Welshofer testified. Welshofer further admitted that during this procedure at times he put his hand over the General's mouth. Mowhoush, as one might expect, suffocated to death. The verdict: Welshofer was ordered to forfeit $6,000 of his salary and was confined to barracks, work, and church for sixty days. During the trial Welshofer stated that top commanders had told him that "the gloves were coming off" and his superiors specifically approved the use of what they called the "sleeping bag technique." The Bush administration, of course, knows all about this because they have directed people to engage in these horrid practices.[13]

The other reason that they can claim with a straight face that the United States does not torture is, of course, because all members of the top leadership are world-class liars. The question here is, why? Why are they, first of all, rather openly employing torture? And secondly, what does this fact tell us about what is up with this brave new world of unspeakable horrors so thinly disguised that no one except the misinformed and gullible would believe the cover stories?

One might think that using torture against putative enemies would be a wholly counterproductive practice for multiple reasons. First, it would endanger Americans who are captured as POWS, since they would have no protection against cruel and unusual punishment and torture, given that the U.S. is openly flouting the Geneva Conventions.

Second, one would think that clearly engaging in torture would make recruitment to this "Army of One" extremely difficult. As it is, recruitment numbers were already depressed since the Iraq war started to bog down, and sufficient troop levels are strained. Many military recruiters have gone AWOL because of these problems. Given the neocons' long-standing plans to go after other rival countries, such as Syria and Iran, this strategy would seem to be counterproductive. The primary reason that Defense Secretary Donald Rumsfeld resisted the brass' insistence that there be a larger footprint of American troops on the ground in the Iraq war (advice that from the standpoint as an invading imperialist and occupational force has proven to be obviously correct) was because he wanted to be able to show that the U.S. could invade and conquer a country without using too many troops, so that it could engage in two or three or more wars in relatively quick succession.

Third, the public-relations fallout from these practices both domestically and internationally, would appear to be unacceptable. The contrast between the U.S.'s public image of the defender of human rights and friend of democracy and the battering that this precious image is taking would seem to be dangerous to these torturers' rule. Why run this risk, particularly in light of my next reason?

Fourth, intelligence experts (and people who have been subjected to torture and survived) point out that information obtained under such duress, extraction of information under pain of death, is virtually worthless information: the interrogatees give whatever information they think the interrogators want to hear. Thus, torture and killing in custody gets the U.S. little to no good information, on top of which the U.S. pays a high price in terms of reputation, both internationally and domestically. The Bush administration claims that its "rough interrogation" techniques have stopped several other terrorist incidents, but if so, then why have there been, outside of Richard Reid and Zacharias Moussaoui, no prosecutions of the conspirators? Furthermore, neither Reid nor Moussaoui represent instances in which incidents were foiled as the result of torture interrogations of the defendant or someone who in turn fingered the defendants.

Of the 80,000 Arabs and Muslim nationals who were required to register after 9/11, the 8,000 brought in for FBI interviews, and the 5,000 locked up in "preventive detention," none has been convicted of a terrorist crime.[14] The one case Bush has pointed to as a successful prevention of an attack involves an alleged plot to fly an airplane into the U.S. Bank (aka Library) Tower in Los Angeles; this plot was uncovered by another country's intelligence service, not our own.

Fifth, the people who are being detained and tortured and killed almost without exception don't know anything useful. Of the four hundred convictions the United States can point to, almost every one has been for minor overstays of visas and the like. The few that aren't trivial have been convicted of nebulous charges of *conspiring to affiliate with or support* groups defined by the government as terrorist, not for being actually involved in a pending terrorist plot. The practice of torturing these people therefore appears to be an attempt at sheer intimidation rather than actual information gathering.

Finally, these inhumane practices fuel hatred of the United States, expand the ranks of suicide bombers, guarantee the further proliferation of IEDs (Improvised Explosive Devices), and therefore result in more killed and maimed American soldiers and others unlucky enough to step on these devices and *more*, produce ever greater probabilities of terrorist incidents aimed at America and Americans.

Why, then, is the Bush administration engaging in this practice? Is it that they are just brutal terrorists who don't care whom they anger because they figure they're too powerful? Or are they merely *insane*? Award-winning journalist Seymour Hersh, who has been described by neocon Richard Perle as the closest thing American journalism has to a terrorist, quotes an intelligence officer in his latest book, *Chain of Command*: "[Senior WH officials] were so crazed and so far out and so difficult to reason with—to the point of being bizarre. Dogmatic, as if they were on a mission from God."

If this were a line from *The Blues Brothers* film, it would be laughable. But it's not. These people are crazy, but there is a method to their madness. I'm going to offer two parts to my answer to this matter. The first has to do with their faith-based, antiscientific, antirationalist worldview; the second deals with their strategy for world conquest and the intrinsic nature of globalization.

Bush and Cheney's Worldview

We know that members of the administration believe, as the *New York Times'* Ron Suskind chillingly recounted in an October 17, 2004, article, that they can make real whatever they want to be real and that they are not bound by what the rest of us are bound by—empirical reality. Not all of them are religious fanatics, but those who aren't, such as Cheney, are arrogant enough to think that they can force things to be true that they desire to be true through sheer power. This is the logic of empires. Think Rome. Think the short-lived thousand-year Third Reich.

If they think they can make real whatever they want to, the corollary to which is an utter hostility to science and reason, then *they do not think that reason and reasoning with people enter into the picture at all.* From their perspective, if *they* aren't true believers through reasoning, why would anybody else be moved by reason? In many respects, especially among their loyal social base of reactionary evangelicals, they reject the Enlightenment and much that has happened since. They literally want to go back to the Dark Ages, except this time with high-tech machinery. They believe in the literal truth of the Bible, where heretics are killed and disobedient children can be stoned to death.

If a man have a stubborn and rebellious son, which will not obey the voice of his father, or the voice of his mother, and [that], when they have chastened him, will not hearken unto them: Then shall his father and his mother lay hold on him, and bring him out unto the elders of his city, and unto the gate of his place; And they shall say unto the elders of his city, This our son [is] stubborn and rebellious, he will not obey our voice; [he is] a glutton, and a drunkard. And all the men of his city shall stone him with stones, that he die: so shalt thou put evil away from among you; and all Israel shall hear, and fear.

—Deuteronomy 21:18–21

Their hostility to reason is truly radical and unprecedented in modern times. It is part of what makes them startlingly similar to their putative enemy, al-Qaeda. When they confront people who don't believe what they believe, whether those people are Iraqis or Democrats or American citizens, their spontaneous inclination is to try to deceive and fool (and thereby "convince") and, failing that, to intimidate, to scare, to blackmail, to coerce, to bludgeon, to torture, or to kill. They do not believe in compromise, and they believe that their principles are not negotiable. Suskind recounts: "A group of Democratic and Republican members of Congress were called in to discuss Iraq sometime before the October 2002 vote authorizing Bush to move forward. A Republican senator recently told *Time* magazine that the president walked in and said: 'Look, I want your vote. I'm not going to debate it with you.' When one of the senators began to ask a question, Bush snapped, 'Look, I'm not going to debate it with you.'"[15]

Even if they weren't zealots, their principles and their practices don't stand up to scrutiny in comparison to the homilies they pronounce about democracy, freedom, and liberty. Make no mistake: they have no illusions themselves about democracy and liberty. They know that they are oligarchs and know that what is good for them is bad for the vast majority of humanity, that an honest description of their policies would go down to ignominious defeat by approbation. That's why they so studiously and carefully conceal their full program for public consumption and attempt to appear more moderate than the irrational extremists that they are.[16]

Bush thinks he's a messenger of God, that he actually talks to God, and Cheney doesn't talk to anyone and doesn't think he *needs* to talk to anyone. This is the bubble that Bush lives in. It's not just his dyslexicon, his facility for mangling the English language, and it's not just the fact that he is a simpleton, lacking in curiosity or humility and, on top of that, stunningly arrogant.

The Bush White House represents a coalescing of two tendencies—radical know-nothing religious zealotry and imperialist empire. Anti-state terrorism *helps them* more than it hurts them. Anti-state terrorism and state-sponsored terror are obverse sides of the same coin. They need and thrive upon each other. Their whole Homeland Security and PATRIOT Act program and clamping down on the borders and immigrants, their militarizing of the police and their spy state, their imperial presidency logic so evident in the comments of Samuel Alito[17] and Alberto Gonzales, their public-order policies that criminalize and call into suspicion activities that previously were either mere nuisances, such as the presence of winos, or the ordinary activities and mere presence of groups of youth, minorities, and immigrants, or legitimate forms of political protest and expression: all of these policies that they justify on the grounds of fighting terrorism and clamping down on "security threats" are *not* designed to prevent and minimize disasters, terrorist or otherwise. Katrina and, before that, their failure to interdict 9/11 are clear demonstrations of this. Their rapidly evolving police state is designed primarily to repress and coerce domestic and international populations, not to resist terrorism. They were already moving in this direction before the 9/11 attacks.

The Neoliberal State

Why is that? The general answer here—and this is my second main point—is that as the New Deal-Keynesian Welfare State is systematically dismantled by the neoliberal state—the political expression of globalization—as privatization takes the place of social programs, as deindustrialization and downsizing and speedups and take-aways proceed, as insecurity of job and livelihood becomes the norm rather than the exception, as the positive incentives, in other words, for normative behavior (jobs and decent pay, and so forth) are increasingly shredded, the state and the corporate world have no choice but to rely more and more heavily upon coercion to ensure cooperation and to forestall rebellion and revolution. Coercion itself must be used more, but even coercion doesn't work in all instances, and sheer terror must be employed given their overweening ambitions for world domination.

The reason that the Bush White House has been (openly) practicing torture and terror is because it plans to reconfigure the U.S. imperialist empire in such a way that brutality—concealed and unconcealed—is a prominent feature. Shut up and take it or we'll censor you, and if that doesn't work we'll lock you up, and we won't shrink if we have to torture and kill you. For we'll do it all with God on our side.

This attitude is consistent with the strategy of the theocratic right that makes up the Bush-Cheney administration's core base. Consider the following:

Our job is to reclaim America for Christ, whatever the cost. As the vice regents of God, we are to exercise godly dominion and influence over our neighborhoods, our schools, our government, our literature and arts, our sports arenas, our entertainment media, our news media, our scientific endeavors—in short, over every aspect and institution of human society.

—D. James Kennedy, Coral Ridge Ministries Pastor, at a "Reclaiming America for Christ" conference in February, 2005[18]

Christians have an obligation, a mandate, a commission, a holy responsibility to reclaim the land for Jesus Christ—to have dominion in civil structures, just as in every other aspect of life and godliness. . . . World conquest. That's what Christ has commissioned us to accomplish.

—George Grant[19]

Here is what Dr. Bruce Prescott, Executive Director of Mainstream Oklahoma Baptists, a critic of the religious right, said in 2005:

Stripped to its barest essentials, here is their [Reconstructionist] blueprint for America. Their ultimate goal is to make the U.S. Constitution conform to a strict, literal interpretation of Biblical law. To do that involves a series of legal and social reforms that will move society toward their goal. Here is their blueprint: 1) Make the ten commandments the law of the land, 2) Strengthen patriarchically ordered families, 3) Close public schools—make parents totally responsible for the education of their children, 4) Reduce the role of government to the defense of property rights, 5) Require "tithes" to ecclesiastical agencies to provide welfare services, 6) Close prisons—reinstitute slavery as a form of punishment and require capital punishment for all of ancient Israel's capital offenses—including apostacy [*sic*], blasphemy, incorrigibility in children, murder, rape, Sabbath breaking, sodomy, and witchcraft.

Some Reconstructionists realize that, sooner or later, there is bound to be a backlash against the kind of society that they intend to create. Many seem to be biding their time until public sentiment turns decisively against the kind of reforms they are seeking. When that happens, I believe that some, if given the opportunity, will be willing to take up arms and wage another civil war. Some of their literature indicates that they believe that such actions can be morally and theologically justified if they follow a lesser magistrate (like the Governor of a state) who claims to be following biblical law while refusing to submit to a rule of law that is imposed by a secular constitutional authority. This kind of crisis could easily be precipitated by the Governor of a state, like Alabama, refusing to execute a Court order to remove a Ten Commandments monument from state government property.[20]

Even if there weren't a lot of religious fanatics at the helm today, they would still be driven by neoliberalism's logic to use the stick increasingly in place of the carrot, which is why Clinton, for example, advocated the death penalty, sought to put a hundred thousand more cops on the streets, went after welfare, pushed NAFTA, and engaged in rendition. During the Clinton-Gore years the biggest gap in history between the wealthy and the poor opened up, only to be subsequently exceeded by Bush-Cheney. Which brings us to the matter of the Democrats.

Even if somehow the Democrats miraculously win the next presidential election, and even if, hypothetically, the Democratic president wishes to curb the radical-right's agenda, the radical right has entrenched itself so thoroughly and strategically in the government, in the military, in business, and in the media that any moves to curb its power and its agenda will be met with the ferocity of a really pissed-off vampire. Look at how angry and vituperative its practitioners are right now, and they have power! Remember how they succeeded in impeaching Clinton even though only 26 percent of the public supported the idea at the time.

Moreover, even if, for the sake of argument, the Democrats were to be alone in power, and the GOP and its theocratic fascist minions were to disappear overnight in a rapture, consider what has been happening internationally over the last thirty years or so. Social democrats worldwide, who are *far* more left wing than our Democratic Party, have been moving to the right as they "adjust" to the dictates of globalization. Neoliberalism is ascendant worldwide and public-order policies are the rule. In other words, the welfare state worldwide has been under fire and is steadily being dismantled. Social democracy accepts the fundamental "rightness" of capitalism and seeks merely to ameliorate its worst effects. *The solution to the issues of our day thus involves breaking decisively with things as they are and taking things in an entirely different direction.*

During the 1960s' Chinese Cultural Revolution revolutionaries had a slogan that applies to our situation today: "Cast Away Illusions, Prepare for Struggle!" As we stand here, history shall judge us. Did we stick our heads in the sand while the theocratic fascists and imperialists proceeded in consolidating power and preventing any opportunity for opposition to arise, or did we recognize the signs, act decisively and without fear? We either drive this regime from power and repudiate the whole movement of which it is the titular head—*something we cannot possibly achieve without also creating a wholly different political dynamic and bringing very large new forces into political motion and life here and around the world*—OR they get to bring down on our heads this heinous new world where truth is falsehood, science is the work of the devil, abortion is criminalized, women are forced back into their "place," torture is the norm, war is peace, and black is white.

This is a fight that must be engaged fully over the next several years and will decide our country's future and very possibly the future of this planet.

Notes:

1.   Eric Heubeck, "The Integration of Theory and Practice: A Program for the New Traditionalist Movement," http://www.theocracywatch.org/yurica_weyrich_manual.htm.

2. See, for example, Steven Kinzer, "Feels Like the Third Time," *The American Prospect* online edition, June 11, 2004, at http://www.prospect.org/web/view-web.ww?id=7829. See also, for example, http://www.rense.com/general19/flame.htm.
3. Limbaugh on May 4, 2004 on Abu Ghraib:
    "This is no different than what happens at the Skull and Bones initiation, and we're going to ruin people's lives over it, and we're going to hamper our military effort, and then we are going to really hammer them because they had a good time. You know, these people are being fired at every day. I'm talking about people having a good time, these people, you ever heard of emotional release? You [ever] heard of [the] need to blow some steam off?" http://www.cbsnews.com/stories/2004/05/06/opinion/meyer/main616021.shtml.
4. Jonah Goldberg, "The Gospel According to Me," *National Review* online, June 18, 2004, at http://www.nationalreview.com/goldberg/goldberg200406181453.asp.
5. January 5, 2003, issue.
6. Michael Ignatieff, "Lesser Evils," *New York Times Magazine*, May 2, 2004, http://www.ksg.harvard.edu/news/opeds/2004/ignatieff_less_evils_nytm_050204.htm.
7. See Howard Friel and Richard Falk, *The Record of the Paper: How the New York Times Misreports Foreign Policy*.
8. "US used front companies to hide CIA flights," *Expatica*, April 5, 2006: http://www.expatica.com/source/site_article.asp?subchannel_id=52&story_id=29054.
9. David Holley and Paul Richter, "Rice Fails to Clarify US View on Torture," *Los Angeles Times*, December 8, 2005, at http://www.truthout.org/docs_2005/120805K.shtml.
10. His signing statement read in relevant part: "in a manner consistent with the constitutional authority of the president to supervise the unitary executive branch . . . and consistent with the constitutional limitations on the judicial power."
11. Mike Allen and Dana Priest, "Memo on Torture Draws Focus to Bush: Aide Says President Set Guidelines for Interrogations, Not Specific Techniques," *Washington Post*, June 9, 2004; Page A03, http://www.washingtonpost.com/wp-dyn/articles/A26401-2004Jun8.html.
12. http://www.truthout.org/docs_2005/101805I.shtml.
13. In his article "Stripping Rumsfeld and Bush of Impunity," Matthew Rothschild wrote,

> The first solid piece of evidence against Bush is his September 17, 2001, "Memorandum of Notification" that unleashed the CIA. According to Bob Woodward's book *Bush at War*, that memo "authorized the CIA to operate freely and fully in Afghanistan with its own paramilitary teams" and to go after al-Qaeda "on a worldwide scale, using lethal covert action to keep the role of the United States hidden."
>
> Two days before, at Camp David, then-CIA Director George Tenet had outlined some of the additional powers he wanted, Woodward writes. These included the power to " 'buy' key intelligence services. . . . Several intelligence services were listed: Egypt, Jordan, Algeria. Acting as surrogates for the United States, these services could triple or quadruple the CIA's resources." According to Woodward, Tenet was upfront with Bush about the risks entailed: "It would put the United States in league with questionable intelligence services, some of them with dreadful human rights records. Some had reputations for ruthlessness and using torture to obtain confessions. Tenet acknowledged that these were not people you were likely to be sitting next to in church on Sunday. Look, I don't control these guys all the time, he said. Bush said he understood the risks."
>
> That this was administration policy is clear from comments Vice President Dick Cheney made on Meet the Press the very next day.
>
> "We also have to work, though, sort of the dark side, if you will," Cheney told

Tim Russert. "We've got to spend time in the shadows in the intelligence world. A lot of what needs to be done here will have to be done quietly, without any discussion, using sources and methods that are available to our intelligence agencies, if we're going to be successful. That's the world these folks operate in, and so it's going to be vital for us to use any means at our disposal, basically, to achieve our objective." (*The Progressive*, July 2005, http://www.truthout.org/cgi-bin/artman/exec/view.cgi/38/11451, accessed March 11, 2006.)

14. David Cole, "Terror: the Bush Deception," *New York Review of Books*, March 9, 2006, p. 17.
15. http://www.truthout.org/docs_04/printer_101704A.shtml.
16. See Jacob S. Hacker and Paul Pierson, *Off Center: The Republican Revolution and the Erosion of American Democracy*.
17. *The New York Times*, Editorial, "Judge Alito, in His Own Words," January 12, 2006, http://www.truthout.org/cgi-bin/artman/exec/view.cgi/48/16903.
18. http://www.theocracywatch.org/#How.
19. *The Changing of the Guard, Biblical Principles for Political Action*, pp. 50—51, http://www.serve.com/thibodep/cr/worldcnq.htm and cited on theocracywatch.org.
20. http://www.talk2action.org/story/2005/11/26/01436/229.

Chapter 6

IRAQ
Phase Two in an Unbounded War on the World

Larry Everest

HELEN THOMAS: I'd like to ask you, Mr. President, your decision to invade Iraq has caused the deaths of thousands of Americans and Iraqis, wounds of Americans and Iraqis for a lifetime. Every reason given, publicly at least, has turned out not to be true. My question is, why did you really want to go to war? From the moment you stepped into the White House . . . what was your real reason? You have said it wasn't oil . . . it hasn't been Israel, or anything else. What was it?

GEORGE W. BUSH: "I didn't want war. To assume I wanted war is just flat wrong, Helen, in all due respect. . . . No President wants war. Everything you may have heard is that, but it's just simply not true.[1]

Three years after invading Iraq, President George W. Bush continues to lie about his administration's reasons for war and its goals in Iraq. As one administration lie after another is exposed, and as it becomes clearer that the U.S. invasion and occupation are creating a brutal nightmare for most Iraqis, public opinion has turned against the war. Yet most still don't have a clear answer to Helen Thomas' question—why *did* the Bush administration launch the war? Nor, consequently, do they understand how profoundly illegal, immoral, and unjust this war and occupation really are.

No current-day Daniel Ellsberg has yet leaked an Iraq-war equivalent of the Pentagon Papers, revealing the government's actual reasons for the invasion.

The administration continues to distort, dissemble, spin, and cover up. Meanwhile the mainstream media and leading Democrats expose and criticize some aspects of the war but refuse to get to the bottom of the enormous deceptions perpetrated to justify it or to expose its true objectives.

Nonetheless, putting together what has been revealed about the record of U.S. actions in Iraq in the 1990s, what is known of Saddam Hussein's WMD programs, the timeline of George W. Bush's decision to go to war, and the strategic thinking of the administration and its dominant figures, the following coherent picture emerges:

- *The U.S. government openly debated and actually attempted to overthrow the Hussein regime for a decade before 9/11*, but not because Iraq posed a military threat or was linked to al-Qaeda. Instead, the U.S. establishment felt that Hussein's regime was undermining its control of the Middle East and impeding its ambitions globally. These were also the core motives for the 2003 war.
- The chronology of Bush's decision to wage war demonstrates that his administration saw 9/11 as an opportunity to invade Iraq as part of a sweeping global agenda long in the works. It cynically used that day's horror to create political support for a war that had nothing to do with preventing such attacks in the future. *The decision to invade Iraq was made by November 2001*, nearly a year before the U.S. attempted to secure the United Nation's sanction of approval in the fall of 2002.
- *The Bush administration's rationalizations for war were deliberate, conscious lies, not an "intelligence failure."* The U.S. and the international community knew that Iraq had been disarmed in the mid-1990s. There was no new evidence to suggest it had rearmed, and the government's own intelligence contradicted the administration's public claims regarding both WMD and Iraq's links to al-Qaeda. In short, the Bush team did not see Iraq as a "grave and gathering threat," but as a target in a broader agenda.
- "Operation Iraqi Freedom" was not waged to eliminate "terrorism," to destroy weapons of mass destruction, or to liberate Iraqis. It was phase two (after Afghanistan in October 2001) in a sweeping campaign, waged under the banner of a "war on terror," to redraw the world's geopolitical map and to solidify and extend U.S. imperial dominance. Occupying

Iraq was intended to tighten America's grip on the oil-rich Persian Gulf and to turn it into a beachhead for controlling the entire arc from North Africa to Central Asia (an effort now focused on Iran)—all to strengthen the U.S.'s hand against rivals, current and future.

- International law and the United Nations Charter provide for only two legal reasons to go to war—individual or collective self-defense in response to an armed attack or an action authorized by the United Nations Security Council. The U.S. had neither, making its 2003 war on Iraq an illegal act of unprovoked aggression—a war crime.

Targeting Iraq—A Decade Before 9/11

The drumbeat for war on Iraq began nearly ten years before September 11, 2001, within the highest levels of the U.S. political establishment. Since the end of World War II, dominating the Middle East and controlling its vast oil supplies have been crucial to U.S. foreign policy under eleven different presidents, Democrat and Republican. Why? Primarily because global capitalism in this era is fueled and lubricated by oil.[2]

Of the world's raw materials, none is more vital to economies, armies, and governments. Petroleum is an essential economic input whose price impacts production costs, profits, and competitive advantage. It is an instrument of rivalry: controlling oil means exercising leverage over those who depend on it and over the world economy as a whole. And it is impossible to project military power globally without abundant supplies of oil. In sum, petroleum, *as one 1944 State Department memo candidly acknowledged, is "a stupendous source of strategic power, and one of the greatest material prizes in world history."*[3]

The heart of the world petroleum industry lies in the Persian Gulf, with 65 percent of the world's known oil reserves, 34 percent of the world's natural gas reserves, and nearly 30 percent of the world's output of each.[4] As the world's thirst for petroleum has grown, so has the Gulf's strategic import.

In pursuit of dominating this region, the U.S. has for decades acted covertly and overtly, employing the carrot of aid and the stick of military assault—installing and overthrowing governments; building Israel into a regional gendarme; exerting economic, political, and military pressure; waging wars; even threatening the use of nuclear weapons. In Iraq, this effort led to helping bring Hussein to power in the 1960s; using, then betraying, the Kurds in the 1970s; and encouraging Iraq's invasion of Iran as well as its acquisition and use of chemical and biological weapons in the 1980s—the very crimes George W. Bush cited as justifications for the 2003 war.

Iraq's invasion of Kuwait in 1990 threatened to upset the U.S.-dominated regional status quo. Yet the goals of George H.W. Bush's administration in the 1991 Persian Gulf War were never limited to its stated objective of expelling Hussein's forces and returning to the status quo ante, but were far broader. Coming when the Soviet Union was spiraling into crisis, "Operation Desert Storm" was an attempt to deepen U.S. regional hegemony and usher in a "new world order" of unfettered American global dominance, as envisioned by the first President Bush's strategists, including Dick Cheney, Paul Wolfowitz, and Lewis Libby. These objectives demanded crushing Iraq as a regional power, removing Saddam Hussein from power (while leaving the Ba'athist state in place), and forcefully demonstrating U.S. military might to the world. "We have to have a war," George H.W. Bush secretly told his war cabinet.[5] The Pentagon later called Desert Storm "a defining event in United States global leadership."[6]

Yet matters didn't work out as planned. Despite a massive bombing campaign that savaged Iraq's military as well as its civilian infrastructure and killed between 100,000 and 200,000 Iraqis, Saddam Hussein remained. Nor did he fall after a decade of crippling sanctions, coup plots, assassination attempts, and frequent American and British bombing strikes.

The Bush I, Clinton, and Bush II administrations all claimed that tensions with Iraq were caused by Hussein's refusal to comply with United Nations resolutions and disarm. This was a lie, a decade-long lie repeated by government officials and the U.S. media alike.

In reality Iraq did disarm, and the international community knew it. In October 1998 the International Atomic Energy Agency certified that Iraq had provided it with a "full, final, and complete" account of its nuclear-weapons programs and that the agency had found no evidence of any prohibited nuclear activities since October 1997.[7] A year later, the United Nations Security Council's disarmament panel concluded, "Although important elements still have to be resolved, the bulk of Iraq's proscribed weapons programmes has been eliminated."[8]

Testifying before the January 2006 International Commission of Inquiry on Crimes Against Humanity by the Bush Administration, former lead United Nations weapons inspector Scott Ritter stated:

While there may have been uncertainty about the final disposition of the totality of Iraq's WMD programs, the entire world including the CIA acknowledged that the United Nations' weapons inspectors had, by 1998, accounted for 95–98% of Iraq's declared stockpiles. There was uncertainty regarding the final disposition of this 5–2% that could not be absolutely verified, but there was no nation, and I will say that again, no nation including the United States, that had any hard factual data to sustain the argument that Iraq a) retained weapons of mass destruction, or b) was actively reconstituting weapons of mass destruction.[9]

The distortions continue. The post-2003 invasion failure to find chemical, biological, or nuclear weapons has strikingly not prompted any in the mainstream media to raise the obvious question: if Iraq didn't have banned weapons, why were sanctions continued—sanctions that killed between one and two millions Iraqis, mainly children and the elderly?[10] (Nor does the media ever mention sanctions' devastating impact when discussing the crippled state of Iraq's economy today.)

Bait & Switch: Seizing Upon 9/11 to Attack Iraq

[T]he process of transformation, even if it brings revolutionary change, is likely to be a long one, absent some catastrophic and catalyzing event—like a new Pearl Harbor.
—"Rebuilding America's Defenses, Strategy,
Forces and Resources For a New Century,"
Project for a New American Century, September 2000 [11]

The Pearl Harbor of the 21st century took place today.
—Diary entry of President George W. Bush, September 11, 2001 [12]

The timeline of Bush's decision to attack Iraq also illuminates the depth of its deceptions and its actual motives for war. Although Bush and his top officials repeatedly cited 9/11 as a justification for the 2003 invasion, they had been trying to find ways to remove Hussein as soon as they took office—nine months before the Towers fell. And then they began planning for war on Iraq immediately after September 11, even though they knew Iraq was not involved and had not rearmed.

Bush's seizure of the presidency in 2000 brought those clamoring for more aggressive action against Iraq—and the world—back into power, and half of their first national-security meeting was spent on Iraq and the Persian Gulf.[13] At the Pentagon, Rumsfeld and Wolfowitz immediately began studying military options for ousting Hussein.[14]

U.S. intelligence had been attempting to link Iraq to al-Qaeda since the first World Trade Center bombing in 1993, but there was no evidence of a connection.[15] Nonetheless, "when the Bush administration took office in 2001," according to the *Wall Street Journal*, "officials at the Pentagon immediately began peppering intelligence agencies with requests for studies on Baghdad's links to terrorism."[16]

Some five hours after hijacked jets crashed into the World Trade Center and then the Pentagon, Rumsfeld told an aide to begin drawing up plans for war—on Iraq. That afternoon the CIA concluded that it was "virtually certain" that the bin Laden network was responsible, not Iraq or other states,[17] but Rumsfeld wanted to know if U.S. intelligence was also "good enough to hit S.H. [Saddam Hussein] at same time. Not only UBL [OBL—Osama bin Laden]." His admonition: "Go massive. Sweep it all up. Things related and not."[18]

Bush and his war cabinet discussed the need to act quickly "to capitalize on international outrage about the terrorist attack."[19] They realized that the attacks gave them a once-in-a-lifetime political opening to act forcefully to "shift the tectonic plates" of global power. One top Bush official who wished to remain anonymous told *The New Yorker's* Nicholas Lemann that September 11 was a "transformative moment," not because it "revealed the existence of a threat of which officials had previously been unaware," but because it "drastically reduced the American public's usual resistance to American military involvement overseas, at least for a while. . . . Now that the United States has been attacked, the options are much broader."[20]

In his book *Plan of Attack*, Woodward confirms that Bush was fixated on Iraq and that by Thanksgiving of 2001 he had told Donald Rumsfeld to prepare a plan for an invasion.[21] On September 12, 2002, *USA Today* reported,

"President Bush's determination to oust Iraq's Saddam Hussein by military force if necessary was set last fall. . . . He decided that Saddam must go more than 10 months ago . . . the president's determination to oust Saddam—the decision he made in the seven weeks following the attacks on Sept. 11—hasn't wavered."[22]

War First, Evidence Later—Or Not

The Bush case against Iraq rested on two lies, repeated early and often: first, that Saddam Hussein was linked to al-Qaeda and the attacks of September 11; and second that his possession of dangerous chemical, biological, and possibly nuclear weapons posed a "grave and growing danger" to the Middle East and to the United States itself. Bush raised the specter that Iraq "could provide these arms to terrorists, giving them the means to match their hatred. . . . The price of indifference would be catastrophic."[23] He also made the Hussein-al-Qaeda link by repeatedly mentioning September 11 in one breath and Iraq in the next, a textbook case of bait-and-switch.

The Bush administration's charges against Iraq were presented in great detail, as concrete immediate threats, not broad general concerns. In his January 2003 State of the Union speech, Bush warned that Saddam Hussein had or could have "biological weapons materials sufficient to produce over 25,000 liters of anthrax; enough doses to kill several million people . . . materials sufficient to produce more than 38,000 liters of botulinum toxin; enough to subject millions of people to death by respiratory failure . . . materials to produce as much as 500 tons of sarin, mustard and VX nerve agent . . . upwards of 30,000 munitions capable of delivering chemical agents." He claimed that during the 1990s the Hussein regime had "an advanced nuclear weapons development program," and then uttered what would become his sixteen infamous words: "The British government has learned that Saddam Hussein recently sought significant quantities of uranium from Africa."[24]

Every single one of these charges, without exception, has now been proved to be untrue, including by the Bush administration's own Iraq Survey Team (IST). The IST scoured Iraq for WMD for nearly two years and found, among other things: Iraq did not possess any WMD stockpiles at the time of the U.S. invasion; Iraq had not started any efforts to reconstitute its nuclear, chemical, or biological weapons program; and it had, as Ritter long insisted, destroyed its WMDs by 1995.[25]

The administration has tried to explain away the stunning conflict between its prewar charges and the utter absence of WMD in Iraq as an honest error— an "intelligence failure" shared by the rest of the international community. In reality the focus on "intelligence failures," a major theme of official and media discussions, doesn't represent an honest admission of error. It's an effort to cover up the fact that the administration knew Iraq had disarmed by the mid-1990s, had no new evidence to the contrary, and knowingly lied about Iraq's weapons to obscure the administration's real reasons for war.

"No nation supported the Bush administration's contention that Iraq maintained viable massive stockpiles of weapons of mass destruction at any time from 1998 up until the eve of the invasion in March of 2003," Scott Ritter states. "We need to make it clear that there was no intelligence failure. The policy was regime change. The intelligence failure was actually an intelligence success, because it was the job of the CIA to put forward a misrepresentation of the facts. The CIA actively suppressed data which sustained Iraq's contention that it had unilaterally disarmed in the summer of 1991."[26]

In the early months of the Bush administration Colin Powell and Condoleezza Rice both admitted as much: On February 24, 2001, Powell stated, "He [Saddam Hussein] has not developed any significant capability with respect to weapons of mass destruction. He is unable to project conventional power against his neighbors." On July 29, 2001, Rice said, "Saddam does not control the northern part of the country. We are able to keep his arms from him. His military forces have not been rebuilt."[27]

The Bush administration's own intelligence—all classified before the war, but some of which has since become public—also contradicted its public charges concerning Iraq's links with al-Qaeda and its WMD capabilities. Here are some key examples (and there are many more).

Links to al-Qaeda:

- In 2002 the *New York Times* reported that the CIA has "no evidence that Iraq has engaged in terrorist operations against the United States in nearly a decade, and the agency is also convinced that President Saddam Hussein has not provided chemical or biological weapons to Al Qaeda or related terrorist groups."[28] This assessment was upheld by

the congressional commission set up in February 2002 to investigate
the 9/11 attacks, which found no Iraqi connection.[29]

- A February 2002 report by the Defense Intelligence Agency (DIA), the
Pentagon's primary intelligence arm, identified a White House source
of the claim that Iraq had trained al-Qaeda members to use biological
and chemical weapons as a likely fabricator, and concluded that he was
intentionally misleading his interrogators. The *New York Times* reports
that as an official intelligence report "the document would have circu-
lated widely within the government, and it would have been available to
the CIA, the White House, and other agencies."[30]

WMD:

- A September 2002 assessment by the Defense Intelligence Agency concluded that there was "no definitive, reliable information" that Iraq either
possessed or was manufacturing chemical or biological weapons.[31]
- In February 2002 former Ambassador Joseph Wilson traveled to Niger
at the behest of the CIA to investigate the claim that Iraq had attempted
to buy uranium; he found that it was "highly doubtful that any such
transaction had ever taken place" and reported as much to the Bush
administration.[32]
- "The CIA sent two memos to the White House in October [2002] voic-
ing strong doubts about a claim President Bush made three months
later in the State of the Union address that Iraq was trying to buy nuclear
material in Africa," the *Washington Post* reported.[33] That same month
the administration, including Bush himself, reviewed a summary of
a National Intelligence Estimate (NIE) that noted a sharp debate on
whether aluminum tubes possessed by Iraq were for the purpose of
developing a nuclear weapon.[34]
- The Downing Street memos prove that the Bush administration knew
Iraq was not a threat but had decided to go to war anyway: "the intelligence and facts were being fixed around policy. . . . Saddam was not
threatening his neighbors and his WMD capability was less than that of
Libya, North Korea, or Iran."[35]

The still-unfolding Plame scandal demonstrates that the Bush administration was fully aware of just how hollow its "evidence" against Iraq was, and

how far it was willing to go to suppress that truth. It was triggered in July 2003 when Joseph Wilson went public about his 2002 trip to Niger—that Bush claims that Iraq had tried to buy uranium were false and that he had reported as much to the CIA in February 2002.

Almost immediately an effort swung into gear to discredit and intimidate Wilson by leaking the identity of his wife, CIA agent Valerie Plame—a crime under U.S. law. Administration officials suggested that Wilson couldn't be trusted because Plame might have helped in selecting him for the Niger mission. Both Lewis Libby and Karl Rove spoke with reporters (Judith Miller and Robert Novak) about this matter shortly before Plame was publicly named in an article by Novak.[36]

Vice President Cheney's top assistant, Lewis "Scooter" Libby has since been charged by a special prosecutor with perjury and obstruction of justice for denying under oath that he disclosed Plame's CIA employment to journalists. It has also been revealed by Libby that Bush himself authorized the declassification of previously secret intelligence on Iraq to defend his decision to go to war, and that he did so when that intelligence had already been questioned within the administration.[37]

In reality and all along the administration saw a weakened Iraq—a country of 25 million, the size of the State of California, which had been battered by twenty-plus years of war and twelve years of sanctions—as a target of opportunity, not a growing threat.[38]

Iraq and Empire

If all the Bush administration's declared reasons for war have been lies, what, then, were its real motives? This question remains unanswered for most people because the mainstream media and Democratic Party critics have refused to expose the link between the Bush regime's avowed strategy of being the world's dominant imperial superpower and the invasion of Iraq. But the Iraq war can only be understood in the context of this overall agenda.

This agenda's core thesis is that the 1991 Soviet collapse had left the U.S. the world's only superpower—with both an enormous opportunity to expand its power and a great necessity to head off future challenges. This has been a central theme in neoconservative theorizing for over a decade beginning with the 1992 Cheney-Libby-Wolfowitz Defense Guidance paper, continuing with the Project for a New American Century's 2000 paper, "Rebuilding America's Defenses," and culminating in the Bush National Security Strategies (NSS) of 2002 and 2006.[39]

The current U.S. ambassador to Iraq, Zalmay Khalilzad, succinctly spelled out this thinking in a 1995 brief for U.S. global hegemony—"From Containment to Global Leadership." Among the new dangers confronting the U.S. imperialists, Khalilzad included the potential for "major regional conflicts, attempts at regional hegemony, and proliferation of weapons of mass destruction," as well as "chaos and fragmentation within states" and possibilities ranging from a "growing number of small wars" to "Russian reimperialization and Chinese expansionism."

Khalilzad noted that "economic growth under way in Asia . . . will produce important changes in relative economic power—with important potential geopolitical and military implications" and "intensified international economic competition." He called China "the most likely candidate" for a global rival. "Over the longer term—the next twenty years—there is a real possibility of efforts by China or Russia or a coalition of states to balance the power of the United States and its allies."

Khalilzad argued that the U.S. should focus on preventing others from having "hegemony over critical regions," including the Persian Gulf. He concluded: "The United States should also resolve to maintain its position of global leadership and preclude the rise of another global rival for the indefinite future. It is an opportunity the nation may never see again."[40]

Bush's 2002 NSS made this strategic vision official policy, arguing that the U.S. had "unparalleled military strength and great economic and political influence"—and that American policy should be to "work to translate this moment of influence into decades of peace, prosperity, and liberty."[41]

The substance of the NSS makes clear that "liberty" means the freedom of American capitalism, its dominant corporate financial elite in particular, to impose its values, interests, and economic system on all others. As the NSS baldly put it, "These values of freedom are right and true for every person, in every society."

The strategy calls for maintaining overwhelming military superiority over all other countries and eliminating challengers before they emerge. It advocates greater freedom for U.S. business and accelerated capitalist globalization, stating that the U.S. will "use this moment of opportunity" to extend "free markets, and free trade to every corner of the world." And it and the Cheney report call for enhancing "energy security" by expanding "the sources and types of global energy supplied, especially in the Western Hemisphere, Africa, Central Asia, and the Caspian region."[42]

In sum, the Bush doctrine calls for striking down adversaries, large and small, and radically recasting global political, military, and economic relations. America's imperial rulers have, as Bob Avakian presciently put it shortly after September 11, "ambitions of essentially reshuffling the whole deck, reordering the whole situation, beginning with the strategic areas of Central and South Asia and the Middle East . . . but, even beyond that, on a world scale."[43] The enormity and sweep of these ambitions prompted the Nobel laureate Harold Pinter to note, "The Bush Administration is the most dangerous force that has ever existed. It is more dangerous than Nazi Germany because of the range and depth of its activities and intentions worldwide."[44]

Why was conquering Iraq key to this agenda, not a "diversion"? Removing Hussein was seen as heading off a U.S. defeat should sanctions crumble, preventing other powers from gaining ground in Iraq, eliminating a potential threat to Israel, and strengthening U.S. control of the Middle East.

Occupying Iraq could give the U.S. direct control of the world's second-largest oil reserves and places its armed forces in the center of the Persian Gulf-Central Asian region, home to some 80 percent of the world's energy reserves. Control of the global flow of oil and natural gas could give the U.S. enormous leverage over Russia, France, Germany, China, Japan, and others.

U.S. actions during the occupation, including its continuing commission of war crimes against the Iraqi population,[45] also flow from its grand strategy—not from its rhetoric of "liberating" Iraqis. For instance, U.S. pro-counsel Paul Bremer enacted a series of "orders," in line with the NSS's goal of opening new areas to U.S. and global capital. His orders dismantled Iraq's state sector and restructured its economy along neoliberal lines—lowering the corporate tax rate, creating a framework for privatization, providing for 100 percent foreign ownership of Iraqi assets, and allowing 100 percent profit repatriation for foreign investors and banks.[46] And the U.S. may now be in the process of building permanent military bases in Iraq.[47]

The Iraq invasion is not a single, discrete war, as was Vietnam, but one part of a much broader imperial crusade, as the current threats against Iran so chillingly demonstrate.[48] For all these reasons the U.S. must leave Iraq now. Every day it remains in Iraq, it will pursue this agenda, whatever tactical adjustments it's forced to make.

While the Bush administration insists that it will stay the course, leading Republican and Democrat "critics" of the war argue that the U.S. must not lose or "precipitously" withdraw. This argument reflects an underlying agreement with the unjust objective of maintaining U.S. regional and global dominance (which is never questioned), even as the critics have tactical and strategic differences with Bush over how to do so. This is why the Democrats voted for the war in 2002, continue to authorize funding for it, and now refuse to speak out against Bush's threatened attack, or war, on Iran.

These "critics" often raise the specter of civil war if the U.S. military were to pull out. But it's the U.S. invasion and occupation that have unleashed and fueled an incipient civil war. It may or may not intensify with the end of the occupation, and if it did, it would be a horror for Iraqis. Yet continuing the occupation and allowing the Bush administration to complete its "mission" would be even worse. It would guarantee ongoing bloodshed and torture by the U.S. and its Iraqi allies. It would mean forging a pro-U.S. neocolony and strengthening the oppression of the Iraqi people in many ways, for decades to come. It would turn Iraq into a staging ground for U.S. intrigue and aggression across the region.

Bush's Criminal Doctrine of "Preemptive" War

The Bush regime's staggering ambitions demand staggering methods—trampling on international law, casting aside global treaties, and eviscerating international organizations. It also means radically restructuring governing norms at home, including undermining the rule of law, eroding civil liberties, breaking down the separation of church and state, and vastly extending presidential power.

Take current international law as one example. It is not, in my view, the ultimate arbiter of what's just and what's not; for instance, the 1991 Persian Gulf War did have United Nations sanction but was still a war whose aims were predatory and unjust. International law is, however, an important measure of the breathtaking lawlessness and profound immorality of the Bush regime.

In its 2002 NSS the Bush administration officially enshrined an Orwellian doctrine of "pre-emptive self-defense" in flagrant violation of international laws and treaties to which the U.S. is a signatory. The NSS states, "America will act against such emerging threats before they are fully formed. . . . We will not hesitate to act alone, if necessary, to exercise our right of self-defense by acting preemptively." In other words, the U.S. has given itself the "right" to launch attacks on other countries without warning, evidence of threat, provocation or international approval.

Even former Secretary of State Henry Kissinger acknowledged that this new doctrine violates 400 years of international law and custom:

> Regime change as a goal for military intervention challenges the international system established by the 1648 Treaty of Westphalia, which established the principle of nonintervention in the domestic affairs of other states. Also, the notion of justified preemption runs counter to modern international law, which sanctions the use of force in self-defense only against actual—not potential—threats.[49]

Many countries have violated international law and waged illegal wars; none in memory has attempted to openly legitimize its right to do so. As the International Commission of Inquiry concluded, "As part of an illegal doctrine of 'preemptive war,' based on deliberate and conscious lies, and with no legitimate claim of self defense, the Bush administration planned, prepared and waged the supreme crime of a war of aggression in contravention of the United Nations Charter, the 1949 Geneva Convention [2] and the Nuremberg Principles."[50]

Bush—and His Agenda—Must Go

Given the criminality of the Iraq war, the predatory imperialist agenda driving it, and the future wars of aggression it guarantees, it is imperative that the Bush administration be driven from power and its whole program, including the so-called war on terror, repudiated.

This rejection cannot be done by criticizing the administration for not waging the war "competently" or not having a strategy for victory. This reproach is simply a call for more efficiently waging an illegal, immoral, and unjust war, which will only mean new horrors and forms of oppression for the Iraqi people. Nor can it be opposed by debating whether the invasion of Iraq is a diversion from the "war on terror." This argument means accepting the framework of George W. Bush's global agenda and the legitimacy of an unbounded imperial war against whomever the administration chooses.

Nor can it be done by simply relying on the powers that be, business as usual, or normal channels in the vain hope that they will set things right. All the institutions of the established order—the Republican and Democratic parties, all branches of government, the media, and the like—have proven unwilling and/or unable to hold Bush to account and to stop the war his administration has declared it will pursue for decades if need be.

Without an unprecedented, determined popular outpouring from below, beyond even what occurred in the 1960s, a massive and public declaration by millions that they refuse to allow this to continue, Bush will not be impeached, indicted, or forced to leave office. With such an outpouring, and the seismic political shift it would represent, all of these options come into view.

Will such a change be easy? Of course not. Can it be done without sacrifice? No. Is it possible? Yes. "The point is this: history is full of examples where people who had right on their side fought against tremendous odds and were victorious," as the World Can't Wait call puts it. "And it is also full of examples of people passively hoping to wait it out, only to get swallowed up by a horror beyond what they ever imagined. The future is unwritten. WHICH ONE WE GET IS UP TO US."[51]

Notes:

1. "Bush President Finally Calls on Helen Thomas, Says He Only Semi-Regrets It," *Editor & Publisher*, March 21, 2006.
2. For a more comprehensive discussion of the history of U.S. intervention in Iraq and the economic, political, and historic roots of the 2003 war, see my book, *Oil, Power & Empire: Iraq and the U.S. Global Agenda* (Monroe, ME: Common Courage Press, 2004).
3. Howard Zinn, *A People's History of the United States* (New York: Harper & Row, 1980), p. 404.
4. Energy Information Administration (EIA), "Persian Gulf Oil and Gas Exports Fact Sheet," April 2003, http://www.eia.doe.gov/emeu/cabs/pgulf.html.
5. Bob Woodward, *Shadow: Five Presidents and the Legacy of Watergate* (New York: Simon & Schuster, 1999), p. 185

6. Patrick E. Tyler, "U.S. Strategy Plan Calls for Insuring No Rivals Develop," *New York Times*, March 8, 1992. This vision was articulated most directly in the Defense Department's 1992 "Defense Planning Guidance." Written by Paul Wolfowitz, Lewis Libby, and Zalmay Khalilzad under the direction of then-Defense Secretary Dick Cheney—all later top officials in George W. Bush's administration—the document argued that the U.S. should insure "that no rival superpower is allowed to emerge in Western Europe, Asia or the territory of the former Soviet Union" and that the United States remain the world's predominant power for the indefinite future. The Defense Guidance envisioned accomplishing these far-reaching objectives by preemptively attacking rivals or states seeking weapons of mass destruction, strengthening U.S. control of Persian Gulf oil, and refusing to allow international coalitions or law to inhibit U.S. freedom of action. Steven R. Weisman, "Pre-emption: Idea With a Lineage Whose Time Has Come," *New York Times*, March 23, 2003.

7. Barbara Crossette, "Clean Bill for Iraqis on A-Arms? Experts Upset," *New York Times*, April 19, 1998.

8. FAIR Media Advisory, "Iraq's Hidden Weapons: From Allegation to Fact," February 4, 2003, www.fair.org/press-releases/iraq-weapons.html.

9. www.bushcommission.org. Ritter also testified that Iraq probably disarmed in 1991: "Hussein Kamal provided testimony, debriefings, to the United Nations Special Commission, to the CIA, and to British MI6 or the Secret Intelligence Service, in August 1995 . . . that all weapons of mass destruction—chemical, biological, nuclear and long-range ballistic missiles, were destroyed unilaterally by the Iraqi government in the summer of 1991. This is a finding, by the way, that has been certified by the Central Intelligence Agency, in specific the Iraq Survey Group, after the invasion of Iraq in March 2003. The CIA today states that the Iraqi government and indeed Hussein Kamal were telling the truth. All weapons were in fact destroyed in the summer of 1991." Former chief of the United Nations' inspection program Hans Blix shares Ritter's assessment that most of Iraq's WMDs "were discovered and destroyed by weapons inspectors and by Hussein Kamel, Saddam's son-in-law, in the early 1990s, after the Gulf War." Thane Peterson, "Hans Blix's Post-Mortem," *Business Week* online, March 26, 2004.

10. UNICEF and Government of Iraq Ministry of Health, "Child and Maternal Mortality Survey 1999: Preliminary Report," July 1999, www.unicef.org, Barbara Crossette, "Children's Death Rates Rising In Iraqi Lands, Unicef Reports," *New York Times*, August 13, 1999, p. A6.

11. www.newamericancentury.org/RebuildingAmericasDefenses.pdf, p. 51.

12. Dan Balz and Bob Woodward, "America's Chaotic Road to War—Bush's Global Strategy Began to Take Shape in First Frantic Hours After Attack," *Washington Post*, January 27, 2002, p. A1.

13. Eric Schmitt and James Dao, "Iraq is Focal Point as Bush Meets With Joint Chiefs," *New York Times*, January 11, 2001, p. A20.

14. Bob Woodward and Dan Balz, "At Camp David, Advise and Dissent—Bush, Aides Grapple With War Plan," *Washington Post*, January 31, 2002, p. A1.

15. Raymond Bonner, "Experts Doubt Iraq Had Role in Latest Terror Attacks," *New York Times*, October 11, 2001; David S. Cloud, "Bush's Efforts to Link Hussein To al Qaeda Lack Clear Evidence," *Wall Street Journal*, October 23, 2002.

16. Cloud, *Wall Street Journal*, October 23, 2002.

17. Woodward and Balz, *op cit.*, January 27, 2002.

18. "Plans for Iraq Attack Began on 9/11," CBS TV, *Evening News*, September 4, 2002.

19. Woodward and Balz, *op cit.*, January 27, 2002; Bob Woodward and Dan Balz, "'We Will Rally the World'—Bush and His Advisers Set Objectives, but Struggled With How to Achieve Them," *Washington Post*, January 28, 2002, p. A1.

20. Nicholas Lemann, "Next World Order," *The New Yorker*, April 1, 2002.

21. Bob Woodward, *Plan of Attack* (New York: Simon and Schuster, 2004), p. 120.

22. Diamond, et al., *USA Today*, September 11, 2002.

23. "Text of President Bush's State of the Union address," Associated Press, January 30, 2002.

24. "Bush's State of the Union speech," CNN.com, January 29, 2003.

25. The Iraq Survey Team (IST) was headed first by David Kay and later by Charles Duelfer. The October 2004 1500-page Duelfer Report went into even greater detail than the earlier Kay Report. Its conclusions included: (1) earlier suggestions by Kay that the Iraqi regime "could be producing 'test amounts' of chemical weapons and researching the use of ricin in weapons" were doubtful; (2) no evidence that so-called dual-use industrial equipment was being converted to weapons production; (3) no significant evidence that WMDs had been smuggled out of the country; (4) Iraq had destroyed its biological weapons stocks in 1995; (5) there was no evidence that Iraq had attempted to make any chemical weapons in twelve years. Julian Borger, "Iraq Had No WMD: The Final Verdict," *Guardian News*, September 18, 2004; Dana Priest and Walter Pincus, "U.S. Almost All Wrong on Weapons," *Washington Post*, October 7, 2004.

26. Ritter testimony, www.bushcommission.org. Ritter also testified that weapons of mass destruction were the only official U.S. justification for invading Iraq, as submitted in a letter from U.S. Ambassador John Negroponte to the United Nations Security Council on the eve of war. "In this letter, Ambassador Negroponte repeatedly refers to Iraq's refusal to disarm, the existence of weapons of mass destruction, and therefore the existence of a clear and present risk to international peace and security that warranted the use of military action on the part of the United States."

27. On May 15, 2001, Powell also stated, "Hussein had not been able to 'build his military back up or to develop weapons of mass destruction' for 'the last ten years.'" "Colin Powell said Iraq was no threat," John Pilger, *Daily Mirror*, September 22, 2003; Edward M. Gomez, "World Views: New 'Downing Street Memo' says Bush, Blair agreed on regime change in 2002," SF Gate.com, June 14, 2005.

28. James Risen, "Terror Acts by Baghdad Have Waned, U.S. Aides Say," *New York Times*, February 6, 2002.

29. "Commissioner: Bush Deliberately Delayed Inquiry Report Until After Iraq War," UPI, July 26, 2003.

30. Douglas Jehl, "2002 report doubted Iraq-al Qaeda informer," *San Francisco Chronicle*, November 6, 2005.

31. Bryan Bender, "Spy report saw no proof of Iraq arms," *Boston Globe*, June 7, 2003.

32. Joseph C. Wilson, "What I Didn't Find in Africa," *New York Times*, July 6, 2003.

33. Dana Milbank and Walter Pincus, "Bush Aides Disclose Warnings from the CIA," *Washington Post*, July 23, 2003.

34. Murray Waas, "Administration: What Bush Was Told About Iraq", *National Journal*, March 2, 2006.

35. In October 2001 the Bush administration set up a new intelligence-operations arm in the Pentagon—the Office of Special Plans—directly under the control of Deputy Defense Secretary Wolfowitz and Undersecretary of Defense for Policy Douglas Feith—precisely to "fix" the "intelligence" to justify war. (Jason Leopold, "CIA Probe Finds Secret Pentagon Group Manipulated Intelligence on Iraqi Threat," Antiwar.com, July 25, 2003; Julian Borger, "The spies who pushed for war," *Guardian*, (UK), July 17, 2003; Paul Pillar, the CIA's national intelligence officer for the Near East and South Asia from 2000 to 2005 and "considered the CIA's leading counter-terrorism analyst," charges that the administration was "cherry-picking," ignoring, and misusing intelligence in order to justify the invasion and downplay the difficulties of the subsequent occupation. Paul R. Pillar, "Intelligence, Policy, and the War in Iraq," *Foreign Affairs*, March/April 2006.

36. Murray Waas, "Prewar Intelligence: Insulating Bush," *National Journal*, March 30, 2006. The *Washington Post* reported in April 2006 that "Special Counsel Patrick J. Fitzgerald for the first time described a 'concerted action' by 'multiple people in the White House'—using classified information—to 'discredit, punish or seek revenge against' a critic of President Bush's war in Iraq. Barton Gellman and Dafna Linzer, "'Concerted Effort' to Discredit Bush Critic," *Washington Post*, April 9, 2006.

37. David Johnston and David E. Sanger, "Cheney's Aide Says President Approved Leak," *New York Times*, April 7, 2006; David E. Sanger and David Barstow, "Iraq Findings Leaked by Cheney's Aide Were Disputed," *New York Times*, April 9, 2006.

38. The *New York Times* reported in September 2002 that the "Bush administration's decision to force a confrontation . . . reflects its low regard for Iraq's conventional armed forces . . . American officials are confident that United States forces would quickly prevail" in war. Michael R. Gordon, "In Bush's Axis of Evil: Why Iraq Stands Out," *New York Times*, September 9, 2002.

39. PNAC's "Rebuilding America's Defenses" singled out Iran, Iraq, and North Korea as immediate targets nearly two years before Bush labeled them an axis of evil, and criticized previous Pentagon planning for giving "little or no consideration to the force requirements necessary not only to defeat an attack but to remove these regimes from power." (See "Rebuilding America's Defenses," pp. 2, 8, 16, 22, 51). Under George W. Bush, Cambone would become Undersecretary of Defense for Intelligence and Abram Shulsky, the Director of Pentagon Office of Special Plans—which helped create the phony "intelligence" used to rationalize the 2003 war on Iraq. Robert Kagan, William Kristol, and other right-wing luminaries also contributed to the study.

40. Zalmay M. Khalilzad, *From Containment to Global Leadership* (Santa Monica, CA: RAND, 1995), pp. 7–8, 30.

41. The White House, "The National Security Strategy of the United States of America," September 2002.

42. National Security Strategy 2002, pp.17, 19, 20.

43. Bob Avakian, "The New Situation and the Great Challenges," *Revolutionary Worker*, March 17, 2002, http://rwor.org/a/036/avakian-new-situation-great-challenges.htm.

44. Harold Pinter, October 31, 2005 message to World Can't Wait, "Voices Speak Out" at www.worldcantwait.net.

45. See Dahr Jamail chapter herein, and the work of the World Tribunal on Iraq (www.worldtribunal.org) and the International Commission of Inquiry on Crimes Against Humanity by the Bush administration (www.bushcommission.org).

46. Naomi Klein, "Baghdad Year Zero," *Harper's*, September 2004.

47. The BBC reports that "the Pentagon has requested hundreds of millions of dollars in emergency funds for military construction in Iraq . . . a 13 March report accompanying the emergency spending legislation . . . said that money was 'of a magnitude normally associated with permanent bases.'" Becky Branford, "Iraq bases spur questions over US plans," BBC News March 30, 2006.

48. "The Iran Plans," Seymour M. Hersh, *The New Yorker*, April 17, 2006.

49. Henry A. Kissinger, "Iraq 'regime change' is a revolutionary strategy," *San Francisco Chronicle*, August 9, 2002.

50. www.bushcommission.org.

51. www.worldcantwait.net.

Chapter 7

THE DOWNING STREET MEMOS, MANIPULATION OF PREWAR INTELLIGENCE, AND KNOWINGLY WITHHOLDING VITAL INFORMATION FROM A GRAND JURY INVESTIGATION

Greg Palast

Here it is. The smoking gun. The memo that has IMPEACH HIM written all over it.

The top-level government memo marked SECRET AND STRICTLY PERSONAL, dated eight months before Bush sent us into Iraq, following a closed meeting with the President, reads, "*Military action was now seen as inevitable. Bush wanted to remove Saddam through military action justified by the conjunction of terrorism and WMD. But the intelligence and facts were being fixed around the policy.*"

Read that again: "The intelligence and facts were being fixed . . ."

For years, after each damning report on BBC TV, viewers inevitably ask me, "Isn't this grounds for impeachment?"—vote rigging, a blind eye to terror and the bin Ladens before 9/11, and so on. Evil, stupidity, and self-dealing are shameful but not impeachable. What's needed is a "high crime or misdemeanor."

Well if this ain't it, nothing is.

The memo uncovered in May 2005 by the *London Times* goes on to describe an elaborate plan by George Bush and British Prime Minister Tony Blair to hoodwink the planet into supporting an attack on Iraq, though they knew full well that the evidence for war was phony.

A conspiracy to commit serial fraud is, under federal law, racketeering. However, the mob's schemes never cost so many lives.

Here's more: *"Bush had made up his mind to take military action. But the case was thin. Saddam was not threatening his neighbors, and his WMD capability was less than that of Libya, North Korea or Iran."*

Really? But Mr. Bush told us, "Intelligence gathered by this and other governments leaves no doubt that the Iraq regime continues to possess and conceal some of the most lethal weapons ever devised."

In April 2005 the Silberman-Robb Commission issued its report on WMD intelligence before the war, dismissing claims that Bush had fixed the facts, with this snooty, condescending conclusion, written directly to the President, "After a thorough review, the Commission found no indication that the Intelligence Community distorted the evidence regarding Iraq's weapons."

We now know that the report was a bogus 618 pages of thick whitewash, intended to let Bush off the hook for his murderous mendacity.

Read on: The invasion build-up was then set, states the memo, *"beginning 30 days before the US Congressional elections."* Mission accomplished.

You should parse the entire memo—reprinted below—and see if you can make it through its three pages without losing your lunch.

Now sharp readers may note that they didn't see this memo printed in the *New York Times.* It wasn't. Rather, it was splashed across the front pages of the *Times* of LONDON.

But in the U.S., barely a word. The *New York Times* covers this hard evidence of Bush's fabrication of a casus belli as some "British" elections story. Apparently, our President's fraud isn't "news fit to print."

My colleagues in the United Kingdom press have skewered Blair, digging out more incriminating memos, challenging the official government factoids and fibs. But in the U.S. press . . . nada, bubkes, zilch. Bush fixed the facts, and somehow that's a story for "over there."

The Republicans impeached Bill Clinton over his cigar and Monica's affections. And the U.S. media could print nothing else.

Now we have the stone-cold evidence of bending intelligence to sell us on death by the thousands of Americans and tens of thousands of Iraqis, and neither a Republican Congress, nor what is laughably called U.S. journalism, thought it worth a second look.

My friend Daniel Ellsberg once said that what's good about the American people is that you have to lie to them. What's bad about Americans is that it's so easy to do.

SECRET AND STRICTLY PERSONAL—UK EYES ONLY
DAVID MANNING
From: Matthew Rycroft
Date: 23 July 2002
S 195 /02
cc: Defence Secretary, Foreign Secretary, Attorney-General, Sir
Richard Wilson, John Scarlett, Francis Richards, CDS, C, Jonathan
Powell, Sally Morgan, Alastair Campbell

IRAQ: PRIME MINISTER'S MEETING, 23 JULY
Copy addressees and you met the Prime Minister on 23 July to
discuss Iraq.

This record is extremely sensitive. No further copies should be
made. It should be shown only to those with a genuine need to
know its contents.

John Scarlett summarised the intelligence and latest JIC assessment. Saddam's regime was tough and based on extreme fear.
The only way to overthrow it was likely to be by massive military
action. Saddam was worried and expected an attack, probably by
air and land, but he was not convinced that it would be immediate
or overwhelming. His regime expected their neighbours to line
up with the US. Saddam knew that regular army morale was poor.
Real support for Saddam among the public was probably narrowly
based.

C reported on his recent talks in Washington. There was a percep-
tible shift in attitude. Military action was now seen as inevitable.
Bush wanted to remove Saddam, through military action, justified
by the conjunction of terrorism and WMD. But the intelligence
and facts were being fixed around the policy. The NSC had no
patience with the UN route, and no enthusiasm for publishing
material on the Iraqi regime's record. There was little discussion
in Washington of the aftermath after military action.

CDS said that military planners would brief CENTCOM on 1–2 August, Rumsfeld on 3 August and Bush on 4 August.

The two broad US options were:

(a) Generated Start. A slow build-up of 250,000 US troops, a short (72 hour) air campaign, then a move up to Baghdad from the south. Lead time of 90 days (30 days preparation plus 60 days deployment to Kuwait).

(b) Running Start. Use forces already in theatre (3 x 6,000), continuous air campaign, initiated by an Iraqi casus belli. Total lead time of 60 days with the air campaign beginning even earlier. A hazardous option.

The US saw the UK (and Kuwait) as essential, with basing in Diego Garcia and Cyprus critical for either option. Turkey and other Gulf states were also important, but less vital. The three main options for UK involvement were:

(i) Basing in Diego Garcia and Cyprus, plus three SF squadrons.

(ii) As above, with maritime and air assets in addition.

(iii) As above, plus a land contribution of up to 40,000, perhaps with a discrete role in Northern Iraq entering from Turkey, tying down two Iraqi divisions.

The Defence Secretary said that the US had already begun "spikes of activity" to put pressure on the regime. No decisions had been taken, but he thought the most likely timing in US minds for military action to begin was January, with the timeline beginning 30 days before the US Congressional elections.

The Foreign Secretary said he would discuss this with Colin Powell this week. It seemed clear that Bush had made up his mind to take military action, even if the timing was not yet decided. But the case was thin. Saddam was not threatening his neighbours, and his WMD capability was less than that of Libya, North Korea or Iran. We should work up a plan for an ultimatum to Saddam to allow back in the UN weapons inspectors. This would also help with the legal justification for the use of force.

The Attorney-General said that the desire for regime change was not a legal base for military action. There were three possible legal bases: self-defence, humanitarian intervention, or UNSC authorisation. The first and second could not be the base in this case. Relying on UNSCR 1205 of three years ago would be difficult. The situation might of course change.

The Prime Minister said that it would make a big difference politically and legally if Saddam refused to allow in the UN inspectors. Regime change and WMD were linked in the sense that it was the regime that was producing the WMD. There were different strategies for dealing with Libya and Iran. If the political context were right, people would support regime change. The two key issues were whether the military plan worked and whether we had the political strategy to give the military plan the space to work.

On the first, CDS said that we did not know yet if the US battleplan was workable. The military were continuing to ask lots of questions.

For instance, what were the consequences, if Saddam used WMD on day one, or if Baghdad did not collapse and urban warfighting began? You said that Saddam could also use his WMD on Kuwait. Or on Israel, added the Defence Secretary.

The Foreign Secretary thought the US would not go ahead with a military plan unless convinced that it was a winning strategy. On this, US and UK interests converged. But on the political strategy, there could be US/UK differences. Despite US resistance, we should explore discreetly the ultimatum. Saddam would continue to play hard-ball with the UN.

John Scarlett assessed that Saddam would allow the inspectors back in only when he thought the threat of military action was real.

The Defence Secretary said that if the Prime Minister wanted UK military involvement, he would need to decide this early. He cautioned that many in the US did not think it worth going down the ultimatum route. It would be important for the Prime Minister to set out the political context to Bush.

Conclusions:

(a) We should work on the assumption that the UK would take part in any military action. But we needed a fuller picture of US planning before we could take any firm decisions. CDS should tell the US military that we were considering a range of options.

(b) The Prime Minister would revert on the question of whether funds could be spent in preparation for this operation.

(c) CDS would send the Prime Minister full details of the proposed military campaign and possible UK contributions by the end of the week.

(d) The Foreign Secretary would send the Prime Minister the background on the UN inspectors, and discreetly work up the ultimatum to Saddam.

He would also send the Prime Minister advice on the positions of countries in the region especially Turkey, and of the key EU member states.

(e) John Scarlett would send the Prime Minister a full intelligence update.

> (f) We must not ignore the legal issues: the Attorney-General would consider legal advice with FCO/MOD legal advisers.
>
> (I have written separately to commission this follow-up work.)
>
> MATTHEW RYCROFT

Rycroft was a Downing Street foreign policy aide.

Now to the above we must add the other evidence and secret memos and documents still hidden from the American public. Other foreign-based journalists could doubtlessly add more, including the disclosure that the key inspector of Iraq's biological weapons, the late Dr. David Kelly, found that the Bush-Blair analysis of his intelligence was indeed "fixed," as the Downing Street memo puts it, around the war-hawk policy. Here is a small timeline of confidential skullduggery dug up and broadcast by my own team for BBC Television and *Harper's* on the secret plans to seize Iraq's assets and oil.

February 2001

Only one month after the first Bush-Cheney inauguration, the State Department's Pam Quanrud organizes a secret confab in California to make plans for the invasion of Iraq and the removal of Saddam. U.S. oil industry advisor Falah Aljibury and others are asked to interview would-be candidates for a new U.S.-installed dictator.

On BBC Television's *Newsnight*, Iraq-born Aljibury himself explained about the early 2001 war plan, "It is an invasion, but it will act like a coup. The original plan was to liberate Iraq from the Saddamists and from the regime."

March 2001

Vice President Dick Cheney meets with oil-company executives and reviews oil-field maps of Iraq. Cheney refuses to release the names of those attending or their purpose. *Harper's* has since learned their plan and purpose: take out Saddam, who was jerking the world price of oil up and down, causing havoc for Big Oil.

October–November 2001

An easy military victory in Afghanistan emboldens then-Deputy Defense Secretary Paul Wolfowitz to convince the administration to junk the State Department "coup" plan in favor of an invasion and occupation that could remake the economy of Iraq. An elaborate plan, ultimately summarized in a 101-page document, scopes out the "sale of all state enterprises"—that is, most of the nation's assets, "especially in the oil and supporting industries."

2002

Grover Norquist and other corporate lobbyists meet secretly with Defense, State, and Treasury officials to ensure that the invasion plans for Iraq include plans for protecting "property rights." The result was a preinvasion scheme to sell off Iraq's oil fields, banks, and electricity systems, and even change the country's copyright laws to benefit the lobbyists' clients. Occupation chief Paul Bremer would later order these giveaways into Iraq law.

Fall 2002

Philip Carroll, former CEO of Shell Oil USA, is brought in by the Pentagon to plan the management of Iraq's oil fields. He works directly with Paul Wolfowitz and Douglas Feith. "There were plans," says Carroll, "maybe even too many plans"—but none disclosed to the public or even the U.S. Congress.

January 2003

Robert Ebel, former CIA oil analyst, is sent, the BBC learns, to London to meet with Fadhil Chalabi to plan terms for taking over Iraq's oil.

March 2003

What White House spokesman Ari Fleischer calls Operation Iraqi Liberation (OIL) begins. (The invasion is rechristened OIF—Operation Iraqi Freedom.)

The Defense Department is told in confidence by U.S. Energy Information Administrator Guy Caruso that Iraq's fields are incapable of a massive increase in output. Despite this intelligence, Deputy Secretary

Wolfowitz testifies to Congress that the invasion will be a free ride. He swears, "There's a lot of money to pay for this that doesn't have to be U.S. taxpayer money. . . . We're dealing with a country that can really finance its own reconstruction and relatively soon"—a deliberate fabrication, promoted by the administration, an insider told the BBC, as "part of the sales pitch" for war.

May 2003

General Jay Garner, whom Bush appointed as viceroy over Iraq, is fired by Defense Secretary Donald Rumsfeld. The general revealed in an interview for the BBC that he resisted White House plans to sell off Iraq's oil and national assets. "That's just one fight you don't want to take on," Garner told me. But apparently the White House wanted that fight. The general also disclosed that these invade-and-grab plans were developed long before the U.S. asserted that Saddam still held WDM: "All I can tell you is the plans were pretty elaborate; they didn't start them in 2002, they were started in 2001."

November–December 2003

Secrecy and misinformation continued even after the invasion. The oil industry objects to the State Department's plans for Iraq's oil fields and drafts for the administration a 323-page plan, "Options for [the] Iraqi Oil Industry." Per the industry plan, the U.S. forces Iraq to create an OPEC-friendly state oil company that supports the OPEC cartel's extortionate price for petroleum.

The Stone Wall

Harper's and the BBC obtained the plans despite official denial of their existence and official footdragging when officials were confronted with the evidence of the reports' existence. To this day the State and Defense Departments and the White House continue to stonewall our demands for the notes of meetings between lobbyists, oil-industry consultants, and key administration officials that would reveal the war's hidden economic motives. What are the secret interests behind this occupation? Who benefits? Who met with whom?

Why won't this administration release these documents of the war's economic blueprint? To date the State and Defense Department responses to our reports are risible, and their answers to our requests for documents range from evasive to downright misleading. Maybe Congress, with its power of the subpoena, can do better.

In April 2006 Dick Cheney's dogsbody, "Scooter" Libby, under indictment for perjury, outed "Mr. Big," the perpetrator of the heinous disclosure of confidential intelligence about preinvasion Iraq. It was the President of United States himself—in conspiracy with his Vice President. Those leaks led to the release of a secret agent's name, Valerie Plame. The pundits got lost arguing over whether our waraholic President had the legal right to leak this national-security information. But that was a fake debate, meant to distract you.

Let's accept the White House alibi that releasing Plame's identity was no crime. But if that's true, they've committed a bigger crime: Bush and Cheney knowingly withheld vital information from a grand-jury investigation, a multimillion dollar inquiry the perps themselves authorized. That's akin to calling in a false fire alarm or calling the cops for a burglary that never happened—but far, far worse. Remember that in the hunt for this noncrime's perpetrator, reporter Judith Miller went to jail.

Think about that. While Miller sat in a prison cell, Bush and Cheney were laughing their sick heads off, knowing the grand-jury testimony, the special prosecutor's subpoenas, and the FBI's terrorizing newsrooms were nothing but fake props in Bush's elaborate charade, Cheney's Big Con.

On February 10, 2004, our not-so-dumb-as-he-sounds President stated, "Listen, I know of nobody—I don't know of anybody in my administration who leaked classified information. If somebody did leak classified information, I'd like to know it, and we'll take the appropriate action. And this investigation is a good thing. . . . And if people have got solid information, please come forward with it."

Notice Bush's cleverly crafted words. He says that he can't name anyone who leaked this "classified" info—knowing full well he'd declassified it. Far from letting Bush off the hook, this ploy worsens the crime. For years I worked as a government investigator, and let me tell you, Bush and Cheney withholding material information from the grand jury is a felony. Several felonies, actually: abuse of legal process, fraud, racketeering, and that old standby, obstruction of justice.

If you or I had manipulated the legal system this way, we'd be breaking rocks on a chain gang. We wouldn't even get a trial—most judges would consider this a "fraud upon the court" and send us to the slammer, using the bench's power to administer instant punishment for contempt of the judicial system.

Why'd they do it? The White House junta did the deed for the most evil of motives: to hoodwink the public during the 2004 election campaign, to pretend that evil anti-Bush elements were undermining the Republic, when it was the Bush element itself at the conspiracy's center. (Let's remember that in 1972 elections trickery motivated Richard Nixon's "plumbers" to break into the Watergate building, then the Democratic Party campaign headquarters.)

Let me draft the indictment for you as I would have were I still a government gumshoe:

> Perpetrator Lewis Libby (alias, "Scooter") contacted Miller while John Doe 1 contacted perpetrators' shill at the *Washington Post*, Bob Woodward, in furtherance of a scheme directed by George Bush (alias "The POTUS") and Dick Cheney (alias, "The Veep") to release intelligence information fraudulently proffered as "classified," and thereinafter, knowingly withheld material evidence from a grand jury empanelled to investigate said disclosure. Furthermore, perpetrator "The POTUS" made material statements designed to deceive investigators and knowingly misrepresent his state of knowledge of the facts.

Statements aimed at misleading a grand jury investigation are hard-time offenses. It doesn't matter that Bush's too-clever little quip was made to the press and not under oath. I've cited press releases and comments in the *New York Times* in court as evidence of fraud. Bush, by not swearing to his disingenuous statement, gets off the perjury hook, but he committed a crime nonetheless: "deliberate concealment."

Here's how the law works (and hopefully, it will). The Bush gang's use of the telephone in this con game constituted wire fraud. Furthermore, while presidents may leak ("declassify") intelligence information, they may not obstruct justice—that is, send a grand jury on a wild goose chase. Under the RICO statute (named after the Edward G. Robinson movie mobster, "Little

Rico," and an acronym of Racketeer Influenced and Corrupt Organizations), the combination of these crimes makes the Bush executive branch a racketeering enterprise.

So, book 'em, Dan-O. Time to read The POTUS and The Veep their rights.

After setting their bail (following the impeachments and removals, of course), a judge will have a more intriguing matter to address. The RICO statute law requires the feds to seize all "ill-gotten gains" of a racketeering enterprise, even before trial. Usually we're talking fast cars and diamond bling. But in this case the conspirators' purloined booty includes a stolen election and a fraudulently obtained authorization for war. I see no reason why a judge could not impound the Eighty-Second Airborne as "fruits of the fraud"—lock, stock, and gun barrels—and bring the boys home.

If justice is to be done, we will also have to run yellow tape across the gates at 1600 Pennsylvania Avenue—CRIME SCENE—DO NOT ENTER—and return the White House to its rightful owners, the American people, the victims of this gangster government.

Chapter 8

PROPAGANDA, LIES, AND PATRIOTIC JOURNALISM

Nancy Snow

Anyone who has the power to make you believe absurdities has the power to make you commit injustices.

—Voltaire

In the early to mid-1990s the U.S. was engaged in a nonideological struggle for the hearts and minds of overseas consumers. It was not their darkness to our light but rather their barren shelves to our megamalls. The U.S. had "won" the Cold War, and the Clinton doctrine directed the United States Information Agency (USIA) to link economic ties to public diplomacy outcomes. The North American Free Trade Agreement (NAFTA) was the apex of the new commercial mission of USIA. Despite the incorporation of public diplomacy efforts, the end of the Cold War spelled trouble for the lifeline of an agency whose birth was a product of the U.S.-Soviet showdown. USIA was officially abolished as an independent agency in October 1999, and all of its programs were shifted to the State Department. Two years passed with little discussion of U.S. propaganda strategies. Then everything changed.

On September 11, 2001, the attacks on the World Trade Center and the Pentagon overcame in a matter of seconds growing doubts about an incompetent, even illegitimate, presidency. A drastic event that impacts a person's sense of well-being is a potent gift to any propagandist, let alone a propaganda administration. In an instant we were a nation at war with both known and unknown enemies and the nations that harbored them, first Afghanistan, then Iraq, with "outed" Axis of Evil coconspirators. Our new struggle would be defined, much like the Cold War, in terms of many decades, not months or just a few years. That kind of public commitment required an unprecedented allegiance to the American executive branch of government in general and the American presidency in particular. A nation turned its eyes to the American president and copresident for comfort through the many storms that lay ahead. As someone who has studied American propaganda strategies since my graduate-school days, it very quickly became apparent that actual truth was being replaced with whatever was believed to be true. Truth was becoming whatever the Bush-Cheney administration told us was true. Since both written and vocal language is the major tool of propaganda, the Bush administration adopted language techniques that followed the gamut from total falsehoods, to incomplete information or misinformation, to no information whatsoever.[1] Through manipulation of public language that was dutifully republished in the patriotic press, they were able to shift public opinion to support measures that were counter to the public interest. How could this happen? They shifted language away from public interest and public accountability to a fear-based warfare style of language infused with appeals to security and threats. Both 9/11 and the subsequent label of the war on terror that followed were used as trump cards that would guide the propaganda lies of the administration and the jingoistic press response that have plagued us to this day.

We are now living in the post-9/11 Age of Terror as defined by Bush-Cheney. We have no other alternative narrative thus far—that is, anything that warrants credibility among the opinion leaders and shapers inside government and the press. Just try to question the very phrase, "Global War On Terror" (GWOT) or "Global Struggle Against Violent Extremism" (GSAVE) or the most recent "Long War," and one's very patriotic core is in question. Spin and information control are at historic levels. The propaganda lies of this administration are not only beyond Nixon in legendary status but rise to the level of impeachable offenses, most notably for deceiving the American public through manipulation of public fear after 9/11 and deliberately lying to Congress by falsely connecting the 9/11 perpetrators to the Saddam Hussein regime. These information offenses were shepherded along by a majority patriotic mainstream media system that acted like a volunteer army of willing conscriptors. So many of the journalistic heavyweight stenographers of the Bush-Cheney 9/11 era—like Judith Miller of the *New York Times* and Bob Woodward of the *Washington Post*—are representative of a matrix of establishment media personalities who generally do not directly challenge the established order but occasionally nibble around its edges at their Washington cocktail parties and book launches. Lewis Lapham, editor of *Harper's* magazine and one of the few committed journalistic voices of protest, has noted that the establishment media operate as sycophants to power:

> I long ago learned that nothing so alarms the assembled company as the intrusion of a new idea. The nature of the business is commercial, not political, and when the speakers on the dais praise one another as ferocious champions of liberty pacing tirelessly to and fro on the ramparts of freedom, the effect is comic. The ladies and gentlemen seated behind the wineglasses enjoy the patronage of very large, very rich, and very timid corporations (Time Warner, General Electric, the Disney Company), and anybody who rises to prominence in their ranks—as editor, political columnist, publisher, anchorperson, theater critic—learns to think along the accommodating lines of an English butler bringing buttered scones to the Prince of Wales.[2]

Norman Solomon, co-founder of FAIR (Fairness and Accuracy in Reporting) and founder of the Institute for Public Accuracy, pointed out in his book *War Made Easy* that "in a wartime frenzy, TV correspondents blend in with the prevailing media scenery. Later, a few briefly utter words of regret, although the next time around they revert to more or less the same pattern of cheerleading the current war."[3]

Their assessment of the patriotic press is much like my experience inside the walls of the federal government: you gain nothing by thinking for yourself and gain the most by supporting the official versions of the truth in the corporate boardroom or the West Wing. Bush and Cheney have turned a Washington habit into tyrannical control. This administration has demonstrated a complete lack of faith in anything outside its own survival. This is why the American public is coddled into believing everyday claptrap such as "They hate America because we love freedom," or the Bush terror doctrine that states, "Either you're with us or you're with the terrorists." The nature of Bush-Cheney propaganda is to control us by making us think that we have already come to the same conclusions. After all, we love freedom, right? We aren't aligned with the terrorists. As Bush told a group of Republican supporters (his favorite audience) in July 2002:

> I want you to know, the doctrine that says either you're with us, or you're with the terrorists, it still stands. And we enforce it every single day. If you harbor a terrorist, if you feed a terrorist, if you finance a terrorist, you're just as guilty as the killers who struck America on September the 11th, and we'll hold you accountable, as well.[4]

The Bush-Cheney administration favors propaganda appeals that warn us against or create fears of other propaganda—namely, that amorphous but technologically savvy enemy propaganda. In a February 17, 2006, speech before the Council on Foreign Relations, Secretary of Defense Donald Rumsfeld warned the American people that our propaganda was being threatened by their propaganda. Apparently theirs is bigger than ours. His speech was picked up in a number of major media, such as CNN and MSNBC and was excerpted verbatim in a *Los Angeles Times* op-ed article days later:

> Our enemies have skillfully adapted to fighting wars in today's media age, but for the most part we—our government, the media or our society in general—have not. Consider that violent extremists have established "media relations committees" and have proved to be highly successful at manipulating opinion elites. They plan and design their headline-grabbing attacks using every means of communication to break the collective will of free people. Our government is only beginning to adapt its operations for the 21st century. For the most part, it still functions as a five-and-dime store in an EBay world.[5]

Rumsfeld's solution is more government and corporate propaganda, not less. The U.S. advantage in this information war, according to the Donald, is that "truth is on our side." Unless the American people subject themselves to the will of the government and military, we may not reach old age:

> We are fighting a battle in which the survival of our free way of life

is at stake. It is a test of wills, and it will be won or lost with our public and the publics of free nations around the world. We need to do all we can to correct the lies being told, shatter the appeal of the enemy and attract supporters to our noble and necessary efforts to defeat violent extremism around the globe.[6]

Many Americans have accepted the ready-alert reaction to government fear rhetoric because of such warnings. If we don't adhere to the standard-issue government line, the enemy goblins will get us. If we don't behave like patriots and support the President the violent extremists will win. Bush, Cheney, Rumsfeld, and Rice, with her transformational diplomacy doctrine, have conditioned us into believing that without *their* ideas, we're nothing. We close our minds to our own ideas or to challenging their ideas because the alternative they present (enemy lies and attacks) seems more dangerous than their manipulation of our free thinking. This is the most effective propaganda out there: to manipulate and massage existing public opinion rather than create new attitudes or opinions. In order to manipulate public opinion, what better anchor than 9/11 and the radioactive fallout it wrought in Afghanistan and Iraq?

In Federalist No. 65, my ancestor Alexander Hamilton described the subject of impeachment as referring to "those offences which proceed from the misconduct of public men, or, in other words, from the abuse or violation of some public trust. They are of a nature which may with peculiar propriety be denominated political, as they relate chiefly to injuries done immediately to the society itself."[7] The Bush-Cheney team has violated the public trust by manipulating public opinion, destroying public trust, and deceiving our public representatives with falsified and trumped-up information about the threat to our national security from Iraq. In the 1930s the Institute for Propaganda Analysis (IPA), an American think tank founded by leading scholars and businesspeople of the day, classified several propaganda techniques that are typically used in any propaganda campaign. These include selecting the issue, promoting the bandwagon (everybody's doing it), exploiting omnibus words (freedom, liberty, democracy), and utilizing a just-plain-folks style of communication (I'm one of you.) At the time the fear was from propaganda appeals that lead a nation to war. Has much changed since then? The rest of this chapter lays out the violations of the public trust through Bush-Cheney warring propaganda.

1. The Big Lie

The issue selected by Bush-Cheney and that most violated the public trust was the Iraq link to 9/11. Selecting this issue anchored any national-security debate in terms of an immediate struggle (for example, imminent threat) and forced a red herring. Public attention was diverted from real security issues (no capture of Osama bin Laden, lack of security on domestic airplanes or seaports) to a trumped-up security threat overseas that required an elective invasion on the part of the United States military. While Bush, Cheney, and Rumsfeld never provided evidence of any real link between Saddam Hussein and 9/11, they repeatedly linked the two in prominent speeches that were then reiterated by the approving press.[8] Just seven months before the attacks of 9/11, on February 12, 2001, Rumsfeld told the Fox News channel, "Iraq is probably not a nuclear threat at the present time." But in testimony before the House Armed Services Committee on September 18, 2002, Rumsfeld reversed himself: "Some have argued that the nuclear threat from Iraq is not imminent—that Saddam is at least 5–7 years away from having nuclear weapons. I would not be so certain. . . . He has, at this moment, stockpiles of chemical and biological weapons, and is pursuing nuclear weapons."[9] Shortly after this testimony the U.S. Congress overwhelmingly supported the administration's position to use "all appropriate means" to remove Saddam Hussein from power.

You might ask yourself how we can live in a country where propaganda works so effectively. Aren't we taught to think for ourselves in the United States? The nature of the Bush administration's informational propaganda is not to overly tax our thinking or cause too many antagonistic emotional responses; rather, the citizenry is instructed to behave as if the administration's behavior and attitudes were its own. In particular, the regular hammering of the Iraq-9/11 link served effectively to create a herdlike response among American citizens. We were conditioned to believe what the government was telling us, with no visible proof, because the alternative—enemy propaganda and control—was too devastating to consider. We shut down to stop thinking for ourselves whenever our government directs us to think alike on such major issues as safety and security. This is what makes such propaganda so insidious and paternalistic. The worst propagandists view their target audience with a great deal of disdain. Bush and Cheney, like Rumsfeld and Rice, are true perpetrators, in that they believe the American people need to be converted to the administration's position for "our own good," not just to serve the power needs of the government. They are guided by a long tradition in American public relations and propaganda history, known as the "engineering of consent," a term first coined by Edward L. Bernays, the father of modern public relations, during the early days of the Cold War. Bernays believed that free speech and a free press must be extended by government's "freedom to persuade" because in a democracy like the United States, the results desirable to the government do not just happen but must be manipulated by expert communication elites.[10]

2. Subversion of the Press with Patriotic Propaganda

Even though the Bush administration selected the issue, it was not an easy sell early on. A Chicago Council on Foreign Relations poll in June 2002 showed that among those Americans surveyed, just 20 percent responded that "the U.S. should invade Iraq even if we have to go it alone," while an overwhelming majority (65 percent) replied that the United States "should only invade Iraq with UN approval and the support of its allies."[11] It was clear that while the American people were open to the overthrow of the despotic Saddam Hussein, the clear method for such overthrow was to favor a multilateral response for Iraq. To support its own agenda, the Bush administration set out to frighten the American people into believing that Saddam Hussein's government was preparing to use weapons of mass destruction against the United States and was lending substantive support to Osama bin Laden's al-Qaeda organization, neither of which was true. Less than nine months later the American people had shifted their support for unilateral war on Iraq. The President was given a blank check to engage in a military invasion and occupation of Iraq.

How did public opinion shift so rapidly? The Bush-Cheney administration purposely manipulated public opinion to anchor misperceptions about Iraq, 9/11, and al-Qaeda's role, and was generously helped along in this process by a patriotic, unquestioning mainstream media. In 2003 the Program on International Policy Attitudes (PIPA) at the University of Maryland teamed up with the polling firm Knowledge Networks (KN) to investigate misperceptions about Iraq and the role of the media. The results indicated three key misperceptions promoted by the Bush administration: Weapons of mass destruction had been found; there was clear evidence that Saddam Hussein was working closely with al-Qaeda; and global public opinion favored the U.S. going to war with Iraq. The PIPA surveys showed a strong correlation between one's media source and the likelihood to misperceive. Eighty percent of viewers of Fox News, the national news channel most closely aligned with the Bush administration, held at least one misperception, followed by CBS News and ABC News. The group least likely to hold at least one of these misperceptions was that of National Public Radio listeners or Public Broadcasting viewers.

Frequency of Misperceptions per Respondent: WMD Found, Evidence of al-Qaeda Link, and World Majority Support for War (percentages) Source: PIPA/Knowledge Networks

Number of misperceptions per respondent	Fox	CBS	ABC	CNN	NBC	Print	NPR/PBS
None of the three	20	30	39	45	45	53	77
One or more misperception	80	71	61	55	55	47	23

These media surveys show clear evidence of the Bush administration leading by falsehood and deception, courting patriotic mainstream media still reeling from 9/11, and convincing the American people that Iraq was the new Ground Zero and the next battleground in the war on terror. President Bush and Vice President Cheney made speeches in which they implied they had evidence supporting all three of these misperceptions. In his March 18, 2003, Presidential Letter to Congress, Bush wrote that the decision to invade Iraq was the proper next step in "the necessary actions against international terrorists and terrorist organizations, including those nations, organizations, or persons who planned, authorized, committed, or aided the terrorist attacks that occurred on September 11, 2001."[12] Later that year on NBC News' *Meet the Press*, Cheney said, "If we're successful in Iraq . . . so that it's not a safe haven for terrorists, now we will have struck a major blow right at the heart of the base, if you will, the geographic base of the terrorists who have had us under assault now for many years, but most especially on 9/11."[13] After the war in Iraq had begun and following his "Mission Accomplished" speech on board the USS *Lincoln* off the coast of San Diego, President Bush was going as far as to defy prewar intelligence altogether by telling an outright lie: "For those who say we haven't found the banned manufacturing devices or banned weapons, they're wrong. We found them."[14] The American people were so swayed by the manufacturing of consent by the Bush administration that a PIPA poll released in June 2003, showed 71 percent of Americans said yes to the following question: "Do you think the Bush administration did imply that Iraq under Saddam Hussein was involved in the September 11th attacks?" Even though there was no evidence of such a link, the American public was aware of the implication. By October 2003 Bush asserted the Iraq-9/11 link once again and reinforced myriad misperceptions:

> And the intelligence that said he [Saddam Hussein] had a weapon system was intelligence that had been used by a multinational agency, the U.N., to pass resolutions. It's been used by my predecessor to conduct bombing raids. It was intelligence gathered from a variety of sources that clearly said Saddam Hussein was a threat. And given the attacks of September the 11th it was—we needed to enforce U.N. resolution for the security of the world, and we did. We took action based upon good, solid intelligence. It was the right thing to do to make America more secure and the world more peaceful.[15]

Where was the American press to challenge the executive branch of government? The PIPA/KN surveys indicate a media system in which plenty of networks, not just Fox News, report the news in a Bush-friendly manner. The period after 9/11 led to enormous patriotic zeal inside newsrooms across America, and this unquestioning "my country, right or wrong" style was ripe for accepting the administration's deceptions at face value. Many news media representatives seemed to believe that it was not the news media's role in wartime to question the government, and once war was declared, they wished to show their bias toward our side. CBS News anchor Dan Rather said on *Larry King Live* on April 4, 2003, "Look, I'm an American. I never tried to kid anybody that I'm some internationalist or something. And when my country is at war, I want my country to win. . . . Now, I can't and don't argue that that is coverage without a prejudice. About that I am prejudiced."[16] This was a position extended at the Fox News channel. Throughout the initial engagement in the war on Iraq, the Fox News channel included a flag in the left-hand corner of the screen that showed agreement with the Defense Department's name for the war in Iraq, "Operation Iraqi Freedom." When Fox was later criticized for being too prowar in its news coverage, Fox News channel moderator Neil Cavuto replied, "So am I slanted and biased? You damn well bet I am. . . . You say I wear my biases on my sleeve? Better that than pretend you have none, but show them clearly in your work."[17] Pulitzer-Prize winning CNN reporter Peter Arnett was fired in March 2003 for violating the patriotic press creed; that is, he told the truth to Iraqi state television: "the first war plan [of the Bush administration] has failed because of Iraqi resistance. Now they are trying to write another war plan. Clearly the war planners misjudged the determination of Iraqi forces. . . . President Bush said he is concerned about the Iraqi people. But if Iraqi people are dying in numbers, then American policy will be challenged very strongly."[18] Around the same time MSNBC reporter Ashleigh Banfield was dismissed after telling a college audience the following about press coverage of the Iraq war, which she had covered extensively since the start:

> There are horrors that were completely left out of [the coverage of] this war. So was this journalism or was this coverage? There is a grand difference between journalism and coverage, and getting access does not mean you're getting the story, it just means you're getting one more arm or leg of the story. And that's what we got, and it was a glorious, wonderful picture that had a lot of people watching and a lot of advertisers excited about cable news. But it wasn't journalism, because I'm not so sure that we in America are hesitant to do this again, to fight another war, because it looked like a glorious and courageous and so successful terrific endeavor, and we got rid of a horrible leader: We got rid of a dictator, we got rid of a monster, but we didn't see what it took to do that.[19]

In response her employer issued a terse statement: "She and we [NBC] both agreed that she didn't intend to demean the work of her colleagues, and she will choose her words more carefully in the future."[20]

A study conducted by Fairness and Accuracy in Reporting (FAIR) found that prowar commentary by guests on television news programs dramatically overshadowed antiwar commentary at the start of the war in Iraq. Steve Rendell and Tara Broughel revealed that the "percentage of U.S. sources that were officials varied from network to network, ranging from 75 percent at CBS to 60 percent at NBC. Fox's *Special Report with Brit Hume* had fewer U.S. officials than CBS (70 percent) and more U.S. antiwar guests (3 percent) than PBS or CBS. Eighty-one percent of Fox's sources were prowar, however, the highest of any network. CBS was close on the Murdoch network's heels with 77 percent. NBC featured the lowest proportion of prowar voices with 65 percent."[21] This volume of prowar commentary corresponds with the tendency to cite Bush administration-reinforced misperceptions about the war, especially among Fox and CBS viewers.

In an article for *Political Science Quarterly*, PIPA director Steven Kull and two research associates wrote that the media's reluctance to question the administration during the buildup and invasion of Iraq amplified misperceptions. They wrote,

> Reluctant to challenge the administration, the media can simply become a means of transmission for the administration, rather than a critical filter. For example, when President Bush made the assertion that WMD had been found, the 31 May 2003 edition of the *Washington Post* ran a front page headline saying, "Bush: 'We Found Banned Weapons.'"[22]

Columbia Journalism Review editor Brent Cunningham believes that the American press tradition in news objectivity has led news journalists to become passive recipients of news from elite sources, most prominently the American president and his closest advisors. Further, some news media do not want to distance themselves from the administration vis-à-vis the war. Cunningham reports in his article, "Rethinking Objectivity," that one of his interns contacted several newspapers during the initial engagement in Iraq to find out the percentage of prowar versus antiwar letters to the editor. The editor of *The Tennessean* told him that while 70 percent of their letters were actually antiwar, the paper decided to run more prowar letters so that it wouldn't lose any of its readership over charges of either a Bush or liberal bias.[23] The PIPA article concludes:

The President's influence is not limitless. He does not appear to be capable of getting the public to go against their more deeply held value orientations. If he did, then it would not be necessary for the public to develop false beliefs. But he is capable of prompting the public to support him by developing the false beliefs necessary to justify the administration's policies in a way that is consistent with the public's deeper value orientations. It also appears that the media cannot necessarily be counted on to play the critical role of doggedly challenging the administration.[24]

The American mainstream media cannot be counted on by the American people to serve as a watchdog of government malfeasance. Many media staff have been conditioned to avoid questioning by an administration that is record-breaking in its use of government propaganda techniques designed to subvert and control opinion.[25]

3. Courting of Select Press

Bush and Cheney have leaked classified material to such most-favored-national journalists as Bob Woodward of the *Washington Post* and Judith Miller of the *New York Times*. These journalists set a dangerous precedent in exchanging access for exclusives. In his book *Bush at War*, Woodward was given access to secretly classified intelligence material because he was friendly to the outcomes of the Bush-Cheney administration. His major source for material was the now discredited Cheney chief of staff, I. Lewis "Scooter" Libby. Woodward has been the ultimate prize for the Bush administration because he is the legendary Watergate reporter credited with helping take down a Republican president. Ironically, it is Woodward's profile of Bush in several post-9/11 works that provides a legitimate rationale for the President's impeachment. In *Bush at War* we read of a president who illegally diverts funds for Afghanistan to Iraq. In a letter to Director of National Intelligence John Negroponte, Senator Jay Rockefeller (D-WV) said that the Bush administration's practice of leaking classified material to select members of the press is a "blatant abuse of intelligence information for political purposes." It is not, as CIA Director Porter Goss wrote in the *New York Times*, the fault of "misguided whistleblowers," but rather of executive branch members pushing a particular policy. Decades ago while running for President, Adlai Stevenson said, "If ignorance, apathy and excessive partisanship are still the greatest enemies of democracy . . . then of course it is up to a free press to help us on all three counts and all the time. Otherwise neither democratic government nor a free press can be sure of permanency."[26]

And is there any more sycophantic example of fawning elite media than Judith Miller? The Bush White House worked very closely with Miller to push a preemptive war rationale against Iraq, and she was a willing servant. The *New York Times*, with its legendary tag line, "All the News That's Fit to Print," is the Gray Lady of responsibility and accountability. It is the newspaper that serves as the lead dog to other American papers. Miller's articles played up the imminent threat of weapons of mass destruction in Iraq and gave Bush and Cheney all the credibility they needed, in part because her front-page stories were published in the leading newspaper in the U.S., known for having a liberal editorial slant. This wasn't a conservative rag but a respectable member of the media. How could this paper get the story wrong too? Miller used such discredited sources as Ahmed Chalabi, founder of the U.S.-government-sponsored Iraqi National Congress, and Cheney's chief of staff Scooter Libby to argue that Saddam Hussein's Iraq was just one large warehouse of missing WMD. The Iraqi National Congress intelligence wasn't in the least bit reliable, due to its habit of using faulty intelligence for administration propaganda purposes, but this intelligence is what fed the presidential and vice-presidential statements on Iraq.[27] It wasn't until well over a year after the start of war in Iraq that the "liberal" *New York Times* published an editor's note pointing out that it got the WMD story all wrong. It did not include the name of the reporter who led the cheering on behalf of the administration. That person was Judith Miller, who had written two-thirds of the botched articles.[28]

How did we get the kind of country where propaganda lies are perpetuated and patriotic journalists dominate? The Bush administration has been helped along by a rise in conservative think tanks and far right media that have not only reached unprecedented numbers in this century but have successfully demonized any opposition to the status quo, including any sustained resistance to war predicated on lies and deceit. Our public-policy problems may not fit neatly into red/blue or left/right categories, but a landscape of self-censorship and deceptive manipulation has permeated the media continuum from public media to traditional corporate mainstream media outlets that are cowed by the charge of being liberal—the new McCarthy charge—from a well-financed conservative-media machine.[29] Rupert Murdoch's Fox News is merely the cherry on top of the conservative-media pie, but the main ingredients include such think tanks as the Cato Institute, the Heritage Foundation, and the American Enterprise Institute, whose ideas end up on the editorial pages of influential newspapers, such as the *Wall Street Journal* and in the banter of such popular right-wing radio and TV hosts as Bill O'Reilly and Rush Limbaugh. Bill Kristol, the former editor of the Murdoch-funded *Weekly Standard*, used Bradley Foundation monies to found the Project for a New American Century (PNAC), an organization credited with the Bush-Cheney war strategy on Iraq.

Conservative pundits, such as Ann Coulter, Sean Hannity, Michelle Malkin, and Cal Thomas are given the main stage in the press, while progressive critique is offered as a sideshow attraction, Cindy Sheehan being the most recent example. There is no sustained progressive critique to challenge the rightward tilt of the press, and certainly no "echo chamber" from liberal and progressive think tanks and activist groups to counter the Bush rhetoric. Academicians are increasingly afraid to speak up out of fear of being tagged too ideological and biased by David Horowitz, William Bennett, and Lynne Cheney, whose American Council of Trustees and Alumni published a November 2001 report, "Defending America: How Our Universities are Failing America," which included pull quotes of alleged anti-American statements after 9/11. This onslaught has narrowed the range of discourse on our college and university campuses, which traditionally have offered corridors for free, open exchange and debate. This is of particular concern as campuses may be our last forum for truth seeking when government and the media fail us. As Jonathan Cole, professor at Columbia University, wrote in a special forum on the chilly climate at college campuses today:

> A rising tide of anti-intellectualism and intolerance of university research and teaching that offends ideologues and today's ruling prince is putting academic freedom—one of the core values of

the university—under more sustained and subtle attack than at any time since the dark days of McCarthyism in the 1950s. . . . Scholars and scientists are often exercising their right to remain silent rather than face the potential scorn, ridicule, sanctions, and ostracism that challenging shoddy evidence and poor reasoning on political sensitive topics can invite."[30]

At the top of the Bush White House agenda today is control of information through perpetual thinking about perpetual war, fear strategies, and campaigns that point to the comparative strategic superiority of our enemies, both within and outside the United States. The Defense Department is moving in the direction of legitimizing propaganda strategies domestically as part of its "Long War" strategy. A secret Pentagon document, "Information Operations Roadmap," which was approved by Rumsfeld in October 2003, calls for "full spectrum" information operations and acknowledges that "information intended for foreign audiences, including public diplomacy and PSYOP (Psychological Operations), increasingly is consumed by our domestic audience and vice-versa."[31] PSYOPs are defined by the U.S. military as "planned operations to convey selected information and indicators to foreign audiences to influence their emotions, motives, objective reasoning, and ultimately the behavior of foreign governments, organizations, groups, and individuals. The purpose of psychological operations is to induce or reinforce foreign attitudes and behavior favorable to the originator's objectives."[32]

Under the Bush administration propaganda agenda, PSYOPs will continue to play overseas and contribute to our already damaged reputation and credibility in the world, but it will also spill over to a domestic American audience despite legal prohibitions against the use of government propaganda on the American public. While the Information Roadmap report calls for "boundaries" between information operations abroad and the news media at home, no such limits are placed on psychological-operation campaigns. As long as the American people are not specifically targeted by PSYOPs, American consumption of such campaigns is acceptable. This development follows the discredited DoD Office of Strategic Influence (OSI) that the *New York Times* reported in 2002 was "developing plans to provide news items, possibly even false ones, to foreign media organizations in an effort to influence public sentiment and policy makers in both friendly and unfriendly countries."[33] Now it looks as if the Bush administration has a blank check on propagandizing as much at home as overseas.

The Pentagon information roadmap includes a strategy for taking over the Internet and controlling the flow of information, viewing the World Wide Web as a potential military adversary. If the Internet is viewed by the Bush administration as equal to an enemy weapon, it may be difficult for Web-based activists to get across their messages and organize social movements without fears of reprisal, surveillance, and restraint. The USA PATRIOT Act already allows the U.S. government to monitor Internet messaging, and such a civil-liberty restriction has been met with little public resistance. In a speech on February 17, 2006, to the Council on Foreign Relations in New York, Defense Secretary Rumsfeld said that the battle over information in America and in the global media would be a crucial front in the Long War (formerly known as the War on Terror). He charged that violent extremists employ media and public-relations specialists proactively while government can only react to information crises. Complicating matters is the fact that the United States' enemies in the global war on terror "propagate lies with impunity—with no penalty whatsoever," while the U.S. has no such "luxury of relying on other sources for information—anonymous or otherwise. Our government has to be the source. And we tell the truth." I assume that Rumsfeld was not taking into account the multimillion-dollar DoD contractor Lincoln Group's efforts to plant positive stories in the Iraqi press. Rumsfeld's prescription for change was to centralize communications in every aspect of the War on Terror, including militarizing international broadcasting efforts, such as the Voice of America (VOA).

We presently have a government dominated by war propagandists and supported by a prowar media majority. Their war includes both a language and a false sense of security. The more our government wages war here at home and overseas, the less secure we are as a nation and the more vulnerable we are to further attacks. We have lost our moral legitimacy in the world through this government's inability to be frank and open with its own people and with our allies abroad. The Bush-Cheney war is an efficient means of centralizing information in order to support their continued power over us—the power to control information and to dominate the discussion, both through message and the threat of force. Unless we challenge this administration's legitimate right to serve the public interest and hold itself accountable to the public, we will continue to get the government we deserve. The choice is ours to make.

Notes:

1. For in-depth background, see Nancy Snow, *Information War: American Propaganda, Free Speech and Opinion Control Since 9/11* (New York: Seven Stories Press, 2004).
2. Lewis Lapham, *Gag Rule* (New York: Penguin Press, 2004), pp. 91–92.
3. Norman Solomon, *War Made Easy* (Hoboken, NJ: John Wiley & Sons, 2005), p. 131.
4. George W. Bush, "Remarks by the President at Coleman/Kline Minnesota Republican Victory 2002 Dinner," http://www.whitehouse.gov/news/releases/2002/07/20020711-8.html.
5. Donald H. Rumsfeld, "War in the Information Age," *Los Angeles Times*, February 23, 2006. This op-ed piece is an excerpt of Rumsfeld's February 17, 2006, speech to the Council on Foreign Relations in New York.
6. *Ibid.*
7. Alexander Hamilton, "The Powers of the Senate," Federalist No. 65, March 7, 1788.
8. BBC News, "Bush administration on Iraq 9/11 link," September 18, 2003. Available online at http://news.bbc.co.uk/2/hi/americas/3119676.stm.
9. Ralph Dannheisser, "Rumfeld Says Issue in Iraq is Disarmament, Not Weapons Inspections," The United States Mission to the European Union, September 18, 2002, available at http://www.useu.be/Categories/GlobalAffairs/Sept1802RumsfeldIraqDisarmament.html.
10. J. Michael Sproule, *Propaganda and Democracy: The American Experience of Media and Mass Persuasion* (Cambridge: Cambridge University Press, 1997), p. 213.
11. Chicago Council on Foreign Relations, "U.S. Report," Worldviews 2002, June, available at http://www.worldviews.org/detailreports/usreport/index.htm.
12. President George W. Bush, "Presidential Letter," March 18, 2003, available at http://www.whitehouse.gov/news/releases/2003/03/20030319-1.html.
13. Vice President Richard Cheney, *Meet the Press*, September 14, 2003.
14. Mike Allen, "Bush: 'We Found' Banned Weapons; President Cites Trailers in Iraq as Proof," *Washington Post*, May 31, 2001.
15. President George W. Bush, "Press Conference," October 28, 2003, available at http://www.whitehouse.gov/news/releases/2003/10/20031028-2.html.
16. Dan Rather, *Larry King Live*, April 4, 2003.
17. David Folkenflik, "Fox News defends its patriotic coverage: Channel's objectivity is questioned," *Baltimore Sun*, April 2, 2003.
18. James Ruttenberg, "NBC News fires Arnett over Iraqi TV interview," *New York Times*, March 31, 2003.
19. "MSNBC's Ashleigh Banfield Slams War Coverage," AlterNet, April 29, 2003, available at http://alternet.org/story/15778/.
20. As released in an MSNBC statement and reported by AlterNet, April 28, 2003.
21. Steve Rendell and Tara Broughel, "Amplifying Officials, Squelching Dissent: FAIR study finds democracy poorly served by war coverage," *Extra!*, May/June 2003, Fairness and Accuracy in Reporting, available at www.fair.org/extra/0305/warstudy.html.
22. Steven Kull, Clay Ramsay, Evan Lewis, "Misperceptions, the Media, and the Iraq War," *Political Science Quarterly*, vol. 118, no. 4, Winter 2003–2004, p. 594.
23. Brent Cunningham, "Rethinking Objectivity," *Columbia Journalism Review*, July 2003.
24. Kull et al., *op cit.*, p. 597.
25. See Michelle Chin, "Behind the White House's Billion-dollar Propaganda Push," *The New Standard*, February 18, 2006, available at http://www.alternet.org/story/32378#comments.
26. Adlai Stevenson, quoted in *Voice of the People: Readings in Public Opinion and Propaganda*, Reo

M. Christenson and Robert O. McWilliams, editors (New York: McGraw-Hill, 1962), p. 141.

27. Robert Dreyfuss, "The Pentagon Muzzles the CIA," *The American Prospect*, vol. 13, no. 22, December 16, 2002.

28. Steven Rendall, Peter Hart, and Julie Hollar, "20 Stories That Made a Difference," *Extra!* January/ February 2006, available at http://www.fair.org/index.php?page=2816.

29. Jessica Clark and Tracy Van Slyke, "Making Connections," *In These Times*, May 9, 2005, pp. 17–22.

30. Jonathan R. Cole, "The New McCarthyism," *Chronicle of Higher Education*, September 9, 2005, pp. B7–B8.

31. See "Rumsfeld's Roadmap to Propaganda" as reported by the National Security Archives, January 26, 2006; available at http://www.gwu.edu/~nsarchiv/NSAEBB/NSAEBB177/index. htm.

32. U.S. Department of Defense (DoD) Dictionary Terms, available at http://jdeis.cornerstoneindustry. com/jdeis/dictionary/qsDictionaryPortlet.jsp?group=dod.

33. Media advisory, "Pentagon plan is undemocratic, possibly illegal," Fairness and Accuracy in Reporting, February 19, 2002, released the same day as the *New York Times* article on the OSI.

Chapter 9

THE CAMPAIGN FOR UNFETTERED POWER
Executive Supremacy, Secrecy, and Surveillance

Barbara J. Bowley

In spite of its glaring ineptitude, its inability to handle national disasters, its know-nothing environmental policy, its absurd claims of winning a global war on terror, and its rapid escalation of our domestic insecurity, the Bush-Cheney administration is performing acts of unrivaled political cunning.

Hidden in the shadows of this administration's team of unbridled incompetents is a cabal of experts who are dismantling the government we know and constructing a federal tyranny, one more suitable to a monarchy than a presidency. In a mere handful of years this cabal has established the Bush administration's dominance over Congress and the Judiciary.

The most aggressive proponents of this perspective belong to the Federalist Society, a group of conservative lawyers and academics who believe that the framers intended "unitariness" of each of the branches of government—a kind of independence that would give each branch more freedom to act without even the figment of the putative balance of power between the three branches.

For the Federalist Society, the executive branch should dominate, hence the Society's frequent use of the term "unitary executive." The unitary executive is a relatively recent doctrine that claims that the President's constitutional powers rest upon his oath to "preserve, protect, and defend the Constitution of the United States." As Federalist Society member and future Supreme Court Justice Sam Alito put it in 2000: "The president has not just some executive powers, but *the* executive power—the whole thing" (italics added).[1] Alito would get no argument from fellow Federalist Society members Supreme Court Justice Antonin Scalia and Supreme Court Justice Clarence Thomas.

Scalia ruled the unitary executive concept constitutional in 1987. He wrote: "it [is] not enough simply to repose the power to execute the laws [in the president], it [is] also necessary to provide him with the means to resist legislative encroachment upon that power . . . [including] the power to veto encroaching laws or even to disregard them when they are unconstitutional."[2]

The Campaign for Executive Unaccountability

This administration may be called conservative, but it has one of the most radical agendas in history. Although it has taken decades for the players, the plan, and the tactics to come together, once the combination of people and ideas found themselves together in one administration, they moved with breathtaking speed.

Part of this notion of the all-powerful executive has its roots in the Reagan administration's Iran-Contra scandal. Without the knowledge of Congress and in contravention of the law, Reagan-Bush attempted to overthrow the Nicaraguan government by supplying arms to the right-wing Contras. It financed the Contras with money obtained from covert arms sales to Iran. After the scandal broke, a bipartisan congressional committee warned the administration: "fundamental processes of government were disregarded and the rule of law was subverted."[3]

But not all members of that bipartisan committee agreed with the conclusion. One dissenter was Dick Cheney, then a Republican congressman from Wyoming. Cheney disdained what he saw as Congress' high-handedness over the executive branch's conduct of foreign policy. He felt that the bipartisan committee had "criminalize[d] a policy difference" between Congress and the president.[4]

Cheney had his legal counsel, David Addington, write a report claiming that presidential prerogatives supersede those of Congress, particularly in the conduct of war. This was the blueprint for running an administration under the concept of the "unitary executive," and Cheney quotes from that report to this day.[5] It is also a manifesto asserting a president's right to operate by fiat, in secret, and with the latitude to ignore any law in the name of "national security." In other words, it was the manifesto of the Bush-Cheney administration.

Dick Cheney has played an especially successful behind-the-scenes role in creating unfettered executive power. His Secret Service name is "Backseat" (a reference to both his secrecy and his covert political maneuvering).[6] But even more elusive is his aide, David Addington. As Cheney's chief of staff, former counsel, and author of the dissenting report on the Iran-Contra affair, Addington is the inspiration behind many of the administration's legal strategies concerning the unitary executive. In the administration's inner circle, Addington is nicknamed "the Octopus,"[7] a reference to his reach into virtually every area of the administration. Addington is a zealot who is the administration's watchdog on presidential authority.

Addington helped to write the Bush administration's infamous torture memo. As members of the administration were crafting the memo, a concerned observer from the State Department opined, "They were arguing for a new interpretation of the Constitution [that] negates Article One, Section Eight, that lays out all of the powers of the Congress."[8] In other words, they were asserting the right to establish a presidency with unchecked power.

Unitary Executive vs. Congressional Authority: Cheney Takes the Lead

But even before Bush's transition team received word in 2001 that the Supreme Court had anointed Bush as president, Cheney, then the CEO of the oil-and-gas company Halliburton, quietly began assembling a task force to chart the administration's energy policy. The task force, whose official title was the National Energy Policy Development Group, would be the Bush administration's opening salvo in the march toward unilateral executive power.

The press eventually learned that the task force was meeting with over a dozen private oil companies, such as the now infamous Enron.[9] Contravening the 1972 Federal Advisory Committee Act, all of the task force's meetings were held in secret, and no public record was made of these meetings.[10]

In April 2001 reports began to emerge indicating that private interests, including campaign contributors, had access to Cheney's group, while the public and consumer groups were excluded.[11] In response, two Democratic Congressmen, Henry Waxman (D-California), ranking member of the Committee on Government Reform, and John Dingell (D-Michigan), ranking member of the Energy and Commerce Committee, asked Cheney to provide Congress' General Accounting Office (GAO)[12] with the composition and activities of the National Energy Policy Development Group. Cheney refused.[13] He claimed that the executive branch had a legal prerogative, called executive privilege, to keep this information from Congress. What was shocking about Cheney's move was not that he used the claim of executive privilege—many presidents have claimed executive privilege throughout the country's history. But Cheney, in a foretaste of the aggressive assault the administration was going to wage, was the first *vice president* to withhold information from Congress using the claim of executive privilege.[14]

After being rebuffed by Cheney, Congress asked the GAO, Congress' primary investigative arm, to request merely the task force's members' names. Cheney wrote to Congress that "the GAO did not have the [legal] 'standing' to review such information."[15] In January 2002 Cheney defended his actions by asserting that there was "an important principle involved" and that releasing the information would reduce the president's traditional prerogatives. In a news conference he stated that he needed to bolster the executive branch's prerogatives because of unwise compromises made over the last several decades.

Though the GAO continued to fight Cheney all the way to the Supreme Court, after a long stretch of legal wrangling Cheney prevailed and was required to release a relatively small number of inconsequential documents concerning the task force. What he left in the wake of that litigation was a historic victory in the march toward a government that could operate outside the traditional bounds of accountability. In his legal battle to undercut the GAO's authority to investigate the executive branch, Cheney began to draw the wall around the administration that would give it legal standing to operate in secret.[16]

Bush's Unitary Executive Campaign

Executive privilege is just one of the Bush administration's pocketful of tactics to create a unitary executive. One of Bush's favorite tactics is to use Executive Orders (EOs). EOs are legally binding directives given by the president to federal administrative agencies. EOs are generally used to guide federal agencies in how to execute congressional laws or policies. However, in many instances the Bush administration has used them as a guide for operating in ways specifically contrary to Congress' intent. In other words, in the Bush administration's hands, EOs are a means of taking away Congress' rightful power to establish the law. This administration simply interprets the law as it sees fit.

The administration has been heavy-handed in using EOs to establish the power of the unitary executive. By 2005 Bush had issued four hundred EOs and in them used the term "unitary executive" ninety-five times.[17] In contrast, prior to the year 2001 presidents issued on average about five EOs per year.[18]

Another administration tactic is the presidential "signing statement" attached to a bill as it is signed into law. Throughout history most presidential signing statements have been pro forma, but the Bush administration has used signing statements repeatedly to interpret the law on its own terms. Bush issued over twenty-five signing statements per year during his first term alone, and in the course of such statements he made 505 different challenges to the Constitution against Congress' legislative intent.[19] His most notorious signing statement was attached to the 2005 McCain Amendment that prohibited torture of detainees.

In signing the McCain Amendment, Bush's little-noticed signing statement stated that he would interpret the bill "in a manner consistent with the constitutional authority of the president to supervise the unitary executive branch . . . and consistent with the constitutional limitations on judicial power." In other words, he claimed that neither the courts nor Congress had the constitutional authority to interfere with his prerogative to act on his own terms. The journalist and legal scholar Jennifer Van Bergen calls this "a form of presidential rebellion against Congress and the courts, and possibly a violation of President Bush's oath of office, as well."[20]

Secrecy and Accountability

In its bid for unbridled power this administration has used a variety of legal and bureaucratic tactics. Its members have asserted their authority over Congress and the Judiciary, but these assertions are not enough. In order to operate in whatever way they see fit, the administration's operatives need to rule in secrecy and without accountability to the people and their putative representatives.

One of Bush's first acts as president was to close off access to presidential records.[21] He claimed executive privilege over his administration's records and the records of those administrations twenty years prior to his, even if the prior president wanted his records released. This claim contravenes the 1978 Presidential Records Act, which requires the release of presidential materials twelve years after the administration leaves office.

Bush's policy will have a severe chilling effect on the amount of information presidential historians and the public will have about presidents and vice presidents. Interestingly, the first former vice president whose papers will now be protected is George H. W. Bush. In the words of the historian Stanley Kutler, "Who knows? Perhaps we might learn something about that vice president's role in Iran-Contra, a role for which he famously denied any knowledge."[22]

Shortly after claiming executive privilege over presidential records, Bush again claimed executive privilege, this time in response to a subpoena by the House's Government Reform Committee seeking Department of Justice records. One set of records concerned the 1996 Clinton-Gore campaign and the other documents related to corruption in the way the FBI handled organized crime in the 1960s and 1970s. Attorney General John Ashcroft, on Bush's orders, refused to comply with the subpoena.[23]

Dan Burton (R-Indiana) and other members of the committee were clearly unhappy about the administration's attempt to withhold information that Congress would normally have access to. Burton called Ashcroft to appear at a hearing on December 13, 2001, but on December 12, the day before the hearing, Bush claimed executive privilege over the documents. In his memorandum, Bush referred to the need "to protect individual liberty," and stated, "congressional access to these documents would be contrary to the national interest."[24]

The hearings proceeded despite Bush's claim of executive privilege, but John Ashcroft did not appear and sent an assistant instead. During the hearings Burton stated angrily, "This is not a monarchy. . . . The legislative branch has oversight responsibility to make sure there is no corruption in the executive branch." He exasperatedly told Ashcroft's assistant, "[W]e've got a dictatorial president and a Justice Department that does not want Congress involved. . . . Your guy's acting like he's king."[25]

By 2002 it was becoming more and more apparent that the administration was making a full-out assault on Congress' right to know. On April 11, 2002,

Congressman Henry Waxman (D-California) convened a hearing on "Secrecy and the Bush Administration" in which the committee discussed the problem of the amount of information being withheld from Congress. The Waxman Committee's final report found that the administration had undermined "laws that are designed to promote public access to information . . . while laws that authorize the government to withhold information or to operate in secret have repeatedly been expanded. The cumulative result is an unprecedented assault on the principle of open government."[26] The committee concluded that the administration used "novel legal theories to justify secret investigations, detentions, and trials. And the Administration has engaged in litigation to contest Congress' right to information."[27]

Then Came 9/11—The Surveillance Wars

Though its early acts showed its intent to establish an unbridled executive, with the tragic events of 9/11 the stage was set for the Bush-Cheney administration to use the President's war powers to justify virtually any act in the name of national security. 9/11 has been one of the most important tools this administration has used to hide its real ambitions about power, unaccountability, and global supremacy. The specter of 9/11 has enabled the administration to assert that the President needs to exercise extraordinary power and to do so in secret because we are in a time of war.

Prior to 9/11 the Bush administration was already well on its way to ensuring that Congress, the Judiciary, and the press posed little threat to Bush's power. The administration would use 9/11 as an excuse to intimidate and control the only other group that could subvert the President's aims: the American public. The events of 9/11 gave Bush the latitude to conduct unimpeded and illegal surveillance of the American people. Using the figleaf of protecting national security, Bush dusted off or breathed new life into a dizzying array of surveillance programs, many of which were unproven or outright dysfunctional, but all of which are turning the country into a surveillance state.

Using programs with Orwellian names, such as Carnivore, MATRIX, Talon, Eagle Eyes, and Total Information Awareness, the administration is exercising an unprecedented level of power over citizens' lives.

Much of the legal basis for this surveillance activity is in the Uniting and

Strengthening America by Providing Appropriate Tools Required to Intercept and Obstruct Terrorism (USA PATRIOT) Act. John W. Whitehead, president of the conservative Rutherford Institute, calls the PATRIOT Act "[a] politician's dream—and a civil libertarian's nightmare. [It broadens] the already immense powers of the federal government, not only in regarding to investigations relating to terrorism, but also to criminal investigations . . . . Hidden within this tome are provisions that turn the FBI, CIA and INS[28] into secret police."[29]

Congress passed the USA PATRIOT Act[30] on Oct. 25, 2001, just six weeks after the 9/11 attacks. The Act filled over 342 pages and passed with no public hearing, conference report, or committee report, and was read in its entirety by almost no members of Congress.[31]

If Congress was unaware of exactly what it was passing, the administration was not. In 2002 the president signed a secret EO that authorized the National Security Agency (NSA)[32] to collect "signal intelligence" (that is, telecommunication and electronic communication information) on U.S. residents while they are in the U.S. It was not until 2005, when the *New York Times* finally blew the whistle on this program (after agreeing for a year to hold off, under pressure from the Bush administration) that it became clear that the Bush administration would unilaterally use the USA PATRIOT Act to justify untrammeled spying within the U.S.[33]

Undoubtedly many more shoes will drop in this domestic spying scandal. In April 2006 the *New York Times* further revealed that "a former AT&T employee has . . . documents [that] suggest the telephone companies may be helping the government engage in wholesale interception of telephone calls, e-mail messages and Web surfing." The former employee stated that "AT&T has maintained a secret room at its San Francisco Internet and telephone hub where its customers' data could be mined by keywords, e-mail addresses and other attributes . . . [and] the National Security Agency was given access to the room and the data. He says other technicians have reported to him that similar rooms exist at other AT&T sites."[34]

In May 2006 *USA Today* revealed that since 2001 the NSA has been illegally and covertly collecting a massive database of calls placed by *tens of millions* of Americans.[35] In May 2006, shortly after this startling revelation, Bush nominated Gen. Michael Hayden to be the new CIA director. As NSA chief from 1999 to 2005 Hayden *oversaw* that agency's massive illegal surveillance. During his confirmation hearings Hayden refused to publicly answer any probing questions about this surveillance, continuing to claim against all evidence that he and the NSA were abiding by the law.

As each new revelation of more massive and more intrusive illegal surveillance comes out, the administration concocts a new cover story, only to subsequently have another whistleblower reveal the falsity of the administration's last rationale. Small wonder that the administration is so intent on criminalizing media coverage of their illegal acts and thus strangling the public's right to know.

On May 16, 2006, ABC News reported that the administration was tracking phone numbers dialed by major news organizations in order to intimidate reporters and those in government who provide leaks to the press. Furthermore, this tracking can be done without court order, using a "national security letter," issued by an agent in the field.[36] This letter can require a phone company or Internet provider to turn over the information without revealing that the act has been done. According to Brian Ross, ABC News' chief investigative correspondent, the Justice Department's figures show that the FBI issued 9,254 of these national security letters in 2005, aimed at surveilling 3,500 U.S. citizens and legal immigrants.[37] This administration is clearly operating surveillance at a magnitude far greater than it has ever represented.

Once the PATRIOT Act was passed libraries became "hunting grounds" for FBI agents, demanding information about their patrons. The American Library Association's executive director has described this practice as a "scary" trend.[38] Librarians, like telephone and Internet carriers, are even prohibited from disclosing that the information was requested of them.[39] The PATRIOT Act, moreover, applies not only to library records but also to all so-called third-party records, including "medical, financial, educational, purchase, rental, and lending records."[40]

This kind of intelligence gathering is patently illegal. The 1978 Foreign Information Security Act (FISA), which Bush violated in spying on U.S. citizens without warrants, was passed by Congress for two reasons: to permit monitoring of potential threats to the U.S. and to prevent the abuses of this monitoring that had been so evident in the Nixon administration, where it had been used against political "enemies," such as the Democratic Party. Nixon's improper use of domestic surveillance was, in fact, included in Article 2, paragraph 2, of the impeachment articles against him.[41]

Given that FISA even allows retroactive approval for surveillance, no legitimate grounds exist for bypassing it. Nonetheless, just days after the September 11, 2001, attacks on New York and the Pentagon, the administration had John Yoo write an internal memorandum arguing that the government might use "electronic surveillance techniques and equipment that are more powerful and sophisticated than those available to law enforcement agencies in order to intercept telephonic communications and observe the movement of persons but *without obtaining warrants* for such uses" (emphasis added).[42]

FISA requires court approval for authorizing electronic surveillance in order to obtain foreign intelligence information. The Foreign Intelligence Surveillance Court (FISC) has direct jurisdiction over FISA activities. It is composed of eleven District Court judges from different circuits, who are appointed by the chief justice of the Supreme Court, and convene only to grant or deny foreign-intelligence surveillance warrants.

Even before ABC News broke the story in the surveillance scandal in May 2006, a FISC judge in 2000 criticized the Justice Department and FBI "for providing the [court] with misleading information" in seventy-five cases in which it "substituted relaxed foreign intelligence gathering wiretapping procedures to evade higher requirements for standard criminal investigations," possibly because "the government is unable to meet the substantive requirements of these law enforcement tools."[43] An FBI memo revealed "that agents illegally videotaped suspects, intercepted e-mails, recorded the wrong phone conversations, and allowed electronic surveillance operations to run beyond their [FISC warrant] deadline."[44]

In 2005 the administration revealed to the head of FISC that information was obtained without proper warrants from the FISA court, but executive branch officials assured her that it would never happen again. Not only would it happen again, the administration had specific plans on how to make it happen.

In fact, the administration's real intent in continuously circumventing the Fourth Amendment's judicial oversight requirement of surveillance activities was revealed shortly after September 11, 2001, in a letter from the Justice Department's Office of Legislative Affairs' Assistant Attorney General Daniel J. Bryant. The letter, addressed to key senators, invoked the unitary executive by recommending, incredibly, the suspension of the Fourth Amendment's requirement for warrants when the executive branch is investigating a threat to national security:

As Commander-in-Chief, the President must be able to use whatever means necessary to prevent attacks upon the United States:
this power, by implication, includes the authority to collect information necessary to its effective exercise. . . . Here, for Fourth
Amendment purposes, *the right to self-defense is not that of an individual, but that of the nation and its citizens*. . . . If the government's
heightened interest in self-defense justifies the use of deadly force,
then it certainly would also justify warrantless searches (emphasis
added).[45]

Specifically, Section 216 of the PATRIOT Act authorized the use of Carnivore (also known as the DCS1000 system). Carnivore, once installed on an
Internet Service Provider (ISP), can intercept a wide array of Internet activities, including e-mail, Web page use, and telephone conversations. The technical problem with applying the FISA restrictions to a system such as Carnivore,
which captures electronic communications, is that the FISA rules were written
before the digital-communication era. The FISA rules are based on using pen-
register and trap-and-trace devices, which capture only telephone numbers
rather than the conversation's content. But with electronic communications,
the FBI's interpretation of a pen-register has changed, as has its surveillance
capability.[46]

Because Carnivore cannot avoid tracking content along with signals, it is
unable to discriminate between targets of an investigation and those who are
not targets.[47] In July 2000 then-Attorney General Janet Reno announced that
the Justice Department would review the new program in light of the fact
that existing statutes were written for analog phone calls and did not relate to
the capture of information in a way that related to digital Internet communication. The Clinton administration promised to maintain strict oversight to
avoid abuses, but as one member of the Carnivore review team stated, "I trust
Reno, but I don't know the intent of her successors. . . . The fact of the matter
is, once it's deployed, there's no guarantee of the intent of successors. Look at
J. Edgar Hoover."[48] Reno never did complete the review of Carnivore, and the
PATRIOT Act's Section 216 made certain it would not be reviewed.[49]

This was not the only time such errors happened in violation of FISA regulations. In 2002 an FBI lawyer noted that Carnivore was prone to cause "the

improper capture of data," and that such unauthorized interceptions needed to avoid capturing data on "innocent third party communications." The lawyer concluded, "I am not sure how we can proceed to test [Carnivore] without inadvertently intercepting [those] communications."[50]

Despite this agent's revelation, FBI Assistant Director Dr. Donald M. Kerr insisted that Carnivore "limits the messages viewable by human eyes."[51] The Bush administration revealed—perhaps inadvertently—how extensive this surveillance is when in January 2006 it filed a lawsuit in the U.S. District Court in San Jose, California, in which the plaintiff complained that Google had refused to turn over *one million* "random Web addresses and records of all Google searches from any one-week period."[52]

New York's U.S. District Judge Victor Marrero has said that the provision's "compulsory, secret, and unreviewable production of information" violate the Fourth Amendment rights against unreasonable searches, as did its requirement for compliance with the burgeoning national security letters issued on FBI letterhead providing a demand for information that, unlike a subpoena, cannot be contested before a judge.[53]

Despite all of this, in his December 10, 2005, call to renew the PATRIOT Act, President Bush noted that the renewal is aimed at "bolstering the Patriot Act's significant *protections* of civil rights" (italics added).[54] While a few essentially cosmetic changes were made to the renewed PATRIOT Act, the law has not fundamentally changed the government's surveillance state.

A Brave New Intelligence World

The Bush administration used 9/11 security concerns to create a new bureaucracy that would enable intelligence gathering to be a priority for an unprecedented number of agencies. In 2002 the Homeland Security Act split up the INS and organized it into different branches. One of these new divisions was ICE (The Office of U.S. Immigration and Customs Enforcement), created in March 2003. ICE was clearly set off from the rest of the divisions as a means of concentrating on activities considered to be threats to national security. In establishing ICE, the administration blurred the historic distinction between criminal and terrorist activity.

One of the most disturbing examples of the conflating of criminals and terrorists is ICE's invitation to businesses and individuals to join a project called Cornerstone. Cornerstone teaches private entities how to recognize suspicious activities and to report them. As ICE's chilling Web site notes, in deploying Cornerstone, "ICE does not differentiate between criminals and terrorists. Any criminal act—whether driven by profit or ideology—is a potential threat to the security of the United States."[55]

Among these suspicious activities are: "Frequent/unusual use of night deposit or ATM machines . . . issuing checks, money orders, or other financial instruments to the same person or business, or to a person or business whose name is spelled similarly . . . [t]ransactions inconsistent with usual and customary business or personal practices . . . [t]ransfer of funds to a commercial account with no logical relationship or connection to the sender of the funds (e.g. jewelry store account wiring money to auto parts exporter)."[56]

The military has also been enlisted in the surveillance war. The Pentagon's Counterintelligence Field Activity (CIFA) was created in 2002, and although its budget and size remain classified, its charge is to collect "raw information reported by concerned citizens and military members regarding suspicious incidents" that "may or may not be related to an actual threat,"[57] but are nonetheless compiled into Threat and Local Observation Notice (Talon) reports.

The government is encouraging us to spy on each other. The U.S. Air Force's Operation Eagle Eyes for example "enlists the eyes and ears of Air Force members and citizens in the war on terror."[58] A 2003 Air Force newsletter stated that Eagle Eyes informants could include family members of Air Force personnel, off-base merchants, contractors, and neighborhoods,[59] and threats might include monitoring by individuals of U.S. facilities using binoculars, taking pictures of facilities, annotating maps or drawings of those facilities, or theft of materials that might be used to create identification cards.[60] As the Washington lawyer Richard Ben-Veniste, a member of the 9/11 Commission, said at the Commission's final news conference: "I am particularly apprehensive about the expansion of our military's role in domestic intelligence gathering."[61]

Spying was planned at the neighborhood level for civilians. In August 2002 the Department of Justice announced its new Operation Terrorist Information and Prevention System (TIPS). The first phase would involve "one million American workers in ten cities whose ranks will include truckers, mail carriers, train conductors, and utility workers, and who will constitute a formal network for reporting suspected terrorist activities."[62]

TIPS did not last long. In response to widespread criticism about the program, Congress prohibited it in 2003.[63]

Data Mining: Collecting Intelligence Information at the Mega Scale

Perhaps the most sinister of the Bush-Cheney administration's electronic surveillance plans are those with the ability to capture information about the physical identity, whereabouts, and behavior patterns of all citizens—and to do so in league with private contractors.

One of the first of these was a database envisioned by the Pentagon's Defense Advanced Research Projects Agency (DARPA). It would be a database "of an unprecedented scale[64] . . . to be used by the intelligence, counterintelligence, and law enforcement communities [and] intends to exploit research and development efforts that have been underway for several years in DARPA and elsewhere, as well as private-sector data-mining technology."[65]

In 2002 DARPA began to create a computer surveillance system out of its Information Awareness Office (IAO). IAO's head was former Admiral John Poindexter (convicted in the Iran-Contra affair for exchanging guns for hostages). Poindexter stated that "the key to fighting terrorism is information" and "[t]o fight terrorism, we need to create a new intelligence infrastructure to allow [national, state, and local] agencies to share information and collaborate effectively and new information technology aimed at exposing terrorists."[66]

But simply breaking down the existing intelligence infrastructure did not seem to be the technology's principle aim. IAO boasted that its programs would include "human network analysis and behavior model-building engines; biometric signatures of humans; story telling, change detection, and truth maintenance; and biologically inspired algorithms for agent control."[67]

One of their programs, Scalable Social Network Analysis (SSNA), caused great controversy when it was discovered. As DARPA explained to Congress in 2003, SSNA would use algorithm-based programs to "simultaneously model multiple connection types (e.g., social interactions, financial transactions, and telephone calls) and combine the results from these models." It was a system designed to analyze "not only a single 'level,' such as connections between people or between organizations, but multiple 'levels' simultaneously, such as interactions among people and the organizations of which they are a part."[68]

Congress did not approve the use of SSNA on individuals acting within the U.S., but in the hands of an administration bent on unfettered power this restriction proved irrelevant.

Surveillance technologies, such as SSNA, would converge to produce the centerpiece of IAO's new system: Total Information Awareness. TIA would mine a variety of data such as personal and commercial communication for patterns of behavior suggestive of terrorist activity.[69] These kinds of programs use complicated algorithms to identify purportedly suspicious activity by comparing information from a vast array of databases. In the case of TIA, which was envisioned as the largest database in the world, some of the information included would be "financial, medical, communication, and travel record information gleaned from multiple sources and fed into the system along with intelligence data."[70]

TIA would use "private and public-sector information holdings . . . to obtain transactional and biometric data."[71] Information might include credit card transactions, communications data, transactions records in a variety of areas such as medical, veterinary, transportation, housing, and critical resources. "Biometric data could include face, fingerprints, gait, and iris data."[72]

In February 2002 a concerned Congress prohibited TIA's use against Americans without congressional approval. But despite TIA's dismantling and warnings that such federal agencies as DARPA do not have the authority to perform domestic intelligence, the administration cleverly renamed the program from "Total Information Awareness" to "Terrorism Information Awareness" and moved many of TIA's counterintelligence machinations, with Senate approval, to the CIA, DoD, and other agencies,[73] or down to the state and local level, hiding them under the cloak of local law enforcement.

One such ambitious program was the Multistate Anti-Terrorism Information Exchange (MATRIX—named without, apparently, a shred of irony given the famous movie), a program that emanated from DHS. The MATRIX intelligence system would search thousands of files looking for "anomalies" that would indicate criminal activity or terrorist threat. One of the most disturbing aspects of the MATRIX is its ability to search a wide array of information including the commonly available information such as drivers licenses and social security numbers as well as credit histories, marriage and divorce records, names and addresses of neighbors, family members, and business associates.[74]

MATRIX was designed to create a "terrorist quotient"[75] measuring the likelihood of an individual being a terrorist. Those carrying a HTF (High Terrorist Factor) would have their information distributed to ICE, the FBI, and the Secret Service. A top Florida police official told the *Washington Post* that the program was so powerful that it was "scary" and that "it could be abused. I mean, I can call up everything about you, your pictures and pictures of your neighbors."[76] (See Chapter 14 in this volume for a discussion of the wealth of information this administration had before 9/11, using old-fashioned information collecting techniques, which they failed to act upon to prevent 9/11.)

The ACLU and others helped bring down MATRIX in 2005. Stated the ACLU, "The message was loud and clear: the Matrix program is not consistent with the American tradition that innocent citizens be 'left alone' by their government."[77]

Despite the failure of at least two of their flagship projects, the administration's fight to continue to gather vast amounts of information on individuals continues unabated. One of the Pentagon's favorite ploys has been to shut down programs in name only, then resume the original operations under a different title, often using the same contractor engaged for the original program. Not surprisingly, most of the information about these programs remains classified, though it is known that some programs under TIA were moved to Advanced Research and Development Activity (ARDA),[78] housed in the NSA, and were awarded late in 2002 to a firm called Hicks & Associates.

Shane Harris of the *National Journal* describes a memo by Brian Sharkey of Hicks & Associates in which Sharkey reveals a project called Basketball. Sharkey played a major role in TIA's development and is a close friend of John Poindexter. The memo reveals that the system was being tested at a center run jointly by the government and Science Advances International Corp (SAIC), a major defense and intelligence contractor and sole owner of Hicks & Associates.[79] Sharkey describes Basketball as a "closed-loop, end-to-end prototype system for early warning and decision-making"—the same verbiage Hicks used when it was awarded the TIA contract in 2002.[80]

Information collection and assessment will not go away. Presumably to allow it to continue undeterred in creating such data-mining systems as TIA and MATRIX, the administration issued Presidential EO 13356, creating the Regional Information Sharing System (RISS) database, whose workings are secret but are similar to MATRIX in that the system links federal, state, and local law-enforcement information in a database that may be shared with private organizations.[81] RISS works in conjunction with the Counterterrorism Collaboration Interoperability Project (CCIP). RISS is being developed by a private company, the Institute of Intergovernmental Research in Florida (IIR).[82] IIR was the company that originally proposed MATRIX.

The administration's ambition to collect massive amounts of data on its citizens is highly disturbing. Along with this concern are the technical problems seen under Carnivore, in which innocent citizens cannot be differentiated from terrorists. A simple example is the CIA "no-fly" list, a watch list that contains an estimated 70,000[83] names in nine databases targeting people who are "paying for a ticket with cash, booking a seat at the last minute, flying one way instead of round trip and even arriving at the airport without luggage."[84]

Screening on the no-fly list has been the airlines' responsibility, but the lack of administrative coordination for the list and the number of errors are examples of just two of its limitations. For example, Senator Edward Kennedy (D-Mass) and Representative Don Young (R-Alaska), Chairman of the House Transportation and Infrastructure Committee, were included on the "no fly" list.[85] Once you have become a target, you may never be able to get your name removed.[86]

Shutting Down the Public's Right to Know

One of the very few means by which ordinary citizens can learn about the workings of the executive branch is the Freedom of Information Act (FOIA), created in 1966. Under the Bush-Cheney administration, FOIA and the right to know about the government are being gutted.

For years, administrations, particularly the Clinton administration, acted in favor of disclosure of information under FOIA, but in October 2001 Attorney General John Ashcroft directed federal agencies to choke off compliance with FOIA requests: "when you have discretion, use it to withhold information." He went on to say that "[you] can be assured the Department of Justice will defend your decisions."[87]

As it hides information by denying FOIA requests, the administration also makes information disappear, aided by information-age tools. Especially vulnerable is scientific information. Steven Aftergood, director on government secrecy of the Federation of American Scientists, notes that an astonishing amount of information has been deleted from federal Web sites during the Bush-Cheney administration; all this information had previously been unclassified. This includes a decades-old NASA database concerning Earth satellites' orbits, the loss of which could hamper "international efforts to mitigate space debris."

Thousands of items of U.S. Army and Air Force Web-based information have been removed. Even the National Geospatial-Intelligence Agency no longer publishes aeronautical maps and other publications—maps of great use to biologists and engineers.[88]

After 9/11 the administration ordered libraries to destroy their U.S. Geological Service CD-ROMs and even restricted the IRS reading room under the guise of national security.[89] And the administration threatened to censor scientists' articles if they did not do so voluntarily. Ironically these kinds of actions may actually compromise our national security. Under government pressure, The National Academy of Sciences agreed to censor articles even though this action might discourage research "on immunization and quarantine strategies that could protect us in the event of a biological attack."[90]

Information that is potentially threatening to the administration's illicit activities may be deleted in the name of national security. On April 8, 2005, the Defense Technical Information Center (DTIC) Joint Electronic Library went offline to remove a report entitled "Joint Doctrine of Detainee Operations."[91]

Unfettered Power in the Information Age

As this administration advances toward unlimited power without accountability, it has refused to explain how gathering massive amounts of data about innocent citizens is aiding the war on terror. It has not explained how our information will be kept out of private hands, including those of the private contractors who help them build these systems, nor has it explained what will happen if government surveillance systems are faulty.

This is the course on which the Bush-Cheney administration has put us. We need security and counterintelligence for our country's protection, but it should not be developed at the draconian costs to our individual liberties by a government that has shown that it has far more of its own agenda in mind than the American people's safety.

Bush has mused out loud that it would be better if he were a dictator.[92] But the aggressive behind-the-scenes strategy to concentrate nearly all power in the executive branch and make it unaccountable to any vestiges of democratic monitoring is more than the product of the efforts of a power-hungry administration. The general trend toward stripping Congress of most of its power (especially its constitutional right to declare war) predates Bush and Cheney and reflects the exigencies of an imperialist superpower bent on having its way in the world, irrespective of what "the people" want. What we see in the Bush-Cheney regime is a great heightening of this general trend and open defiance of any congressional attempts to monitor and investigate. Like the proverbial story of the frog in the pot—in which if you were to drop a frog into a pot of boiling water, it would immediately jump out, but if you put a frog into a pot of cold water and slowly warm it up, the frog will be cooked before it knows what hit it—the American people and "rule of law" have been getting the heat turned up on them.

This administration is tearing down the rule of law while it builds an impenetrable wall around its actions. It has been painful over the last several years to see the executive branch usurp so much power from Congress, the people's putative representatives. It is hard to see the judicial branch remain so inactive, allowing this usurpation to go unchallenged. It is difficult to accept that our press has been so thoroughly intimidated by these political thugs.

Perhaps you have not yet been a victim of the secret government and its campaign toward unchecked power. Perhaps you haven't been on a "no-fly" list only to find that you can't get off it. Perhaps you aren't an environmental scientist whose government's removal of federal reports has permanently jeopardized your work. But these actions happen every day, and they have happened to millions of innocent American citizens.

If you want to get just a small sense of what it feels like to be an innocent person in the midst of a power-hungry secret government, I invite you to go to the Web and look at some of the programs and policies of the military and intelligence departments of the executive branch. Use the tools of the information age to peer in the small peephole they allow you to access. Look at their missions. Look at their programs.

Perhaps you will see, in your innocent research about the federal government, something such as I did when I clicked on the "Privacy and Security Notice" of the Air Force District of Washington, DC's Web site: "Your interaction with this system is not anonymous. By using this system you are consenting to the monitoring of your activity. Raw data logs will only be used to identify individual users and their usage habits for authorized law enforcement investigations or national security purposes."[93]

President Bush, I am scared, and I've done nothing wrong. But I think you have, and you and Vice President Cheney need to leave office.

Notes:

1.　Jess Bravin, "Judge Alito's View of the Presidency: Expansive Powers," *Wall Street Journal*, January 5, 2006, http://online.wsj.com/article_email/SB113642811283938270-lMyQjAxMD E2MzA2NDQwMjQ4Wj.html.
　　　Even as early as 1787 anti-Federalists were concerned about the potential for tyranni-cal power resting in the newly conceived position of U.S. president. Said one anti-federal-ist: "[The] President will be in time a King for life; and after him, his son . . . will be King also. View your danger, and find out good [congressional representatives]—men of your own profession and station in life. Rich men can live easy under any government, be it ever so tyrannical while the greater part of the common people are led by the nose, and played about by these very men, for the destruction of themselves and their class. Be wise, be virtuous, and catch the precious moment as it passes, to refuse this newfangled federal government, and extricate yourselves and posterity from tyranny, oppression, aristocratical or monarchical government." A Farmer and a Planter, "The Use of Coercion by the New Government (Part I)," *The Antifederalist Papers* (no. 26), originally printed in the *Maryland Journal* and *Baltimore Advertiser*, April 1, 1788.
2.　*Freytag v. Commissioner*, 501 U.S. 868 (1991), *Id.* at 906 (Scalia, J., concurring), http://66.102.7.104/search?q=cache:_BN-tYBrzCoJ:www.usdoj.gov/olc/nonexcut.htm.
3.　Daniel K. Inouye and Lee H. Hamilton. Report of the Congressional Committees Investigat-ing the Iran-Contra Affair (Washington, DC: U.S. Government Printing Office), 1987, p. 11.
4.　Bob Woodward, "Cheney Upholds Power of the Presidency," *Washington Post*, January 20, 2005, p. A7.
5.　"Vice President's Remarks to the Traveling Press," December 20, 2005, www.whitehouse. gov/news/releases/2005/12/20051220-9.html. Cheney referred to his Iran-Contra minority report as "very good in laying out a robust view of the President's prerogatives with respect to the conduct of especially foreign policy and national security matters." In these matters "[t]he President of the United States needs to have his constitutional powers unimpaired."
6.　Sidney Blumenthal, "The Long March of Dick Cheney," salon.com, November 24, 2005, http://dir.salon.com/story/opinion/blumenthal/2005/11/24/cheney/index.html.
7.　Jane Mayer, "The Memo: How an Internal Effort to Ban the Abuse and Torture of Detainees Was Thwarted," *The New Yorker*, February 27, 2006, posted February 20, 2006, www.newyorker. com/fact/content/articles/060227fa_fact.
8.　Mayer, *op cit.* The so-called Torture Memo is officially titled "Memorandum from Jay S. Bybee, Assistant Attorney General, to Alberto Gonzales, Counsel to the President. Stan-dards of Conduct for Interrogation. Aug. 1, 2002." http://news.findlaw.com/hdocs/docs/doj/bybee80102ltr.html. According to the Torture Memo, "The Framers understood the [Commander-in-Chief] Clause as investing the President with the fullest range of power understood at the time of the ratification of the Constitution as belonging to the military

commander."

9. John Nichols, "Enron: What Dick Cheney Knew," *The Nation*, April 15, 2002, posted March 28, 2002, http://www.thenation.com/doc/20020415/nichols/2. Nichols notes that Enron memos show that "Cheney and his aides met at least six times with Kenneth Lay" in preparing the Task Force's final report, and "in April 2001 Lay gave Cheney a . . . 'wish list' of corporate recommendations," many of which found their way into the Task Force's final report.

10. Dana Milbank and Eric Pianin, "Bush's Panel on Energy Works Off the Record," *Boston Globe*, April 17, 2001, p. A2. Originally cited in Philip H. Melanson, *Secrecy Wars: National Security, Privacy, and the Public's Right to Know* (Washington, DC: Brassey's, Inc., 2001), p. 86.

11. U.S. House of Representatives, Committee on Government Reform, Minority Staff Special Investigations Division, "Secrecy in the Bush Administration," September 14, 2004, p. 70, http://democrats.reform.house.gov/features/secrecy_report/pdf/pdf_secrecy_report.pdf.

12. The General Accounting Office (GAO) is now called the Government Accountability Office. Its charge has remained to work "for Congress and the American people. Congress asks GAO to study the programs and expenditures of the federal government. [As] the investigative arm of Congress [it is] nonpartisan." "What is the GAO?" http://www.gao.gov/about/what.html.

13. "Letter from David S. Addington, Counsel to the Vice President, to Anthony Gamboa, General Counsel, General Accountability Office (June 7, 2001)," http://democrats.reform.house. gov/ features/secrecy_report/pdf/pdf_secrecy_report.pdf.

14. Throughout U.S. history, presidents have claimed that the separation of powers permits the executive branch to deny requests, including those for information, from the other two branches by exerting executive privilege. Michael C. Dorf, "A Brief History of Executive Privilege, from George Washington through Dick Cheney," FindLaw.com February 6, 2002, http://writ.news.findlaw.com/scripts/printer_friendly.pl?page=/ddorf/20020206.html.
    Notes John Dean, presidential secrecy expert from the Watergate era: "[E]xecutive privilege is one of the strongest tools of presidential secrecy." John W. Dean, *Worse Than Watergate: The Secret Presidency of George W. Bush* (NY: Little, Brown and Company, 2004), pp. 83–84.

15. U.S. House of Representatives Committee on Government Reform, Minority Staff Special Investigations Division, "Secrecy in the Bush Administration," September 14, 2004, p. vii, http://www.fas.org/sgp/library/waxman.pdf.

16. T. J. Halstead, "The Law: Walker v. Cheney: Legal Insulation of the Vice President from GAO Investigations," *Presidential Studies Quarterly*, Washington: September 2003, vol. 33.3, p. 635.

17. Jennifer Van Bergen, "The Unitary Executive: Is The Doctrine Behind the Bush Presidency Consistent with a Democratic State?" Findlaw.com., January 9, 2006, http://writnews.find-law.com/commentary/20060109_bergen.html.

18. William G. Howell, "Unilateral Powers: a Brief Overview," *Presidential Studies Quarterly*. Washington: September 2005, vol. 35, 3, p. 417.

19. John W. Dean, "The Problem with Presidential Signing Statements: Their Use and Misuse by the Bush Administration," Findlaw.com. January 13, 2006, http://writ.news.findlaw.com/.

20. Van Bergen, *op cit.*

21. Mark J. Rozell, *Executive Privilege: Presidential Power, Secrecy, and Accountability* (Lawrence, KS: University Press of Kansas, 2002: 2nd ed., revised), p. 147.

22. Quoted in Nancy Chang, *Silencing Political Dissent* (NY: Seven Stories Press, 2002), p. 127.

23. George W. Bush, "Memorandum for the Attorney General: Congressional Subpoena for Executive Branch Documents," December 12, 2001, http://www.fas.org/sgp/bush/121201_execpriv.html.

24. *Ibid.*

25. Glen Johnson, "Bush Halts Inquiry of FBI and Stirs Up a Firestorm," *Boston Globe*. Decem-

ber 14, 2001, Boston.com.
26. U.S. House of Representatives Committee on Government Reform, Minority Staff Special Investigations Division, "Secrecy in the Bush Administration," September 14, 2004, p. iii, http://www.fas.org/sgp/library/waxman.pdf.
27. Ibid.
28. After 9/11, the Immigration and Naturalization Service was renamed U.S. Immigration and Customs Enforcement (ICE) and was given a greater role in law enforcement and surveillance.
29. John W. Whitehead, "The President Is Wrong: The USA Patriot Act Should Be Terminated," The Rutherford Institute, January 26, 2004, www.rutherford.org/articles_db/commentary.asp?record_id=262.
30. Pub. L. 107–56 stat. 349.
31. Chang, op cit., p. 43.
32. "The National Security Agency/Central Security Service is America's cryptologic organization. It coordinates, directs, and performs highly specialized activities to protect U.S. government information systems and produce foreign signals intelligence information." Introduction to NSA/CSS, http://www.nsa.gov/about/.
33. James Risen and Eric Lichtblau, "Bush Lets U.S. Spy on Callers Without Courts," New York Times, December 16, 2005, p. A1.
34. "AT&T and Domestic Spying; [Editorial]," New York Times, April 17, 2006, p. A20.
35. Leslie Cauley, "NSA Has Massive Database of American's Phone Calls," USAToday.com, May 11, 2006, www.usatoday.com/news/washington/2006-05-10-nsa_x.htm.
36. Amy Goodman, "Freedom of the Press Under Attack: Government Begins Tracking Phone Calls of Journalists," Interview with Brian Ross, DemocracyNow.org, May 16, 2006, www.democracynow.org/pring.pl?sd=06/05/16/145201.
37. Ibid.
38. Chang, op cit., p. 50.
39. Van Bergen, op cit., p. 132.
40. Ibid.
41. Jennifer Van Bergen, "The Unitary Executive: Is The Doctrine Behind the Bush Presidency Consistent with a Democratic State?" Findlaw.com, January 9, 2006, http://writ.news.findlaw.com/commentary/20060109_bergen.html.
42. Risen and Lichtblau, op cit.
43. "FISA Court Chastises DOJ, FBI," Electronic Privacy Information Center: Foreign Intelligence Services Act, October 10, 2002, http://www.epic.org/privacy/terrorism/fisa/.
44. "Memo Reveals FBI Wiretap Violations," Electronic Information Privacy Center: Foreign Intelligence Services Act, August 23, 2002, http://www.epic.org/privacy/terrorism/fisa/.
45. Quoted in Chang, op cit., p. 56.
46. According to "Daily E-Mail Alert," Tech Law Journal, no. 1, 110, April 6, 2005, http://www.techlawjournal.com/alert/2005/04/06.asp., "The statutes for wiretaps and PR&TTD orders were drafted with analog Public Switched Telephone Network (PSTN) voice service in mind. Originally, 18 U.S.C. § 3127 provided that a pen register records the numbers that are dialed or punched into a telephone, while a trap and trace device captures the incoming electronic or other impulses which identify the originating number of an instrument or device from which a wire or electronic communication was transmitted. The Patriot Act expanded the scope of surveillance under pen register and trap and trace authority to include internet routing and addressing information. That is, an e-mail address in the 'To:' line of an e-mail message is somewhat analogous to the number dialed in a PSTN voice call. However, this expanded authority also applies to new technologies for collecting addressing and routing information, such as the FBI's Carnivore system."

47. Chang, *op cit.*, p. 55.
48. Richard Stengler, "Justice Department Mum About Who Will Review 'Carnivore,'" CNN.com, September 7, 2000, http://archives.cnn.com/2000/TECH/computing/09/07/carnivore/index.html.
49. Section 216 extends telephone-monitoring laws to cover Internet usage.
50. "FBI's Carnivore System Disrupted Anti-Terror Investigation," Electronic Privacy Information Center, May 28, 2002. www.epic.org/privacy/carnivore/5_02_release.html.
51. Donald M. Kerr, "Internet and Data Interception Capabilities Developed by the FBI," Statement for the Record, U.S. House of Representatives, the Committee on the Judiciary, Subcommittee on the Constitution, July 24, 2000, http://www.cdt.org/security/carnivore/000724fbi.shtml.
52. "New Updates from Citizens for Legitimate Government," legitgov.org, January 19, 2006, http:www.legitgov.org.
53. Nikki Swartz, "Patriot Act Provision Ruled Unconstitutional," *Information Management Journal: Lemexa*, Nov/Dec 2004, vol. 38, no. 6, p. 6.
54. "Bush Says Congress Needs to Act Quickly to Extend Patriot Act," Bloomberg.com, December 10, 2005, http://www.bloomberg.com/appsnews?pid=10000087&sid=aLNyP6.EvyKM&refer=top_world_news.
55. U.S. Immigration and Customs Enforcement, "ICE: Immigration Enforcement and Highlights," www.ice.gov, http://www.ice.gov/doclib/pi/news/factsheets/021406ice.pdf.
56. U.S. Immigration and Customs Enforcement, "Partners: Red Flag Indicators," http://www.ice.gov/partners/cornerstone/redflag.htm.
57. Walter Pincus, "Defense Facilities Pass Along Reports of Suspicious Activity," *Washington Post*, December 11, 2005, p. A12.
58. "Eagle Eyes Program," Air Force Office of Special Investigations Web site, http://public.afosi.amc.af.mil/eagle/index.asp.
59. Pincus, *op cit.*
60. *Ibid.*
61. *Ibid.*
62. Chang, *op cit.*, p. 97.
63. Nat Hentoff, "The Death of Operation TIPS: Volunteer Spying Corps Dismissed," Villagevoice.com, December 13, 2002, http://www.villagevoice.com/news/0251,hentoff,40587,6.html.
64. Quoted in "Government Technology Surveillance: Privacy Overview: Information Access and Citizen Protections," *Congressional Diges*, April 2003, vol. 82, no. 4, p. 1.
65. *Ibid.*, p. 2.
66. "Vision Statement of the Information Awareness Office of the Defense Advanced Research Projects Agency, U.S. Department of Defense," quoted in "DARPA's Information Awareness Office," *Congressional Digest*, April 2003, vol. 82, no. 4, p. 1.
67. *Ibid.*
68. Dr. John M. Poindexter, "Report to Congress Regarding the Terrorism Information Awareness Program, In Response to Consolidated Appropriations Resolution, 2003, Pub. L.18-07, Div. M. § 111 (b), May 20, 2003, "http://wyden.senate.gov/leg_issues/reports/darpa_tia.pdf.
69. "Government Technology Surveillance: Foreword," *Congressional Digest*, April 2003, vol. 82, no. 4, p. 1.
70. Quoted in "Government Technology Surveillance: Privacy Overview: Information Access and Citizen Protections," *Congressional Digest*, April 2003, vol. 82, no. 4, p. 2.
71. *Ibid.*
72. *Ibid.*
73. Noah Shactman, "Homeland Security: The Bastard Children of Total Information Awareness," Slate.com, February 2, 2004, http://www.wired.com/wired/archive/12.02/start.html?pg=4.

74. American Civil Liberties Union, "ACLU Unveils Disturbing New Revelations About MATRIX Surveillance Program," ACLU Web site, May 20, 2004, http://www.aclu.org/privacy/spying/15234prs20040520.html.

75. American Civil Liberties Union, "Feature on MATRIX," ACLU Web site, March 8, 2005, http://www.aclu.org/privacy/spying/15701res20050308.html.

76. Quoted in American Civil Liberties Union, "ACLU Applauds End Of 'Matrix' Program," ACLU Web site, April 15, 2005, http://www.aclu.org/privacy/spying/15324prs20050415. html.

77. *Ibid.*

78. ARDA is "an Intelligence Community (IC) center for conducting advanced research and development related to Information Technology (IT)." ARDA is being taken out of the NSA and will be called the "Disruptive Technology Office," which Shane Harris of the the *National Journal* calls "a reference to a term of art describing any new invention that suddenly, and often dramatically, replaces established procedures." Shane Harris, "TIA Lives On," *National Journal,* February 23, 2006, http://nationaljournal.com/about/njweekly/stories/2006/0223nj1.htm.

79. *Ibid.*

80. *Ibid.*

81. Chang, *op cit.*, p. 114.

82. Institute for Intergovernmental Research Web site., http://www.iir.com.

83. Pam Fessler, "Problems Plague 'No-Fly' List, TSA Considers Changes," *NPR Morning Edition,* Washington, DC, April 26, 2005.

84. Christopher Elliot, "Getting Off a Security Watch List Is the Hard Part," *New York Times,* November 2, 2004, p. C8.

85. Keith Alexander, "A Common Name Can Be a Curse," *Washington Post,* October 12, 2004, p. E1.

86. Elliot, *op cit.*

87. U.S. Department of Justice, Office of Information and Privacy, "FOIA Post: New Attorney General FOIA Memorandum Issued," www.usdoj.gov/oip/foiapost/2001foiapost19.htm.

88. Steven Aftergood, "The Age of Missing Information: the Bush Administration's Campaign against Openness," Slate.com, posted Thursday, March 17, 2005, http://www.slate.com.

89. "John Podesta Remarks to Heinz School of Public Policy: The War at Home: Democracy, Debate and Dissent," Center for American Progress, May 18, 2003, http://www.americanprogress.org/site/apps/nl/content3.asp?c=biJRJ8OVF&b=837247&ct=48225.

90. *Ibid.*

91. Laura Gordon-Murnane, "Shhh!!: Keeping Current on Government Secrecy," *Searcher* vol. 14, no. 1, January 2006, p. 36.

92. "Meeting with House and Senate Republican Leadership." Aired on "Transition of Power: President-Elect Bush Meets With Congressional Leaders on Capitol Hill," *CNN Newsday,* aired December 18, 2000, transcript at http://transcripts.cnn.com/TRANSCRIPTS/0012/18/nd.01.html.

93. Air Force District of Washington Web site www.afdw.af.mil/dsiclaimer.htm.

Chapter 10

BUSH-CHENEY'S WAR
ON THE ENLIGHTENMENT

Mark Crispin Miller

I

Although the United States, God knows, has had its share of shady leaders, we have never seen anything like this. No prior presidential team, however infamous in its own day, is even faintly comparable to the gang that has now taken power. In its venality this regime has no precedent. What with its ongoing fire sale of all government services and public property; its deep, dark roots in Enron; its symbiotic partnerships with Halliburton-KBR and Lockheed Martin (just to name two); and its blood relations with the Carlyle Group and countless other surreptitious players—the Bush administration makes the tawdry dealings of Ulysses S. Grant or Warren Harding look like child's play; and it even makes the epic pig-out of Big Bill McKinley's term—the presidency most admired by Karl Rove—seem trivial by comparison. The racketeering of the Bush regime dwarfs even Richard Nixon's crookedness (the income-tax evasion, ITT and Dita Beard, the milk fund, Dwayne Andreas, Tom Pappas, "I am not a crook," and so on), and even the big-money scandals under Reagan-George H. W. Bush (Wedtech, HUD, the S&L calamity, the Superfund imbroglio at EPA, and the like).

Bush-Cheney's greed is staggering, and yet such vast self-dealing is, in fact, the least remarkable of this regime's high crimes and misdemeanors. Far more dangerous than all its merely larcenous activity is its imperial crusade for total power. In this regard as well it has attained new heights. Mainly through the PATRIOT Act, but also through such steps as the establishment of "First Amendment Zones" and other wholly arbitrary measures, this regime has outdone every prior presidential stroke of war time tyranny, from John Adams' Alien and Sedition Acts to Lincoln's imposition of martial law to Woodrow Wilson's Sedition Act to all of the repressive legislation of the Cold War's first ten years. Such dictatorial strokes, however dangerous, were meant to stay in force no longer than the conflicts that had spawned them, and in every case the enemy was largely massed somewhere, or thought to be, on Planet Earth. (Even the Cold War, however daunting its projection, could be seen as some-day ceasing through the Kremlin's victory or surrender.)

This war is something else entirely. Since "terror" is only what Bush-Cheney say it is, their war against it is no likelier to conclude than, say, a "War on Dark-ness," or a "War on Smoke." *This* war, in other words, is no mere terminable clash, like all the prior wars in human history, but an unprecedented national crusade to wipe out all the evil in the world—a total struggle that can only end when all the world, and human history itself, have ended too. Since this war must be *final*, then, it has necessarily entailed a program of repression far more comprehensive than the mere draconian decrees of 1798 or 1917. Whereas such prior measures were meant just to silence the dissenters of the moment, Bush-Cheney's ongoing crackdown is intended to stamp out all opposition or divergence absolutely—not just the dissent we hear (or not) today, but any dissidence that *could* break out, should there be any place where it might be permitted to arise, or any medium through which it might find marginal expression.

In working to shut off contemporaneous debate, Bush-Cheney and their apparat have utterly surpassed the dictatorial half-steps of previous U.S. administrations by doing everything they could to silence all dissenting voices and suppress all contradictory (or incriminating) information. This regime has gagged and persecuted whistle-blowers, blackballed journalists, muzzled scientists, punished candid soldiers, hounded uncooperative nonprofits, and above all, smeared its critics, slandering them with a vindictive gusto that makes even Richard Nixon seem restrained. And while thus pounding everyone who dares to disagree, the Bush regime has also arrogated to itself a new monopoly on public information, repeatedly misleading both the Congress and the pub-lic by burying (or distorting) inconvenient data, classifying (or reclassifying) contrary government reports, and otherwise concealing its activities and plans behind an Iron Curtain of its own design. If the law requires transparency, the Bush regime ignores it. Thus Cheney early on refused to name the members of the working group that helped him formulate the nation's energy policy (and he continued to refuse, although several judges told him to comply); and thus, in November 2001, the President grandly overturned the 1978 Presidential Records Act by signing Executive Order 13233, which granted him the power to hold back presidential papers from 1980 on—papers that the law earmarked specifically for publication.

Through such strokes of intimidation, lawlessness, and outright censorship, Bush-Cheney and their men have run the government just as they managed their campaign events in 2004—as a closely scripted, tightly managed, wholly empty *show* of happy unanimity. And yet Bush-Cheney do not merely want to suppress all disagreement in the present (and erase all memory of contradiction in the past). While striving thus to fake a rosy picture for us in the here and now, they are engaged as well in waging an immense and various preemptive war against all disagreement in the future. Strategically their goal is to create a populace that *cannot argue*, as there won't be any space or medium for argument nor any citizens still able, or inclined, to think out loud against the status quo (or, for that matter, think at all). The regime now pursues that dual crusade on every front. For instance, these people have all but finished off "the liberal media" (although that weary phantom had, in fact, already largely vanished by 2000, or Bush-Cheney never would have been "elected"). The regime has crushed CBS News, castrated NPR and PBS, and cowed the broadcast networks through a daunting range of threats ("indecency" lawsuits) and promises (more "deregulation"). Dissent has moved, predictably, to cyberspace—and so Bush-Cheney are now working to destroy the Internet, by allowing the big telephone and cable companies to monopolize it. That maneuver, along with heavy new constraints on the political expression of nonprofits, would effectively transform the Internet into a vast online equivalent of Fox News TV.

While it makes such efforts to contain the media, the Bush regime works also, more directly, to constrain the people, carefully inducing them to see no evil, hear no evil, speak no evil of the Bush regime. "People should watch what they say," as Ari Fleischer put it shortly after 9/11. That blunt warning is the subtext of many, if not most, of the regime's domestic policies. Certainly Bush-Cheney's counterterrorism program does far more to intimidate the people than it does to catch or hinder any terrorists (a goal that would appear to call for heightened port security, increased protection of America's borders, and strict safeguards on the nation's petrochemical facilities, to name a few of the precautions that the Bush-Cheney government has failed to take). Intimidation also has been key to the regime's low-key campaign to neutralize the colleges and universities, which still, to some extent, encourage critical reflection. Using such ideologues as David Horowitz to generate publicity, the ruling party has recruited undergraduates to spy on leftish faculty on campuses throughout the nation, as a way to cow the vulnerable (that is, the untenured) into parroting the party line, whatever it may be. Although such tactics are appalling, at this time they pose a negligible threat to the nation's intellectual development.

More fundamentally, however, the regime has apparently done great and lasting damage to American politics and civic life in general, through its (bipartisan) "reforms" in public education. As altered by the No Child Left Behind Act, our public schools now teach our children not to reason, not to grasp complexity, not to read for pleasure or for deeper understanding of the world, but only to pass endless simple tests concocted by the government itself. Primarily through that regressive policy—along with massive budget cuts in education and the gradual suffusion of curriculums and textbooks with religious myth, including "abstinence-based sex education"—our public schools have been converted into mills for the production of compliant troops as homogeneous and ignorant as clams, frightened of unpleasant truths, worshipful toward those in charge, and therefore fundamentally incapable of governing themselves. The regime's drive to dominate the media and regulate the public mind is not conservative, of course, but radical, like any other program of totalitarian control.

In their transgression Bush and Cheney are also unprecedented in another way; no prior U.S. chief executives have been as *brazen* in the perpetration of their crimes and misdemeanors. If we compare this regime with the major presidential malefactors of the years since World War II, we note in the misdeeds of Bush and Cheney an anomalous overtness. Where other presidents were secretive because they did not want their crimes exposed, Bush and Cheney boast about their crimes right out in public, or advise their critics to go fuck themselves, or offer alibis so feeble that it's obvious that they themselves don't even buy them.

Whereas Nixon mounted an elaborate cover-up to hide the crimes of Watergate, desperate as he was to keep the world from learning of the sabotage and the surveillance, Bush has openly, indignantly, defiantly affirmed his right to have his agents read our mail and "eavesdrop" on our phone calls. Whereas, back in the 1970s, the CIA was circumspect about its use of dirty tricks and torture and its programs of assassination, Bush, Cheney, Rumsfeld, and Gonzales have made very clear that they see nothing wrong with such dark practices as long as it is "we" who use them. And whereas Ronald Reagan's men meticulously hid their efforts to subvert the will of Congress, so that their Iran-contra plot came as a huge surprise in 1986, Bush-Cheney openly despise their adversaries in Congress, ignoring both their laws and their inquiries; and while the Reagan team obtained its war in Nicaragua covertly, Bush and Cheney and their men lied openly, demonstrably, to engineer their war against Iraq, fabricating evidence with such overt dishonesty that they could not have pulled it off without the acquiescence of the press (and all too many of the Democrats).

II

What is it that accounts for this regime's unprecedented shamelessness? What, exactly, drives these leaders to attempt to gain dominion over all the world? Why do they believe themselves to be "above the written law" (as Fawn Hall infamously put it at the Iran-Contra hearings)? And what could possibly explain the wild apocalyptic thrust of their agenda? For this regime is not conservative, nor does it represent your grandpa's GOP. They do not merely serve the corporate juggernaut, as the Republicans *and* Democrats have both been doing for at least a hundred years. To see this regime, and the movement that has pushed for its success, as motivated just by greed is to mistake its revolutionary program for a purely rational endeavor—and this regime is utterly *irrational*. However dangerous it can be, capital is not inclined to die; and yet Bush-Cheney's policies, across the board, are ultimately suicidal, motivated not by any purely economic logic but by the rapturous eschatology of the quasi-Christian ultraright.

This is not to say that the regime is guided *only* by religious zealotry. Modern revolutions tend, at first, to serve a broad array of interests, and so does this one: an enterprise conjointly headed by apocalyptic Christianists, eager for worldwide theocracy, and an influential network of Straussian neoconservatives, who, although mostly atheists themselves, prefer religious government

to any other, as the system likeliest to create a docile populace. The Strauss-
ians work for empire, while the Christianists want Jesus to return (which, they
think, he will do only *after* they have sanctified the world). The two groups have
collaborated brilliantly so far, with much support from Israel (both groups
being militantly Zionist, for very different reasons), and, far more important,
from the multinational cartels—weapons systems, agribusiness, automotives,
media conglomerates, pharmaceuticals, petrochemicals, healthcare, junk
food, banks, and oil, and so on—which are, of course, forever following the
money. And yet even their motives can be complicated, as the revolution heavily depends on a cabal of pious billionaires whose money making is insepa-
rable from their religious activism: Pete Coors, Richard DeVos (Amway), Tom
Monaghan (Domino's Pizza), Phillip Anschutz, the Rev. Sun Myung Moon,
and the tireless Howard Ahmanson are but a few of Bush-Cheney's stealthy
angels, who are both theocrats and plutocrats at once.

Who, in this schizoid revolution, finally calls the shots? It is a reasonable
question, and one to which we reasonable people like to give this tranquil-
lizing answer: "That Christian nonsense is all smoke and mirrors, craftily
deployed by Cheney and his agents to delude the mass of dopes who actually
believe that stuff. Thus Wall Street is, as usual, in charge, and taking all those
bumpkins for a ride." It is a rational interpretation—and, therefore, fatally
inaccurate, attesting less to truly rational analysis of this regime than to the
tendency of rational observers to project their rationality onto others, even
when those others are insane. (Hitler was thus misconceived for years.) In
fact, the theocrats and neocons are not equivalent forces. Whereas the neocons have no grass-roots constituency, the Christianists command a seasoned
national army of devoted troops who have long since infiltrated the political
establishment at both the state and federal levels and who now run both the
GOP and the regime's executive departments, while also dominating Congress and, increasingly, the Supreme Court. The neocons, in other words, do
not comprise a full-blown movement but are nothing more, or less, than a
highly influential coterie, and so to cast them as the theocrats' full partners is
to overstate their numbers and their power.

A careful survey of Bush-Cheney's policies exposes an agenda more
perverse than Democrats, and leftists generally, have as yet been willing to
acknowledge. For all its plutocratic ruthlessness, its fealty to the multination-
als, its laissez-faire mythology and rampant cronyism, this regime cannot be

explicated purely in economic terms. For this regime is ultimately suicidal; and capital, however dangerous it can be, is not inclined to blow itself to smithereens.

Bush-Cheney's economic policy, for example—Reaganomics to the max— is ruinous to the economy's health in general, however magical its influence on profits in the short run. Although today the Laffer Curve has just about as much respectability as crystal meth, this regime pursues "supply-side economics" with a vengeance—spending a cool trillion on "defense" while slashing taxes to the bone. While it exhilarates some buccaneering types, this manic program is entirely unsustainable, as the world's financial elites fully understand. This is why the annual mood at Davos has been dismal since Bush came to power, and why both the *Financial Times* and the *Economist* endorsed John Kerry in 2004, and why Bush-Cheney's reelection was also opposed by 169 tenured business professors, who a few weeks prior to election day publicly deplored the regime's economic recklessness. (That open letter was conceived and drafted at the Harvard Business School, where Bush went for his MBA.)

A suicidal impulse drives Bush-Cheney's military policy, which courts disaster on two fronts. First of all, the regime seems peculiarly intent on the destruction of the military itself. Through serial adventurism, pointless penny-pinching, and (what would appear to be) astonishing incompetence, Bush-Cheney have demoralized the troops, lost countless able officers, and for all their tough talk, left this nation largely unprotected, as hurricane Katrina made quite clear. Although Bush-Cheney now spend more on arms than all the other nations of the world combined, such extravagance is only hastening the military's breakdown, as that largesse goes mainly to the likes of Halliburton-KBR, Blackwater USA, and Lockheed Martin, while the regime slashes veterans' benefits, closes schools on military bases, sticks the troops with poor equipment, and makes wounded soldiers pay for their own meals. Such bald exploitation, and the ever rising carnage in Iraq, have dragged recruitment down to crisis levels, as many officers have warned repeatedly and publicly, yet the President says that all is well and seems to mean it.

And while it ravages its own war machine, the regime has also been using it to touch off a catastrophe far larger; for these wars are not only "about oil" and/or the hot new chain of U.S. military bases in Iraq and/or the role of Israel in U.S. foreign policy. Such concerns are worldly, whereas Bush himself, and an influential circle of his military men, have Armageddon on their minds. As Seymour Hersh has pointed out, Commander Bush is driven largely by "messianism," with Rove and Cheney generally keeping him "in the gray world of religious idealism, where he wants to be anyway."[1] As Defender of the Faith, Bush yearns to "bring it on," as he affirmed quite openly in July 2003; nor was the President misspeaking when he came out with that boyish challenge. "George sees this as a religious war," a member of his family explained around that time. "He doesn't have a p.c. view of the war. His view of this is that they are trying to kill the Christians. And we the Christians will strike back with more force and more ferocity than they will ever know."[2]

Although it would be nice to think that Bush is all alone in such medieval zeal, there is every indication that a hardy theocratic cult has flowered within the military, and that it's with Bush all the way. In June 2003 the Pentagon announced that Lt. Gen. William "Jerry" Boykin would henceforth serve as Deputy Undersecretary of Defense for Intelligence, a new position at the right hand of Stephen Cambone, Rumsfeld's top capo in the "war on terror." Now Boykin was in charge of the Pentagon's "High Value Target Plan" to track and nab the kingpins of Islamist terror—a job that gave him broad authority over "enemy combatants" held at Abu Ghraib and elsewhere. It may not have been the wisest of appointments, as Boykin was already famed for the weird light in his own eyes. For over a year he had been touring U.S. churches nationwide, in his full-dress uniform delivering fierce lay sermons on America's Christian war against Islam. "We're a Christian nation," he would tell the pious, "and the enemy is a guy called Satan." Bush is in the White House, he would say, "because God put him there for a time such as this." So keen was Boykin's zealotry that he often sounded like an Islamist himself. "We in the army of God, in the house of God, kingdom of God have been raised for such a time as this," he said on June 30, 2002, at the First Baptist Church in Broken Arrow, Oklahoma. "Heaven is your reward. You are here as soldiers to take on the enemy," he said on February 6, 2003, at a prayer breakfast at Fort Dix. And just as the Islamists do, Boykin would repeatedly describe "our" war against the unbelievers as *defensive*. "They're after us because we're a Christian nation."[3]

Given Boykin's fervent Manichaeanism, and his important place atop the U.S. gulag archipelago, the atrocities at Abu Ghraib (and other sites) should not have come as a surprise, nor is it credible that they were merely the aberrant work of some "bad apples" acting on their own. The scale and virulence of the abuse, and the bizarre intensity of the religious torture in particular (the taunts and ridicule, the constant sexual humiliation and the holy books profaned) suggest a general atmosphere suffused with that Islamophobic lunacy that Boykin had been uttering in churches all across the land. Nor has that crusading spirit surged only in the Army, Boykin's home, for it has metastasized throughout our military. That spirit pervades the Air Force Academy in Colorado Springs, where the predominating born-agains—instructors and cadets alike—have proselytized aggressively inside the classrooms, in the hallways, on the playing fields, and after hours, harassing those of insufficient zeal, and the Jewish cadets especially. The spirit is also strong among Marines (although the U.S. press has not reported on this occurrence). Before they joined in the destruction of Fallujah, a company of leathernecks cavorted and hallooed in pious ecstasy as chaplains supervised their prayers and Christian rock blared over them. "'You are the sovereign. Your name is holy. You are the pure spotless lamb,' a female voice cried out on the loudspeakers as the Marines clapped their hands and closed their eyes, reflecting on what lay ahead for them." The scene was reported by Agence France-Presse on Nov. 6, 2004.

Between the service's electric guitar religious tunes, marines stepped up on the chapel's small stage and recited a verse of scripture, meant to fortify them for war.

One spoke of their Old Testament hero, a shepherd who would become Israel's king, battling the Philistines some 3,000 years ago.

"Thus David prevailed over the Philistines," the marine said, reading from scripture, and the marines shouted back "Hoorah, King David," using their signature grunt of approval.

The marines then lined up and their chaplain blessed them with holy oil to protect them.

"God's people would be anointed with oil," the chaplain said, as he lightly dabbed oil on the marines' foreheads.

The crowd then followed him outside their small auditorium for a baptism of about a half-dozen marines who had just found Christ.[4]

Such warlike ecstasy among our troops is no mere matter of religious free-dom, any more than the Islamists have a right to use *their* creed to justify mass murder. Whichever faith appears to motivate the killers, there is a direct relationship between the certainty of their belief and the atrociousness of their behavior because a fierce self-righteousness is capable of anything. At Fallujah the Marines used napalm and white phosphorous—weapons banned by inter-national law—to *immolate* the people living there, and saw that it was good; for in King David they thought they could see themselves. Agence France-Presse observed: "The marines drew parallels from the verse with their pres-ent situation, where they perceive themselves as warriors fighting barbaric men opposed to all that is good in the world." And yet, as lethal as it was, those soldiers' faith was far less dangerous than the religiosity of those responsible for all Bush-Cheney's wars, which all alike tend toward apocalypse, whether through the use of napalm in Fallujah or tactical nuclear weapons in Iran, or through the ruination of the planet and/or the economy, or through whatever other terminal development that Bush & Co. deliberately allow to happen or conspire to bring about.

III

The President, Gen. Boykin, Justice Roberts, James Dobson, Paul Weyrich, Pat Robertson, Tim and Beverly LaHaye, Tom Coburn, James Inhofe, Bill O'Reilly, Sean Hannity, Tom Monaghan, Richard DeVos, Howard Ahmanson, and all the other players in Bush-Cheney's "faith-based" movement have the right to their religious views and practices. They also have the right to organize politi-cally around those views, as Americans have done from the beginning of this republic's history. And yet those visionaries have *no* right to subvert the Con-stitution, however much they think God wants them to. All good Americans must now consider what this crucial prohibition means.

First of all it means that we must reacquaint ourselves with one of the essential principles of the American revolution: that this nation was quite pointedly conceived by our forefathers—and, no less important, cherished by the American majority—as a wholly secular republic. The separation of church and state was not some alien notion stealthily imposed upon the godly people of the United States of America by Thomas Jefferson and his French friends but a doctrine quintessentially American, backed wholeheartedly by the majority of Framers, and understood by many a good Christian citizen as crucial to the preservation of religious liberty. Indeed, America's immense religious energy from that time on, the peculiar multiplicity and vibrancy of the nation's actual faith-based community, was itself a healthy consequence of the church-state separation, as de Tocqueville so astutely noted. Although the deist founders and certain of their more observant fellow citizens had very different reasons for endorsing separation, they were allies in that support, and that alliance was definitive, creating the unprecedented secular republic that the theocratic movement is now trying to subvert.

This new movement might be understood as a revival of the early theocratic counterdrive against establishing our secular republic: the abortive push to Christianize the Constitution, followed by the Federalists' hysterical crusade, in 1800, to keep Thomas Jefferson from being elected president. And yet, although that counterdrive was virulent, it seems somewhat restrained by contrast with the theocratic movement reigning now; for this new movement is not just much wealthier and, in its propaganda methods, vastly more sophisticated than the early counterdrive, but also far more savagely nostalgic, far more blatant in its disrespect for scientific reason, and far more heavily fixated on apocalypse. (It is more a product of the twentieth than of the eighteenth century, as the dominionist movement grew largely out of the John Birch Society.) What threatens our democracy today is, literally, the theocratic countermovement *with a vengeance*, its members openly inclined to call black "white," or break the laws of man *and* God, if that is what (they think) God wants.

Thus do the "faith-based" operatives assert, against a massive library of evidence, that the U.S. *is* a "Christian republic," having been deliberately conceived as such by Washington, Jefferson, Madison, and their fellows. The Christianist far right has flogged this fiction endlessly, not only through their own almighty Wurlitzer, but also through the Fox News channel and its giant imitators in the corporate media. With the bright-eyed confidence of true believers (for they themselves believe it to be true), they dismiss the church-state separation as "a myth"—"like 'global warming,'" as Jerry Falwell often honks derisively. They generally try to make this argument by dazzling us with reverential factoids yanked from history. That the authors of the Constitution dated it September 17, 1787, "in the Year of our Lord" (a mere calendrical formality), and/or that Ben Franklin suggested that the Framers say a little prayer to consecrate their enterprise (an idea that they all rejected), and/or that "In God We Trust" is printed on our currency (because of legislation passed in 1956), and so on—the Christianists seize on such bits to *prove* that their God made the United States of America entirely for themselves.

We now find that our taxes also pay directly for the proselytizing work of theocratic activists. Officially, Bush-Cheney's Office of Faith-Based and Community Initiatives is just a way to help religious groups help folks in need, by subsidizing social-service programs that just happen to be run by faith-based organizations: churches, synagogues, and mosques—all equally benevolent, all equally effective, and all equally American. In fact, that "office" is devoted, not to strengthening "the armies of compassion," but to funding an enormous network of pro-Bush extremist groups that specialize in propaganda on two fronts. On the one hand they seek converts to their creed while also pushing Christianist home-schooling, abstinence-based sex education, corporal punishment, creationism, male supremacy, "pro-life" ideology, and other very bad ideas. And as they thus do what they deem the work of God, they also, on the other hand, serve as agents of Karl Rove, who closely oversees the funding process, so that no pro-Bush group gets left behind—and no unsympathetic types get any help at all. The "office" is, to say the least, discriminating, funding mostly far-right Christianist outfits while stiffing liberal Christian groups, and also handing small amounts to just enough Muslim and Jewish entities to give the scam some cover.[5]

The "office" is, in fact, a bold and radical assault on constitutional principle. Perversely, and tellingly, Bush first publicly proposed the office's formation in Philadelphia on Independence Day, 2001. Standing right in front of Independence Hall, Bush pitched his program with a speech that carefully identified the history of the United States with the Old Testament. It was a masterpiece of theocratic innuendo, heavily implying that the U.S. is, in fact, a "Christian republic" after all, the Framers and our Constitution notwithstanding. While our president and Congress, once upon a time, may well have claimed, and even actually believed, that America is no theocracy ("the Government of the United States is, in no sense, founded on the Christian religion," proclaims the Treaty of Tripoli, signed in 1796), Bush and his coreligionists say otherwise and certainly think otherwise—and, in their faith-based system, that's enough.

As egregious as it is, the Office of Faith-Based and Community Initiatives is only one example of Bush-Cheney's long crusade to undermine the Constitution. To note the action on another front, the entire process for selecting members of the federal bench has long since been subverted by the theocratic right, whose activists routinely and overtly agitate *for* militantly rightist Christian nominees and, pointedly, *against* all jurists who strike them either as too secular or as insufficiently devoted to the program of the Christian Coalition. Insofar as such activists, as staunch adherents of "originalism," purport to honor every jot and tittle of the Constitution, they contradict themselves completely. To quote Article VI, Section 3, of that essential document:

> The senators and representatives before-mentioned, and the members of the several state legislatures, and all executive and judicial officers, both of the United States and of the several states, shall be bound by oath or affirmation, to support this constitution; *but no religious test shall ever be required as a qualification to any office or public trust under the United States* (emphasis added).

Although back in the days of Jefferson and Paine religious tests were more straightforward than the tacit "litmus test" used by the theocratic movement now, there is no way to argue that the Framers would have smiled upon the latter. Their ban was categorical: "*no* religious test" *of any kind* "shall *ever* be required" of *any* officers in the United States. In fact, one might argue that Congress has violated that injunction by approving not just Bush-Cheney's judicial nominees but also countless of the regime's nominations *and* appointments, considering the theocrats' enormous sway throughout the Bush administration. For the sake of clarity, however, those Americans who respect the Constitution and expect their government to honor it should start simply by studying the public statements of those on the theocratic right (such as John Roberts, Harriet Miers, and Sam Alito) since Election Day 2004.

And yet such an exercise would, of course, certainly not count for much in any effort to impeach this president and, no doubt, neither would a thorough accounting of the funds awarded by the Office of Faith-Based Initiatives. (The latter task may be impossible, as there are evidently no clear records of the office's disbursements.) Such research should certainly be done, not just in honor of the Constitution, but for our fuller understanding of the history of these benighted times. As for its legal and political utility in Washington today, however, such idealistic research would be likely to accomplish nothing. Congress, after all, approved the Office of Faith-Based Initiatives and has failed to look into its books (if any) and so it is complicit in that scandal. Nor can we blame the Bush regime alone for the subversion of the process whereby federal jurists are approved, for Congress is complicit in that too. Those particular departures from the Constitution may have less to do with the impeachability of Bush per se than with a civic rot far more extensive, involving a fanatical minority intent on triumph over all, an "opposition" that refuses to confront it, and a press unwilling to report on it.

However, even if this president cannot be tried for such specific constitutional infractions, the impeachment effort must be largely driven by a full awareness of the regime's theocratic animus—which is, in fact, the force inspiring *all* Bush-Cheney's crimes and misdemeanors, from the election fraud, bald cronyism, and intelligence manipulation to the torture, the surveillance, and the covert propaganda (and the "reelection" fraud). It is their sense that God has chosen them, that they can do no wrong, that they are wholly unaccountable on earth, that they can break the laws of this world with impunity while making up their own laws as they see fit; that "reality" is only what they say it is, means only what they say it means, so that their say so counts for infinitely more than any counter-claims by reason, science, history, or the evidence of your own senses; that God hates their enemies as much as they do, "the enemy" being anyone and everyone who won't see things exactly as they do or give them everything they want (and what they want is everything); and that the world, and everything, must finally end with them, because it's all *for* them, so that, when they go, it too has to go, because it cannot go to anybody else (there being only them). That sort of crackpot certitude is not just a result of greed or an inordinate appetite for power, but is a reexpression of the very same fanatical mentality that Jefferson, Paine, Madison and (at his sanest) Adams, among others, all regarded as a clear and present danger—always—to life, liberty, and the pursuit of happiness.

Despite their cowboy posturing, their endless cries of "Treason!" and those little metal flags on their lapels, Bush-Cheney's view of life is just as un-American as Bolshevism or Islamism. At their best, Americans have always been devoted to the rational improvement of this world and our lives on it. This regime looks at the world, and at our lives, and obviously wants to *get it over with*—an impulse radically opposed to the ideals of the Enlightenment that brought this nation forth and made it strong, while God just watched, perhaps, and called it good. For their dogged and perverse commitment to so alien a view of life, Bush-Cheney must now be impeached (at least), so that we finally can resume our long, slow progress toward the founding vision of the Framers and the countless common folk who fought along with them. In honor of their memory, and to protect what's left of their accomplishment, we must impeach not only Bush himself but all of his accomplices. This is finally no mere partisan affair but a tremendous civic obligation, one that we, the people—not the Democratic Party, or the press—must now endeavor to fulfill; for God helps those who help themselves, and that is not an empty piety, but, rightly understood, the very essence of American democracy.

Notes:

1. Seymour M. Hersh, "Up in the Air," *The New Yorker*, December 5, 2005.
2. Peter and Rochelle Schweizer, *The Bushes: Portrait of a Dynasty* (NY: Doubleday, 2004), p. 517.
3. Lisa Myers, "Top terrorist hunter's divisive views," NBC News, November 15, 2004, www.msnbc.com/news/980764.asp; Spc. Eugene Roaché, "Prayer Breakfast Mixes Faith with Food," Outlook, July 3, 2003, http://schema-root.org/_stacks/www.dix.army.mil/PAO/post03/post030703/outlook.html.
4. "Evangelical Marines Prepare To Battle Barbarians," Agence France-Presse, November 7, 2004, available online at Common Dreams, http://www.commondreams.org/headlines 04/1107-02.html.
5. See Esther Kaplan, *With God on Their Side: How Christian Fundamentalists Trampled Science, Policy, and Democracy in George W. Bush's White House* (New York: New Press, 2004), pp. 45 ff.; Michelle Goldberg, *Kingdom Coming: The Rise of Christian Nationalism* (New York: W.W. Norton, 2006), pp. 120 ff.

Chapter 11

DENYING DISASTER
Hurricane Katrina, Global Warming, and the Politics of Refusal

Kevin Wehr

The Bush administration's mishandling of one of our time's most crucial issues—global climate change—constitutes a clear and extremely serious case of the abuse of power and therefore an impeachable offense. Further, their stunning incompetence and criminal recklessness in the face of hurricane Katrina also constitutes a sufficient justification for their removal from office.

A Human-Made Disaster: Predictable Tragedy

There are few totally "natural" disasters. We put a city in the way of a natural, predictable storm and then call the resulting destruction a natural disaster. But this is a social disaster. Social disasters don't just come about from the ignorance of putting a city on a fault line, in a floodplain, or in the way of forest fires. Social disasters also come from the state's actions (poor planning, cronyism, and ideologically motivated politics) and the needs of capital (continued growth and consumption of resources without concern for the future).

What happened in New Orleans was a preventable social disaster. The hurricane's strength was due in part to global warming. Destroying wetlands and dredging canals for development prior to the storm exacerbated the flooding. The evacuation, such as it was, was inextricably linked to race and class, and also with the encouraging ability of people to organize themselves.

What caused hurricane Katrina's devastation? First, the delta's natural waterways were reconstructed, canals were cut and dredged, the river was rerouted, and levees were built, all of which denied the delta the natural changes it needs, causing the city to sink. Then the wetlands were drained for subdivisions. White flight to the suburbs on those drained wetlands left the city underfunded in terms of taxation, and it concentrated communities of color and poverty. The rural outlying areas are also subject to this urban and classist framing of the disaster: while New Orleans gets the lion's share of money and media attention, whole (poor, rural) towns in Mississippi were literally wiped off the map and got almost no media coverage.

What hath Katrina wrought? A fabled and unique city ruined; 1,282 people killed, 1,000 still missing, 2 million people displaced;[1] 302,000 housing units destroyed or damaged, 71 percent of these low-income units;[2] more than 500 sewage plants destroyed, over 170 point-source leakages of gasoline, oil, or natural gas; more than 2,000 gas stations, the Agriculture Street landfill, a superfund site with homes on it, DuPont chemical plants, and 8 oil refineries submerged and 8 million gallons of oil spilled.[3] Toxic materials from all of the above seeped into floodwaters and spread through much of the city. The full truth of what happened has yet to be determined, and we may not know for some years. But we do know that the exposure of people to this toxic brew will have serious adverse health effects.

Decision-Based Fact Making

The Bush administration has upended the normal fact-based decision-making process. These officials make decisions and then mold the facts to fit the decision. Blind emphasis on pro-business and anti-environmental policies, such as the refusal to negotiate or ratify the Kyoto accord, the promulgation of ineffectual voluntary pollution-control measures, broad development policies based on market needs, and privatized solutions to public problems, all add together to constitute an abuse of power in the face of scientific consensus on global climate change. Virtually all credible scientific studies now agree that the earth is warming at least in part because of anthropogenic (that is, human-induced) causes. And yet since his days as governor of Texas, George W. Bush has championed private solutions to public problems, where "voluntary" pollution controls generally amount to no pollution controls at all.

Dick Cheney's energy task force is a case in point. In 2001 Cheney proceeded to solicit the energy industry's advice and wrote it into policy. No one else was consulted—not scientists, not conservation groups, not antipollution groups, not even alternative-technology experts. When this process came to light, the Bush administration went to court rather than reveal details about the committee and finally partially lifted the veil of secrecy only when forced to do so by court order. The resulting revealed truth was that the Bush administration gave energy industry executives carte blanche to write their own government regulations on energy and the environment.

Bush and Cheney's energy policy has focused on market solutions—and lately on technological innovation—to solve problems that are at root systemic. Our dependence on fossil fuels loads the atmosphere with carbon, and simple lip service to conservation, pollution trading, or domestic sourcing will not address this issue. And of course, we are busy *not* conserving our use of fossil fuels, as witnessed by the Bush administration's refusal to raise fuel efficiency standards, as well as the passage of tax credits encouraging purchase of the biggest gas guzzlers.[4] What needs to happen is a global reduction in carbon loading, a change that necessarily means regulation on the national and international levels. Even though since 1979 the National Academy of Sciences has made it clear that in order to address global climate change, the U.S. and other nations need to reduce the emission of carbon and other gasses and pollutants, we are today producing more carbon than we did fifteen years ago.[5] Even if we were somehow able to stop *all* carbon emissions *today*, because of the momentum of these changes, we will face further temperature increases and thus further disruptions to the global climate. It has been clear for decades that reducing carbon in the atmosphere is the only fruitful approach, but the Bush administration has not only denied this fact, it has also aggressively attempted to stop scientists from alerting the public to the enormity of the problem and the appropriate solutions.

On January 29, 2006, the *New York Times* reported on one case, part of a pattern that the administration exhibits of denying or silencing evidence inconvenient to its policy positions. James Hansen, NASA's senior climate scientist, was warned of "dire consequences" if he continued to speak out about global climate change and the need for reducing emissions of associated gasses. Hansen was told that he could no longer talk to the press, give lectures, or post material on the Web without review of his work by the public-affairs office. George Deutsch, a Bush-appointed NASA public-affairs officer, stated that the job of this office is "to make the President look good." Indeed, Deutsch's two credentials for the job were a degree in journalism from Texas A&M and working on Bush's campaign. He even lied about the degree—he never graduated.[6]

The denial of scientific evidence that would cast doubt on the administration's positions is pervasive. The National Oceanic and Atmospheric Administration was forced to censor its Web site on climate change. Donald Kennedy, editor-in-chief of *Science*,[7] wrote that empirical studies published in several journals have contradicted the science presented on the NOAA Web site.

Furthermore, at the National Institutes of Health it is an open secret that in order for research grants to be approved, they must not mention certain trigger words. Research has been suppressed at the EPA on endangered species and on the effects of mountaintop removal for mining, on forest management, on mercury emissions, and on the interactive effect of multiple air pollutants. The Centers on Disease Control was forced to change its Web site regarding condom usage, and studies questioning the efficacy of abstinence approaches have been repressed.[8]

Global Warming: Denying Science, Refusing Reality

The science demonstrating global climate change is clear, and there is consensus among the scientific community on the topic. The literature on this topic is truly voluminous; the most important of research outlets, including *Science* and *Nature*, have published many reports on the topic, definitively showing the globe's rising temperatures. Figure 1 shows the average increases.

While the ten hottest years since record keeping began in 1861 have all happened since 1990, Timothy J. Osborn and Keith R. Briffa, in a recent article in *Science*, have also shown that "the continuing warmth of the late 20th century is the most widespread and longest temperature anomaly of any kind" in the last twelve hundred years.[9] David B. Field and his fellow researchers show that the water off the California coast "has become warmer during the late 20th century than it was at any time during the past 1400 years." They conclude that these changes are "apparently anthropogenic."[10] The voice of the scientific community is clear.

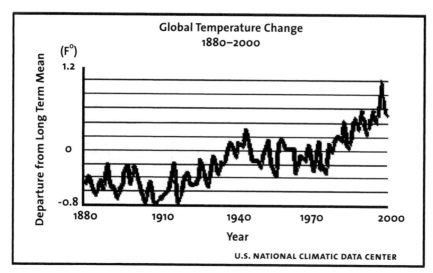

FIGURE I. GLOBAL AVERAGE TEMPERATURES

The trifling amount of controversy that actually does exist centers on the question of whether these changes are caused by humans or represent cyclical fluctuations. The National Academy of Sciences has published reports on global climate change since the early 1970s. Its 2001 report, "Climate Change Science: An Analysis of Some Key Questions"[11] opens with a simple statement of the situation: "Greenhouse gases are accumulating in Earth's atmosphere as a result of human activities, causing surface air temperatures and subsurface ocean temperatures to rise."

The report also goes on to explain that some amount of the recorded changes may be due to natural variation but it states unequivocally that human actions are responsible for the overwhelming amount of measurable global warming and associated climate change. CO_2 is a particularly important example, since ice core samples from Greenland glaciers indicate that natural carbon levels in the atmosphere had never been above 280 parts per million (ppm), but since the Industrial Revolution the carbon load has soared to its current level of 370 ppm (and climbing at a rate of 1.5 ppm per year). The report concludes that *it could take hundreds of years to remove these gasses from the atmosphere, assuming that we start now and cease producing any new pollutants.*

How can this change be blamed on human action? The strongest of causal arguments can be made since we know previous levels have a temporal sequence, and strong and significant correlations exist (see Figures 2 and 3). The burning of fossil fuels since the Industrial Revolution is the clearest source of anthropogenic greenhouse gases.

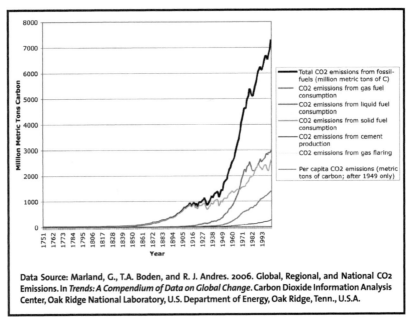

FIGURE 2. ANTHROPOGENIC EMISSIONS

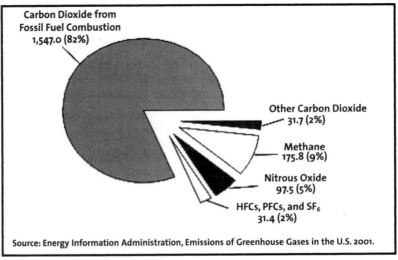

FIGURE 3. MAJOR SOURCES OF ANTHROPOGENIC CARBON EMISSIONS

In 2002 NAS released a report on global climate change, updated to address the issue of "abrupt climate change."[12] The report found that startlingly fast changes can take place: "Roughly half the north Atlantic warming since the last ice age was achieved in only a decade, and it was accompanied by significant climatic changes across most of the globe. . . . Abrupt climate changes were especially common when the climate system was being forced to change most rapidly."

While the overwhelming community of scientists has agreed that climate change is happening, and there is wide consensus that much of the change is anthropogenic, it is now being acknowledged that the change is faster than anyone imagined even just ten years ago. Recent research on Greenland glacier melting rates shows that massive climactic shifts can happen not just on a geologic timescale but in the very human time scale of perhaps three years. The proposed explanation for this rapidity is the stalling of the oceanic conveyer belt—a system in which ocean water cools and sinks as it flows north toward Greenland, thus reversing direction and flowing back south toward the Indian Ocean, where it warms, rises, and reverses yet again (see Figure 4). As global climate change melts the sea ice around the North Pole, fresh water reduces the salinity of the northern Atlantic, and the conveyor belt stalls out. Two recent articles in *Nature* prove this scenario to be of the utmost importance: One article demonstrated empirically that the Gulf Stream has weakened by *70 percent* in the last ten years because of fresh water melting off of the Greenland glaciers, while another computer simulation confirms the stalling of the ocean circulation current.[13] NASA recently confirmed that ice sheets at both poles are melting.[14] All of a sudden the 2004 apocalyptic global-warming film *The Day After Tomorrow* doesn't look so fanciful. The time, clearly, is now.

This time scale—and the dangers that it represents—has been recognized by some officials at the Pentagon. A report from the Defense Advanced Planning Research Projects Agency (the Pentagon's research arm and the folks who brought you the Internet), released in October 2003, declared that global climate change perhaps posed the greatest danger to national security. Two years after the tragedy of 9/11 the report concluded that the threat of global climate change was greater even than terrorism.[15] It proposed scenarios and contingency plans for how to deal with the repercussions of abrupt changes in climate, sea level, and the potential for aggressors to take advantage of the situation.

One of the scarier problems of global climate change is that there are a number of potential outcomes, from the micro (increases in pollen spells bad news for those who suffer from hay fever[16]) to the macro (global climate change is likely to decrease agricultural production yields[17]). Such changes could, at worst, render most of North America and Europe uninhabitable. *At best* it would mean that agriculture would be impossible in these regions. But there are also a number of feedback loops, where increased global temperatures lead to even more greenhouse gas releases. As the Artic permafrost thaws, for example, biomass that has remained frozen since the last ice age 12,000 years ago will begin to rot, releasing methane, thereby increasing global warming. Less ice in the ice caps means that less solar radiation is reflected away from the earth, thus increasing temperatures yet again.

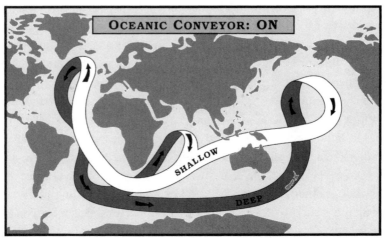

FIGURE 4. THE OCEANIC CONVEYOR BELT. James Kennett and Jeff Jones, University of California at Santa Barbara.

The most important outcome of global warming for the present discussion is an increase in the power of hurricanes. MIT Professor Kerry Emanuel, in several papers published in *Nature* between 1987 and 2005, has demonstrated that "in most cases, the evolution of hurricane intensity depends mainly on three factors: the storm's initial intensity, the thermodynamic state of the atmosphere through which it moves, and the heat exchange with the upper layer of the ocean under the core of the hurricane." The warmth of the ocean is directly affected by global climate change: the warmer the globe, the warmer the ocean and the stronger the hurricane.[18]

In the face of such overwhelming evidence the Bush administration has done nothing; not only has it neglected global warming, it has continued to deny the reality of our impending socio-ecological nightmare: global climate change in the context of the end of cheap oil. While the administration gives lip service to the integrity of science, the actions the President and his advisors have taken belie this stance. Nowhere is this clearer than in the major international attempt to reduce atmospheric carbon, the Kyoto Protocol. According to voluntary reporting, in 2004 the U.S. produced 7,122 million metric tons of carbon dioxide, or *25 percent* of the world's total emissions (the U.S. has only 5 percent of the world's population). Kyoto needs the biggest emitter, the U.S., in order to succeed.[19]

In March 2001 Bush announced that the U.S. would no longer negotiate the Kyoto accord. The Protocol went into effect early in 2005, with the agreement of some 150 nations and requiring emissions reductions in advanced economies. The U.S. is the single largest user of fossil-fuel energy and the largest producer of greenhouse gases. How could the U.S. be expected to reduce emissions and curtail economic growth? As Bush said most clearly in an interview on British television, "The Kyoto treaty didn't suit our needs."[20] It would, in fact, be expensive to the U.S.; there is no doubt on that score. But even prominent members of the corporate world support the Kyoto Protocol, including General Electric and DuPont, who see "greening" their image as good for the bottom line. Business opportunities notwithstanding, refusing to take action on climate change and denying the scientific reality will be far more costly to the U.S. and the world in the future. Back in 1979 the National Academy of Sciences found that "if CO_2 levels continue to increase [there] is no reason to doubt that climate changes will result and no reason to believe that these changes will be negligible." It found that "we may not be given a warning until the CO_2 loading is such that an appreciable climate change is inevitable." The costs of inaction may be akin to the bumper sticker that I saw the other day: "Maybe if we ignore the environment, it'll go away."[21]

The 2006 State of the Union Address is a classic take-back proposal. In the speech Bush claimed that the U.S. is "addicted to oil" and the solution to this is alternative energy development and reduction of reliance on foreign oil sources, such as those in the Middle East. The U.S. imports nearly 60 percent of its oil, only some 20 percent comes from the Middle East, and alternative fuels are not currently sufficient to offset such a reduction. What is left out of the picture is any reasonable notion of conservation, let alone the idea of sustainable levels of use. But even this half-measure proposed in the evening speech was hollowed out the next morning by Bush's press secretary, who told gathered reporters that the President had not meant the comment literally.[22]

Bush and Cheney must be held accountable for denying global climate change and for not taking appropriate actions. This abuse of power connects to the fury of hurricane Katrina as it destroyed New Orleans and much of the Gulf Coast. Katrina could not have been stopped—if we put cities in the way of nature, we have to expect devastation. But global warming fueled the power of Katrina, and action should have been taken years ago to reduce the probability of such supercharged storms. These conditioning factors are ideologically driven and reflect a *gross* incompetence by those in power. And yet even the solutions to Katrina's devastation are similarly ideological: large private firms have benefited from no-bid contracts (just as with Iraq), pollution controls were "temporarily" put on hold, a gulf opportunity zone has been established similar to export zones in developing nations not subject to normal state controls, and money, rather than careful thought and analysis, has been thrown at the problem.

In the face of global warming, national security threats, and a state that exacerbated the potential devastation of the Gulf Coast through pro-growth, anti-environmental policies, what did the Bush administration do to respond to the disaster? Too little, too late. The Bush administration's response to hurricane Katrina is emblematic: the denial of the perils of global warming foreshadowed the denial of disaster in New Orleans.

Hurricane Katrina: Fiddling While New Orleans Floods

The President's response to Katrina was criminally delayed, indifferent, and inept. As Kanye West's public comment lays bare, many observers concluded, "George Bush doesn't care about black people." Just after the disaster in New Orleans, Bush spoke of "taking aggressive action against deep and persistent poverty with roots in a history of racial discrimination." In the span of about two weeks, however, the Republicans were busy blaming the victims themselves, stating that the poverty of the evacuees was clear evidence that the last three decades of governmental poverty-alleviation programs had clearly not worked. Such comments denigrated the people of New Orleans, suggesting that entitlement programs were at fault for creating dependency amongst the destitute. And yet the most damaging form of entitlement is the gift of a political office based on political connections rather than ability, and this cronyism contributed directly to the devastation. The president's mother, Barbara "let them eat cake" Bush, while visiting evacuees in Texas, summed up the perspective of much of the superrich, white, conservative point of view when she ventured the opinion, "What I'm hearing which is sort of scary is they all want to stay in Texas. Everyone is so overwhelmed by the hospitality. And so many of the people in the arena here, you know, were underprivileged anyway, so this—this [she chuckles slightly] is working very well for them." At this juncture one might expect that an administration that was set on "taking aggressive action" against poverty might propose a strategy or specific programs to Congress. The administration made no such suggestions, and Congress voted to cut the budget for existing poverty programs in an attempt to offset the cost of rebuilding the Gulf Coast. And so the relief is perhaps worse than the sickness: we have a social disaster compounded by extremes of poverty and racism, the solution for which is the reduction of programs addressing deep-seated racialized poverty.[23]

That New Orleans is extremely vulnerable to tropical storms has been long understood. Indeed, FEMA's 2001 list of the top three most likely and most devastating disasters were a San Francisco earthquake, a terrorist attack on New York, and a category-four hurricane hitting New Orleans. As former President Clinton advisor Sidney Blumenthal wrote, "No one can say that they didn't see it coming."[24] A five-day hurricane simulation exercise was undertaken in 2004, mimicking a Katrina-like event. This exercise combined the National Weather Service, the U.S. Army Corps of Engineers, the Louisiana State University Hurricane Center, and other state and federal agencies; FEMA's regional director suggested that great progress was made in developing emergency response plans.[25] These plans, however, were not implemented, in part as the result of the federal slashing of funds for protection. Thus, while Bush and Cheney speak virtually daily of the dangers of terrorism, they ignored completely the number one item on their list of likely disasters.

From the Bush administration's first days, FEMA received little attention, and any notice it got was for potential budget cuts. Bush's first appointee as head of FEMA was a Texas crony, Joe Allbaugh, who had no prior disaster experience. In late 2001 the Bush administration announced that it wanted to privatize and downsize much of FEMA, with Allbaugh claiming that "many are concerned that federal disaster assistance may have evolved into . . . an oversized entitlement program."[26] Allbaugh soon left FEMA to start a consulting business and was replaced by another crony, Michael Brown. As part of the federal government's reorganization, the Bush administration brought FEMA into the new Department of Homeland Security and demoted it to a non-cabinet-level position.

In the year before hurricane Katrina hit, the Bush administration continued to cut budgets and deny grants to the Gulf Coast. In June of 2004 the Army Corps of Engineers levee budget for New Orleans was cut, and it was cut again in June of 2005, this time by $71.2 million, or 44 percent of the budget. Adding insult to injury, in 2004 FEMA denied a Louisiana disaster-mitigation grant request. As Walter Maestri, the Jefferson Parish emergency management chief told the *New Orleans Times-Picayune*:

> It appears that the money has been moved in the president's budget to handle homeland security and the war in Iraq, and I suppose that's the price we pay. Nobody locally is happy that the levees can't be finished, and we are doing everything we can to make the case that this is a security issue for us.[27]

Bush, in other words, did worse than nothing. The administration slashed budgets for levee restoration, downgraded FEMA from a cabinet position, and considered privatizing the entire agency. Given that its budget was cut nearly in half, the Corps was forced to stop levee-improvement projects, discontinue a study of how best to protect New Orleans, and institute a hiring freeze. This in the midst of what would become the longest and strongest hurricane season in recorded history. The budget cuts stand in stark contrast to the infrastructure investment of other nations that face such threats.[28]

Since Watergate the classic question has become "What did they know, and when did they know it?" The answer in this situation is that they knew it all, and they knew at least twenty-four hours in advance. The White House was given multiple warnings that hurricane Katrina had a high likelihood of causing serious damage to New Orleans and the Gulf Coast. At 10 a.m. on Sunday,

August 28, 2005, the day before the storm hit, the National Weather Service published an alert under the title "DEVASTATING DAMAGE EXPECTED," the text of which was printed in all capital letters:

HURRICANE KATRINA . . . A MOST POWERFUL HURRI-CANE WITH UNPRECEDENTED STRENGTH . . . MOST OF THE AREA WILL BE UNINHABITABLE FOR WEEKS . . . AT LEAST ONE HALF OF WELL CONSTRUCTED HOMES WILL HAVE ROOF AND WALL FAILURE. . . . HIGH RISE OFFICE AND APARTMENT BUILDINGS WILL SWAY DANGEROUSLY . . . A FEW TO THE POINT OF TOTAL COLLAPSE. ALL WIN-DOWS WILL BLOW OUT. . . . POWER OUTAGES WILL LAST FOR WEEKS. . . . WATER SHORTAGES WILL MAKE HUMAN SUFFERING INCREDIBLE BY MODERN STANDARDS.[29]

The Homeland Security Department also briefed the White House on the scenario, warning of levee breaches and severe flooding. According to the *New York Times*, "a Homeland Security Department report submitted to the White House at 1:47 a.m. on Aug. 29, hours before the storm hit, said, 'Any storm rated Category 4 or greater will likely lead to severe flooding and/or levee breaching.'"[30] This document, made public by a Senate investigation, clearly contradicts the statements made by both President Bush and Homeland Security Director Michael Chertoff immediately after the storm, to the effect that such devastation could not have been predicted. On September 1, 2005, President Bush said, "I don't think anyone anticipated the breach of the levees." But the devastation was predicted, and both Bush and Chertoff were informed, and then they lied about it.

So the weather service told them it was coming, as did the only FEMA agent on the ground and the Department of Homeland Security itself. What was it that administration officials did while New Orleans flooded? Bush, Cheney, and other members of the cabinet were not inconvenienced: the President gave an unrelated speech at a naval air station in San Diego, comparing himself favorably to FDR, with a media photo-op of him strumming a guitar (not fiddling, as Nero did). The Vice President remained fly-fishing on vacation in Wyoming. Other senior members of the administration vacationed in Maine, and the *New York Daily News* reported that Condoleezza

Rice went shopping at Ferragamo on Fifth Avenue and bought several thousand dollars' worth of shoes.[31]

In the immediate aftermath of hurricane Katrina on August 31, 2005, Marty Bahamonde, the only FEMA employee posted by Brown in New Orleans, e-mailed Michael Brown from his mobile device regarding the conditions. The e-mail is urgent and detailed: "The situation is past critical. . . . Hotels are kicking people out, thousands gathering in the streets without food or water. . . . Estimates are many will die within hours. . . . We are without food and running water at the [Super]dome."

Brown's reply was emblematic of the administration's entire response to the catastrophe: "Thanks for the update. Anything specific I need to do or tweak?" Further e-mails showed him to be incomprehensibly removed from the reality of victims' pain and suffering. Brown seemed to be more concerned with his appearances and fashion sense than addressing the crisis in New Orleans. On August 29, 2005, he replied to Marty Bahamonde, who had made a comment about feeling nauseous: "If you'll look at my lovely FEMA attire you'll really vomit. I am a fashion god." On the same day, again via e-mail, Cindy Taylor told Brown that he looked fabulous, to which he replied, "I got it at Nordstrom. Email McBride and make sure she knows. Are you proud of me? Can I quit now? Can I go home?"[32]

The FEMA and DHS response was beyond inept. The secretary of Homeland Security, Michael Chertoff, seemed completely out of the loop during the week following Katrina. First he claimed that there were two separate catastrophes: a hurricane and then a flood, as if these were somehow unconnected. Chertoff did not declare an emergency, did not mobilize the federal resources, and seemed to not even know what was happening on the ground until reporters told him. In a remarkable exchange with Robert Siegel on National Public Radio, Chertoff claimed that "there is a more than adequate law enforcement presence in New Orleans." It became clear during the interview that Chertoff had no idea that several thousand people had gathered at the Ernest N. Morial Convention Center, that they had been turned away from the Superdome, that they had no food or water, that there was no law enforcement or medical facilities, that the people were living "like animals" in squalor. When asked how many days it would take to deliver food and water to them, Chertoff at first confused the Convention Center with the Superdome, stating that the Superdome had plenty of food and water. He then backtracked, claiming that there was enough food and water and medical care for all the people of New Orleans if they would just get to designated gathering centers. When faced with the descriptions of the Convention Center, Chertoff attempted to deny the reports, stating that they were "rumors" and "anecdotal versions" that should not be extrapolated from. But of course these were not anecdotes or rumors; these were reports from CNN, NPR, and other credible news agencies, which had more information than the federal officials. Similarly, Mike Brown found out about the problems at the Convention Center on Thursday while being interviewed on ABC's *Nightline*. The following morning he lied on the NBC *Today* show, saying that the Convention Center refugees had been receiving food and water every day. Those in charge of disaster response privileged illusion over reality: they claimed to be in control when they were not, they had less knowledge than the news media, and yet they felt it acceptable to lie to the public about the situation.[33]

Aaron Broussard, President of Jefferson Parish, on *Meet the Press* said that New Orleanians had "been abandoned by our own country." He called for "whoever is at the top of this totem pole, that totem pole needs to be chainsawed off and we've got to start with some new leadership."[34] Broussard is right that leadership failed in New Orleans, and the totem pole goes all the way up to the crony appointment of Brown as head of FEMA, Chertoff, Bush, and Cheney themselves. But Broussard did not stop in calling for "someone to be fired," he went on to give examples of the ineptitude of the federal response:

> We had Wal-Mart deliver three trucks of water, trailer trucks of water. FEMA turned them back. . . . We had 1,000 gallons of diesel fuel on a Coast Guard vessel docked in my parish. . . . When we got there with our trucks, they got a word. "FEMA says don't give you the fuel." . . . FEMA comes in and cuts all of our emergency communication lines. They cut them without notice. Our sheriff, Harry Lee, goes back in, he reconnects the line. He posts armed guards on our line and says, "No one is getting near these lines." . . .
>
> The guy who runs this building I'm in, emergency management, he's responsible for everything. His mother was trapped in St. Bernard nursing home and every day she called him and said, "Are you coming, son? Is somebody coming?" And he said, "Yeah, Mama, somebody's coming to get you. Somebody's coming to get

you on Tuesday. Somebody's coming to get you on Wednesday. Somebody's coming to get you on Thursday. Somebody's coming to get you on Friday." And she drowned Friday night. She drowned Friday night.

Broussard explained who was at fault:

It's not just Katrina that caused all these deaths in New Orleans here. Bureaucracy has committed murder here in the greater New Orleans area, and bureaucracy has to stand trial before Congress now.

Gross incompetence is clearly demonstrated by ignoring the warnings and by the actual response once the federal government got under way. But the administration initially questioned whose responsibility it was to come to the aid of the hurricane victims. The "blame game," however, was a mere media ploy. The debate was over *legal* responsibility, but the undercurrent of the discussion was clearly about *moral* responsibility. The Bush administration was trying to absolve itself of responsibility by claiming that it had no legal authority to respond. But on Friday, August 26, 2005, Governor Kathleen Blanco declared a state of emergency in Louisiana, and Governor Haley Barbour of Mississippi followed suit the following day. Also on that Saturday, Governor Blanco asked President Bush to declare a federal state of emergency, and on August 28, 2005, the Sunday before the storm hit, Mayor Ray Nagin declared a state of emergency in New Orleans.[35] This is significant on many levels. First, it shows that the local authorities knew how bad the destruction was going to be and that they were anticipating being overwhelmed. Secondly, and more importantly, it sent a clear message to the Bush administration that its assistance was immediately required. Lastly, and most crucially, this declaration of a state of emergency obviated all legal debates. When an emergency is officially declared, the federal government has the ability, the legal right, and the moral responsibility to do whatever it can to remedy the crisis. It does not have to ask the locals for permission to do anything or go anywhere: the declaration of a state of emergency is a blank check to mitigate the effects of a natural disaster. Failure to act under these circumstances demonstrates criminal negligence—the equivalent of leaving the wounded on the battlefield.

This was a disaster they knew was coming. And the administration dares to declare itself our best hope against terrorism and disasters? The U.S. turned down assistance from a nation that has to constantly face hurricanes: Cuba.[36] Regardless of ideology, it is indefensible to turn down help, especially in the first hours and days when people can be saved. In legal terms this is criminal negligence. In moral terms it is inexcusable: in the 2004 South Asia tsunami, the U.S. military got water to victims within twenty-four hours, while in some areas of New Orleans it took several days. FEMA also turned down offers of material assistance from other government agencies, including the Interior Department.[37] With the Louisiana National Guard largely deployed to Iraq, New Orleans had to look to its own police force, surrounding sheriffs' offices, and very quickly, mercenary security forces, such as Blackwater.[38] This situation had clear and disastrous implications.

In Congressional hearings Michael Brown blamed his own incompetent response on the lack of resources given to his agency by the Department of Homeland Security, which, he argued, was focused on terrorism. While this statement is clearly accurate, it does not absolve Brown from responsibility in the bungled response. Indeed, it does show a skewed priority on the part of the Secretary of Homeland Security, Michael Chertoff, and on the part of Bush and the larger administration. Michael Brown, whose qualifications apparently amounted to no more than having a falsified resume and being the Judges and Stewards Commissioner for the International Arabian Horse Association, was clearly one of the worst possible choices to head FEMA. Bush and Chertoff are responsible for hiring Brown, and their ineptitude and cronyism amount to negligence and corruption. This situation allowed for the lawlessness and insecurity of the larger disaster to take place.

What did people do in response to this lawlessness, this lack of security, this climate of uncertainty, death, and destruction? They organized themselves so as to overcome. What is most brilliant in this disaster is the ability of the people themselves to solve the problems that the authorities cannot solve or will not face. The people of New Orleans did not all act with integrity—that much is clear. But most of them did, most of the time. While race and class clearly affected the chances of individuals to get out, these same folks responded to such indignities by developing the types of systems that actually solve problems in the face of governmental incompetence.

Denise Moore was evacuated to the Ernest N. Morial Convention Center.

She was there for two days without food or water. This shelter was not conducive to human existence since it was, in her words, nightmarish:

> Inside the convention center, the place was one huge bathroom. . . . Most people stayed outside because the smell was so bad. But outside wasn't much better: between the heat, the humidity, the lack of water, the old and very young dying from dehydration . . . and there was no place to lay down, not even room on the sidewalk. Young men went to Canal Street and "looted," and brought back food and water for the old people and the babies, because nobody had eaten in days.

She saw some men shoot at the police because after some time "all the people thought the cops were coming to hurt them, to kill them all." They all believed that they were sent there to die, and it was the looters who saved them: "If it wasn't for them," she said, "we wouldn't have had the little water and food they had found. I will never look at thugs and gangsters the same way again."[39]

In the face of disaster and official incompetence, we see the ability of people to solve their own problems. Without the assistance of those in power, people banded together and established a semblance of order. Young men, who in other times would have been feared as "thugs" or "gangsters," organized the crowd and kept violence to a minimum. All this as the National Guard, the Army, and what police were left drove by with their guns pointed at the people whom they are sworn to serve and protect, treating them like criminals, not citizens.

The Politics of Refusal

Global climate change was denied, science was suppressed, budgets were cut, warnings were ignored, the response was bungled, and the people were left to their own devices. What is to be done to fix New Orleans and the Gulf Coast infrastructure? The federal government has promised $3.1 billion to rebuild levees in New Orleans, half of which will go to fixing Katrina-damaged levees. Bush has asked Congress for another $1.5 billion, of which a measly $250 million will be used to restore wetlands. But the U.S. Army Corps of Engineers has raised the estimated cost to $9.5 billion.[40] Chertoff announced in spring of 2006 that the levee reconstruction would be completed by June 1, 2006, but a number of independent experts immediately pointed out that this would be physically impossible because of the protracted way that levees must be built.[41] New Orleans, apparently, will just have to pray that another bad storm doesn't hit them in 2006. Moreover, back in 2002 the Corps completed a study that determined what needed to be done to protect New Orleans, and it concluded that further study was needed—a study that would take six years to complete.

Local contractors have been tapped to do some of the levee work, but many of the billions of dollars will go to the same corporations that are "rebuilding" Iraq (after the Bush administration bombed the infrastructure in the first place): Halliburton, Bechtel, and others with strong connections to the administration.[42] More cronyism is not the answer.

The environmental consequences of Katrina will take years to manifest themselves. We are likely to see more cancer clusters among those exposed to toxins and hazardous materials. We will see much contaminated soil and water that will cost billions to clean up. We will see whole neighborhoods wiped off the map, some so that new expensive homes can be built and others perhaps so that green space can act as a buffer for future flooding.

With full foreknowledge the Bush administration ignored the disaster. These leaders denied its existence. Then they denied its severity. They denied their responsibility to protect and rescue people. And they have denied its real cause: global warming. Bush has refused to engage with environmental reality. There has been a real need to address the coming environmental crisis for at least a decade; the refusal to do so and the criminally negligent response to the disaster of Hurricane Katrina is emblematic of how the Bush administration has denied the environmental consequences of its inaction. This gross incompetence—the startlingly inept (non)reaction to hurricane Katrina, the denial of global warming, the refusal to ameliorate environmental damages—constitutes a most egregious case of the abuse of power and stands on its own as reason enough to impeach the President and his administration.

Notes:

1. Shaila Dewan, "Storm's Missing: Lives Not Lost but Disconnected," *New York Times*, March 1, 2006; Bill Quigley, "Eight Months After Katrina," CommonDreams.org, April 26, 2006.

2. National Low Income Housing Coalition, "Hurricane Katrina's Impact on Low Income Housing Units Estimated 302,000 units lost or damaged, 71% Low Income," Research Note #05–02, September 2005.

3. Timothy Dwyer, Jacqueline L. Salmon, and Dan Eggen, "Katrina Takes Environmental Toll, Water Could Be Unsafe for Years," *Washington Post*, September 7, 2005; Sustainable Energy and Economy Network http://www.seen.org/pages/Katrina/pollution.shtml; Matthew Brown, "N.O. Spots Are Testing Positive for Toxins," *The New Orleans Times-Picayune*, March 6, 2006.

4. Keith Bradsher, *High and Mighty: The World's Most Dangerous Vehicles and How They Got That Way* (New York: Perseus Books, 2002).

5. National Academy of Sciences, "Carbon Dioxide and Climate: A Scientific Assessment," 1979; "Meeting the Challenge of Climate," 1982; "Carbon Dioxide and Climate," 1982.

6. Andrew Revkin, "Climate Expert Says NASA Tried to Silence Him," *New York Times*, January 29, 2006; Andrew Revkin, "A Young Bush Appointee Resigns His Post at NASA," *New York Times*, February 8, 2006.

7. Donald Kennedy, "The New Gag Rules," *Science*, February 17, 2006, vol. 311 (5763), p. 917.

8. Union of Concerned Scientists, "Scientific Integrity in Policymaking: An Investigation into the Bush Administration's Misuse of Science," March 2004.

9. Timothy J. Osborn and Keith R. Briffa, "The Spatial Extent of 20th-Century Warmth in the Context of the Past 1200 Years," *Science*, February 10, 2006, pp. 841–844.

10. David B. Field, Timothy R. Baumgartner, Christopher D. Charles, Vicente Ferreira-Bartrina, and Mark D. Ohman, "Planktonic Foraminifera of the California Current Reflect 20th-Century Warming," *Science*, January 6, 2006, pp. 63–66.

11. National Academy of Sciences, National Research Council, Committee on the Science of Climate Change, "Climate Change Science: An Analysis of Some Key Questions," 2001.

12. National Academy of Sciences, National Research Council, Committee on Abrupt Climate Change, "Abrupt Climate Change: Inevitable Surprises" 2002.

13. Eric Rignot and Pannir Kanagaratnam, "Changes in the Velocity Structure of the Greenland Ice Sheet," *Science*, February 17, 2006, pp. 986–990; Detlef Quadfasel, "Oceanography: The Atlantic Heat Conveyor Slows," *Nature*, December 1, 2005, pp.438, 565–566; Thomas F. Stocker and Christoph C. Raible, "Climate Change: Water Cycle Shifts Gear," *Nature*, April 14, 2005, pp. 434, 830–833 .

14. http://www.nasa.gov/vision/earth/environment/ice_sheets.html.

15. Defense Advanced Planning Research Projects Agency, Peter Schwartz and Doug Randall, "An Abrupt Climate Change Scenario and Its Implications for United States National Security," October 2003.

16. Rachel Williams, "Climate Change Blamed for Rise in Hay Fever," *Nature*, April 28, 2005, pp. 434, 1059.

17. John Porter, "Rising Temperatures Are Likely to Reduce Crop Yields," *Nature*, July 14, 2005, pp. 436, 174.

18. Kerry Emanuel, "Thermodynamic Control of Hurricane Intensity," *Nature*, October 14, 1999, pp. 401, 665–669; "The Dependence of Hurricane Intensity on Climate," *Nature*, April 8, 1987, pp. 326, 483–485; "Increasing Destructiveness of Tropical Cyclones Over the Past 30 Years," *Nature*, August 4, 2005, pp. 436, 686–688; "Reply," *Nature*, December 22, 2005, p. 438. See also Kevin Trenberth, "Uncertainty in Hurricanes and Global Warming," *Science*, June 17, 2005, vol. 308.

19. National Energy Information Center, Energy Information Administration, Office of Inte-

grated Analysis and Forecasting, "Voluntary Reporting of Greenhouse Gases," March 2006.

20. Elizabeth Kolbert, "Storm Warnings," *The New Yorker*, September 19, 2005.

21. Elizabeth Kolbert, "Climate of Man," *The New Yorker*, May 9, 2005.

22. Knight-Ridder, "Administration Backs off Bush's Vow to Reduce Mideast Oil Imports," February 1, 2006.

23. Katherine Boo, "Shelter and the Storm," *The New Yorker*, November 28, 2005.

24. "No One Can Say They Didn't See It Coming," Salon.com, August 31, 2005.

25. FEMA Region IV Press Release # R6-04-093, "Hurricane Pam Exercise Concludes," release date July 23, 2004.

26. Testimony of Federal Emergency Management Agency Director Joe M. Allbaugh, before the Veterans Affairs, Housing and Urban Development and Independent Agencies Subcommittee of the Senate Appropriations Committee, http://www.fema.gov/library/jma051601.shtm.

27. *New Orleans Times-Picayune*, June 8, 2004.

28. Molly Ivins, "Why New Orleans Is in Deep Water," Creators Syndicate, September 1, 2005.

29. NWS alerts for Katrina are archived at http://www.nhc.noaa.gov/archive/2005/KATRINA.shtml?.

30. Eric Lipton, "White House Was Told Hurricane Posed Danger," *New York Times*, January 24, 2006.

31. Lloyd Grove, "Daily Dish," *New York Daily News*, September 7, 2005. Photo can be viewed at http://talkleft.com/new_archives/012058.html.

32. Michael Brown's e-mail exchanges can be viewed at http://i.a.cnn.net/cnn/2005/images/11/03/brown.emails.pdf.

33. National Public Radio, *All Things Considered*, September 1, 2005, http://mediamatters.org/items/200509080002.

34. NBC, *Meet the Press with Tim Russert*, transcript from September 4, 2005.

35. CNN, "New Orleans Braces for Monster Hurricane: Crescent City Under Evacuation; Storm May Overwhelm Levees," August 29, 2005, ThinkProgress Web site Hurricane Katrina Timeline, http://www.thinkprogress.org/katrina-timeline.

36. Stephen Zunes, "Bush Administration Refuses Cuban Offer of Medical Assistance Following Katrina," *Foreign Policy in Focus*, October 19, 2005.

37. Eric Lipton, "FEMA Overlooked Resources From Agencies, Report Says," *New York Times*, January 30, 2006.

38. Jeremy Scahill, "Blackwater Down: Fresh From Iraq, Private Security Forces Roam the Streets of an American City With Impunity," *Democracy Now*, September 23, 2005, http://www.democracynow.org/article.pl?sid=05/09/23/1338246&mode=thread&tid=25.

39. Personal Communication with Lisa Moore, Denise Moore's cousin. Portions of this e-mail have been published in the French journal *Liberation*, September 6, 2005, and *Essence*, "After Katrina," January 2006; Denise Moore was also interviewed on *This American Life*, "After the Flood," September 9, 2005.

40. National Public Radio, "Cost of Levee Repairs Rises in New Orleans," March 31, 2006; Environmental News Service, "New Orleans Levee Repair Price Tag Triples," March 31, 2006.

41. National Public Radio, "Louisiana Levee Critics Now Less Critical," April 13, 2006.

42. Pratap Chatterjee, "Big, Easy Iraqi-Style Contracts Flood New Orleans," CorpWatch.org, September 20, 2005.

Chapter 12

IGNORING PEAK OIL
Beyond Incompetence

Richard Heinberg

While it would be difficult to create an airtight legal case for impeaching George W. Bush based on his ignoring the very real threat posed by Peak Oil, nevertheless I believe that his actions—and inaction—in this regard constitute dereliction of duty on an unprecedented scale.

It is part of the job of leaders to foresee problems and either steer around them or prepare for them. A head of state is analogous to the captain of a ship, who is responsible not only for keeping his vessel on course but also for avoiding hazards such as storms and icebergs. Some problems are not foreseeable; others are. A ship's captain who loses his vessel to a freak "perfect storm" may be blameless, but one who steers his passenger liner directly into a foggy ice field, having no sonar or radar, is worse than a fool: he is criminally negligent.

The argument I will make, in brief, is this:

- Peak Oil is foreseeable.
- The consequences are also foreseeable and are likely to be ruinous.
- The Bush administration has been repeatedly warned.
- Actions could be taken to reduce the impact, but the longer those actions are delayed, the worse the impact will be.
- The administration, rather than taking steps to mitigate these looming catastrophic impacts, has instead done things that can only worsen them.

Let us go through these points one by one.

Is Peak Oil Foreseeable?

Peak Oil—the point at which the rate of global production of petroleum begins its inevitable historic decline—is a subject of growing public interest. The basic concept is derived from experience: during the past century and a half all older oil wells have been observed to peak and decline in output. The same has been noted with entire oilfields and with the collective oil endowment of whole nations. Indeed, most oil-producing nations have already seen their output enter terminal decline. Few informed observers doubt that the rate of oil production for the world in total will reach a maximum at some point and then slowly wane.

The science of Peak Oil was worked out in the 1950s by the veteran geophysicist M. King Hubbert, who successfully used his method to predict the U.S. peak (1970). Declassified CIA documents show that by the late 1970s the Agency was using similar methods to forecast the Soviet Union's oil peak.[1]

We do not know exactly when the global peak will occur, but it will almost certainly happen between now and 2035.

Considering the importance of the peaking event, the range of uncertainty regarding its timing is disturbing. If the peak were to occur within the next five years, our national economy would be unable to adjust quickly enough to avert calamity (as we will discuss below), while a peak thirty years from now would present a much greater opportunity for adaptation.

Ford Motor Company Executive Vice President Mark Fields, in his keynote address in October 2005 at the Society of Automotive Engineers' Global Leadership Conference at the Greenbrier, noted the seven most serious challenges to his industry, one of which was that "oil production is peaking."[2] Volvo motor company has for several years acknowledged in its company literature that a global oil production peak is likely by 2015.[3]

The legendary petroleum geologist T. Boone Pickens, who cofounded Mesa Petroleum and Petroleum Exploration, told the eleventh National Clean Cities conference in May 2005 that "Global oil [production] is 84 million barrels [a day]. I don't believe you can get it any more than 84 million barrels. . . . I think they are on decline in the biggest oil fields in the world today and I know what it's like once you turn the corner and start declining, it's a treadmill that you just can't keep up with."[4]

Royal Dutch Shell Chief Executive Jeroen Van Der Veer has said, "My view is that 'easy' oil has probably passed its peak."[5]

On March 1, 2006, the *New York Times* published an editorial by Robert Semple, Associate Editor of the editorial page for the *Times* since 1998, in which he wrote, "The concept of peak oil has not been widely written about. But people are talking about it now. It deserves a careful look—largely because it is almost certainly correct."[6]

In short, the science behind Peak Oil is well established, and, while there is some disagreement about exactly when the global peak will arrive, there can be no excuse at this stage for ignoring the problem.

Does the Administration Know About Peak Oil?

The *New York Times* knows about Peak Oil, but does the President? On this point the evidence is conclusive.

First of all, agencies within the government clearly understand the problem, and therefore relevant information must be readily available to the chief executive if he wishes to have it.

Explicit warnings of Peak Oil have started to turn up in official U.S. government literature. For example, a paper prepared for the U.S. Army Corps of Engineers titled "Energy Trends and Implications for U.S. Army Installations" (September 2005) includes the following tidbit: "The supply of oil will remain fairly stable in the very near term, but oil prices will steadily increase as world production approaches its peak. The doubling of oil prices in the past couple of years is not an anomaly, but a picture of the future. Peak oil is at hand."[7]

Then there is the following from the U.S. Department of Energy, Office of Deputy Assistant Secretary for Petroleum Reserves, Office of Naval Petroleum and Oil Shale Reserves, dated March 2004:

> The disparity between increasing production and declining reserves can have only one outcome: a practical supply limit will be reached and future supply to meet conventional oil demand will not be available. The question is when peak production will occur and what will be its ramifications. Whether the peak occurs sooner or later is a matter of relative urgency. . . . In spite

of projections for growth of non-OPEC supply, it appears that non-OPEC and non-Former Soviet Union countries have peaked and are currently declining. The production cycle of countries . . . and the cumulative quantities produced reasonably follow Hubbert's model. . . . The Nation must start now to respond to peaking global oil production to offset adverse economic and national security impacts.[8]

And finally there is the 2005 Report, "Peaking of World Oil Production: Impacts, Mitigation and Risk Management," commissioned by the U.S. Department of Energy, about which we will have more to say below.[9]

If none of this is specific enough (in fairness, we cannot expect George W. Bush to spend his evenings poring over obscure Army Corps of Engineers studies), we have the fact that Representative Roscoe Bartlett, Republican from Maryland's sixth district—who has made many speeches about Peak Oil on the floor of Congress—has spent thirty minutes in private conversation with the president explaining the science of Peak Oil and seeking to convey the enormity of the problem.[10]

But what if Bush wasn't able to understand what Bartlett was telling him? Perhaps Bartlett was using words that were too big, or concepts too abstruse for our president to grasp.

Even if that were the case, we have evidence that Bush's second-in-command, Vice President Cheney, understands Peak Oil; given time, Cheney could surely make the concept comprehensible to his superior. In a speech in 1999 (while he was still CEO of Halliburton Corporation, the giant oil-services company) to the Petroleum Institute in London, Cheney pointed out that:

By some estimates there will be an average of two per cent annual growth in global oil demand over the years ahead along with conservatively a three per cent natural decline in production from existing reserves. That means by 2010 we will need on the order of an additional fifty million barrels a day.[11]

This is a fair statement of the depletion dilemma: fifty million barrels per day is almost five times the current output of Saudi Arabia.

Finally, there is the fact that Bush and Cheney are themselves former oilmen: their inside knowledge of the industry should give them enhanced insight into the problem of Peak Oil. Some would say that these officials' former ties to the petroleum industry imply a conflict of interest. (They have been accused of giving perks to oil companies, even to Halliburton—perish the thought!) However, some of the most outspoken authorities on Peak Oil are retired petroleum geologists and engineers who have spent decades working for oil companies. Having former industry insiders in public office today could be good, if these officials used their technical knowledge to benefit the country by warning of the consequences of continued oil dependency. But as we will see below, there is no evidence that the particular former oilmen currently occupying the highest offices in the land are doing any such thing—at least not genuinely or effectively.

In sum, while it is impossible to say whether Mr. Bush understands Peak Oil, no one could credibly argue that that he simply hasn't heard about it.

How Serious Is the Threat?

Addressing this question requires some speculation: the peaking of global oil production is an event that has never occurred before. However, we need not speculate baselessly; for guidance, we have a U.S. government–funded study that could hardly be more relevant: "The Peaking of World Oil Production: Impacts, Mitigation and Risk Management," prepared by Science Applications International (SAIC) for the U.S. Department of Energy and released in February 2005. The project leader for the study was Robert L. Hirsch, who has had a distinguished career in formulating energy policy. The report on the study will hereinafter be referred to as The Hirsch Report.

The first paragraph of the Hirsch Report's executive summary states:

The peaking of world oil production presents the U.S. and the world with an unprecedented risk management problem. As peaking is approached, liquid fuel prices and price volatility will increase dramatically, and, without timely mitigation, the economic, social, and political costs will be unprecedented. Viable mitigation options exist on both the supply and demand sides, but to have substantial impact, they must be initiated more than a decade in advance of peaking.[12]

As the Hirsch Report explains in detail, as a result of our systemic dependence on oil for transportation, agriculture, and the production of plastics and chemicals, every sector of society will be impacted.

The Hirsch Report effectively undermines the standard free-market argument that oil depletion poses no serious problem, now or later, because as oil becomes scarcer the price will rise until demand is reduced commensurate with supply; meanwhile, higher prices will stimulate more exploration, the development of alternative fuels, and the more efficient use of remaining quantities. While it is true that rising prices will do all of these things, we have no assurance that the effects will be sufficient to avert severe, protracted economic, social, and political disruptions.

First, price increases may or may not stimulate more exploration or do so sufficiently or productively. During the early twentieth century, more exploration resulted in more oil being discovered. In recent decades, however, expanded exploration efforts have turned up fewer and fewer finds. It is difficult to avoid the obvious conclusion that there simply isn't much oil left to discover.

Higher prices for oil will also no doubt spur new investment in alternative fuels. But the time required to produce substantial quantities of alternative fuels will be considerable, given the volume of our national transportation-fuel consumption. Moreover, the amount of investment required will be immense. And it would be unrealistic to expect most alternatives to fully or even substantially replace oil at any level of investment, even with decades of effort, given practical, physical constraints to their development.

Higher prices will also no doubt spur efficiency measures, but the most productive of these will likewise require time and investment. For example, raising the fuel efficiency of the U.S. auto fleet would require years for industry retooling and more years for consumers to trade in their current vehicles for more efficient replacements.

James Schlesinger, who served as CIA director in the Nixon administration, defense secretary in the Nixon and Ford administrations, and energy secretary in the Carter administration, in November 2005 testimony before the Senate Foreign Relations Committee urged lawmakers to begin preparing for declining oil supplies and increasing prices in the coming decades. "We are faced with the possibility of a major economic shock and the political unrest that would ensue," he said.[13]

Schlesinger was far from overstating the threat. In fact, it would be no exaggeration to view Peak Oil as potentially representing the economic, social, and political impact of a hundred Katrinas. And that impact will not subside in a few days' or years' time: once global oil production has peaked, the energy shortfalls for transportation and agriculture will be ongoing, relentless, and cumulative.

What Should the Administration Be Doing?

Responsible and competent people who have studied the problem of Peak Oil, (including Robert Hirsch and his colleagues) agree that efforts will be needed to create alternative sources of energy, to reduce demand for oil through heightened energy efficiency, and to redesign entire systems (including both cities and the rural agricultural economy) to operate with less petroleum.

The Hirsch Report's methodology involved the examination of three scenarios:

- Scenario I assumed that action is not initiated until peaking occurs.
- Scenario II assumed that action is initiated ten years before peaking.
- Scenario III assumed action is initiated twenty years before peaking.

In all three scenarios the Hirsch study assumed a "crash program" scale of effort (that is, all the resources of government and industry are marshaled to the tasks of creating supplies of alternative fuels and reducing demand through efficiency measures). The study found that, because of the time required to start efforts and the scale of mitigation required, Scenario I will result in at least twenty years of fuel shortfalls. With ten years of preparation, a ten-year shortfall is likely. And with twenty years of advance mitigation effort, there is "the possibility" of averting fuel shortages altogether. The Report also concludes that "Early mitigation will almost certainly be less expensive than delayed mitigation."[14]

In other words, if global Peak Oil is twenty years away or fewer, *or we believe it might be*, we must begin immediately with a full-scale effort to address the problem.

Most Americans would understandably prefer to solve the dilemma simply by switching to alternative fuels, thus enabling them to maintain their current habits. But, as we have already noted, there are problems with that strategy.

Biofuels (ethanol, wood methanol, and biodiesel) require land area for production and are plagued by the problem of low net-energy yields. According to the calculations of Jeffrey Dukes of the University of Massachusetts, over a hundred tons of ancient plant matter are concentrated in every gallon of gasoline we use today.[15] Granted, modern methods of biofuels production are more efficient than nature's slow means of producing crude oil, but still this analysis should give us pause: trying to replace a substantial fraction of our twenty million barrels per day of national oil consumption with biofuels could potentially overwhelm an agricultural system already destroying topsoil and drawing down ancient aquifers unsustainably.

It is possible to produce liquid transportation fuels from coal and natural gas. However, natural gas is itself a problematic fuel in North America (domestic production peaked in 2001), and coal—a low-quality hydrocarbon—would present a host of environmental and practical quandaries if we tried to increase mining sufficiently to replace a significant proportion of our oil budget. In the end, coal is also a depleting fossil fuel: while it is often said that we have hundreds of years' worth of the stuff, that assumes current rates of consumption and ignores variable quality. Assuming dramatic *increases* in consumption (for oil replacement) and taking into account the fact that much coal offers a low energy yield, those centuries shrink to a very few decades.[16]

Which brings us to the strategies of conservation, efficiency, and curtailment. These clearly present the best opportunities, though efforts along these lines will eventually require significant changes in Americans' habits and expectations.

Our automobiles could be made much more fuel efficient, though this effort will require government leadership via higher Corporate Average Fuel Economy (CAFE) standards. But over the long term automobiles and trucks simply aren't good options for transportation, given their inherent energy inefficiency. Thus the nation will need a much-expanded freight and passenger rail system. Our cities, most of which have been designed for the automobile, need to be made more neighborhood-oriented and walkable and provided with light-rail transit systems. Meanwhile agricultural production must be freed, as quickly and completely as possible, from fossil-fuel inputs. All of these efforts will require substantial investment and many years of work.

If, as the Hirsch Report tells us, the market will be incapable of shifting investment incentives quickly enough away from the old oil-based, energy-guzzling energy infrastructure and toward the new alternatives-based, super-efficient one, then government will have to lead the way through a sustained commitment of effort on a wartime scale. The estimated one to three trillion dollars consumed so far in the invasions and occupations of Afghanistan and Iraq, had they been spent instead on domestic energy security, would probably have represented an appropriate level and rate of funds allocation.

What Has the Administration Done?

Before examining what Bush and Cheney have done (and not done), we should in fairness note that previous administrations are far from blameless. During the Clinton-Gore years, imports of oil increased while CAFE standards languished. However, in a court of law the incompetence or even criminality of others is seldom a viable defense for one's own culpable actions.

That said, in light of the threat and the needed effort, what has the current president actually accomplished?

First of all, the administration effectively buried the Hirsch Report. For many months it was available only on a high-school Web site, then on the Project Censored site; only toward the end of 2005 did it appear on a Department of Energy site. There has been no public mention whatever of the Report by any official in the executive branch. Thus the administration has sought not to respond to warnings of approaching crisis but simply to muffle them.

During the past six years funding for renewable energy programs and for energy efficiency has not increased substantially. Meanwhile the administration has consistently sought to remove subsidies for the nation's passenger rail system, Amtrak, while continuing to support immense subsidies for highways.

To be sure, Bush has occasionally spoken about the need for an energy policy, as in a speech to the nation in April 2005:

First, we must better use technology to become better conservers of energy. And secondly, we must find innovative and environmentally sensitive ways to make the most of our existing energy resources, including oil, natural gas, coal and safe, clean nuclear power. Third, we must develop promising new sources of energy, such as hydrogen, ethanol or bio-diesel. Fourth, we must help growing energy consumers overseas, like China and India, apply new technologies to use energy more efficiently and reduce global demand of fossil fuels.[17]

I would disagree with a few of these suggestions, but over all this is not a bad summary of what actually needs to happen. But talk is cheap, and talk that accomplishes next to nothing is, in this situation, a criminally negligent diversion and waste of time. The words just quoted were spoken in the context of the president's promotion of an energy bill that actually did very little except increase tax breaks to the fossil-fuel industry.

In his 2006 State of the Union address Bush said that the U.S. is "addicted to oil" and put forward the goal of reducing oil imports from the Middle East. The following day his staff backpedaled, stating that this goal was only an "example."[18]

Five years into the Bush administration the nation is more dependent on imported oil than ever before. It is facing an impending energy crisis that a government-funded study notes will be "unprecedented" in scope and consequences. And needed preparation efforts are nowhere to be seen.

Given all this, how will impeachment help? While it would be justified as a punishment for ineptitude or criminality, impeachment will not materially assist the nation to deal with Peak Oil unless current officials are replaced with ones who understand the problem and who are prepared to implement policies that radically shift America's priorities in terms of energy, transportation, urban infrastructure, and agriculture. Looking out over the current political landscape in Washington, it is difficult to identify who those new officials might be. Nevertheless, it would help the nation to start now with a clean slate, and with a popular mandate for the new team of leaders to move rapidly to achieve energy security.

Notes:

1. See discussion of this topic in my book *Powerdown: Options and Actions for a Post Carbon World* (New Society, 2004), pp. 40–41.
2. http://www.greencarcongress.com/2005/10/ford_exec_oil_p.html (accessed 13 March, 2006).
3. http://www.volvo.com/NR/rdonlyres/A9A59F6A-AA6F-F48E-A048-BF9D6DE505DB/0/ future_fuels_large.pdf (accessed March 13, 2006).
4. Michael DesLauriers, "Famed Oil Tycoon Sounds Off on Peak Oil," *Resource Investor*, June 23, 2005, http://www.resourceinvestor.com/pebble.asp?relid=10766 (accessed March 13, 2006).
5. Jeroen Van Der Veer, "Vision for Meeting Energy Needs Beyond Oil," *Financial Times*, January 24, 2006, http://news.ft.com/cms/s/fb775ee8-8d0e-11da-9daf-0000779e2340.html (accessed March 13, 2006).
6. Robert B. Semple, Jr., "The End of Oil," *New York Times*, March 1, 2006, http://select.nytimes.com/gst/tsc.html?URI=http://select.nytimes.com/2006/03/01/opinion/01talkingpoints.html&OQ=_rQ3DiQ26pagewantedQ3Dall&OP=65dfb2d8Q2F)GQ24E)DQ5CH00D)Q22rrI) ri)rK)0LQ2AQ7EQ2A0Q7E)rKDQ26.Q7BQ2AQ7EgLoQ2AQ7EDQ5CxkD2 (accessed March 13, 2006).
7. Adam Fenderson and Bart Anderson, "US Army: Peak Oil and the Army's Future," *Energy Bulletin*, March 13, 2006, http://www.energybulletin.net/13737.html (accessed March 13, 2006).
8. "Strategic Significance of America's Shale Oil Resource," vol. 1, "Assessment of Strategic Issues," Office of Deputy Assistant Secretary for Petroleum Reserves, Office of Naval Petroleum and Oil Shale Reserves, U.S. Department of Energy, March 2004, www.fe.doe.gov/programs/reserves/publications/Pubs-NPR/npr_strategic_significancev1.pdf.
9. Robert L. Hirsch, *et al.*, "The Peaking of World Oil Production: Impacts, Mitigation and Risk Management," February 2005, http://www.projectcensored.org/newsflash/the_hirsch_report.pdf (accessed March 13, 2006).
10. Staff, "Congressman Bartlett Discusses Peak Oil with President Bush," *Energy Bulletin*, June 29, 2005, http://www.energybulletin.net/7024.html (accessed March 13, 2006).
11. http://www.energybulletin.net/559.html (accessed March 13, 2006).
12. Hirsch, *op. cit.*
13. http://www.senate.gov/~foreign/testimony/2005/SchlesingerTestimony051116.pdf (accessed March 13, 2006).
14. Hirsch, *op. cit.*
15. "Price of Gas," *ScienCentral News*, July 28, 2005, http://www.sciencentral.com/articles/view.php3?article_id=218392605&cat=all (accessed March 13, 2006).
16. Gregson Vaux, "The Peak in US Coal Production," *From the Wilderness*, May 27, 2004, http://www.fromthewilderness.com/free/ww3/052504_coal_peak.html (accessed March 13, 2006).
17. http://www.whitehouse.gov/news/releases/2005/04/20050428-9.html (accessed March 13, 2006).
18. http://www.whitehouse.gov/stateoftheunion/2006/index.html (accessed March 13, 2006).

Chapter 13

THE OTHER REGIME CHANGE
Overthrowing Haiti's President Jean-Bertrand Aristide

Lyn Duff and Dennis Bernstein

In early 2002 several hundred crates of assault rifles were taken from their storage facility on an East Coast military base and loaded into a shipping container by the United States Navy's 841 Transportation Battalion. These crates, containing 20,000 M-16 semiautomatic assault rifles with 20-round magazines, were due to be shipped to Dominican Republic, a small country occupying the Western two-thirds of the island of Hispanola. Along with four UH-1H helicopters, the weapons were purportedly a gift from the Bush administration to the Dominican Republic's border patrol.[1]

However, the Dominican border patrol has less than 3,000 employees. This number includes only 900 border-patrol agents who are authorized to carry weapons; the remaining number encompasses everyone from secretaries to janitors working in the country's immigration offices at airports and border crossings.[2]

Why would the United States send 20,000 M-16s to a force of only 900 border-patrol agents? The answer to that question lies in events on the other half of the island, in the struggling and impoverished country of Haiti.

Long rocked by political turmoil and economic interference from outside forces—including American companies—Haiti had been struggling to establish a stable democracy since the country's first free election in 1990. Progress had been stymied by a bloody three-year coup reportedly financed by the United States in 1991,[3] and by several attempted coups in the years since.[4]

In 2000 Jean Bertrand Aristide, a leader in the country's prodemocracy movement, was elected, with 91 percent of the popular vote to serve a second, nonconsecutive term as president.[5] From the moment he took office, the Bush administration attempted to destabilize the democratic government of Haiti, eventually funding and backing a bloody two-year coup in which an untold number were killed and an estimated 15,000 women and girls were subjected to politically motivated mass rape.[6]

The saga began in May 2000, when the Fanmi Lavalas party won landslide victories in national legislature and local elections. Observers from the Organization of American States hailed the elections, which featured the largest number of voters in Haiti's history, as a success, saying that they were both "free and fair." However elections monitors did criticize the method used to calculate runoff votes in seven senate races. Six months later the political opposition used the senate runoff votes as an excuse to boycott presidential elections.[7]

In November 2000, in an election with voter turnout exceeding 50 percent, Jean-Bertrand Aristide was elected President with more than 90 percent of the votes. Observers from the OAS and the International Organization of Independent Observers reported that again the elections were free and fair. On February 7, 2001, Aristide was sworn into office for a five-year term to end in 2006. Without exception the international community recognized him as the duly elected president of Haiti.

But this wasn't good enough for the Bush administration, which repeatedly refused to release international aid to Haiti unless Aristide made concessions to his political opposition, whom the United States government had backed and funded in the 2000 elections. Eventually six senators from the Fanmi Lavalas party and one independent senator resigned and agreed to new elections. Pressured by United States Secretary of State Colin Powell, President Aristide and his party agreed to early elections and even agreed to negotiate a power-sharing arrangement with the opposition.[8]

But bolstered by support from the Bush administration, including $2.4 million in "democracy enhancement" funds from USAID, Haiti's political opposition systematically refused to compromise or agree to a new election, insisting that President Aristide immediately resign and that they, the unelected political opposition, be invited to form a transitional government.[9] These demands doomed negotiations from the start, yet the United States continued to push Haiti's democratic government to accept the terms, even though they violated Haiti's constitution and the rights of Haitian citizens to freely elect their leaders.[10]

At the same time, allegedly in response to irregularities with Haiti's May 2000 senate runoff elections, the United States imposed an international aid embargo on Haiti, withholding almost all assistance to the Haitian government and blocking bilateral assistance from other organizations and countries.[11] The United States directed the Inter-American Development Bank (IADB) to block four loans to Haiti that had already been approved for health, education, potable water distribution, and rural transportation.[12] Not only did this violate the IADB's own internal regulations, but using the bank as leverage in a political dispute breached the IADB's charter.[13] IADB representatives state that Bush administration officials "forced" them to comply with American sanctions against Haiti.[14]

United States Funding of the Political Opposition

During the same period that the Bush administration was blocking aid to the elected government, the United States government was providing generous financing to the political opposition. According to Pamela Callen, deputy director of USAID in Haiti, the agency distributed more than $2.4 million for "democracy enhancement" programs to create, train, and fund the political opposition.[15]

One of the programs was the Federation des Etudiants Universitaire Haitienne,[16] a student organization formed, trained, and funded by the United States through the International Republican Institute[17] and paid for by the United States taxpayers. Callen states that leaders of FEUH were trained in the Dominican Republic during late 2003, staying at the same hotel[18] as the rebel leader, Guy Philippe. The students returned to Haiti to create an "anti-Aristide" organization on their campus that advocated the violent overthrow of the democratically elected government and called for the establishment of a government run by the mulatto elite.[19]

The "democracy enhancement" programs were implemented by the International Foundation for Electoral Systems (IFES),[20] which, during the years leading up to the 2004 coup, created and supported a network of political, professional, business, and legal organizations for the express purpose of generating public support for overthrowing Haiti's elected leaders.[21] IFES financed activities of the Group of 184, the main force leading the political opposition, which was organized by an American citizen, Andrè Apaid Jr., a sweatshop owner in Port-au-Prince. The Group of 184 also received generous financing from the European Union,[22] but it was American monies from IFES that paid for organizing several illegal demonstrations in which middle-class students attacked police officers, market women, peaceful bystanders, and participants in a prodemocracy counterdemonstration.

Meanwhile former members of Haiti's demobilized army, and other armed groups associated with drug traffickers, began military training in the Dominican Republic.[23] From 2001 to 2004, despite protests from the Haitian government, Dominican authorities stood by while these groups conducted periodic raids across the border against targets in Haiti.

And in December 2002 the 20,000 M-16 semiautomatic assault rifles shipped by the United States Navy arrived in the Dominican Republic.[24] Within weeks, according to senior United States military officials and Noble Espejo, a general in the Dominican armed forces, the guns were in the hands of demobilized Haitian soldiers.[25] This appears to be a clear violation of international law, believes Karen Parker, a constitutional law expert from the Association of Humanitarian Lawyers. "According to treaties of the United States, which are the law of the land by our constitution, the United States cannot interfere with the internal affairs of another country."[26]

By shipping weapons and helicopters to the rebels, Parker notes, the Bush administration clearly violated Haiti's sovereignty. "You can't violate another country by arming opposition groups or establishing opposition groups," she states, and yet the Bush administration took both of these actions.

"Is it a civil war if it is [fought by] mercenaries supported, aided, and financed by an outside power? Is this an internal insurgency that we saw in Haiti, or is the United States intervening in the internal affairs of another state?" Arming the rebels was "an impeachable offense" committed by President Bush, states Parker. "Those weapons were given with a string attached. . . . They were given to the rebels, who [the Bush administration] was not just arming, but was also supporting both verbally and diplomatically. This wasn't some normal arms deal."[27]

The weapons were quickly distributed among the demobilized soldiers, who had re-formed into a "rebel front" and were planning to stage a coup against Aristide.[28]

On February 5, 2004, the group made good on its promise, attacking and taking the port city of Gonaïves. Another rebel group, led by Louis Jodel Chamblain and Guy Philippe, crossed the border from the Dominican Republic into Haiti on February 6. Chamblain states that his goal was to kill Lavalas members, "our target was the *chimères* [a derogatory term which has been used simultaneously for both terrorists and Aristide supporters]; I do not know how many died. The battle began at one and ended at four in the afternoon. . . .We were well armed and we would take Cap-Haïtien."[29]

Several weeks later, on the afternoon of February 22, the rebels captured Cap-Haïtien, Haiti's second-largest city.

Embargo as a Weapon of War

How was a group of several hundred armed men able to overthrow an entire government?

The answer to that question, say observers, lies in the actions of the Bush administration.

Since 1995 the United States government had an arms embargo against the elected Haitian government, preventing its national police force from purchasing police revolvers.[30] In 2001, when Aristide took office, the Bush administration expanded this embargo to include standard law-enforcement equipment, such as tear gas, riot shields, and other crowd-control equipment.[31] When the rebels attacked, many police officers were killed simply because they were unarmed and unable to defend themselves, much less defend the city they were charged with protecting.[32]

The rebels were further bolstered by public comments from the White House. On February 26, as the capital of Port-au-Prince was being surrounded by rebels who had openly bragged to the international press about killing unarmed civilians, United States Secretary of State Colin Powell told reporters that Aristide should step down.[33]

The same day CARICOM, the association of Caribbean states, asked the UN Security Council to authorize the urgent deployment of a multinational force to assist in the restoration of law and order.[34] President Aristide asked the United States and the international community for "a few dozen peacekeeping troops" to help avoid a slaughter of his citizens. Not only did the Bush administration refuse to send help, it also blocked the Security Council, of which the United States is one of five permanent members, from sending peacekeeping troops to prevent the overthrow of the elected government. The Bush administration did send a contingent of fifty Marines to Haiti that week, but ordered them to hold off on protecting anything other than American assets until after the rebels reached Port-au-Prince and Aristide's departure was imminent.[35]

On the afternoon of February 28 the Steele Foundation, an American firm contracted by the Haitian government to guard the president, informed President Aristide that the United States State Department had asked it to withdraw all of its personnel from Haiti. Furthermore, the Steele Foundation administrators told Aristide that officials from the Bush administration were preventing the firm from flying a plane of security personnel from San Francisco International Airport to Haiti.[36]

The following day, the Bush administration released a statement condemning Aristide for "orchestrating violence" in Port-au-Prince, claiming that he had directed armed gangs to target civilians, humanitarian programs, and international organizations.[37]

With an overwhelmed security force hemmed in by armed rebels, Aristide was in a desperate situation the night of February 29, 2004. Late that evening, Luis Moreno, United States Embassy deputy director, accompanied by a contingent of United States Marines, confronted Aristide in his home, telling him that if he did not leave the country, he and his supporters would be executed. At the same time, a group of American Marines was, without the permission of the Haitian government, seizing control of the National Palace (Haiti's equivalent of the White House) and the Port-au-Prince International Airport.[38]

Aristide, unaware that American Marines now occupied the National Palace, decided to travel there to speak to the news media and issue a televised appeal to the Haitian people to remain calm and peaceful. He was accompanied by Moreno, who instead directed the driver to take President Aristide to the airport, where a United States-chartered plane was waiting. At the airport, Aristide says, he was given the choice of either signing a letter of resignation and getting on the plane or staying and causing "a bloodbath" in which, American diplomats told him, thousands of innocent Lavalas members would be killed and he and his wife would be executed.

Aristide wrote and signed a cryptic letter that Professor Bryant Freeman, an expert in the Haitian Creole language hired by the United States State Department, later claimed was not in fact a resignation at all.[39] Nevertheless, Aristide and his wife were rushed onto the plane. He was followed by uniformed American troops, who changed into civilian clothes on board. According to witnesses, the soldiers confiscated Aristide's cell phone and prevented him and his wife from raising the window blinds during a refueling stop or calling anyone on the plane's satellite phones.

The couple was kept incommunicado for days, not told where they were flying to, and prohibited from using the phone, says Aristide. No one, including family members, Aristide's attorney, or representatives from the elected Haitian government, was told where United States agents had taken the president. Even the couple's two school-aged daughters, who were staying with their grandparents in Miami, were not told where their parents were.

Several days later, Aristide surfaced in Bangui, capital of the Central African Republic, where he and his wife were being held under armed military guard, without access to the press and prohibited from using the phone or e-mail. At one point Aristide called United States Congresswoman Maxine Waters and Randall Robinson, a friend who is the former executive director of the TransAfrica Forum, on a cell phone that had been smuggled in to him. Both began alerting the world to the Bush administration's removal of Aristide, which Waters called akin to a kidnapping.

"It's clear that the Bush administration illegally violated Haiti's sovereignty in removing a duly elected president from office. Regardless of the interpretation of the content of [the resignation letter], it cannot be considered a voluntary resignation, because United States government officials forced President Aristide to sign the letter under threat," states human-rights attorney Brian Concannon of the Institute for Justice and Democracy in Haiti.[40] "The United States government also claimed that it took President Aristide to the Central African Republic because South Africa had refused him asylum. The South African government denied this report, saying that it had not even received a request for asylum. In fact they extended an offer to Aristide and his family to stay in their country as guests of the South African government."

CARICOM immediately called for an investigation into the forced departure of Aristide, noting, "The removal of President Aristide in these circumstances sets a dangerous precedent for democratically elected governments anywhere and everywhere."[41] The Africa Union Commission agreed that "the unconstitutional way by which President Aristide was removed set a dangerous precedent for a duly elected person and wishes that no action be taken to legitimize the rebel forces" in Haiti.[42]

Haitian Supreme Court Chief Justice Boniface Alexandre was quickly sworn in as Haiti's new president, a move that would only have been constitutionally legal if the office had in fact been vacant, but wasn't legal because Aristide never officially resigned and was prevented from fulfilling his presidential duties only by intervention of the United States. Not a single elected official was present at Boniface's investiture (although officials from the United States embassy were in attendance).

In a move reminiscent of U.S. actions in Afghanistan, a "Council of Wise Men" was established to appoint a new prime minister of Haiti. Yvon Neptune, who had been the current prime minister, was forced from office and went into hiding soon after. On June 27, 2004, he was arrested by the interim government and incarcerated without trail for more than two years.

Haiti's Hamid Karzai was Gérard Latortue, a wealthy businessman from Boca Raton, Florida. Latortue, who has close connections with both the World Bank and the International Monetary Fund, is an American citizen of Haitian descent. The Haitian constitution requires prime ministers to have lived in Haiti for five years preceding their nominations; Latortue had lived in Boca Raton for more than eighteen years and had not even visited Haiti in recent years. His appointment was backed by the United States but was never confirmed by parliament, as is required by the constitution.

The interim government of Haiti quickly solidified its power by dismissing the remaining members of Parliament, illegally firing five supreme court judges[43] and allowing paramilitary death squads led by former soldiers to operate with impunity throughout the countryside. The United States responded by providing the interim government of Haiti with generous financing not previously available to the democratically elected governments because of the Bush administration's foreign-aid embargo against Aristide.

This influx of cash and aid programs was insufficient to win the hearts and minds of the Haitian people, who continued to demand the return of the leaders they elected. To control public dissent, rebel leaders were given free reign to terrorize the populace. Mass rapes became common. Thousands disappeared. The bodies of prodemocracy activists, union leaders, and members of peasant organizations were found dumped in shallow graves, their hands bound and their bodies marked by torture.

Rape, Terror, and Political Repression

In March 2004 the director of the State Morgue told an investigator from the National Lawyer's Guild that "many bodies" had come into the morgue since March 1, including numerous "young men with their hands tied behind their backs, plastic bags over their heads, [who had] been shot." He told human-rights investigators that eight hundred bodies were "dumped and buried" by the morgue on March 7, and another two hundred bodies were dumped on March 28, an unusual number, as the average in Port-au-Prince before the coup was less than a hundred bodies per month.[44]

Not only were citizens murdered, but many women were also subjected to politically motivated mass rape. Maria Pascal, thirty-two, was one of the many women raped by armed men from the disbanded Haitian army. Speaking about her experience, she said, "The repression against women has been taken to a new level. . . . Twelve years ago, when the former military was in power, rape was used to terrorize. But today it is more horrible than anyone could have imagined."[45]

The Bush administration's support for this policy of rape and terror was brought into clearer focus when, on March 20, 2004, Latortue traveled aboard a United States helicopter to Gonaïves. There he honored the rebels, including at least one who had been involved in mass rape, in a ceremony at the Place Publique, next to the courthouse that had been destroyed by rebel forces a month earlier. With Ambassador David Lee, head of the Organization of American States' Special Mission in Haiti, at his side, Latortue thanked fugitive and convicted murderer Jean Tatoune for his work in overthrowing the democratic government of Haiti, referring to the rebels as "freedom fighters."[46]

Another "freedom fighter" lauded by Latortue was Louis Jodel Chamblain, a former sergeant in the Haitian army who was second in command of the Front for the Advancement and Progress of Haiti (FRAPH), a paramilitary death squad organized with United States backing in Haiti in 1992. FRAPH was created specifically to terrorize the Haitian people by publicly executing, torturing, raping, maiming, and burning alive members of the prodemocracy populace.[47] FRAPH's first-in-command, Emmanuel "Toto" Constant, con-firmed during an interview with CBS's *60 Minutes* that he was on the CIA payroll beginning in 1992. According to U.S. State Department documents, as well as public statements made by both Chamblain and Constant, after Aristide's bloody United States-orchestrated ouster in September 1991, Colonel Patrick Collins, a U.S. Defense Intelligence Agency attaché who was stationed in Haiti from 1989 to 1992, directed Chamblain and Constant to organize a front that could "balance" the pro-Aristide movement and do intelligence work against it.[48]

Chamblain went into exile in the Dominican Republic to avoid prosecution after the United States invasion of Haiti in 1994 and was, along with seven others, convicted in absentia in 1995 for the shooting death of Antoine Izmery, a businessman who had been dragged from his church during mass and executed in the street for his support of Lavalas.[49] In November 2000, Chamblain was again convicted of murder for his role in the 1994 massacre of prodemocracy activists in the neighborhood of Raboteau.

In April 2004 Chamblain requested a new trial, and Minister of Justice Bernard Gousse responded by telling reporters that he would pardon Chamblain if he were reconvicted. In August of that year the interim government of Haiti retried Chamblain in an event Amnesty International described as a "mockery" of a trial and which United Nations Secretary General Kofi Annan said "tarnishes the credibility of [Haiti's] justice system." In the one-day trial no witnesses testified, and no evidence was presented; Chamblain was acquitted.[50]

After his acquittal Chamblain rejoined his compatriots in the Haiti's countryside, where they were acting as de facto authorities, controlling the local municipalities and patrolling the roads. Amnesty International investigators witnessed some rebel leaders presiding over impromptu trials of prodemocracy activists, and reports began to surface that, armed with U.S. supplied weaponry, the rebels were continuing to hunt down and execute suspected Lavalas supporters while supporting themselves by extorting money and goods from the populace.

The justice system may have been ineffective in convicting an admitted murderer and human-rights violator, but it was quite effective in the mass arbitrary detention of political activists. In April 2005 a human-rights report from the Inter-American Commission found "approximately 90 percent of individuals held in detention centers in Haiti's 10 geographic departments [had] not been tried or convicted." On one visit to the National Penitentiary, Commission investigators discovered that of the 1,054 inmates in the prison, only nine had been convicted of a crime.[51]

Many were not convicted, claim human rights investigators, because they were arrested and jailed for purely political reasons. Some were picked up during mass arrests in the popular zones, believed to be a hotbed of prodemocracy activity, while others were Lavalas leaders or elected members of the overthrown government who were arrested and jailed without charge for months or years.[52]

The threat of arbitrary arrest was not enough to prevent mass opposition to the interim government, so in the cities a force of 4,000 American Marines was enlisted to suppressed popular protest against the coup. During the first two months of the American occupation, the Marines, many of whom were transferred to Haiti directly from Iraq and Afghanistan, killed an estimated 300 civilians, including numerous children.[53]

One of the victims was sixteen-year-old Evens Dubuisson, a high-school student from Bel Air, Port-au-Prince, who dreamed of becoming a veterinarian. On the night of March 12 Dubuisson's mother sent him to buy groceries at an outdoor market several blocks away. Shortly after 8 p.m. Dubuisson reports, he saw American Marines enter his neighborhood.[54]

"There was a light rain, so the area was not as busy as it usually was," the lanky teen recalls. "And then the shooting started. It was loud and I felt pain and then I felt nothing at all."

The street quickly emptied as residents ran for cover. "We'd heard about the Marines killing and shooting people, like they shot that man who was out after curfew getting asthma medication for his child," explained fifteen-year-old Ulrick Pierre, referring to a late-night checkpoint incident a week earlier in which two people had been shot by Marines in Port-au-Prince. "No one wanted to be near the white military. We weren't taking any chances."[55]

No dispersal order was given to the small crowd of shoppers patronizing the street vendors, say the over two dozen witnesses who spoke with reporters. No civilians in the area had weapons, they say, and no one threatened or attacked the Marines. But something happened (some theorize that the Marines were spooked by a flash of metal they thought was a gun) and in a three-minute barrage of gunfire dozens were shot and at least twelve killed, say witnesses. Dubuisson was shot in the back.

In the growing darkness American Marines marked the bodies with green glow sticks and called for an ambulance parked a few blocks away to fetch the dead. The wounded, however, were denied medical treatment. Witnesses say that they begged Marines to take victims to a hospital, but their pleas were met with abuse as Marines hit them with the butts of their rifles and threatened to arrest those who gathered near the wounded.

So many were killed that Marines ran out of body bags, said one witness who watched from a nearby hiding place. "When the Americans went back to get more bags, we quickly ran into the street and dragged back two bodies, which we hid from the Marines." After returning to find the bodies missing, the Marines reportedly became enraged and searched the neighborhood for over an hour, at times shooting into people's homes.[56]

While soldiers searched for the missing two bodies, Dubuisson's mother approached the very Marines who had shot her son to ask them to bring a doctor, but as the high-school student lay bleeding, she says, Marines refused to provide medical attention and threatened her with their guns. Eventually neighbors took Dubuisson to a clinic, where he underwent emergency surgery to remove a bullet lodged next to his spine.

Two years later Dubuisson has not returned to school. He still experiences physical pain and has difficulty standing and sitting. Dubuisson's mother says that she is angry at President Bush and holds him directly responsible for her son's injuries. "My son didn't do anything to the Americans. Why did they have to shoot him? The Americans came to our country, kidnapped our president, and then shot my son in the back. The Americans treated us like animals. What kind of a man shoots a child in the back?"

While the actions of the United States marines are reprehensible, legal experts say that it was the decision of George Bush to directly undermine the democratic government and to fund the political opposition that violated international law and for which he could be impeached.

Under the supremacy clause of the United States Constitution the president has the responsibility to faithfully abide by all sanctioned international treaties. Among these, front and center, is the United Nations Charter, explains Michael Ratner, president of the Center for Constitutional Law. Violating the United Nations Charter is a direct breach of the president's oath to faithfully carry out the laws of the land.

Article Two of the United Nations charter requires the leaders of all member states to "refrain in their international relations from the threat or use of force against the territorial integrity or political independence of any state, or in any other manner inconsistent with the purposes of the United Nations."

The actions of George Bush in destabilizing Haiti and in arming the opposition while creating embargoes against the democratically elected government is, Ratner notes, "definitely grounds for impeachment."

Others agree. In early 2006 a coalition of human-rights lawyers, including Bureau des Avocats Internationaux in Port-au-Prince and the Allard K. Lowenstein International Human Rights Clinic at Yale Law School, filed a complaint with Santiago Canton, executive secretary of the Inter-American Commission on Human Rights, alleging the Bush administration violated the integrity, sovereignty, and self-determination of the Haitian people.[57]

The Bush administration, the complaint states, violated the rights of the Haitian people through a "long-term, systematic plan" that included "(a) undermining the democratically elected Haitian government through a development-assistance embargo and by supporting both unarmed and armed opposition groups; (b) overthrowing the democratically elected Haitian government and kidnapping its President in February 2004; and (c) replacing it with a government with no constitutional or electoral legitimacy."

When it comes to Haiti, President Bush is guilty, agrees Ratner, because "he is neither preserving and protecting the Constitution, nor is he faithfully executing the laws when he is undermining, subverting, and trying to overthrow another country, interfering with its political process and territorial sovereignty."

Whether the Inter-American Commission on Human Rights acts on the complaint is yet to be seen.

Meanwhile, in Port-au-Prince, the mother of shooting victim Evens Dubuisson believes that impeachment is not severe enough punishment for President Bush. "He should be kidnapped and taken to Africa, like he did to our president. . . . We need justice for the victims. We need the truth to be exposed. If President Bush will not confess all of his crimes and admit what he did, then he should be put into a prison cell and be eaten by mosquitoes."

Notes:

1. Evidence of the weapons shipment was first raised in February 2004 and detailed during an interview on February 25, 2004, on Pacifica Radio with Ira Kurzban, then legal counsel to the Haitian government. Rachel Stohl, a senior analyst at the Center for Defense Information in Washington, reviewed part of the documentation provided by the U.S. Defense Security

Cooperation Agency, which organized the shipment of weapons. The "end user certificate" required after the shipment of weapons indicated that the M-16s and helicopters were to be given to the Dominican border patrol. However, Dr. Luis Barrios, a professor of criminal justice at John Jay College in New York City, traveled to the Dominican Republic in 2004, where he says members of the rebel forces claimed that not only were they armed by U.S.-supplied weapons, but that 200 rebels also received specialized training from U.S. military forces in the Dominican Republic during 2003 on Dominican military bases on or near the Haitian border. For more information on the shipment of U.S. weapons to American allies abroad, see the DSCA's homepage, http://www.dsca.mil/.

2.   According to a March 11, 2004, interview with Flavio Dario Espinal, the Dominican Republic's ambassador to the United States. During the interview he acknowledged that the numbers were "estimates," since he did not have access to a current roster of all border-patrol employees. However, the estimated total is still far below the number of weapons transferred to his agency by the U.S. Defense Security Cooperation Agency. During the interview he was unable to confirm that the border patrol had in fact received the weapons and the helicopters, stating, "I don't know anything about this. I can't comment. I don't know why or, well, I don't know that they [the United States] are giving us these weapons or well, uh, why they would be doing so."

3.   FRAPH death squad leader, Emmanuel Constant, confirmed in an interview with CBS *60 Minutes* in 1995 that he received funds from the Central Intelligence Agency to finance elements of the 1991 coup against Jean-Bertrand Aristide. Further documentation of U.S. funding for the 1991–1994 coup was exposed by Jim Lobe of IPS on October 11, 1996, the *Miami New Times* on February 26, 2004, and the *Miami Herald* on August. 1, 2001.

4.   In 2001 there were two attempted coups against the democratically elected government. The second, which took place on December 17, 2001, involved thirty armed men led by former Haitian military officer Guy Philippe. One civilian and two police officers were killed when the men broke into the National Palace using heavy weaponry and grenades. After stealing a two-way radio from a security office, the attackers broadcast their intentions to take over the Palace, stating that they were on a mission for the demobilized Haitian army and that Guy Philippe was their leader. After an exchange of gunfire with Palace security, one ex-solider, Chavne Milot, was killed and the rest fled the area on foot. As news of the attack on the Palace was broadcast on the radio, thousands poured into the streets to block the attackers as they tried to flee back to the Dominican Republic. At civilian-created roadblocks the attackers shot unarmed civilians, killing one and wounding twelve. Citizens in Terre Rouge apprehended one attacker and turned him over to the police. In Thomazeau four men suspected of being involved in the attack on the Palace (because of their military uniforms and gunshot wounds) were apprehended by citizens, who extrajudicially executed them before police arrived.

5.   See Organization of American States Press release, "Haitian Election Results," November 30, 2000.

6.   For a quantitative study of the human-rights situation in Haiti during 2004–2005, see "The Frequency and Intensity of Human Rights Violations in Port-au-Prince," a study of 1260 households in the Port-au-Prince metropolitan area conducted by Dr. Royce A. Hutson and Athena R. Kolbe, MSW, of Wayne State University in Detroit. The study measured the frequency and severity of five types of human-rights violations occurring during the Latortue regime: looting and vandalism, physical assault, sexual assault, murder, and arbitrary arrests/detention. The study found that 7 percent of households had a member who had been sexually assaulted since February 29, 2004. Of these, 14 percent were raped or sexually assaulted by members of the Haitian National Police. Military irregulars, including ex-soldiers and members of armed anti-Lavalas groups, assaulted another 15 percent of the victims. In addition to vaginal rape, victims reported that they were sodomized, raped with inanimate objects

(such as a piece of metal rebar), and forced to have sexual contact with another unwilling participant. Notably, more than half the sexual assault victims were children.

7.   See CNN report, November 25, 2000.
8.   While these events were widely covered in the national and international press at the time, a good chronology is recorded in a complaint filed with the Inter-American Commission on Human Rights against the Interim Government of Haiti, the governments of the United States of America, and the Dominican Republic for violations of Haitian citizens' rights under Articles 1, 23, and 24 of the American Convention and Article XX of the American Declaration. The complaint was filed in 2006 by Bureau des Avocats Internationaux, the Institute for Justice and Democracy in Haiti, the Allard K. Lowenstein International Human Rights Clinic at Yale Law School, and the TransAfrica Forum. It can be download at www.ijdh. org.
9.   This was also widely reported at the time. A copy of the demands of the political opposition was included as an addendum to Resolution 806, adopted by the OAS Permanent Council in January 2002, which called on the Haitian government to "address its political stalemate."
10. http://pdba.georgetown.edu/Constitutions/Haiti/haiti1987.html.
11. During a press conference in 2002, then U.S. Ambassador Brian Dean Curran said that the economic embargo was "a reorganization of resources directing funding towards the private sector . . . to force political change. . . that is favorable to U.S. interests. " For a compelling account of the impact this statement had on Haiti's poor, see Carl Hiaasen, "U.S. Denies Crucial Funds to Help Haiti," *Miami Herald*, June 16, 2002.
12. See Paul Farmer, Mary C. Smith Fawzi, and Patrice Nevil, "Unjust Embargo of Aid for Haiti," *The Lancet*, 2003.
13. See Tracy Kidder, "Trials of Haiti," *The Nation*, October 27, 2003.
14. Unpublished interview with Lyn Duff, September 14, 2003.
15. Pamela Callen made this statement during an interview with Lyn Duff in March 2004 conducted at the United States embassy in Port-au-Prince.
16. This organization is part of the "Group of 184" that supported the 2004 coup. See the organization's "unity statement" at http://haitipolicy.org/content/452.htm (in French).
17. Not only did the IRI fund the political opposition, but on February 8, 2001, Stanley Lucas, the IRI's senior program officer for Haiti, also implied that President Aristide should be assassinated, he did so during an interview on Port-au-Prince's Radio Tropicale. For more on this interview, and a good chronology of the IRI's efforts to destablize that Haitian government, see Max Blumenthal, "The Other Regime Change," published on Salon.com July 16, 2004.
18. The trainings took place at the Hotel Santo Domingo in April, June, and December 2003, while the rebel leader Guy Philippe was a registered guest, according to the hotel's management. Philippe told reporters that he and his compatriots enjoyed a "warm relationship" with IRI leaders.
19. For a description of the IRI's role in the formation of a political movement advocating the overthrow of the democratically elected government, see Walt Bogdanich and J. Nordberg, "Mixed U.S. Signals Helped Tilt Haiti Toward Chaos," *New York Times*, January 29, 2006.
20. For their stated mission in Haiti, see www.ifes.org/haiti.html.
21. A good overview of the role of IFES can be found in Tom Griffin, "Haiti Human Rights Investigation: November 11–21, 2004," University of Miami School of Law, 2004. The report can be downloaded at www.ijdh.org.
22. An account of funding provided to IFES is also detailed in the 2006 complaint filed by Bureau des Avocats Internationaux, *et al.* with the Inter-American Commission on Human Rights.
23. See "US Accused of Training Haitian Rebels in Dominican Republic," *Xinhuanet*, a Chinese wire service, March 29, 2004.
24. Information based on unpublished interviews with Haitian and Dominican officials con-

ducted with the authors in April 2004.

25. This account is also supported by the 2006 complaint filed by Bureau des Avocats Interna-tionaux, *et al.* with the Inter-American Commission on Human Rights.

26. Karen Parker, interview with Dennis Bernstein, January 2006.

27. *Ibid.*

28. Philippe and other rebel leaders stated as much during numerous interviews with the inter-national press in February and March 2004.

29. See Sue Montgomery, "Mastermind Tells How Plot Evolved: Former Montrealer Leads Politi-cal Wing of Group That Overthrew Haiti's Aristide," *Montreal Gazette*, March 9, 2004.

30. See Jim Lobe, "U.S. Lifts Haitian Arms Embargo as Tensions Mount," *Inter Press Service*, October 21, 2004.

31. For the U.S. perspective on this action, see the Congressional Research Service report by Maureen Taft-Morales, "Haiti: Developments and U.S. Policy since 1991 and Current Con-gressional Concerns," January 19, 2005.

32. Based on conversations and interviews conducted in March 2004 with nine former police officers who were assigned to St. Marc, Cap Haïtien, and Gonaïves during the armed conflict. As one officer stated, "the rebels came in, executed people, and then partied in the streets. . . . We could not defend ourselves; we had no bullets and only one revolver, which was jammed. We fled and we hid in houses nearby or the fields. [Name withheld] took a boat out onto the water and tried to hide. But he was found. The rebels whipped the people into a frenzy and told them to kill him, so they did. I was afraid for my wife and children but they were also found . . . the rebels raped my wife. There was nothing I could do to protect her. I was a police officer but I was powerless against these men."

33. See Peter Slevin and Kevin Sullivan, "Powell Puts Pressure on Haitian Leader to Resign," *Washington Post*, February 27, 2004.

34. See Thalif Deen, "Ignoring Urgent Pleas from Caribbean, Security Council Demurs on Haiti Action," *Inter Press Service*, February 27, 2004.

35. For an interesting account of the U.S. involvement in the events of February 29, 2004, see David Pratt, "Aristide's Final Hours: The Marines Moved in and Revealed the True Power Behind the Haitian 'Revolt,'" *Scotland Sunday Herald*, March 7, 2004.

36. See Juan Tamayo, "US Allegedly Blocked Extra Bodyguards," *Miami Herald*, March 1, 2004.

37. The BBC News broadcast the statement on February 29, 2004.

38. See Gary Younge and Sibylla Brodzinsky, "Cajoled or Abducted? Mystery of Aristide's Final Hours," *Guardian*, March 3, 2004.

39. In a March 2004 interview with the authors, which was broadcast on KPFA's *Flashpoints*, Dr. Freeman said that he was faxed a copy of the resignation letter on March 8 by Mary Ellen Gilroy, director of the Office of Caribbean Affairs at the U.S. State Department, who asked him to provide an independent translation. He did so and discovered that the letter had been initially mistranslated by the U.S. Embassy and that Aristide did not actually resign in the let-ter. The incorrect translation had already been disseminated to the press by the U.S. Embassy in Port-au-Prince, and the State Department continued to distribute the incorrect translation even after Dr. Freeman corrected it. See also, Jennifer Byrd, "KU Prof Asked to Translate Aristide's Statement," *Lawrence Journal-World*, March 11, 2004.

40. Brian Concannon, interview by Dennis Bernstein, February 2006.

41. This statement from Jamaican Prime Minister P.J. Patterson was released March 1, 2004, and can be found at http://www.cnn.com/2004/WORLD/americas/03/01/aristide.claim/.

42. "Aristide's 'Removal' from Haiti 'Unconstitutional': African Union," Agence France-Presse, March 9, 2004.

43. For a good analysis of the events, see "Caribbean Guyana Institute for Democracy Condemns Termination of Haitian Judges," a press release from the Caribbean Guyana Institute for

Democracy dated December 23, 2005, posted on www.alterpresse.org.

44. See Thomas Griffin, "Center for the Study of Human Rights Special Report: Haiti Human Rights Investigation," University of Miami School of Law, 2004.

45. Maria Pascal as told to Lyn Duff, "The Rape of Haiti," interview in full published at http://www.sfbayview.com/110905/rapeofhaiti110905.shtml.

46. The ceremony was broadcast on Haitian television and several national radio stations. It was widely commented on in the international press outside of North America. See also "Haiti: Powell Should Back Rebel Prosecutions," policy statement from Human Rights Watch, April 5, 2004.

47. Survivors of gross human-rights abuses committed by the FRAPH death squads filed suit against FRAPH leaders on January 14, 2005. For a moving account of the motivation for this lawsuit, see the press release titled "Haitian Death Squad Leader, Toto Constant, to Be Brought to Justice For His Campaign of Rape and Murder" on the Web site of the Center for Justice and Accountability.

48. See Mark Weisbrot, "Regime Change in Haiti: A Coup by Any Other Name," Knight-Ridder/Tribune Media Services, March 2, 2004.

49. See Jody A. Benjamin, "INS Arrests 14 Immigrants for Alleged Human Rights Abuses in Their Countries," *Florida Sun-Sentinel*, November 11, 2000.

50. See Kevin Sullivan, "Aristide Foe Acquitted in Brief Retrial," *Washington Post*, August 18, 2004.

51. The sheer number of arbitrary arrests and illegal detentions became so high that even the U.S. State Department was forced to acknowledge the problem in its "Country Report on Human Rights Practices: 2005" released March 8, 2006.

52. See Mary Turck, "Violence, Resistance and Repression," Resource Center of the Americas, October 2005.

53. Numerous reports of civilian deaths at the hands of American Marines were reported in the international and national press throughout March and April 2004. For one example, see "U.S. Marines Kill Two in Haiti" by the Associated Press, March 14, 2004.

54. For a complete account of Evens Dubuisson's story, see Lyn Duff and Dennis Bernstein, "Haiti: The Untold Story," *Censored 2005: The Top 25 Censored Stories* (New York: Seven Stories Press, 2004). Photographs of the victims of the March 12 attack can be found on www.sfbayview.com and www.haitiprogres.com.

55. *Ibid.*

56. *Ibid.*

57. The complaint can be found at The Institute for Justice and Democracy in Haiti Web site www.ijdh.org.

Chapter 14

THE GLOBAL DOMINANCE GROUP
A Sociological Case for the Impeachment of George W. Bush and Richard Cheney

Peter Phillips, Bridget Thornton,
Lew Brown, and Andrew Sloan

The leadership class in the U.S. is now dominated by a neoconservative group of people with the shared goal of aggressively asserting U.S. military power worldwide. George W. Bush, Richard Cheney, and Donald Rumsfeld are the most powerful public members of this *global dominance group* (GDG). The GDG also includes interlocking public-private partnerships, the corporate media, private foundations, military contractors, policy elites, and government officials. We ask the traditional sociological questions regarding who wins, who decides, and who facilitates action inside the world's most powerful military-industrial complex and how collectively this group has benefited from September 11, 2001. As a remedy we advocate the immediate impeachment and removal from office of Bush, Cheney, and their military-dominance cohorts.

A long thread of sociological research documents the existence of a dominant ruling class in the U.S., which sets policy and determines national political priorities. The American ruling class is complex and intercompetitive, maintaining itself through interacting families of high social standing who have similar lifestyles, corporate affiliations, and membership in elite social clubs and private schools.[1]

This American ruling class is mostly self-perpetuating,[2] maintaining its influence through policy-making institutions, such as the National Manufacturing Association, National Chamber of Commerce, Business Council, Business Roundtable, Conference Board, American Enterprise Institute, Council on Foreign Relations and other business-centered policy groups.[3] C. Wright Mills, in his 1956 book *The Power Elite*, documents the ways World War II solidified a trinity of power in the U.S., comprised of corporate, military, and government elites in a centralized power structure motivated by class interests and working in unison through "higher circles" of contact and agreement. Mills described the power elite as those "who decide whatever is decided" of major consequence.[4]

The *higher circle policy elites* (HCPE) are a segment of the American upper class and are the society's principal decision-makers. While having a sense of "we-ness," they tend to have disagreements on specific policies and necessary actions in various sociopolitical circumstances.[5] These disagreements can block aggressive reactionary responses to social movements and civil unrest, as was the case with the 1930s labor movement and the 1960s civil rights movement. During these two periods, liberal elements of HCPE tended to dominate the decision-making process and supported passing the National Labor Relations and Social Security Acts in 1935, as well as the Civil Rights and Economic Opportunities Acts in 1964. These pieces of national legislation were seen as concessions to the ongoing social movements and civil unrest based on their assessment that it was better to make some concessions than risk further and unpredictable social upheaval.

During periods of putative external threats—World War I and World War II—more conservative elements of the HCPE were able to advance their agendas more forcefully. During and after World War I, the U.S. instituted repressive responses to social movements through the Palmer Raids, the passage of the 1917 Espionage Act, and the 1918 Sedition Act. After World War II, the McCarthy-era attacks on liberals and radicals, as well as the 1947 National Security Act and the antilabor Taft-Hartley Act, were encouraged by HCPE.

The Cold War led to a continuing arms race and a further consolidation of military and corporate interests. President Eisenhower warned of this increasing concentration of power in his 1961 address to the nation.

> Our military organization today bears little relation to that known by any of my predecessors in peacetime, or indeed by the fighting men of World War II or Korea. Until the latest of our world conflicts, the United States had no armaments industry. American makers of plowshares could, with time and as required, make

swords as well. But now we can no longer risk emergency impro-
visation of national defense; we have been compelled to create a
permanent armaments industry of vast proportions. Added to this,
three and a half million men and women are directly engaged in
the defense establishment. We annually spend on military security
more than the net income of all United States corporations.

This conjunction of an immense military establishment and a
large arms industry is new in the American experience. The total
influence—economic, political, even spiritual—is felt in every city,
every Statehouse, every office of the Federal government. We recognize the imperative need for this development. Yet we must not
fail to comprehend its grave implications. Our toil, resources and
livelihood are all involved; so is the very structure of our society.

In the councils of government, we must guard against the acquisition of unwarranted influence, whether sought or unsought, by
the military industrial complex. The potential for the disastrous
rise of misplaced power exists and will persist.[6]

The top hundred military contractors from WWII acquired over $3 billion
in new resources between 1939 and 1945, representing a 62 percent increase
in capital assets in just six years. Five main interest groups—Morgan, Mellon,
Rockefeller, Dupont, and Cleveland Steel—controlled two-thirds of the WWII
prime contractor firms and were key elements of HCPE seeking continued
high-level military spending.[7]

Economic incentives, combined with Cold War rivalry, led the HCPE to
advance an unprecedented military readiness, which resulted in a permanent
military-industrial complex. From 1952 to the Soviet Union's collapse, the
U.S. maintained defense funding in the 25–40 percent range of total federal
spending, with peaks during Korea, Vietnam, and the Reagan presidency.[8]

The breakup of the Soviet Union eliminated the rationale for high Cold
War military spending. Some within the HCPE, while celebrating their victory over Communism, saw the possibility of balanced budgets and peace
dividends in the 1990s. In early 1992 Edward Kennedy called for the taking
of $210 billion out of the defense budget over several years and spending
$60 billion on universal health care, public housing, and improved transpor-
tation.[9] However, by the spring of 1992 strong resistance to major cuts in the

military budgets had widespread support in Washington. That year the Senate, in a 50:48 vote, failed to close Republican and conservative Democratic debates against a proposal to shift defense spending to domestic programs.[10] In 1995 Defense Secretary Les Aspin—who during his tenure under Clinton made minor cuts to Pentagon budgets—argued that spending needed to remain high especially for intelligence on "targeting terrorism and narcotics."[11] By 1999, editorials bemoaning the loss of the peace dividend were all that was left of widely anticipated major military spending cuts.[12]

At the same time as HCPE's liberal elements were pushing for a peace dividend, a neoconservative group was arguing for using the Soviet Union's decline as an opportunity to consolidate the U.S. as an unrivaled superpower.

Foundations of the Global Dominance Group

Leo Strauss, Albert Wohlstetter, and others at the University of Chicago's Committee on Social Thought receive wide credit for promoting the neoconservative agenda through their students Paul Wolfowitz, Allan Bloom, and Bloom's student Richard Perle.

The Canadian cultural review magazine *Adbusters*, defines neoconservatism as "The belief that Democracy, however flawed, was best defended by an ignorant public pumped on nationalism and religion. Only a militantly nationalist state could deter human aggression. . . . Such nationalism requires an external threat and if one cannot be found it must be manufactured."[13]

The neoconservative philosophy emerged as a reaction to the 1960s era of social revolutions. Numerous officials and associates in the Reagan and George H.W. Bush presidencies were strongly influenced by the neoconservative philosophy, including John Ashcroft, Charles Fairbanks, Richard Cheney, Kenneth Adelman, Elliot Abrams, William Kristol, and Douglas Feith.[14]

Within the Ford administration there was a split between Cold War traditionalists seeking to minimize confrontations through diplomacy and détente and neoconservatives advocating stronger confrontations with the Soviet's "Evil Empire." The latter group became more entrenched when George H.W. Bush became CIA Director. Bush allowed the formation of "Team B," headed by Richard Pipes along with Paul Wolfowitz, Lewis Libby, Paul Nitze, and others, who formed the Committee on the Present Danger to raise awareness of the Soviet threat and the continuing need for a strong aggressive defense policy. Their efforts led to strong anti-Soviet positioning during the Reagan administration.[15]

The journalist John Pilger recalls his interview of neoconservative Richard Perle during the Reagan administration:

> I interviewed Perle when he was advising Reagan; and when he spoke about 'total war,' I mistakenly dismissed him as mad. He recently used the term again in describing America's "war on terror." "No stages," he said. "This is total war. We are fighting a variety of enemies. There are lots of them out there. All this talk about first we are going to do Afghanistan, then we will do Iraq . . . this is entirely the wrong way to go about it. If we just let our vision of the world go forth, and we embrace it entirely and we don't try to piece together clever diplomacy, but just wage a total war . . . our children will sing great songs about us years from now."[16]

The 1988 election of George H.W. Bush to the presidency, Cheney's appointment as secretary of defense, the expanded presence of neoconservatives within the government, and the fall of the Berlin Wall in 1989 opened the door to the formal initiation of a global-dominance policy.

In 1992 Cheney supported Lewis Libby and Paul Wolfowitz in producing the "Defense Planning Guidance" report, which advocated U.S. military dominance around the globe in a "new order." The report called for the U.S. to prevent any new rivals from rising up to challenge us. Using such words as "unilateral action" and military "forward presence," the report advocated that the U.S. dominate friends and foes alike. It concluded that the U.S. could attain this position by making itself "absolutely powerful."[17]

The Defense Policy Guidance report, leaked to the press, came under heavy criticism from many members of the HCPE. The *New York Times* reported on March 11, 1992 that "Senior White House and State Department officials have harshly criticized a draft Pentagon policy statement that asserts that America's mission in the post-cold-war era will be to prevent any collection of friendly or unfriendly nations from competing with the United States for superpower status."[18]

One administration official, familiar with senior staff reactions at the White House and State Department, characterized the document as a "dumb report" that "in no way or shape represents U.S. policy." Senator Robert C. Byrd, Democrat of West Virginia, called the draft Pentagon document "myopic, shallow and disappointing."[19] Many HCPE were not yet ready for a unilateral global dominance agenda. With Bill Clinton's election in 1992 most neoconservative HCPE lost direct power during the following eight years.

Both political parties cooperate in encouraging Congress to protect U.S. business interests abroad and corporate profits at home. To maintain defense contractors' profits, Clinton's Defense Science Board called for a globalized defense industry obtained through mergers of defense contractors with transnational companies that would become partners in U.S. military readiness.[20]

The Clinton administration generally stayed away from promoting global dominance as an ideological justification for continuing high defense budgets. Instead, to offset profit declines for defense contractors after the fall of the Berlin Wall, the Clinton administration aggressively promoted international arms sales, raising the U.S. share of world arms exports from 16 percent in 1988 to 63 percent in 1997.[21]

Outside the Clinton administration, neoconservative HCPE continued to promote a global-dominance agenda. On June 4, 1994, some two thousand regional and national elites attended a neoconservative "Lakeside Chat" at the San Francisco Bohemian Club's summer encampment.

A University of California at Berkeley political science professor presented the talk, entitled "Violent Weakness." The speaker argued that increasing violence in society was weakening our social institutions. Contributing to this violence and "decay" of our institutions, he said, is bisexualism, entertainment politics, multiculturalism, Afrocentrism, and a loss of family boundaries. The professor claimed that to avert further "deterioration," we need to recognize that "elites, based on merit and skill, are important to society and any elite that fails to define itself will fail to survive. . . . We need boundaries and values set and clear! We need an American-centered foreign policy . . . and a President who understands foreign policy." He went on to conclude that we cannot allow the "unqualified" masses to carry out policy, but that elites must set values that can be translated into "standards of authority." The speech received an enthusiastic standing ovation.[22]

During the Clinton administration, neoconservatives within the HCPE were still active in advocating military global dominance. Many of the neo-conservatives and their global-dominance allies found various positions in conservative think tanks and with Department of Defense contractors. They continued close affiliations with each other through the Heritage Foundation, American Enterprises Institute, Hoover Institute, Jewish Institute for National Security Affairs, Center for Security Policy, and several other conservative policy groups.

HCPE advocates for a U.S.-led "new world order," along with Reagan-Bush hard-liners and other military expansionists, founded Project for a New American Century (PNAC) in June of 1997. Their Statement of Principles set forth their aims as follows:

- We need to increase defense spending significantly if we are to carry out our global responsibilities today and modernize our armed forces for the future.
- We need to strengthen our ties to democratic allies and to challenge regimes hostile to our interests and values.
- We need to promote the cause of political and economic freedom abroad.
- We need to accept responsibility for America's unique role in preserving and extending an international order friendly to our security, our prosperity, and our principles.
- Such a Reagan-ite policy of military strength and moral clarity may not be fashionable today. But it is necessary if the United States is to build on the successes of this past century and to ensure our security and our greatness in the next.[23]

The signatories of this statement include: Elliott Abrams, Gary Bauer, William J. Bennett, Jeb Bush, Richard Cheney, Eliot A. Cohen, Midge Decter, Paula Dobriansky, Steve Forbes, Aaron Friedberg, Francis Fukuyama, Frank Gaffney, Fred C. Ikle, Donald Kagan, Zalmay Khalilzad, I. Lewis Libby, Norman Podhoretz, Dan Quayle, Peter W. Rodman, Stephen P. Rosen, Henry S. Rowen, Donald Rumsfeld, Vin Weber, George Weigel, and Paul Wolfowitz. Of the twenty-five founders of PNAC, George W. Bush appointed twelve to high-level positions in his administration.[24]

Since its founding PNAC has attracted numerous others who have signed policy letters or have participated in the group. Within PNAC eight individuals associate with the number one defense contractor, Lockheed Martin, and seven associate with the number three defense contractor, Northrop Grumman.[25] PNAC is one of several institutions that connect global dominance HCPE and large U.S. military contractors.[26]

In September 2000 PNAC produced a seventy-six-page report entitled *Rebuilding America's Defenses: Strategy, Forces and Resources for a New Century*.[27] The report was similar to the *Defense Policy Guidance* document written by Lewis Libby and Paul Wolfowitz in 1992. This similarity is not surprising in that Libby and Wolfowitz were participants in the production of the 2000 PNAC report. Steven Cambone, Doc Zakheim, Mark Lagan, and David Epstein were also heavily involved. Each of these individuals would go on to hold high-level positions in the George W. Bush administration.[28]

Rebuilding America's Defenses called for homeland protection, the ability to wage simultaneous theater wars, perform global constabulary roles, and control space and cyberspace. It claimed that the 1990s was a decade of defense neglect and that the U.S. must increase military spending to preserve American geopolitical leadership as the world's sole superpower. The report claimed that in order to maintain a Pax Americana, potential rivals—such as China, Iran, Iraq, and North Korea—needed to be held in check. The report also noted that "the process of transformation . . . is likely to be a long one, absent some catastrophic and catalyzing event such as a new Pearl Harbor."[29] The events of September 11, 2001, were exactly the kind of catastrophe that the authors of *Rebuilding America' Defenses* needed to accelerate a global-dominance agenda.

Before 9/11 members of Congress and liberal HCPE, who continued to hold a détente foreign-policy frame, traditionally advocated by the Council of Foreign Relations and the State Department, challenged strategic global-dominance policies.

9/11 so shocked the liberal/moderate HCPE that they immediately gave full support to the PATRIOT Act, Homeland Security, and legislation to support military action in Afghanistan and, later, Iraq. The resulting permanent war on terror has led to massive government spending, huge deficits (caused also in part by the Bush tax cuts), and the rapid acceleration of the neoconservative HCPE plans for military control of the world.[30]

Understanding Global-Dominance Advocates Within the HCPE

A group of Department of Defense (DoD) and Homeland Security contractors benefited significantly from expanded military spending after 9/11. We include in this study the top seven military contractors who derive at least one-third of their income from DoD contracts. We also added the Carlyle Group and Bechtel Group, Inc., because of their high levels of political influence and revolving door personnel within the Reagan and both Bush administrations.[31] These corporations benefited significantly from post-9/11 policies. We seek to understand the sociological phenomena of how, as collective actors, the GDG within the HCPE had the motive, means, and opportunity to gain from 9/11 and the war on terrorism, and how their most public figures—Bush, Cheney, Rumsfeld, and Rice—use the U.S. government to expand the GDG agenda.

To establish a GDG parameters list, we included the boards of directors of the nine DoD contractors identified above as those corporations earning over one-third of their revenue from the government or having high levels of political involvement. Additionally we have included members of sixteen leading conservative global-dominance-advocating foundations and policy councils.

Connections and associations listed in our GDG are not always simultaneous but rather reflect links extending for close to two decades inside an increasingly important group within the HCPE. The list includes 237 names of people who hold or have held high-level government positions in the George W. Bush administration, sit on the boards of directors of major DoD contracting corporations, and/or are close associates of the above, serving as GDG advocates on policy councils or advocacy foundations.

GDG Advocacy Organizations

Key GDG advocacy groups for the past decade include: Project for a New American Century (PNAC), Hoover Institute (HI), American Enterprise Institute (AEI), Hudson Institute (HI), National Security Council (NSC), Heritage Foundation (HF), Defense Policy Board (DPB), Committee on Present Danger (CPD), Jewish Institute of National Security Affairs (JINSA), Manhattan Institute (MI), Committee for the Liberation of Iraq (CLI), Center for Security Policy: Institute for Strategic Studies (CSP), Center for Strategic and International Studies (CSIS), National Institute for Public Policy (NIPP), and the American Israel Public Affairs Committee (AIPAC).

Core elements of each of these groups, in cooperation with major defense contractors, have encouraged and supported U.S. military expansion, a powerful U.S. presence in the world, and containment of rivals vis-à-vis policies of détente and statesmanship.

Some key examples of global dominance advocacy follow.

Condoleezza Rice, Hoover Senior Fellow, stated in 2000, "As the world's leading superpower, the United States has special responsibilities. I like to think about this as a great train that's going down the track, and there's markets and competition for private capital," Rice said. "Clearly the United States is kind of in the conductor's seat. With this position of leadership comes a responsibility to keep the peace," Rice said, and then suggested that the Clinton administration's military policies were not the ideal. "Clearly there has to be a rebalancing of America's military missions and America's military resources," she said, focusing on keeping weapons of mass destruction out of the hands of such countries as Iraq and North Korea. (AP, November 17, 2000.)

Tom Donnelly of the American Enterprise and PNAC quoted in the *Washington Post*. "The Pentagon's restructuring in Asia and the president's trip imply that the administration can be quite sober about what China's rise really means. Make no mistake, the competition already underway with Beijing is critical: America has a vital interest in sustaining its place as the guarantor of Asia's security. Its leadership has led to the region's peace and prosperity. And still there is more at stake. China is an increasingly important player in the Middle East and indeed globally. Ultimately, if the Bush Doctrine is not successfully applied to East Asia, and China can export its bad behavior to the Middle East, the strategy of promoting democracy will fail there, too." (*Washington Post*, November 27, 2005, p. B5.)

Richard Perle with American Enterprise Institute, PNAC and Committee to Liberate Iraq, and former Assistant Secretary of Defense, on NPR. "I think when others have thought this through, it will be recognized that the ability of the United States to defend itself is a stabilizing feature for our security, and depending on what situations we may be concerned, it can be stabilizing for others. For example, suppose we had, as I think we're technologically capable of producing, a ballistic missile defense based on ships. And suppose there was a sharp increase in tension on the Asian subcontinent, the India-Pakistan dispute. Imagine if an American president could say, 'I am dispatching an Aegis cruiser with a ballistic missile defense on it, and we will intercept the first missile fired by either side in this conflict.' Would that be a bad thing for the Indians or the Pakistanis? It seems to me it could very possibly bring stability to a very dangerous situation." (National Public Radio, *All Things Considered*, June 20, 2000.)

Peter Brooks on National Public Radio, October 18, 2005: "Chinese leaders believe that if its economic growth continues apace, China will overcome 150 years of humiliation at the hands of foreign powers, returning to its past glory as the 'Middle kingdom,' . . . this economic growth will allow it to be able to challenge the world's most powerful nations, including the United States."

In each of the above cases we see an underlying assumption that the U.S. is the dominant global power and that rivals (China, Iraq, and Iran) need to be contained through expanded military spending and tough U.S. policies. Collectively these fifteen global-dominance-advocacy groups, in cooperation with the top military contractors, have a controlling lock on U.S. military and foreign policy within the current administration and represent a rising power with the traditional higher circles policies elites in the U.S.

Who Funds GDG Groups?

The 1960s went poorly for the ultraright elites. Goldwater lost in 1964, and the Vietnam War engendered a widespread movement of the disaffected, which posed a threat to elites. Conservatives needed to get their message out in a more widespread and effective manner—they needed to reach not only the policy makers but the voters as well. By the early 1970s the primary source of funding for a new conservative movement came from a handful of family foundations that focused on building a phalanx of conservative think tanks. The wealth generated by the founders of such companies as Vick-Richardson, White Star Oil, Koch Oil, the Carnegie-Mellon fortune, Brady Corporation, Bradley-Allen Manufacturing, and Noble Oil had been passed on to their heirs primarily through these nonprofit organizations, sidestepping the inheritance tax along the way. A detailed search of public databases, such as Rightweb International Relations Center, Media Transparency, Source Watch, as well as the individual Web sites of the foundations involved, reveals a telling picture. Over the last thirty years a total of $177,623,700 has gone to fund the policy directives of the global dominance group. Of this amount, about 96 percent has flowed from the coffers of ten families controlling fourteen foundations. See Appendix C for a listing of the top ten funders of the neoconservative GDG movement.

Who Profits from GDG Policies?

Lockheed Martin has benefited significantly from the post-9/11 military expansion promoted by the GDG. The Pentagon's budget for buying new weapons rose from $61 billion in 2001 to over $80 billion in 2004. Lockheed Martin's sales rose by over 30 percent at the same time, with tens of billions of dollars on the books for future purchases. From 2000 to 2004, Lockheed Martin's stock value rose 300%.

The *New York Times* reporter Tim Weiner wrote in 2004, "No contractor is in a better position than Lockheed Martin to do business in Washington. Nearly 80% of its revenue comes from the U.S. Government. Most of the rest comes from foreign military sales, many financed with tax dollars."[32]

As of August 2005 Lockheed Martin stockholders had made 18 percent on their stock in the prior twelve months.[33] Northrup-Grumann has seen similar growth in the last three years, with DoD contracts rising from $3.2 billion in 2001 to $11.1 billion in 2004.[34]

Halliburton, with Vice President Richard Cheney as former CEO, has seen phenomenal growth since 2001. Halliburton had defense contracts totaling $427 million in 2001; by 2003 the company had $4.3 billion in defense contracts, of which approximately one-third were sole-source agreements.[35] Cheney, not incidentally, continues to receive a deferred salary from Halliburton. According to financial disclosure forms, the company paid Cheney $205,298 in 2001; $162,392 in 2002; $178,437 in 2003; and $194,852 in 2004; his 433,333 Halliburton stock options rose in value from $241,498 in 2004 to $8 million in 2005.[36]

The Carlyle Group, established in 1987, is a private global-investment firm that manages some $30 billion in assets. Numerous high-level members of the GDG have been involved in The Carlyle Group, including Frank

Carlucci, George H. W. Bush, James Baker III, William Kennard, and Richard Darman. The Carlyle Group purchased United Defense in 1997. The Group sold its shares in the company after 9/11, making a profit of $1 billion.[37] Carlyle continues to invest in defense contractors and is moving into the homeland-security industry.[38]

Profits for defense contractors have been so good that the *New York Times* in May 2005 described how some $20 to $30 billion is sitting in the coffers of the top military contractors as a result of record Pentagon budgets and robust government spending on homeland security. The *New York Times* reported that Boeing had $6.5 billion in cash on hand.[39]

Pro-Israel Lobbies and the Global Dominance Group

Two pro-Israel lobby organizations in the U.S. work closely with the GDG to influence U.S. policy in the Middle East. The Jewish Institute of National Security Affairs (JINSA) and, more significantly, the American Israel Public Affairs Committee (AIPAC), seek to align U.S. GDG policies with Israeli agendas. These pro-Israel lobby groups have established a strong presence at the American Enterprise Institute, Center for Security Policy, the Foreign Policy Research Institute, the Heritage Foundation, the Hudson Institute, and the Institute for Foreign Policy Analysis. Over $3 billion in annual U.S. foreign aid goes to Israel, with most of the money returned to the U.S. for weapons purchases from U.S. military contractors.

Since 1982, the U.S. has vetoed thirty-two Security Council resolutions critical of Israel, more than the *total* number of vetoes cast by *all* the other Security Council members. The U.S. has also blocked Arab states' efforts to put Israel's nuclear arsenal on the International Atomic Energy Agency's (IAEA) agenda.

An even more one-sided pro-Israel policy has emerged under the Bush-Cheney administration than in past administrations. Fervent advocates of Israeli issues include Elliot Abrams, John Bolton, Douglas Feith, I. Lewis Libby, Richard Perle, Paul Wolfowitz, and David Wurmser.

The following are key segments of Vice President Dick Cheney's keynote address at the AIPAC Policy Conference on March 7, 2006.

Some of us are Republicans; some of us are Democrats, yet all of

us share a fundamental belief—that the freedom and security of
Israel are vital interests to the United States of America. . . . There
is no doubt that America's commitment to Israel's security is solid,
enduring and unshakeable. . . . Israel, and the United States, and
all civilized nations will win the war on terror. To prevail in this
fight, we must understand the nature of the enemy. As Israelis
have seen so many times, and as America experienced on September 11th, 2001, the terrorist enemy is brutal and heartless.
This enemy wears no uniform, has no regard for the rules of warfare, and is unconstrained by any standard of decency or morality.
We are dealing with enemies who plot and plan in secret, then
attempt to slip into a country, blend in among the innocent, and
kill without mercy. . . . This enemy also has a set of clear objectives.
The terrorists want to end all American and Western influence
in the Middle East. Their goal in that region is to seize control of
a country, so they have a base from which to launch attacks and
wage war against governments that do not meet their demands
. . . ultimately to establish a totalitarian empire that encompasses
a region from Spain, across North Africa, through the Middle East
and South Asia, all the way around to Indonesia.

They have made clear, as well, their ultimate ambitions: to arm
themselves with chemical, biological and even nuclear weapons
to destroy Israel, to intimidate all Western countries and to cause
mass death here in the United States . . . we are determined to
deny the terrorists the control of any nation, which they would use
as a home base and a staging ground for terrorist attacks against
others. . . . And that is why we are fighting the Saddam remnants
and terrorists in Iraq. . . . On 9/11, the United States learned that
problems boiling in a far-off region of the world could lead directly
to a sudden and murderous attack right here on our own soil. . . .
America supports, as well, the democratic aspirations of the people of Iran. Iranians have endured a generation of repression at
the hands of a fanatical regime. That regime is one of the world's
primary state sponsors of terror. . . . We will not allow Iran to have
a nuclear weapon.[40]

Cheney's speech is the mantra for the Global Dominance agenda. Evil terrorists everywhere are plotting for the ruin of "civilized" nations. A global war on terrorism requires the U.S. and Israel to stand together as the defenders of freedom and democracy.

Public-Private Partnerships: Media and the GDG

While it is important not to underestimate the profit motive within the ranks of the top military defense contractors, the promotion of a global-dominance agenda includes both neoconservative ideological beliefs and the formation of extremely powerful permanent public-private partnerships at government's highest levels to create interlocking networks of global control.

A global-dominance agenda includes penetration into U.S. corporate media's boardrooms. A Sonoma State University research team recently finished conducting a network analysis of the ten big U.S. media organizations' boards of directors. The team found that only 118 people comprise the entire membership. These 118 individuals, in turn, sit on the corporate boards of 288 national and international corporations. Four of the top ten media corporations in the U.S. have GDG-DoD contractors on their boards of directors, including:

William Kennard: New York Times, Carlyle Group
Douglas Warner III: GE (NBC), Bechtel
John Bryson: Disney (ABC), Boeing
Alwyn Lewis: Disney (ABC), Halliburton
Douglas McCorkindale: Gannett, Lockheed Martin.[41]

Given an interlocked media network, big media in the U.S. effectively represent corporate America's interests. The media elites, a key component of the HCPE in the U.S., are the watchdogs of acceptable ideological messages, the controllers of news and information content, and the decision makers regarding media resources. Corporate media elites are subject to the same pressures as the higher-circle policy makers in the U.S., and are therefore equally susceptible to a reactionary response to our most recent Pearl Harbor.

U.S. corporate media has shown an expanding dependency on GDG spokespersons as sources for news. Below we compare a few of the major conservative think tanks' exposure in mainstream media in 2000 as compared to 2005:[42]

AEI: American Enterprise Institute
New York Times: 2000: 55; 2005: 99; 80 percent increase
Washington Post: 2000: 87; 2005: 157; 80.4 percent increase
Transcripts*: 2000: 137; 2005: 148; 8 percent increase

CSIS: Center for Strategic and International Studies
New York Times: 2000: 25; 2005: 61; 144 percent increase
Washington Post: 2000: 54; 2005: 81; 50 percent increase
Transcripts: 2000: 46; 2005: 98; 113 percent increase

* Transcripts represented: ABC News Transcripts, CBS News Transcripts, CNN, National Public Radio, and NBC News.

GDG and 9/11

A significant portion of the GDG had every opportunity to know in advance that the 9/11 attacks were imminent. Afghanistan, Argentina, Britain, the Cayman Islands, Egypt, France, Germany, Israel, Italy, Jordan, Morocco, Russia, and the U.S. intelligence community all warned the U.S. of imminent terrorist attacks. Some of the 9/11 prewarnings include:

1996–2001
Federal authorities knew that suspected terrorists with ties to bin Laden received flight training at schools in the U.S. and abroad. An Oklahoma City FBI agent sent a memo warning that "large numbers of Middle Eastern males" were getting flight training and could have been planning terrorist attacks. (CBS, May 30, 2002.) One convicted terrorist confessed that his planned role in a terror attack was to crash a plane into CIA headquarters. (*Washington Post*, September 23, 2001.)

June 2001
German intelligence warned the CIA, Britain's intelligence agency, and Israel's Mossad that Middle Eastern terrorists were planning to hijack

commercial aircraft and use them as weapons to attack "American and Israeli symbols which stand out." (*Frankfurter Allgemeine Zeitung*, September 11, 2001; *Washington Post*, September 14, 2001; Fox News, May 17, 2002.)

June 28, 2001

George Tenet wrote an intelligence summary to Condoleezza Rice stating, "It is highly likely that a significant al-Qaeda attack is in the near future, within several weeks." (*Washington Post*, February 17, 2002.)

June–July 2001

President Bush, Vice President Cheney, and national security aides were given briefs with headlines such as "Bin Laden Threats Are Real" and "Bin Laden Planning High Profile Attacks." The exact contents of these briefings remain classified, but according to the 9/11 Commission, they consistently predicted upcoming attacks that would occur "on a catastrophic level, indicating that they would cause the world to be in turmoil, consisting of possible multiple—but not necessarily simultaneous—attacks." (*9/11 Commission Report*, April 13, 2004.)

July 26, 2001

Attorney General Ashcroft stopped flying commercial airlines because of a threat assessment. (CBS, July 26, 2001.) The report of this warning was omitted from the *9/11 Commission Report*. (Griffin, May 22, 2005.)

August 6, 2001

President Bush received a classified intelligence briefing at his Crawford, Texas, ranch, warning that bin Laden might be planning to hijack commercial airliners; this briefing was entitled "Bin Laden Determined to Strike in the United States." The entire memo focused on the possibility of terrorist attacks inside the U.S. and specifically mentioned the World Trade Center. (*Newsweek*, May 27, 2002; *New York Times*, May 15, 2002; *Washington Post*, April 11, 2004; White House, April 11, 2004; Intelligence Briefing, August 6, 2001.)

August 2001

Russian President Vladimir Putin warned the U.S. that suicide pilots were training for attacks on U.S. targets. (*Fox News*, May 17, 2002.) The head of Russian intelligence also later stated, "We had clearly warned them" on several occasions, but they "did not pay the necessary attention." (*Agence France-Presse*, September 16, 2001.)

September 10, 2001

A group of top Pentagon officials received an urgent warning that prompted them to cancel their flight plans for the following morning. (*Newsweek*, September 17, 2001.) The *9/11 Commission Report* omitted this report. (Griffin, May 22, 2005.)[43]

Foreknowledge of 9/11 enabled the GDG to act quickly to accelerate its global-dominance agenda. People in the GDG wanted an invasion of Afghanistan long before 9/11. The House of Representatives' International Relations Committee's Subcommittee on Asia and the Pacific met in February 1998 to discuss removing Afghanistan's government from power. The U.S. government told India in June 2001 that a planned invasion of Afghanistan was set for October, and *Jane's Defence Weekly* reported in March 2001 that the U.S. planned to invade Afghanistan later that year. The BBC reported that the U.S. told the Pakistani foreign secretary prior to 9/11 of a planned invasion of Afghanistan in October.[44]

Bush and Cheney delayed the formation of a 9/11 Commission for 411 days, and the final report did not come out until July 2004. Remaining unanswered in the 9/11 Commission's report are numerous key questions of governmental malfeasance and incompetence that threaten the Bush-Cheney administration's very legitimacy. The university theologian David Ray Griffin, in his book *The 9/11 Commission Report: Omissions and Distortions*, documents extensive cover-ups and contradictions in the government's official version of what happen on 9/11.[45] A national committee of over one hundred university professors and professional researchers has formed Scholars for 9/11 Truth to evaluate the discrepancies in the 9/11 Commission report.[46]

Recent research by the Brigham Young University physicist Steven E. Jones establishes that the government's explanation for the collapse of World Trade Center buildings 1, 2, and 7 violates the laws of physics.[47]

Without a doubt 9/11 hastened the GDG's unfolding agenda. The questions of preknowledge or involvement of the Bush-Cheney administration awaits investigation and/or impeachment proceedings, aided by Congress's subpoena powers.

The National Call for Impeachment of Bush and Cheney

There are many undeniable correlations between the current influence of neoconservative policy and the American fascism that Vice President Henry Wallace predicted in 1944 and Eisenhower's concern regarding the concentration of power in a military-industrial complex.

Vice President Wallace wrote in the *New York Times* on April 9, 1944,

> The really dangerous American fascist . . . is the man who wants to do in the United States in an American way what Hitler did in Germany in a Prussian way. The American fascist would prefer not to use violence. His method is to poison the channels of public information. With a fascist the problem is never how best to present the truth to the public but how best to use the news to deceive the public into giving the fascist and his group more money or more power.

Wallace then added,

> They claim to be super-patriots, but they would destroy every liberty guaranteed by the Constitution. They demand free enterprise, but are the spokesmen for monopoly and vested interest. Their final objective toward which all their deceit is directed is to capture political power so that, using the power of the state and the power of the market simultaneously, they may keep the common man in eternal subjection.[48]

At the beginning of 2006 the Global Dominance Group has well established its agenda within higher-circle policy councils and inside the U.S. government. It works hand in hand with defense contractors in promoting deployment of U.S. forces in over seven hundred bases worldwide.

Penn State University's Ken Cunningham writes, "current War-on-Terror levels [of expenditures] surpass the Cold War averages by 18%. . . . 9/11 and the War on Terror have enabled the assertion of an aggressive, preemptive, militarist bloc within the government and the National Security State. . . . The gravity of the current militarism is the nebulous, potentially limitless [permanent war]."[49]

Without the broad social movements and the citizen unrest that threatens the stability of HCPE's socioeconomic agendas and corporate profits, there will be little, if any, serious challenge to the GDG. Should the 2006 election bring Democratic control to the House or Senate, we are likely to see only a slight slowing of the GDG agenda but certainly not a reversal without a strong impeachment movement.

Many people in the U.S. are having serious doubts about the moral and practical acceptability of financing world domination and about the dangers to personal freedoms permanent war implies. U.S. polls show that nearly a majority of Americans already favor impeachment *despite* the near total absence of any calls for impeachment by political leaders and mass media. In October 2005 Public Affairs Research found that 50 percent of Americans believed that President Bush should be impeached if he lied about the war in Iraq. A Zogby International poll from early November 2005 found that 53 percent of Americans agree that, "If President Bush did not tell the truth about his reasons for going to war with Iraq, Congress should consider holding him accountable through impeachment."

Bush and Cheney are the most public figureheads for the Global Dominance Group in the U.S. Impeaching them and firing Rumsfeld and their other cohorts in government is a solid first step to resisting the GDG agenda of total military control of the world.

Challenging the neoconservatives and GDG agenda is only the beginning of reversing the long-term conservative reactions to the gains of the 1960s. Readdressing poverty, the United Nations Declaration of Human Rights, and our own weapons of mass destruction is a long-term agenda for progressive scholars and citizens.

Appendix A

Figures in Appendix A courtesy of Mergent Online Database.

Company	Defense Contracts 2004	Total Revenue 2004	% from DoD
Lockheed Martin Corporation	$20,690,912,117	$35,526,000,000	58%
General Dynamics Corporation	$9,563,280,236	$19,178,000,000	50%
Raytheon Company	$8,472,818,938	$20,245,000,000	42%
Northrop Grumman Corporation	$11,894,090,277	$29,853,000,000	40%
Halliburton Company	$7,996,793,706	$20,464,000,000	39%
Science Applications International	$2,450,781,108	$7,187,000,000	34%
The Boeing Company	$17,066,412,718	$52,457,000,000	33%
The Carlyle Group	$1,442,680,446	N/A	N/A
Bell Boeing Joint Program	$1,539,815,440	(Boeing)	NA

Appendix B

In selecting the sixteen important neoconservative GDG advocacy organizations, we relied for the most part on the International Relations Center Web site, http://rightweb.irc-online.org/, The Center for Public Integrity at: www.publicintegrity.org, and other sources cited in this paper.

Global Dominance Group Advocacy Organizations

PNAC	Project for a New American Century
HO	Hoover Institute
AEI	American Enterprise Institute
HI	Hudson Institute
NSC	National Security Council
HF	Heritage Foundation
DPB	Defense Policy Board
CPD	Committee on Present Danger
JINSA	Jewish Institute of National Security Affairs
MI	Manhattan Institute
CLI	Committee for the Liberation of Iraq
CSP	Center for Security Policy: Institute for Strategic Studies
CSIS	Center for Strategic and Int'l Studies
NIPP	National Institute for Public Policy
AIPAC	American Israel Public Affairs Committee
Team B	Presidents Foreign Advisory Board

Important Agencies and Other Organizations

CIA	Central Intelligence Agency
DoD	Department of Defense
DoS	Department of State
CFR	Council on Foreign Relations
DoJ	Department of Justice
DoC	Department of Commerce
WHOMB	White House Office of Management and Budget
DoE	Department of Energy
DPB	Defense Policy Board
DoT	Department of Transportation
NSA	National Security Agency

Appendix C

Principal Funders of Global Dominance Group Advocacy Organizations

1. SCAIFE: Richard Mellon-Scaife of Pittsburgh inherited the Mellon-Scaife fortune in 1965. He became the preeminent funder of the neoconservative movement. Through three foundations, he has contributed over $57 million since 1974 directly to GDG organizations.

Sarah Scaife Foundation	Lifetime Grants to GDG Advocates
PNAC	$50,000.00
CSIS	$7,773,000.00
CPD	$210,000.00
MI	$2,905,000.00
CSP	$2,801,000.00
NIPP	$1,050,000.00
Hudson	$2,183,000.00
AEI	$4,836,000.00
Hoover	$7,820,500.00
Heritage	$18,035,000.00

Scaife Family Foundation	Lifetime Grants to GDG Advocates
CSIS	$200,000.00
MI	$25,000.00
Hudson	$221,000.00
AEI	$590,000.00
Heritage	$702,640.00

The Carthage Foundation (Scaife)	Lifetime Grants to GDG Advocates
Pacific/CSIS	$195,000.00
CSIS	$50,000.00
CPD	$200,000.00
MI	$1,138,000.00
CSP	$875,000.00
NIPP	$125,000.00
Hudson	$715,000.00
AEI	$600,000.00
Hoover	$1,223,400.00
Heritage	$2,759,000.00

2. BRADLEY: The sale of Bradley-Allen to Rockwell for $1.65 billion funded this foundation. Solid neoconservative activists, such as Michael Grebe, President and CEO, write the checks, not Bradley family members.

The Lynde and Harry Bradley Foundation, Inc.	Life Time Grants to GDG Groups
PNAC	$500,000.00
CSIS	$1,548,402.00
MI	$2,796,560.00
CSP	$481,624.00
NIPP	$282,683.00
Hudson	$5,574,946.00
AEI	$15,892,797.00
Hoover	$1,928,500.00
Heritage	$13,283,702.00

3. OLIN: in a 1977 interview John Olin stated that he created his foundation in an effort "to see free enterprise re-established in this country. Business and the public must be awakened to the creeping stranglehold that socialism has gained here since World War II." Olin Corporation made its fortune from Winchester bullets, copper mining, chlorine, and caustic soda. Through the years over $370 million poured from this foundation into a wide variety of conservative organizations. It closed its doors in 2005.

John M. Olin Foundation, Inc.	Lifetime grants to GDG advocate Groups
Pacific/CSIS	$25,000.00
CSIS	$2,112,318.00
MI	$4,899,500.00
CSP	$261,000.00
NIPP	$43,500.00
Hudson	$3,034,840.00
AEI	$7,022,124.00
Hoover	$5,015,660.00
Heritage	$8,320,835.00
PNAC	$50,000.004.00

4. SMITH RICHARDSON: H.S. Richardson, founder of the Vicks-Richardson company (Vicks Vapo-Rub), had numerous correspondences with conservative politicians and influence in many anti-communist and anti-immigration policies.[50]

Smith Richardson Foundation	Lifetime Grants to GDG Groups
JINSA	$350,000.00
Pacific/CSIS	$932,545.00
CSIS	$4,421,868.00
MI	$1,165,981.00

NIPP	$1,659,317.00
Hudson	$1,400,212.00
AEI	$4,566,713.00
Hoover	$1,456,612.00
Heritage	$195,000.00

5. NOBLE: Initially founded by the developer of the world's largest offshore oil exploration company to help agriculture in Oklahoma and to enable small farmers to succeed.

Samuel Roberts Noble Foundation	Lifetime Grants to GDG Groups
CSP	$185,000.00
Hudson	$25,000.00
Hoover	$35,000.00
Heritage	$7,000,000.00

6. BRADY: William H. Brady built his father's business into an international concern. His commitment to the right was evident from the beginning, William F. Buckley was a close personal friend, and Brady sat on the board of the local Bradley foundation. He established the W.H. Brady Foundation in 1956 in Milwaukee. It focused its grants on national policy research and education and aimed to strengthen democratic capitalism and self-government at home and abroad. During the 1990s it began to work on influencing the institutional foundations of a free society: (1) morality and public life, (2) family and community, and (3) competitive educational structures.[51] The foundation currently supports the scholarly work of Lynne Cheney, senior fellow at American Enterprise Institute.

W.H. Brady Foundation	Lifetime Grants to GDG Advocates
MI	$820,000.00
CSP	$22,000.00
Hudson	$75,000.00
AEI	$5,032,500.00
Heritage	$14,000.00
JINSA	$1,000.00

7. COORS: According to *Axis of Ideology: Conservative Foundations and Public Policy*, the Coors family has multiple relations with right-wing organizations. Holland Coors, for example, is a board member of the Heritage Foundation and a trustee of the Intercollegiate Studies Institute, and Jeffrey Coors is the director of Free Congress Research and Education and a board member of the Independence Institute. [52]

Castle Rock Foundation (Coors)	Lifetime Grants to GDG Advocates
MI	$105,000.00
Hudson	$85,000.00
AEI	$345,000.00
Hoover	$25,000.00
Heritage	$2,348,760.00

8. DONNER: The Union Steel fortune first went to establish a cancer research center, after William H. Donner's son died of the disease in the 1930s. Since then the foundation has passed into the hands of his children and grand-children, splitting into two different foundations; one based in Philadelphia continues to fund medical research, the other, The William H. Donner Foundation in New York, has been extremely active in funding conservative policies. Robert Donner, Jr., now runs the foundation.

William H. Donner Foundation	Lifetime Grants to GDG Advocates
CSIS	$242,500.00
MI	$340,500.00
CSP	$190,000.00
Hudson	$762,500.00
AEI	$285,000.00

9. KOCH: Texas-based Koch Oil nets about $25 billion a year, making the brothers David and Charles two of the wealthiest men in the country. They funnel their wealth through three organizations: David H. Koch Foundation, the Charles G. Koch Charitable Foundation, and the Claude R. Lambe Charitable Foundation.

Claude R. Lambe (Koch) Charitable Foundation	Lifetime Grants to GDG Advocates
MI	$325,000.00
Hudson	$12,650.00
Heritage	$1,409,000.00

Charles D. Koch Charitable Foundation	Lifetime Grants to GDG Advocates
Hoover	$5,000.00
Heritage	$78,000.00

David H. Koch Charitable Foundation	Lifetime Grants to GDG Advocates
MI	$50,000.00
Hudson	$20,000.00

10. EARHART: Harry B. Earhart started the foundation in 1929 with the fortune he made with White Star Oil Company, a fortune facilitated by his close relationship with Rockefeller and Standard Oil. The foundation was family

run until 1949, when Earhart converted the board into an independent operation. David Kennedy served as the board's president until 2004, when Ingrid Gregg took over.

Earhart Foundation	Lifetime Grants to GDG Advocates
CSIS	$15,600.00
MI	$315,000.00
CSP	$3,000.00
NIPP	$44,945.00
Hudson	$71,783.00
AEI	$448,800.00
Hoover	$380,474.00

Appendix D

Individuals Within the Global Dominance Group and Their Affiliations

1. Abramowitz, Morton I.; PNAC, NSC, Asst. Sec. of State, Amb. to Turkey, Amb. to Thailand, CISS, Carlyle
2. Abrams, Elliott; PNAC, Heritage, DoS, HU, Special Asst. to President Bush, NSC
3. Adelman, Ken; PNAC, CPD, DoD, DPB, Fox News, CPD, Affairs, Commander I in Chief Strategic Air Command, Northrop Grumman, Arms Control Disarmament Agency
4. Aldrige, E.C. Jr.; CFR, PNAC, NSA, HU, HF, Sec. of the Air Force, Asst. Sec. of State, Douglas Aircraft, DoD, LTV Aerospace, WHOMB, Strategic Systems Group, Aerospace Corp.
5. Allen, Richard V.; PNAC, HF, HO, CFR, CPD, DPB, CNN, U.S. Congress, CIA Analyst, CSIS, NSC
6. Amitay, Morris J.; JINSA, AIPAC
7. Andrews, D.P.; SAIC
8. Andrews, Michael; L-3 Communications Holdings, Deputy Asst. Sec. of Research and Technology, Chief Scientist for the U.S. Army

9. Archibald, Nolan D.; Lockheed Martin
10. Baker, James III; Carlyle, Sec. of State (Bush), Sec. of Treas. (Reagan)
11. Barr, William P.; HF, HO, PNAC, CFR, NSA, U.S. Congress, Asst. to the President (Reagan), Carlyle
12. Barram, David J.; Computer Sciences Corporation, U.S. DoC
13. Barrett, Barbara; Raytheon
14. Bauer, Gary; PNAC, Under-Sec. of Ed.
15. Bechtel, Riley; Bechtel
16. Bechtel, Steve; Bechtel
17. Bell, Jeffrey; PNAC, MI
18. Bennett, Marcus C.; Lockheed Martin
19. Bennett, William J.; PNAC, NSA, HU, Sec. of Education
20. Bergner, Jeffrey; PNAC, HU, Boeing
21. Berns, Walter; AEI, CPD
22. Biggs, John H.; Boeing, CFR
23. Blechman, Barry; DoD, CPD
24. Bolton, John; JINSA, PNAC, AEI, DoS, DoJ, Amb. to UN, Agency Int'l Devel. Under-Sec. State Arms Control-Int'l Security
25. Boot, Max; PNAC, CFR
26. Bremer, L. Paul; HF, CFR, Administrator of Iraq
27. Brock, William; CPD, Senator, Sec. of Labor
28. Brooks, Peter; DoD, Heritage, CPD
29. Bryen, Stephen; JINSA, AEI, DoD, L-3 Network Security, Edison Int'l, Disney
30. Bryson, John E.; Boeing
31. Bush, Jeb; PNAC, Governor of Florida
32. Bush, Geroge H. W.; President, Carlyle, CIA Dir.
33. Bush, Wes; Northrop Grumman
34. Cambone, Stephen; PNAC, NSA, DoD, Los Alamos (specialized in theater nuclear weapons issues), Ofc. Sec. Defense: Dir. Strategic Def., CSIS, CSP
35. Chabraja, Nicholas D.; General Dynamics
36. Chain, John T. Jr.; Northrop Grumman, Sec. of the Air Force, Dir. of Politico-Military Affairs, DoS, Chief of Staff for Supreme Headquarters Allied Powers Europe, Commander in Chief Strategic Air Command
37. Chao, Elaine; HF, Sec. of Labor, Gulf Oil, U.S. DoT, CFR
38. Chavez, Linda; PNAC, MI, CFR
39. Cheney, Lynne; AEI, Lockheed Martin

40. Cheney, Richard; JINSA, PNAC, JINSA, AEI, HU, Halliburton, Sec. of Defense, VP of U.S.

41. Cohen Eliot A.; PNAC, AEI, DPB, DoD, CLI, CPD

42. Coleman, Lewis W.; Northrop Grumman

43. Colloredo-Manfeld, Ferdinand; Raytheon

44. Cook, Linda Z.; Boeing

45. Cooper, Dr. Robert S.; BAE Systems, Asst. Sec. of Defense

46. Cooper, Henry; CPD, DoD, Heritage, Depty Asst. Sec. Air Force, U.S. Arms Control Disarm. Strategic Def. Initiative, Applied Research Assoc, NIPP

47. Cox, Christopher; CSP, Senior Associate Counsel to the President, Chairman: SEC

48. Crandall, Robert L.; Halliburton, FAA Man. Advisor Bd.

49. Cropsey, Seth; PNAC, AEI, HF, HU, DoD, Under-Sec. Navy

50. Cross, Devon Gaffney; PNAC, DPB, HF, CPD, HO

51. Crouch, J.D.; CSP, Depty. National Security Advisor, DoD, Amb. to Romania

52. Crown, James S.; General Dynamics, Henry Crown and Co.

53. Crown, Lester; General Dynamics, Henry Crown and Co.

54. Dachs, Alan; Bechtel, CFR

55. Dahlburg, Ken; SAIC, DoC, Asst. to Reagan, WHOMB

56. Darman, Richard G.; Carlyle, Dir. of the U.S. Office of Management and Budget, President Bush's Cabinet, Asst. to the President of the U.S., Deputy Sec. of the U.S. Treasury, Asst. U.S. Sec. of Commerce

57. Dawson, Peter; Bechtel

58. Decter, Midge; HF, HO, PNAC, CPD

59. Demmish, W.H.; SAIC

60. DeMuth, Christopher; AEI, U.S. Office of Management and Budget, Asst. to Pres. (Nixon)

61. Derr, Kenneth T.; Halliburton

62. Deutch, John; Dir. CIA, Deputy Sec. of Defense, Raytheon

63. Dine, Thomas; CLI, U.S. Senate, AIPAC, U.S. Agency Int'l Development, Free Radio Europe/Radio Liberty, Prague, Czech Rep., CFR

64. Dobriansky, Paula; PNAC, HU, AEI, CPB, DoS, Army, NSC European/Soviet Affairs, USIA, ISS

65. Donnelly, Thomas; AEI, PNAC, Lockheed Martin

66. Downing, Wayne; Ret. Gen. U.S. Army, NSA, CLI, SAIC

67. Drummond, J.A.; SAIC

68. Duberstein, Kenneth M.; Boeing, WH Chief of Staff
69. Dudley, Bill; Bechtel
70. Eberstadt, Nicholas; AEI, CPD, PNAC, DoS (consultant)
71. Ebner, Stanley; Boeing, McDonnell Douglas, Northrop Grumman, CSP
72. Ellis, James O. Jr.; Lockheed Martin, Retired Navy Admiral and Commander, U.S. Strategic Command
73. Epstein David; PNAC, Office of Sec. Defense
74. Everhart, Thomas; Raytheon
75. Falcoff, Mark; AEI, CFR
76. Fautua, David; PNAC, Lt. Col. U.S. Army
77. Fazio, Vic; Northrop Grumman, Congressman (CA)
78. Feith, Douglas; JINSA, DoD, L-3 Communications, Northrop Grumman, NSC, CFR, CPS
79. Feulner, Edwin J. Jr.; HF, HO, Sec. HUD, Inst. European Def. & Strategy Studies, CSIS
80. Foley, D.H.; SAIC
81. Fradkin, Hillel; PNAC, AEI,
82. Frank, Stephen E.; Northrop Grumman
83. Fricks, William P.; General Dynamics
84. Friedberg, Aaron; PNAC, CFR, NSA, DoD, CIA consultant
85. Frost, Phillip (M.D.); Northrop Grumman
86. Fukuyama, Francis; PNAC, CFR, HU
87. Gates, Robert; CIA Dir., NSA, SAIC
88. Gaffney, Frank; CPD, PNAC, Washington Times, DoD
89. Gaut, C. Christopher; Halliburton
90. Gedmin, Jeffrey; AEI, PNAC, CPD
91. Gerecht, Reuel Marc; PNAC, AEI, CIA, CBS
92. Gillis, S. Malcom; Halliburton, Electronic Data Systems Corp.
93. Gingrich, Newt; AEI, CFR, HO, DPB, U.S House of Reps., CLI, CPD
94. Goodman, Charles H.; General Dynamics
95. Gorelick, Jamie S.; United Technologies Corporation, Deputy Attorney General, DoD, Asst. to the Sec. of Energy, National Com. Terrorist Threats Upon the U.S., DoJ, Nat'l Security Adv., CIA, CFR
96. Gouré, Daniel; DoD, SAIC, DoE, DoS (consultant), CSP
97. Haas, Lawrence J.; Communications WHOMB, CPD
98. Hadley, Stephen; NSA advisor to Bush, Lockheed Martin

99. Hamre, John J.; ITT Industries, SAIC, U. S. Dep. Sec. of Defense, Under-Sec. of Defense, Senate Armed Services Committee

100. Hash, Tom; Bechtel

101. Haynes, Bill; Bechtel

102. Hoeber, Amoretta; CSP, Defense Industry consultant, CPD, CFR, DoD

103. Horner, Charles; HU, CSP, DoS, Staff member of Sen. Daniel Patrick Moyihan

104. Howell, W.R.; Halliburton, Dir. Deutsche Bank

105. Hunt, Ray L.; Halliburton, Electronic Data Systems Corp, President's Foreign Intelligence Advisory Board

106. Inman, Bobby Ray; Ret. Adm. U.S. Navy, CIA Dep. Dir., CFR, NSA, SAIC

107. Ikle, Fred; AEI, PNAC, CPD, HU, DPB, Under-Sec. DoD, Def. Policy Board

108. Iorizzo, Robert P.; Northrop Grumman

109. Jackson, Bruce; PNAC, NSA, AEI, CFR, Office of Sec. of Def., U.S. Army Military Intelligence, Lockheed Martin, Martin Marietta, CLI, CPD

110. Jennings, Sir John; Bechtel

111. Johnson, Jay L.;General Dynamics, Retired Admiral, U.S. Navy

112. Jones, A.K.; SAIC, DoD

113. Joseph, Robert; Under-Sec. of State for Arms Control and Int'l Security Affairs, DoD, CSP, NIPP

114. Joulwan, George A.; General Dynamics, Retired General, U.S. Army

115. Kagan, Frederick; PNAC, West Point Military Academy

116. Kagan, Robert; PNAC, CFR, DoS (Deputy for Policy), *Washington Post*, CLI, editor, *Weekly Standard*

117. Kaminski, Paul G.; General Dynamics, Under-Sec. of U.S. Department of Defense

118. Kaminsky, Phyllis ; JINSA, CSP, NSC, Int'l Pub. Rel. Society

119. Kampelman, Max M.; PNAC, JINSA, CPD, Sec. Housing and Urban Development, CPD

120. Keane, John M.; General Dynamics, Retired General, U.S. Army, Vice Chief of Staff of the Army, DoD Policy Board

121. Kennard, William; Carlyle, *New York Times*, FCC

122. Kemble, Penn; PNAC, DoS, U.S.IA

123. Kemp, Jack; JINSA, HF, Sec. of HUD, U.S. House of Reps., CPD

124. Keyworth, George; CSP, HU, Los Alamos, General Atomics, NSC

125. Khalilzad, Zalmay; PNAC, Amb. to Iraq

126. King, Gwendolyn S.; Lockheed Martin

127. Kirkpatrick, Jeane; AEI, JINSA, CFR, CPD, NSA, Sec. of Defense Commission, U.S. Rep. to UN, CLI, CPD, Carlyle
128. Kramer, H.M.J. Jr.; SAIC
129. Kristol, Irving; CFR, AEI, DoD, *Wall Street Journal* Board of Contributors
130. Kristol, William; PNAC, AEI, MI, VP Chief of Staff 1989, CLI, Domes. Policy Adv. To VP, 1989
131. Kupperman, Charles; CPD, Boeing, NIPP
132. Lagon, Mark; PNAC, CFR, AEI, DoS
133. Lane, Andrew; Halliburton
134. Larson, Charles R.; Retired Admiral of the U.S. Navy, Northrop Grumman
135. Laspa, Jude; Bechtel
136. Ledeen, Michael; AEI, JINSA, DoS (consultant), DoD
137. Lehman, John; PNAC, NSA, DoD, Sec. of Navy
138. Lehrman, Lewis E.; AEI, MI, HF, G.W. Bush Oil Co. partner
139. Lesar, Dave; Halliburton
140. Libby, I. Lewis; PNAC, Chief of Staff to Richard Cheney, DoS, Northrup Grumman, RAND, DoD, House of Rep., Team B
141. Livingston, Robert; House of Rep., CSP, DoJ
142. Loy, James M.; Lockheed Martin, Retired U.S. Navy Admiral
143. Malone, C.B.; SAIC, Martin Marietta, DynCorp, Titan Corp., CLI, CPD
144. Martin, J. Landis; Halliburton
145. McCorkindale, Douglas H.; Lockheed Martin
146. McDonnell, John F.; Boeing
147. McFarlane, Robert; National Security Advisor (Reagan), CPD, Bush's Transition Advisory Committee on Trade
148. McNerney, James W.; Boeing, 3M, GE
149. Meese, Edwin; HF, HO, U.S. Attorney General, Bechtel, CPD
150. Merrill, Philip; CSP, DoD, Import-Export Bank of U.S.
151. Minihan, Kenneth A.; Ret. General U.S. Air Force, BAE Systems, DoD, Defense Intelligence Agency
152. Moore, Frank W.; Northrop Grumman
153. Moore, Nick; Bechtel
154. Moorman, Thomas S.; CSP, Aerospace Corporation, Rumsfeld Space Commission, U.S. Air Force: Former Vice Chief of Staff
155. Mundy, Carl E. Jr.; General Dynamics, Retired General, U.S. Marine Corps Commandant

156. Muravchik, Joshua; AEI, JINSA, PNAC, CLI, CPD
157. Murphy, Eugene F.; Lockheed Martin, GE
158. Nanula, Richard; Boeing
159. Novak, Michael; AEI, CPD
160. Nunn, Sam; GE, U.S. Senator, Chairman Senate Armed Services Committee
161. O'Brien, Rosanne; Northrop Grumman, Carlyle
162. Odeen, Philip A.; Defense and Arms Control Staff for Henry Kissinger, TRW, Northrop Grumman
163. Ogilvie, Scott; Bechtel
164. Owens, William; Ret. Adm. U.S. Navy, DPB, Joint Chiefs of Staff, SAIC
165. Perle, Richard; AEI, PNAC, CPD, CFR, NSA, JINSA, HU, DoD, DPD, CLI, Carlyle
166. Peters, Aulana L.; Northrop Grumman, SEC
167. Pipes, Daniel; PNAC, CPD, Team B
168. Podhoretz, Norman; PNAC, CPD, HU, CFR
169. Poses, Frederic; Raytheon
170. Precourt, Jay A.; Halliburton
171. Quayle, Dan; PNAC, VP U.S.
172. Ralston, Joseph W.; Lockheed Martin, Retired Air Force Gen., Vice Chairman of Joint Chiefs of Staff
173. Reed, Deborah L.; Halliburton, Pres. Southern CA. Gas & Elec.
174. Rice, Condoleezza; Hoover Institute, Foreign Policy Advisor to George H. W. Bush, Secretary of State
175. Ridgeway, Rozanne; Boeing, Asst. Sec. of State, Europe and Canada, Amb. German Democratic Republic, Finland, DoD
176. Riscassi, Robert; L-3 Communications Holdings, UN Command/Korea, Army Vice Chief of Staff, Joint Chiefs of Staff
177. Roche, James; Sec. of the Air Force, CSP, Boeing, Northrop Grumman, DoS
178. Rodman, Peter W.; PNAC, NSA, Asst. Sec. of Defense for Int'l Security Affairs, DOS
179. Rowen, Henry S.; PNAC, HO, CFR, DPB, DoD
180. Rubenstein, David M.; Carlyle, Deputy Asst. to the President for Domestic Policy (Carter)
181. Rubin, Michael; AEI, CFR, Office of Sec. of Defense
182. Rudman, Warren; U.S. Senator, Raytheon
183. Ruettgers, Michael; Raytheon

184. Rumsfeld, Donald; PNAC, HO, Sec. of Defense, Bechtel, Tribune Co.
185. Sanderson, E.J.; SAIC
186. Savage, Frank; Lockheed Martin
187. Scaife, Richard Mellon; HO, HF, CPD, Tribune Review Publishing Co.
188. Scheunemann, Randy; PNAC, Office of Sec. of Defense (consultant), Lockheed Martin, CLI Founder/Dir., CPD
189. Schlesinger, James; DoE, Atomic Energy Commission, Dir. CIA, CSP
190. Schmitt, Gary; PNAC, CLI, DoD (consultant), CLI
191. Schneider, William, Jr.; BAE Systems, PNAC, DoS, House of Rep./Senate staffer, WHOMB, CSP, NIPP
192. Schultz, George; HO, AEI, CPD, CFR, PNAC, Sec. of State, Sec. of Treasury, Bechtel, CLI, CPD
193. Shalikashvili, John M.; Boeing, Retired Chairman of Joint Chiefs of Staff, DoD, Ret. Gen. U.S. Army, CFR
194. Sharer, Kevin; Northrop Grumman, U.S. Naval Academy, Ret. Lt. Com. U.S. Navy
195. Sheehan, Jack; Bechtel, DPB
196. Shelman, Thomas W.; Northrop Grumman, DoD
197. Shulsky, Abram; PNAC, DoD
198. Skates, Ronald L.; Raytheon
199. Slaughter, John Brooks; Northrop Grumman
200. Sokolski, Henry; PNAC, HF, HO, CIA, DoD
201. Solarz, Stephen; PNAC, HU, DoS, CPD, Carlyle
202. Spivey, William; Raytheon
203. Statton, Tim; Bechtel
204. Stevens, Anne; Lockheed Martin
205. Stevens, Robert J.; Lockheed Martin
206. Stuntz, Linda; Raytheon, U.S. DoE
207. Sugar, Ronald D.; Northrop Grumman, Association of the U.S. Army
208. Swanson, William; Raytheon, Lockheed Martin
209. Tkacik, John; PNAC, HF, U.S. Senate
210. Turner, Michael J.; BAE Systems
211. Ukropina, James R.; Lockheed Martin
212. Van Cleave, William R.; Team B, HO, CSP, CPD, DoD, NIPP
213. Waldron, Arthur; CSP, AEI, PNAC, CFR
214. Walkush, J.P.; SAIC

215. Wallop, Malcolm; Heritage, HU, CSP, PNAC, Senate
216. Walmsley, Robert; General Dynamics, Retired Vice-Admiral, Royal Navy, Chief of Defense Procurement for the UK Ministry of Defense
217. Warner, John Hillard; SAIC, U.S. Army/Airforce Assn.
218. Watts, Barry; PNAC, Northrop Grumman
219. Weber, John Vincent (Vin); PNAC, George W. Bush Campaign Advisor, NPR
220. Wedgewood, Ruth; CLI, DoD, DoJ, DoS, CFR
221. Weldon, Curt; House of Rep., CSP
222. Weyrich, Paul; HF, PNAC, U.S. Senate
223. White, John P.; L-3 Communications, Chair of the Com. on Roles and Missions of the Armed Forces, DoD
224. Wieseltier, Leon; PNAC, CLI
225. Williams, Christopher A.; PNAC, DPB, Under-Sec. for Defense, Boeing (lobbyist), Northrop Grumman (lobbyist), CLI
226. Winter, Donald C.; Northrop Grumman
227. Wolfowitz, Paul; PNAC, HF, HU, Team B, Under-Sec. Defense, World Bank, Northrop Grumman, DoS
228. Wollen, Foster; Bechtel
229. Woolsey, R. James; PNAC, JINSA, CLI, DPB, CIA Dir., Under-Sec. of Navy, NIPP
230. Wurmser, David; AEI, Office of VP Middle East Adviser, DoS
231. Yearly, Douglas C.; Lockheed Martin
232. Young, A.T.; SAIC
233. Zaccaria, Adrian; Bechtel
234. Zafirovski, Michael S.; Boeing
235. Zakheim, Dov S.; PNAC, HF, CFR, DoD, Northrop Grumman, McDonnell Douglas, CPD
236. Zinni, Anthony C.; Retired General U.S. Marines, BAE Systems, Commander in Chief U.S. Central Command
237. Zoellick, Robert; PNAC, U.S. Trade Representative, DoS, CSIS, CFR, DOJ

Notes:

1. G. William Domhoff, *Who Rules America?*, 5th ed. (New York: McGraw Hill, 2006); Peter Phillips, *A Relative Advantage: Sociology of the San Francisco Bohemian Club*, 1994, http://library.sonoma.edu/regional/faculty/phillips/bohemianindex.html.

2. Early studies by Charles Beard in the *Economic Interpretations of the Constitution of the United States* (1929), established that economic elites formulated the U.S. Constitution to serve their own special interests. Henry Klein, in his book *Dynastic America* (1921), claimed that wealth in America has power never before known in the world and was centered in the top 2 percent of the population owning some 60 percent of the country. Ferdinard Lundberg wrote *America's Sixty Families* (1937) documenting intermarrying self-perpetuating families where wealth is the "indispensable handmaiden of government." C. Wright Mills determined ("American Business Elites," *Journal of Economic History*, December 1945) that nine out of ten business elites from1750 to 1879 came from well-to-do families.

3. See R. Brady, *Business as a System of Power* (New York: Columbia University Press, 1943) and Val Burris, "Elite Policy Planning Networks in the United States," American Sociological Association paper, 1991.

4. C. Wright Mills, *The Power Elite* (New York: Oxford University Press, 1956).

5. T. Koenig and R. Gobel, "Interlocking Corporate Directorships as a Social Network," *American Journal of Economics and Sociology*, vol. 40 (1981); Peter Phillips, "The 1934–35 Red Threat and The Passage of the National Labor Relations Act," *Critical Sociology*, vol. 20, no. 2 (1994).

6. Public Papers of the Presidents, Military-Industrial Complex Speech, Dwight D. Eisenhower, 1961, pp. 1035–1040.

7. *Economic Concentration and World War II*, A report of the Smaller War Plants Corporation to the Special Committee to Study Problems of American Small Business, U.S. Senate, U.S. Government Printing Office, Washington, DC, 1946.

8. U.S. Office of Management and Budget, Budget of the United States Government, Historical Tables, Fiscal Year 1995 (Washington, DC, Government Printing Office, 1994). pp. 36–43, 82–87.

9. Michael Putzel, "Battle Joined in Peace Dividend," *Boston Globe*, January 12, 1992, p. A1.

10. Eric Pianin, "Peace Dividend Efforts Dealt Blow," *Washington Post*, March 27, 1992, p. A4.

11. Sam Meddis, "Peace Dividend is no Guarantee, Aspin Says," *USA Today*, December 6, 1994.

12. Margaret Tauxe, "About that Peace Dividend: The Berlin Wall Fell, But a Wall of Denial Stands," *Pittsburgh Post-Gazette*, November 12, 1999, p. A27.

13. Guy Caron, "Anatomy of a Neo-Conservative White House," *Canadian Dimension*, May 1, 2005.

14. Alain Frachon and Daniel Vernet, "The Strategist and the Philosopher: Leo Strauss and Albert Wlhlestetter," *Le Monde*, April 16, 2003, English translation, *Counterpunch*, June 2, 2003.

15. Anne Hessing Cahn, "Team B; The Trillion-Dollar Experiment," *Bulletin of the Atomic Scientists*, volume 49, no. 03, April 1993.

16. John Pilger, "The World Will Know The Truth," *New Statesman* (London), December 16, 2002.

17. Peter Phillips, "The Neoconservative Plan for Global Dominance," *Censored 2006* (New York: Seven Stories Press), http://www.projectcensored.org; excerpts from the 1992 Draft "Defense Planning Guidance" can be accessed at http://www.pbs.org/wgbh/pages/frontline/shows/iraq/etc/wolf.html.

18. Patrick E. Tyler, "Senior U.S. Officials Assail Lone-Superpower Policy," *New York Times*, March 11, 1992, p. A6.

19. *Ibid.*

20. Anna Rich and Tamar Gabelnick, "Arms Company of the Future: BoeingBAELockheedEADS, Inc.," *Arms Sales Monitor*, January 2000.

21. Martha Honey, "Guns 'R' Us," *In These Times*, August 1997.

22. Peter Phillips, "A Relative Advantage: Sociology of the San Francisco Bohemian Club," 1994, http://libweb.sonoma.edu/regional/faculty/phillips/bohemianindex.html, p. 104, Note: While

I heard this speech myself, a preagreement with my host required that the names of the speakers and others participants be kept confidential.

23. Project for a New American Century, *Statement of Principles*, June 3, 1997, http://www.newamericancentury.org.

24. Positions held by PNAC founders in the George W. Bush administration: Elliot Abrams, National Security Council; Richard Cheney, Vice President; Paula Dobriansky, Department of State, Under-Sec. of Global Affairs; Aaron Friedberg, Vice President's Deputy National Security Advisor; Francis Fukuyama, Presidents Council on Bioethics; Zalmay Khalilzad, U.S. Ambassador to Afghanistan; Lewis Libby, Chief of Staff for the Vice President; Peter Rodman, DoD, Assist. Sec. Of Defense for International Security; Henry S. Rowen, Defense Policy Board, Comm. On Intelligence Capabilities of U.S. regarding WMDs; Donald Rumsfeld, Secretary of Defense; Vin Weber, National Commission Public Service; Paul Wolfowitz, Dep. Sec. Of Defense, Pres. World Bank.

25. Ted Nace, *Gangs of America* (San Francisco: Berrett-Koehler Publishers Inc., 2003), p. 186.

26. For a full review of the Global Dominance Group listing key advocates for military expansion and affiliates of the major defense contractors see Appendix A.

27. The Project for a New American Century, *Rebuilding America's Defenses, Project for a New American Century: Strategy, Forces and Resources for a New Century*, September 2000, www.newamericancentury.org.

28. David Epstein, Office of the Sec. Of Defense; Steve Cambone, NSA; Dov Zakheim, CFO Dept. of Defense; Mark Lagan, Dep. Assist. Sec. Of State.

29. The Project for a New American Century, *Rebuilding America's Defenses: Strategy, Forces and Resources for a New Century*, www.newamericancentury.org.

30. William Rivers Pitt, "The Root of the Bush National Security Agenda: Global Domination and the Preemptive Attack on Iraq First," www.Truthout.org, February 27, 2003.

31. See Appendix A for listing of the Top 20 DoD Contractors from 2004.

32. Tim Weiner, "Lockheed and the Future of Warfare," *New York Times*, November 28, 2004, Sunday Business p. 1.

33. Jerry Knight, "Lockheed Rules Roost on Electronic Surveillance," *Washington Post*, August 29, 2005, p. D1.

34. See The Center for Public Integrity, "Pentagon Contractors: Top Contractors by Dollar," www.publicintegrity.org.

35. *Ibid.*

36. Raw Story, "Cheney's Halliburton Stock Options Rose 3,281% Last Year, Senator Finds," October 11, 2005, www.rawstory.com.

37. M. Asif Ismail, "Investing in War: The Carlyle Group Profits from Government and Conflict," November 18, 2004, www.publicintegrity.org.

38. M. Asif Ismail, "The Sincerest Form of Flattery: Private Equity Firms Follow in Carlyle's Footsteps," November 18, 2004, www.publicintegrity.org.

39. Leslie, Wayne, "Arms Makers Find Being Cash-Heavy is Mixed Blessing," *New York Times*, May 12, 2005, p. C1.

40. AIPAC Policy Conference, March 7, 2006, http://www.aipac.org/PDFDocs/PC06_Transcript_Cheney.pdf.

41. We searched the LexisNexis database for the number of appearances using the dates 1/1/2000 to 12/31/2000 and 1/1/2005 to 12/31/2005. While some of the quotes do not directly relate to global dominance, we tried to illustrate the increase of influence these organizations exert in shaping the opinions of the U.S. public via major media outlets.

42. See Jessica Froiland's 9/11 prewarnings in Peter Phillips, *Censored 2006*, (New York: Seven Stories Press, 2005) p. 205.

43. George Arney, "India in Anti-Taliban Military Plan," Indiareacts.com, June 26, 2001, BBC

News, September 18, 2001; Rahul Bedi, "India Joins Anti-Taliban Coalition," *Janes Defense News*, March 15, 2001.

44. David Ray Griffin, *The 9/11 Commission Report: Omissions and Distortions*, (Redford, MI: Olive Branck Press, 2005).

45. See Scholars for 9/11 Truth, www.scholarsfor911truth.org.

46. Steven E. Jones, "Why Indeed Did the WTC Buildings Collapse?" http://www.physics.byu.edu/research/energy/htm7.html.

47. Cited from Davidson Loehr, *"Living Under Fascism,"* Unitarian Universalist Church, November 7, 2004, http://www.uua.org/news/2004/voting/sermon_loehr.html.

48. Ken Cunningham, "Permanent War? The Domestic Hegemony of the New American Militarism," *New Political Science*, vol. 26, no. 2, December 2004.

49. Henry Smith Richardson Papers, Library of the University of North Carolina, at Chapel Hill, Manuscripts Department, Southern Historical Collection, located at http://www.lib.unc.edu/mss/inv/r/Richardson,Henry_Smith.html.

50. American Enterprise Institute, W. H. Brady Program in Culture and Freedom, www.aei.org/research/contentID20041110114710420/default.asp, accessed, April 10, 2006.

51. Jeff Krehely, Meaghan House, and Emily Kernan, *Axis of Ideology: Conservative Foundations and Public Policy* (National Committee for Responsive Philanthropy. March 2004), pp. 37, 44.

Chapter 15

BEYOND IMPEACHMENT
Rebuilding a Political Culture

Cynthia Boaz and Michael Nagler

To reclaim our colonized political spaces we will have to reclaim our colonized cultural spaces.

—David Korten

The present drive toward world domination by "the remaining superpower" could be said to have begun in the fall of 1964, when five or six wealthy conservatives invited then–political unknown Ronald Reagan to give a speech supporting Barry Goldwater's presidential campaign. With this impromptu "kitchen cabinet," as it has come to be called, Reagan was able to snatch the seeds of victory from Goldwater's overwhelming defeat and begin the long march toward the presidency—and what is now the "neocon(servative) revolution" that has succeeded in inscribing "full spectrum dominance" as the U.S.'s national "security" policy. Nothing is more important for an understanding of the present crisis and how the U.S. became a rogue superpower threatening the existence of democracy, peace in the world, and possibly the survival of life on Earth, than to understand something of Ronald Reagan's power. An insight into that power was voiced by Rosalynn Carter on the eve of Reagan's defeat of her husband in 1980: "The trouble with that man [Reagan] is that he makes us feel good about our prejudices."

This points us to a question central to understanding the forces that have driven us to the present crisis: what has made so many of us feel-good individuals who can be so easily swayed by appeals to our private comforts and our egotism, that we forsake our values and our own well-being, values that we as a nation have cherished over two centuries of our existence, and well-being that is the native desire of everything living?

According to two recent estimates, residents of North America are exposed to an average of 1500 to 3000 commercial messages a *day*. The *underlying* message in all such ads, regardless of what product they are advertising, is, *feel good. Pursue your own private happiness* (on sale today at . . .). Much has been written about this unending message's harmful impact, which today, thanks to mass media technology, has become pretty much the dominant culture of the West and of all societies dominated by the industrialized West. However, little attention has been paid to its political outcome, which is precisely what has now become the primary threat to our survival.

There are various dimensions to this connection. Take, for example, the little question of *truth*. George W. Bush lied egregiously when he directed British and American security personnel to "fix the facts and the intelligence" to support his drive to war in Iraq. The shock here is not that the President lied or that he expected that millions would obediently follow him, which they did, or even that the outrageous lie was bound to be exposed some short time after he launched the horrific attack that has now so severely endangered our already compromised security. The real shock is that he expected that when his mendacity would be exposed *it would not matter*. It is as if the real world to which we are all responsible no longer existed. You cannot sustain a democratic political culture on a civic culture of delusion.

In a devastating documentary called *Ground Truth*, an Iraq veteran observes that billboards that "sell" the war are no different from the billboards that sell cigarettes—except that there's no Surgeon General's warning. We should be thinking about not one but three levels on which commercial culture feeds the domination system eating away at our civil liberties and the hope of world progress toward peace:

- First and best known is the outright political lying. A documentary filmmaker we know saw with his own eyes how CNN filmed a house in Baghdad being struck with a tank round; how the family poured out of the house, the grandmother dragging her severed leg, and how not one second of this scene or anything like it ever made it to our television screens.
- Second is the general violence. So effective is violent 'entertainment' that when the Army faced the task of desensitizing young men to overcome their human instinct against killing (by forcibly suppressing their

innate capacities for fear, compassion, and empathy), they did it with off-the-shelf video games our young people are watching by the millions.[1] It is not that the games are realistic that allows them to desensitize the soldiers, but that by the time they have done it, killing is *un*realistic. Soldier after soldier reports thinking that the victims of his violence were not really people and are not really dead. Often they add, "It was like a video game."

- Finally, there is the representation of the human being portrayed relentlessly not only by advertisements but by "news" and "entertainment" as a separate, material fragment condemned to struggle against others in a hostile world with scarce resources—and even scarcer meaning.[2] In this characterization of reality, all human interaction is conflict and all exchange is zero-sum. People who are trapped in that worldview are easy victims of scare tactics and other modes of manipulation.

The advertising media are absolutely essential for the success of the neo-conservative agenda, for it is through them that all of us are encouraged to become self-centered, insensitive, childish, and naïve. They are effectively destroying our democracy and it is essential that we find a way to break their spell. But we hope that the foregoing analysis shows that impeachment, even if it succeeds, will be only part of the road back to civic health. In fact, it could be a potential distraction from the real task at hand, because it focuses on two people who are only the figureheads of a network of operatives who are in turn only the expression of a strange and unhappy economy and culture. This is not an argument to abandon the impeachment campaign—quite the contrary. It is a reminder that this presidency did not come from nowhere and an urgent plea that if we want to get things back on track we will have to do much more than remove two individuals from office. Absent an accompanying shift in consciousness that eventually permeates the culture as a whole, those individuals will simply be replaced with like-minded successors.

An ailing civic culture acts like a weakened immune system under the threat of a virus. It provides the ideal host for corrupt, inept, or treacherous governance. Among their other nefarious features, bad governments (historically, but not exclusively, nondemocracies) have one distinct characteristic. Simply put, they force their publics to choose between being good citizens and good people. Government policy and truth cannot but come into conflict in these regimes. Loyalty to the nation-state—which is built into propaganda about extreme "patriotism" in which (to compensate for its distance from the truth) government policy is conflated with religious imagery—takes the place of compassion for the larger community. The state, essentially an abstraction, assumes precedence over the real people and their well-being, whom and which it was designed to serve; and the mechanism for this substitution is the language of xenophobia, racism and intolerance, all of which cannot but replace truth-telling in the public discourse. Ironically, the values claimed as most prized by the regime—that is, liberty and justice—are traded away for the promise of more security.

Take the example of Stalinist Russia, where ratting out one's comrades or family members for crimes under the flimsiest of pretexts could expose your loved one to conviction as an "enemy of the people," and land him or her in a forced labor camp, prison, or worse. The behavior of the informant was often revered in Soviet lore as the epitome of patriotism, and the informer held up as a paragon of civic virtue. Young Pavlik Morozov (1918–1932) was turned into a model of Soviet patriotism after his denunciation of his own father (for hiding grain during a famine) resulted in the latter's relocation to Siberia. Taken to its extreme, a state bent only on its own enrichment has a way of getting people to justify these kinds of choices to themselves; even those choices that are against human nature, and against Truth. Pavlik lived in a time before cable news and the Internet, and a place where corporations functioned without marketing departments. Today it is difficult to overstate the power of propaganda to permeate our collective consciousness. We dare not say that what they did to Pavlik "could not happen here," when dehumanization resonates from and within our culture's most repetitive messages.

In contrast to the systems described above, the goal of a healthy democratic government is to bring human compassion in line with civic virtue. H.G. Wells put it fittingly when he said that "our true nationality is mankind." Good governments should not only make it possible to be a good citizen and a good person simultaneously, but should actively support the natural resonance of these two domains. This is why we have stressed the corrosive effects of popular culture on personal life as an infrastructure, if you will, of regressive politics—and why we will be addressing both domains in a moment when we turn to solutions.

Consider the circumstances under which George W. Bush initially took power. Those unhappy chickens have come home to roost. Imagine for a moment that a presidential election in Russia had unfolded in the same manner as the 2000 U.S. presidential election. If the election that brought Putin to power had been tainted by widespread charges of vote corruption, flawed and inconsistent election standards, hints of nepotism, and finally the intervention of a court whose members owed a political debt to the eventual victor (who had actually received fewer votes than his competitor), it would have been only hours until scholars and pundits declared Russian democracy a fraud. But in the U.S. there was no such reaction. At least, not officially. It should now be clear that a system founded on treachery is not stable. Nearly three thousand Americans and uncounted tens or hundreds of thousands of Iraqis have paid with their life for this error in judgment. It is time to set things right.

In order to restore our democracy to civic health, we must start by holding it accountable—which presupposes, of course, that we make peace with our own responsibility. There are many strategies we can employ to accomplish this. Here are just some of what seem to us the simplest and most effective:

Unspinning the Media

In an ideal democratic society, media's job is to act as an independent channel of information between citizens and policymakers. Discussions about media "bias" only scratch the surface. The concentration of media ownership (globally, as well as within the U.S.) undermines the quest for truth in information because the democratic imperative of free expression comes into conflict with the capitalist need for profit. To confront this, civic-minded people have to *become* the media. One very modern way of doing this is by using the "blogosphere." These blogs allow users to exchange information directly and instantaneously, without the filters of media editors, publishers, and advertisers. Our need for authentic exchange is so great that some blogs have replaced print media or television as the primary source of information for media consumers. Political blogs, in particular, are extremely popular. Arianna Huffington's blog, huffingtonpost.org, receives between *40 and 50 million* visits a month. Start a blog of your own. Or contribute to existing blogs. Call radio news shows. Write letters to the editor of your local (and national) papers. Make it a point to be an *active media participant*, not merely a passive recipient of the line of the day. And of course, at the same time, do not ignore the deeper dimensions of the present media's corrosiveness as they act on our own minds and hearts. Give yourself and encourage your friends and children to give themselves a permanent respite from the commercial, violent, vapid messages of the mainstream media, not only in the news but in advertising and "entertainment."

Holding Leaders Accountable

While it would be ideal to have representatives who entered public service to *do* something rather than *be* something (namely a power-holder), civic-conscious citizens can and should use their collective strength to force representatives to be accountable. Citizen activists have a responsibility to let their elected officials know their interests, and to make sure they are served. Groups such as CODEPINK: Women for Peace are especially effective with this strategy. This group has recently addressed Hillary Clinton for her lack of responsiveness on her constituents' concern about the Iraq war—members of the group show up to each of her public appearances with signs and chants, they flood her office with calls, faxes, e-mails, and postcards, and they invite media to every event in order to grab headlines intended to put Clinton on the spot. We believe, and Gandhi apparently did also, that there is no harm in using the mainstream's media when they will respond, as long as we don't rely on them unduly. This proactive strategy requires more from the voter than just a threat to take one's vote elsewhere (especially when it might not be counted!). It requires citizens to doggedly track the behavior of their representatives, and to let them know they are being monitored. When it comes to holding the president and vice president accountable for impeachable offenses, citizens have to first compel their representatives to do their job by letting them know that they will lose their job if they don't perform. It is especially critical to focus energy on the Democrats, whose job it is to act like a real opposition party. We point to the efforts of groups like MoveOn.org and *Democracy Now!*, which take the task of organizing constituents to hold their leaders accountable seriously.

Joining (or Starting) a Grassroots Organization

It is no coincidence that dozens of social justice movements have emerged, or blossomed, in the days following George W. Bush's first inauguration. It is not only antiwar groups that have made their presence known, but groups concerned with immigrant rights, women's issues, environmental protections, legal jurisprudence, labor unions, racism, and the preservation of democracy have all emerged or been revitalized. In September of 2005, these groups joined together in a mass mobilization in Washington DC for Three Days of Action. An estimated 750,000 people participated in the events, which were intended to force Bush to change course on his administration's policy in Iraq, among other things. While the president and his team of policymakers and spokespeople can choose, for now, to ignore and (attempt to) marginalize these demonstrations of civic outrage, becoming involved in direct political activism has additional benefits besides bringing attention to the message—it gives citizens a direct means to channel their frustrations, empowers participants with a sense of political efficacy, and unites people through the exercise of some of the most critical of democratic values—freedom of speech, expression, assembly, and petition.

Civil Disobedience

When using existing democratic channels does not prove fruitful, it becomes incumbent on concerned citizens to obey their conscience and use means of proven effectiveness to exert deeper pressures on the system. Civil disobedience, a form of nonviolent resistance, encompasses the active refusal to obey certain laws or commands of a governing power without resorting to the use of physical force. In the twentieth century strategies of nonviolent resistance ended imperial rule in India, challenged Nazi occupation in Europe, and dismantled dictatorships from Chile to Czechoslovakia and South Africa to Serbia. Political philosophers from Thoreau to Gandhi to Martin Luther King Jr. have written about the right and duty of citizens to actively oppose the injustices of their governance. The act of engaging in civil disobedience requires a principled commitment to civic justice and strict use of nonviolence. It also includes the recognition of the consequences (both favorable and unfavorable) of one's actions. Active forms of civil disobedience in democratic societies have included peaceful blockades or the occupation of facilities. These sorts of actions—often used in conjunction with the kinds of groups discussed above—are generally a last, but sometimes necessary, resort of a disaffected citizenry.

These steps, doable and effective, outline a new civic reality for all—and let us hope it will be many—who take them up. They will be necessary whether or not President George W. Bush gets to finish out his final term of office. At the same time, in line with our earlier discussion, we emphasize the need to do something about our *individual* participation in the current crisis, which arises from cultural tendencies that have evolved—or should we say, devolved—over a long period. While these tendencies can also be addressed in groups and organizations (one thinks of letter-writing campaigns to corporate media managers regarding their abuse of violent images, or classrooms who have gone off television), it is our feeling that the effectiveness of even these efforts will depend on individual decisions to withdraw from the prevailing commercial way of life—e.g. by living simply on the material level—*and* to withdraw from the ideas, images, and values; in a word, the culture, that props up that kind of life—e.g. by turning to healthier, and usually much less corporate, sources for news and entertainment. It is a politically potent act to have tea with friends instead of seeing 'action movies' and to read serious journals for awareness of the real events taking place in this world instead of watching what our students call "Faux News."

Gandhi explained that the power of civil disobedience lay in what he called the "law of suffering": "Things of fundamental importance to the people are not secured by reason alone but have to be purchased with their suffering . . . if you want something really important to be done you must not merely satisfy the reason, you must move the heart also."[3]

What a bracing antidote to the culture of comfort and apathy that has brought us to present crisis. And yet, in actual fact most activists have experienced considerably *more* comfort with themselves and life in general when they repossess their minds from the world of commercial media, not to mention standing up for their conscience in acts of civil disobedience which Thoreau and Gandhi called the first duty of the citizen.

The first reaction some people have to these suggestions is, "Yes, but I'm only one person; I can't make a difference, especially just by changing how I think." We remind you that is *the* necessary lie (or "illusion," to cite Noam Chomsky) that has allowed the neocon "revolution" to prevail over compassion and sanity. Is it not what we think and do, person by person, that has brought us to this pass? Seeing through this lie—and sharing that vision, which is the objective of the book you are holding—is the first act of truth that will guide the rebuilding of our civic and political culture.

Notes:

1. See Lt. Col. Dave Grossman, *Stop Teaching Our Kids to Kill*, (New York: Crown Publishers, 1999).
2. See also Neil Postman's *Amusing Ourselves to Death* on the devastating effects of technological media on civic responsibility and attention span.
3. N.K. Bose, Ed., *Selections From Gandhi* (Ahmedabad: Navajivan, 1948), pp.146–147.

Chapter 16

WHAT CAN BE DONE?

Dennis Loo and Peter Phillips

If nothing else, the Bush-Cheney regime has demonstrated how easily a radical right-wing agenda can be foisted upon the U.S. government and the mainstream media. To oust their regime will require a powerful social movement, not only to overcome Bush-Cheney and those who have been complicit with them, but to create a completely different political atmosphere.

A social movement is, in its earliest stages, one or two people with a vision, an unflinching determination and a sense of the moment pregnant with possibility and necessity. We are in such a time, and if we who wrote this book have done our job, you—*and many, many more*—want, as they used to say in the 1960s, to be part of the solution, not part of the problem. Millions of people seeking a very different world than the one that Bush and Cheney have in mind are ready to support and, in varying ways, join with those who are willing to stand up.

The powers we must overcome have mountains of money and their hands on the levers of institutional power, including most of the mass media. But we have three things they don't and can't have: justice, truth, and the majority of people on our side. You can douse a rotting pile of manure with as much perfume as you want, but it's still going to smell. The gap between what the government and their apologists say they're doing and what they are actually doing grows wider by the day. They can say that Homeland Security and FEMA are on the job, but New Orleans proves them wrong. They can claim they're winning the war on terror and the war in Iraq, but every day the facts belie their claims. They can assure us that they're protecting our civil liberties and doing everything by the book, but nearly every week brings fresh revelations of their lawbreaking.

In the 1960s this gap was dubbed the credibility gap and forced President Lyndon Johnson to forego running for another term in office. His successor, Richard Nixon, was forced to resign because of the leak of the Pentagon Papers by whistleblower Daniel Ellsberg and because of the revelations about Watergate through whistleblower Deep Throat. Today our government threatens reporters and civil servants with jail and prison for blowing the whistle on its illegal deeds. Yet there is a reason more and more whistleblowers are stepping forward and risking their careers: their consciences won't allow them to sleep at night. The more that information and truth gets out there, the less credible the radical right-wing forces in power today become and the more powerful the opposition forces become.

The first, and most critical, step in mobilizing people against this regime is recognizing and using the power of information. One of the best things that you can do to spread the word is by using the book you have in your hands. Encourage your friends and family, your coworkers and your neighbors to read it. Form reading circles around the book and plot strategy. Spread the word through the Internet. Contact Seven Stories Press and post flyers publicizing this book. Arrange bulk consignment sales and set up book tables at your school, in your community, at club events, at large or small gatherings, at demonstrations, and anywhere you can think of to sell the book to others. Use your book tables to sign people up for actions and activities. Contact us to arrange speakers. All of our authors are available to speak at gatherings.

Polls and the talk in the streets indicate that there is a sleeping giant inside the country and inside ourselves that needs direction and leadership at all levels. We encourage you to check out and join groups that have taken a stand against Bush and Cheney such as the groups listed below. As we go to press, the 2006 midterm elections approach. The stranglehold that the GOP holds over Congress must be broken for impeachment proceedings, the accompanying necessary investigations into their crimes, and their Senate trial, to proceed.

Things You Can Do Right Away

- Put a bumper sticker on your car supporting impeachment.
- Give "Impeach Bush and Cheney" yard signs to all your friends or have a sign-making party.

- Start an impeachment group in your school or at your workplace.
- Plan and execute a rally or demonstration at your school calling for impeachment.
- Send a letter to your local newspapers demanding Bush and Cheney's ouster.
- Send a letter to your local political party central committee (Democrat, Republican, Green, Libertarian, or Independent) demanding they take a public position favoring impeachment of Bush and Cheney. *(Even Republicans who honestly look at their traditional Republican values know that they do not include torture, regime change, global military domination, foreign invasions, massive spying on U.S. citizens, and suspending human rights.)*
- Attend candidate debate nights and political rallies and ask, if elected, will the candidates support impeachment.
- Petition your local city council to pass a resolution supporting impeachment.
- Join pro-impeachment action groups and organize meetings with your local elected officials to ask for impeachment.
- Send out press releases to regional media and hold public impeachment rallies with speakers, posters, and lists of impeachment grievances.
- Raise enough money to rent a full-size highway billboard with an Impeachment Now message.
- Print up hundreds of "Impeach" stickers and paste then in public places.
- Read the Declaration of Human Rights and U.S. Bill of Rights in public places while calling for the impeachment of Bush and Cheney.

Afterword

THE IMPEACHMENT OF GEORGE BUSH
—A WORLD WIDE PARTY

Edward Sanders

Today they impeached George Bush
and the world began to party

Flowers bloomed spontaneously
Trombones came out of attics by themselves
and began to play the "Celebration Waltz"

Out in Des Moines the birds in the pet shops
suddenly knew "All you need is love"
and every single puppy could hold a D minor yowl!

In Italy they turned on all the ancient fountains
and the ghosts of Roman poets wrote encomia!

Through the Arc de Triomphe
400,000 lily-carrying children sang
the two words of impeachment
"Égalité . . . . . Liberté"

It was '45 all over again

In Bohemia the state glass works
produced a million blue plates of Absolute Joy!
to be given out free to the tourists of Prague!

654,000 tapdancers were seen in Santiago
surging past the house of Pablo Neruda
while the stolen books of '73 were repaired

Petrarch and Laura appeared holding hands
and watching the boat races along the Arno
beneath the bridge of sighs

Out of the mound of Troy
came the mother of Patroclus
with a basket of pomegranates
to heal the soul-wounds of Bush's many killings

On the cliffs of Leucadia
ancient Sappho sang
"There'll be freedom to live as we love now
that he is gone"

The voice of Thomas Jefferson
came across Virginia to ask that all citizens' debts
to banks be forgiven

Anita Ekberg swam naked and alone in the Trevi Fountain
she was so excited at George's barring
and Catullus wrote three poems at the marvel

500,000 legless humans from U.S. and Chinese land mines
clicked their crutches to the beat as
Stevie Wonder's "Superstition" played from giant helicopters
to lift the millions of unexploded land mines
out of the blood fields
& into U.N. casks

Paul Bowles sent a waterpipe from Tangier
to Corso, Ginsberg and Orlovksy
in room 27 of the Beat Hotel on rue Git le Coeur
to celebrate the good news

Cassandra stands on Pennsylvania Avenue
and weeps this time with surprise
because the world at last is listening to her words,
"Goodbye George, your house has fallen without ashes!"

Party yay! party say!
Time to dance all day!

INDEX

ABOUT THE CONTRIBUTORS

DENNIS BERNSTEIN, executive producer for Pacifica Radio's Flashpoints News Magazine, is an award-winning print and radio journalist whose articles and essays have appeared widely in the *New York Times, Newsday*, the *Boston Globe, The Nation*, and many others. His work has been honored numerous times by the national media watchdog group Project Censored. dbernstein@igc.org.

CYNTHIA BOAZ is Assistant Professor of Political Science and International Studies at the State University of New York at Brockport. Her major research and teaching interests include media and politics, political development, and democratization. She has published previously in *Comparative Political Studies, Peace Review, Feminist Media Studies*, and *Sojourners Magazine*. cboaz@brockport.edu.

BARBARA J. BOWLEY is an Associate Professor at Woodbury University in Burbank, California, where she is Director of Library Services and Director of General Education. She received her MA in Anthropology and her MS in Library Service from Columbia University. Her research interests include the critical examination of the role of information in society and issues concerning the future of higher education. Barbara.bowley@woodbury.edu.

JEREMY BRECHER, JILL CUTLER, and BRENDAN SMITH are the coeditors of *In the Name of Democracy: American War Crimes in Iraq and Beyond* (New York: Metropolitan/Holt, 2006) and the founders of www.warcrimeswatch.org. Jeremy Brecher is a historian who has written and edited more than a dozen books on social movements, including *Strike!* He has received five regional Emmy Awards for his documentary film work. Jill Cutler is an assistant dean at Yale College, where she is also a lecturer in the Department of English. She has edited many books, including *Global Visions: Beyond the New World Order*. Brendan Smith is the coauthor of *Globalization from Below* and has written for the *Los Angeles Times, The Nation*, and the *Baltimore Sun*. He holds a law degree from Cornell University. blsmith28@gmail.com.

LEW BROWN has been a political activist, deckhand, ironworker, disc jockey, teacher, guide, and friend to the developmentally disabled. He graduated cum laude with department honors and a BA in Psychology from Sonoma State University in 2006. He holds membership in two national honors societies and has won awards for public speaking, writing, and research. Today he is an independent research analyst in the private sector and a loving husband and father.

LYN DUFF is a journalist currently based in Port-au-Prince, Haiti. In 1995 she traveled to Haiti to help establish that country's first children's radio station and has since covered Haiti extensively for Pacifica Radio's Flashpoints, the San Francisco *Bay View*, and other local and national media. LynDuff@aol.com.

LARRY EVEREST is the author *of Oil, Power & Empire: Iraq and the U.S. Global Agenda* from Common Courage Press (2004). Everest has covered the Middle East and Central Asia for over twenty-five years for *Revolution* newspaper (www.revcom.us) and other publications. In 1986, Everest wrote *Behind the Poison Cloud: Union Carbide's Bhopal Massacre.* In 1991, he traveled to Iraq and shot the award-winning video *Iraq: War Against the People.* In 2005, he testified at the culminating session of the World Tribunal on Iraq in Istanbul, Turkey and helped organize the 2005-2006 International Commission of Inquiry on Crimes Against Humanity by the Bush Administration. www.bushcommission.org. larryeverest@hotmail.com.

RICHARD HEINBERG is the author of seven books including *The Party's Over: Oil, War and the Fate of Industrial Societies* (New Society, 2003, 2005), *Powerdown: Options and Actions for a Post-Carbon World* (New Society, 2004), and *The Oil Depletion Protocol* (New Society, 2006). He is a journalist, educator, editor, lecturer, and a Core Faculty member of New College of California, where he teaches a program on "Culture, Ecology and Sustainable Community," and is widely regarded as one of the world's foremost Peak Oil educators.

DAHR JAMAIL has spent over eight months reporting from inside occupied Iraq as an independent journalist. He writes regularly for Inter Press Service and the *Asia Times.* His articles have also been printed in *The Independent, The Guardian,* the *Sunday Herald* in Scotland, and *The Nation.* In Iraq he reported for *Democracy Now!* and the BBC World Service and was the Flashpoints/Pacifica special correspondent. mail@dahrjamailiraq.com.

DENNIS LOO is Associate Professor of Sociology at Cal Poly Pomona. He graduated with honors in Government from Harvard and received his M.A. and Ph.D. in Sociology from the University of California at Santa Cruz. His recent article, "No Paper Trail Left Behind: the Theft of the 2004 Presidential Election" was honored by Project Censored in 2006. He is a former journalist and his research specialties include polling, public policy making, social movements, and criminology. *Impeach the President* is his first book. ddloo@csupomona.edu.

MARK CRISPIN MILLER is a Professor of Culture and Communication at New York University. His books include *The Bush Dyslexicon: Observations on a National Disorder* and *Fooled Again: How the Right Stole the Election of 2004, and How They'll Steal the Next One Too (Unless We Stop Them).* His off-Broadway show, *A Patriot Act,* is available on DVD, at markcrispinmiller.com. mcm7@MAIL.nyu.edu.

MICHAEL NAGLER is Professor Emeritus of Classics and Comparative Literature at UC, Berkeley, where he founded and still teaches nonviolence and other courses in the Peace and Conflict Studies Program. His most recent books are *The Search for a Nonviolent Future* (American Book Award, 2002) and *Our Spiritual Crisis.* He has been nominated for the 2006 Jamnalal Bajaj prize for Gandhian work outside India. www.mettacenter.org.

GREG PALAST is a former racketeering investigator and author of *Armed Madhouse: Dispatches from the Front Lines of the Class War* (Penguin-Dutton, 2006). "The man widely considered as the top investigative journalist in the United States, is persona non grata in his own country's media" (*Asia Week*) has received five Project Censored Awards for his investigations of elections manipulation, World Bank skullduggery, U.S. involvement in the coup in Venezuela, and other stories for Britain's *Guardian* papers, BBC Television *Newnight,* TomPaine.com, and *Harper's.* Palast, an economist by training, is a world-recognized authority on corporate governance and coauthor of the United Nations guide to utility privatization, *Democracy and Regulation.* Stories by him that were rejected by U.S. mainstream media are gathered in the international bestseller, *The Best Democracy Money Can Buy.* gregpalast@gregpalast.com.

PETER PHILLIPS is a Professor of Sociology at Sonoma State University and director of Project Censored, a media research organization. He is the editor of ten volumes of *Censored: Media Democracy in Action* (1997 to 2007). Phillips regularly publishes sociopolitical op-eds in newspapers, magazines, and Web sites including Commondreams.org, counterpunch.org, buzzflash.org, and projectcensored.org. peter.phillips@sonoma.edu.

ANDREW SLOAN is a liberal studies major at Sonoma State University. He has published a study of the Israel Lobby and the Global Dominance Group in *Censored 2007*.

NANCY SNOW received her Ph.D. in international relations at The American University, Washington, DC, and her BA in political science at Clemson University. She was a Fulbright Scholar in political science in Germany and a former government propagandist at the U.S. Information Agency (1992–1994). She is currently an Associate Professor at the College of Communications, California State University, Fullerton; Adjunct Professor at the USC Annenberg School for Communication; and a senior research fellow at the USC Center on Public Diplomacy. She has written *Information War; Propaganda, Inc.; War, Media and Propaganda;* and *America the Beautiful?* nsnow@fullerton.edu.

BRIDGET THORNTON is a senior level research assistant for Project Censored at Sonoma State University. She has published research reports in *Censored 2006, Censored 2007,* and is coauthor of a chapter in *9/11 & American Empire: Intellectuals Speak Out* by David Ray Griffin and Peter Dale Scott.

JUDITH HALFPENNY VOLKART is an award-winning lawyer, educator, and civil rights activist. A graduate of Hastings College of Law, she teaches constitutional law and other legal courses at Sonoma State University and University of California, Berkeley. An outspoken critic of the USA PATRIOT Act, Judith has addressed audiences throughout northern California and her speeches have aired nationally. jhv@sonic.net.

KEVIN WEHR is an Assistant Professor of Sociology at Cal State, Sacramento. He received his MS and Ph.D. in Sociology from the University of Wisconsin, Madison, and his BA in Sociology from University of California at Santa Cruz. His publications include *America's Fight Over Water: The Environmental and Political Consequences of Large-Scale Dams in the American West.* kwehr@csus. edu.

HOWARD ZINN is the author of the best-selling *A People's History of the United States* and many other books, including *The Zinn Reader* (Seven Stories Press, 2000), and, most recently, *Voices of a People's History of the United States* (Seven Stories Press, 2004).

RESOURCES FOR IMPEACHMENT

Vote to Impeach Bush: Advocates impeachment of the President, solicits donations to finance ads in major newspapers, and features views of former U.S. Attorney General Ramsey Clark. www.votetoimpeach.org.

CODEPINK: A women-initiated grassroots peace and social justice movement working to end the war in Iraq, stop new wars, and redirect our resources into healthcare, education, and other life-affirming activities. CODEPINK rejects the Bush administration's fear-based politics that justify violence, and instead calls for policies based on compassion, kindness, and a commitment to international Indict President Bush. Support The Movement To Indict Bush. http://www.codepink4peace.org/article.php?list=type&type=3.

Movement to impeach George W. Bush—Wikipedia, the free encyclopedia: http://en.wikipedia.org/wiki/Movement_to_impeach_George_Bush.

Francis Boyle: Draft Impeachment Resolution Against George W. Bush: www.counterpunch.org/boyle01172003.htm.

Impeach Bush: Editorials and Information on How to Impeach Bush: http://www.impeachbush.tv/.

Petition To Impeach President Bush And Vice President Cheney: We, the undersigned, believe George W. Bush and Richard Cheney should be impeached for the following high crimes and misdemeanors. http://elandslide.org/elandslide/petition.cfm?campaign=impeach&refer=home.

The Four Reasons: The Four Reasons why "**We the People**" must uphold the Constitution of The United States of America and hold those who violate it accountable. http://www.thefourreasons.org/.

Topplebush.com: Inspired by the combined outrage and frustration of several good friends and family members with the Bush Administration's blatant corporate cronyism, which became magnified when Bush invaded Iraq based on lies. http://www.topplebush.com/index.shtml.

SourceWatch: The case for impeachment of President George W. Bush is outlined below in books, Web sites, documents, articles, and resources related to what are believed to be Bush's impeachable offenses. http://www.sourcewatch. org/index.php?title=The_case_for_impeachment_of_President_George_W._Bush#Books.

Veterans for Peace: Veterans Working Together for Peace & Justice Through Non-violence. Wage Peace! http://www.veteransforpeace.org/impeachment/impeachment.htm.

Petition for the Impeachment of President George W. Bush: http://www.petitiononline.com/911911/petition.html.

AfterDowningStreet.org: Articles Of Impeachment Against George W. Bush, President Of The United States, . . . Calls for the impeachment of President George W. Bush and cohort. http://www.afterdowningstreet.org/?q=taxonomy/term/17.

World Can't Wait: As the call from the World Can't Wait puts it: "The point is this: history is full of examples where people who had right on their side fought against tremendous odds and were victorious. And it is also full of examples of people passively hoping to wait it out, only to get swallowed up by a horror beyond what they ever imagined. The future is unwritten. WHICH ONE WE GET IS UP TO US." http://www.worldcantwait.org/.